The Rise of the Sharing Economy

The Rise of the Sharing Economy

Exploring the Challenges and Opportunities of Collaborative Consumption

Pia A. Albinsson and B. Yasanthi Perera, Editors

Foreword by Russell Belk

An Imprint of ABC-CLIO, LLC

Santa Barbara, California • Denver, Colorado

Copyright © 2018 by Pia A. Albinsson and B. Yasanthi Perera

Library of Congress Cataloging-in-Publication Data

Names: Albinsson, Pia A., 1975– editor. | Perera, B. Yasanthi, editor.
Title: The rise of the sharing economy : exploring the challenges
    and opportunities of collaborative consumption / Pia A. Albinsson
    and B. Yasanthi Perera, editors ; foreword by Russell Belk.
Description: Santa Barbara, California : Praeger, [2018] | Includes
    bibliographical references and index.
Identifiers: LCCN 2017037578 (print) | LCCN 2017046359 (ebook) |
    ISBN 9781440851872 (ebook) | ISBN 9781440851865 (alk. paper)
Subjects: LCSH: Sharing—Economic aspects. | Cooperation. |
    Consumption (Economics) | Economics.
Classification: LCC HD2961 (ebook) | LCC HD2961.R57 2018 (print) |
    DDC 334—dc23
LC record available at https://lccn.loc.gov/2017037578

ISBN: 978-1-4408-5186-5 (print)
        978-1-4408-5187-2 (ebook)

22 21 20 19 18   1 2 3 4 5

This book is also available as an eBook.

Praeger
An Imprint of ABC-CLIO, LLC

ABC-CLIO, LLC
130 Cremona Drive, P.O. Box 1911
Santa Barbara, California 93116-1911
www.abc-clio.com

This book is printed on acid-free paper (∞)

Manufactured in the United States of America

*To David, Emmelie, and Evelynne whom I love and
share my life with.*
—*Pia A. Albinsson*

For my dear parents, B. C. and Diana Perera.
—*B. Yasanthi Perera*

Contents

Foreword: The Sharing Economy

Russell Belk

Sharing is nothing new. It is as old as humankind and has been necessary for our survival as a species (Belk 2014). Everatt and Solanki (2008) found that sharing is pervasive in South Africa and is highest among the lowest socioeconomic classes. Stack (1974) also found that poor blacks in the United States were more likely to share. Widlok (2017) notes that in contemporary Germany rather than selling their labor on the market, the majority of citizens make their livings as family dependents, pensioners, or social benefit recipients. That is, they depend on sharing by the family or the state. As Wolf and Ritz (this volume) report, in former East Germany people shared because it was necessary to make do in an economy of scarcity. The same was true across Eastern Europe under communism (Axelova and Belk 2009; Drakulič 1991). Together, such findings affirm that sharing has often been a survival mechanism.

But the age and ubiquity of sharing is not to say that there is nothing new about the nature of sharing in today's world. As the contributions in this volume attest, there are many new twists on sharing in the so-called sharing economy. Some of these twists involve applying the label of sharing to short-term rental of cars, homes, rooms, and rides. This is not really sharing in the original sense of allowing others to regard possessions as ours rather than mine and yours (Belk 2014; Eckhardt and Bardhi 2015). Sharing also takes on a different character when what is being shared is information or digital goods that are not rivalrous and are not seen as part of a zero-sum game (see Harvey, Smith, and Golightly, Kamilaris and Prenafeta-Boldú, and Teubner and Hawlitschek in this volume). Likewise, John (2017) sees the photos, videos, likes, and updates that we post on social media as involving "fuzzy objects" or non-objects. Thus, both the types of things we may share and the ways in which we may share them have greatly expanded. Moreover, sharing is now becoming a convenience rather than a survival mechanism, although in the long run it may aid the continued survival of our environment.

But contemporary sharing outside of the home and neighborhood may not be unproblematic. While the broad hope that information wants to flow freely online (e.g., Benkler 2006; Ghosh 2005; Giesler 2008; Hyde 2010; Lessig 2004) is now largely dead, there remain pockets of free shared content in open-source software, wickis, blogs, BitTorrent applications, social media, and creative commons applications (e.g., Hemetsberger 2012; Tapscott 2008). Nevertheless, as with the banner of sharing, monetization has become a part of most online offerings to the extent that some see willing consumer participation in such media as another form of corporate exploitation of consumer labor and freely provided consumer content (e.g., Zwick, Bonsu, and Darmody 2008). In this view, we have gone from "what's mine is yours" (Botsman and Rogers 2010) to "what's yours is mine" (Slee 2015). There are many charges that consumer-producers are also exploited in the gig economy of ridesharing and home-sharing apps as well (Belk 2017b). But this isn't all due to corporate exploitation either, as illustrated by consumers' grudging sharing of "club goods" within settings like gated communities (Belk 2017c). For similar reasons, many voluntary and noncommercial sharing organizations have foundered or become difficult to sustain (Philip, Ozanne, and Ballantine, this volume; Schor et al. 2016).

In spite of its problems, the overall impact of the rise of the sharing economy and collaborative consumption has been positive. It has opened us up to thinking about new models of ownership and use (Hyde 2010; Rudmin 2016). It has led us to reexamine the distinctions between gift giving, sharing, and marketplace exchange (Belk 2010; Widlok 2013). It has caused us to consider more sustainable forms of using limited resources (e.g., Lawrie 2012) and to consider more equitable models of resource distribution (e.g., Ferguson 2015; Gollnhofer, Hellwig, and Morhart 2016; Widlok 2017). And it has moved us to reconsider how we may come to value cooperation over competition (e.g., Leadbeater 2009; Sennett 2012; Tomasello 2009). It has even caused us to imagine alternative forms of economy (Eckhardt and Bardhi 2016). With cryptocurrencies like Bitcoin and innovative business models lacking corporate hierarchies and middle persons, we may be poised for the rise of distributed autonomous corporations and organizations that take over our economies (Belk 2017a; Sundararajan 2016; Tapscott and Tapscott 2016). The result might be either sharing the profits with all or forcing us into government programs of guaranteed incomes that are not contingent on work. Therefore, while there may be nothing new in the basic concept of sharing, the stir caused by the sharing economy is reshaping the way we live and the ways we think about production and consumption. This volume offers a highly welcome emersion into a range of these issues.

References

Axelova, Eleonora, and Russell Belk. 2009. "From Saver Society to Consumer Society: The Case of the East European Consumer." *Advances in Consumer Research* 36: 824–825.

Belk, Russell. 2010. "Sharing." *Journal of Consumer Research* 36 (5): 715–734.

Belk, Russell. 2014. "Sharing versus Pseudo-Sharing in Web 2.0." *The Anthropologist* 18 (1): 7–23.

Belk, Russell. 2017a. "Consumers in an Age of Autonomous and Semi-Autonomous Machines." In *Currents in Consumer Culture Theory,* edited by John Sherry Jr. and Eileen Fischer. 5–32. London: Routledge.

Belk, Russell. 2017b. "Sharing, Materialism, and Design for Sustainability." In *Routledge Handbook of Sustainable Product Design,* edited by Jonathan Chapman. 160–172. London: Routledge.

Belk, Russell. 2017c. "Sharing without Caring." *Cambridge Journal of Regions, Economy, and Society* 10 (2): 249–261.

Benkler, Yochai. 2006. *The Wealth of Networks: How Social Production Transforms Markets and Freedom.* New Haven, CT: Yale University Press.

Botsman, Rachel, and Roo Rogers. 2010. *What's Mine Is Yours: The Rise of Collaborative Consumption.* New York: Harper Business.

Drakulić, Slavenka. 1991. *How We Survived Communism and Even Laughed.* New York: W. W. Norton.

Eckhardt, Giana M., and Fleura Bardhi. 2015. "The Sharing Economy Is Not about Sharing at All." *Harvard Business Review.* https://hbr.org/2015/01/the-sharing-economy-isnt-about-sharing-at-all.

Eckhardt, Giana M., and Fleura Bardhi. 2016. "The Relationship between Access Practices and Economic Systems." *Journal of the Association for Consumer Research* 1 (2): 210–225.

Everatt, David, and Geetesh Solanki. 2008. "A Nation of Givers? Results from a National Survey of Social Giving." In *Giving and Solidarity: Resource Flows for Poverty Alleviation and Development in South Africa,* edited by Adam Habib and Brij Maharaj. 45–78. Pretoria: Human Sciences Research Council Press.

Ferguson, James. 2015. *Give a Man a Fish: Reflections on the New Politics of Distribution.* Durham, NC: Duke University Press.

Ghosh, Rishab, ed. 2005. *CODE: Collaborative Ownership and the Digital Economy.* Cambridge, MA: MIT Press.

Giesler, Markus. 2008. "Conflict and Compromise: Drama in Marketplace Evolution." *Journal of Consumer Research* 34: 739–753.

Gollnhofer, Johanna, Katharina Hellwig, and Felicitas Morhart. 2016. "Fair Is Good, but What Is Fair? Negotiations of Distributive Justice in an Emerging Nonmonetary Sharing Model." *Journal of the Association for Consumer Research* 1 (2): 226–245.

Hemetsberger, Andrea. 2012. "'Let the Source Be with You!'—Practices of Sharing in Free and Open-Source Communities." In *Cultures and Ethics of Sharing,* edited by Wolfgang Sützl, Felix Stalder, Ronald Maier, and Theo Hug. 117–128. Innsbruck: Innsbruck University Press.

Hyde, Lewis. 2010. *Common as Air: Revolution, Art, and Ownership.* New York: Farrar, Strauss and Giroux.

John, Nicholas. 2017. *The Age of Sharing.* Cambridge: Polity Press.

Lawrie, Magnus. 2012. "Sharing and Sustainability across Institutional and Self-Instituted Forms." In *Cultures and Ethics of Sharing,* edited by Wolfgang Sützl, Felix Stalder, Ronald Maier, and Theo Hug. 59–70. Innsbruck: Innsbruck University Press.

Leadbeater, Charles. 2009. *We-Think: Mass Innovation, Not Mass Production.* London: Profile.

Lessig, Lawrence. 2004. *Free Culture: The Nature and Future of Creativity.* New York: Penguin.

Rudmin, Floyd. 2016. "The Consumer Science of Sharing: A Discussant's Observations." *Journal of the Association for Consumer Research* 1 (2): 193–197.

Schor, Juliet, Connor Fitzmaurice, Lindsey Carfagna, and Will Attwood-Charles. 2016. "Paradoxes of Openness and Distinction in the Sharing Economy." *Poetics* 54: 66–81.

Sennett, Richard. 2012. *Together: The Rituals, Pleasures and Politics of Cooperation.* New Haven, CT: Yale University Press.

Slee, Tom. 2015. *What's Yours Is Mine: Against the Sharing Economy.* New York: O/R Books.

Stack, Carol. 1976. *All Our Kin: Strategies for Survival in a Black Community.* New York: Harper & Row.

Sundararajan, Arun. 2016. *The Sharing Economy: The End of Employment and the Rise of Crowd-Based Capitalism.* Cambridge, MA: MIT Press.

Tapscott, Don. 2008. *Wikinomics: How Mass Collaboration Changes Everything.* New York: Penguin.

Tapscott, Don, and Alex Tapscott. 2016. *Blockchain Revolution: How the Technology behind Bitcoin Is Changing Money, Business, and the World.* Toronto: Portfolio.

Tomasello, Michael. 2009. *Why We Cooperate.* Cambridge, MA: MIT Press.

Widlok, Thomas. 2013. "Sharing: Allowing Others to Take What Is Valued." *Hau: Journal of Ethnographic Theory* 3 (2): 11–31.

Widlok, Thomas. 2017. *Anthropology and the Economy of Sharing.* London: Routledge.

Zwick, Detlev, Sammy Bonsu, and Aron Darmody. 2008. "Putting Consumers to Work: 'Co-Creation' and New Marketing Govern-Mentality." *Journal of Consumer Culture* 8 (2): 163–196.

PART 1

The Sharing Economy: How Did We Arrive Here?

CHAPTER ONE

Introduction: Sharing in Modern Societies

B. Yasanthi Perera and Pia A. Albinsson

This collection of writings on the sharing economy is timely as the term seems to be everywhere as of late. A range of outlets from blogs to long-standing publications such as the *New York Times* have covered various aspects of this phenomenon, and dictionaries such as those published by *Merriam Webster* and *Oxford* now provide definitions for this noun, indicating that it has become a part of the mainstream vernacular. A 2014 survey by Nielsen, an information and measurement company, which polled over 30,000 Internet-based consumers in 60 countries, found that 68% of respondents were open to sharing or renting their personal belongings for payment and that approximately 66% were likely to use products offered through sharing opportunities. A more recent poll collaboratively conducted by *Time,* the Aspen Institute, and Burson-Marsteller, a strategic communications and global public relations firm, indicates that 44% of adult North American Internet users have participated as both sharing economy providers and users and that 71% of these individuals report positive experiences (Steinmetz 2016). As John Burbank, president of Strategic Initiatives at Nielsen, notes, "There is now an established comfort level that has opened the door for sharing personal property via the Internet that may have seemed unfathomable even a few short years ago. Connecting online for activities such as shopping, managing finances, conducting research or watching videos have become an integral part of the daily routines for many. . . . Just about anything is fair game for sharing" (Nielsen 2014). Based on its increasing popularity, Pricewater-houseCoopers, the multinational professional services firm, estimates that the travel, car-sharing, finance, staffing, and music and video streaming sectors of the sharing economy, currently valued at $15 billion, will be worth $335 billion by 2025 (PwC 2015). Thus, gaining a better understanding of what the sharing economy entails would be of use in capitalizing on its potential and in engaging in meaningful research.

From a broad perspective, the sharing economy includes traditional government-to-peer (G2P) (e.g., public libraries, transportation, parks, and land) and business-to-peer (B2P) initiatives; however, much of the attention has focused on peer-to-peer (P2P) or collaborative consumption-based initiatives. "Collaborative consumption" is defined as "the set of resource circulation systems which enable consumers to both obtain and provide, temporarily or permanently, valuable resources or services through direct interaction with other consumers or through the mediation of a third-party" (Ertz, Durif, and Arcand 2016, 15). Producers and users engaging in collaborative consumption efforts interact directly in order to share, swap, trade, or rent (Botsman 2011) as well as barter, lend, and gift (Botsman and Rogers 2010). While sharing has been commonplace across cultures for millennia, in the modern marketplace and the sharing economy, technology is a critical component that facilitates sharing (Belk 2014; Chapter 5, Harvey, Smith and Golightly; Chapter 6, Kamilaris and Prenafeta-Boldú, this volume). Thus, current definitions of the sharing economy reference online activity. For example, Hamari, Sjöklint, and Ukkonen (2015, 1) define it as "the peer-to-peer-based activity of obtaining, giving, or sharing the access to goods and services, coordinated through community-based online services." Schor (2015) speaks of "economic activity that is Peer-to-Peer, or person-to-person, facilitated by digital platforms," and the *Oxford Dictionary* explains it as "an economic system in which assets or services are shared between private individuals, either free or for a fee, typically by means of the Internet." With technology as a facilitator, sharing opportunities can be scaled. As a result, "this type of 'stranger sharing' is new" (Schor 2015).

A wide range of collaborative consumption-based businesses or "platforms," enabled by technology, exist in the marketplace, and their offerings affect the lives of millions of individuals who choose to engage with them. In terms of categorization, they (1) recirculate existing goods (e.g., eBay), (2) increase the use of underutilized durable assets (e.g., Lyft, Uber, and Airbnb), (3) facilitate service exchanges (e.g., TaskRabbit or Kutoto), and (4) encourage the sharing of productive assets (e.g., co-working spaces or educational platforms) (Schor 2014). These entities may be further differentiated based on whether they are nonprofit or for-profit oriented and whether they are P2P or B2P providers (Schor 2014). But, on a practical level, what does it mean for individuals to consume in the sharing economy? For a start, those who do not own a vehicle but yet want to occasionally use one may sign up for member-ship with various collaborative consumption-based car-sharing services such as Turo or Getaround. While Zipcar, now owned by Avis, provides individuals with the means to engage in access-based consumption of vehicles (see Bardhi and Eckhardt 2012), some would argue that this model does not vary mean-ingfully from those that simply rent vehicles to consumers. From this perspec-tive, while technology and businesses serve as facilitators, the "sharing" in the sharing economy occurs between peers. Thus, as Zipcar inventory is owned by a company and Turo's and Getaround's stock comprises idle vehicles that belong to other consumers, the latter organizations fall under collaborative consumption. To get around town, in lieu of waiting for public transportation or taxicabs, consumers can conveniently secure rides from other consumers with cars through Uber's, or Lyft's smartphone applications. In addition, those with tasks to be done, ranging from furniture assembly to staffing public rela-tions events, can connect with one or several vetted individuals willing to complete these tasks for self-set fee rates through sites such as TaskRabbit that "connects you to safe and reliable help in your neighborhood" (TaskRabbit n.d.). Consumers with clothes and accessories that they no longer want can sell them and purchase those that belong to others on sites such as Poshmark or Vinted, and they can connect with other local individuals to share physical good through NeighborGoods, and Fluid, and even through local clothing libraries (Chapter 9, Albinsson and Perera), and so on. In Chapter 8 of this volume, Philip, Ozanne, and Ballantine examine online swapping, and P2P renting in order to understand consumers' experience, and assess what might make such means of collaborative consumption more effective and appealing. When on the road, consumers can secure unique and oftentimes less-expen-sive or free accommodations through Airbnb or Couchsurfing instead of tra-ditional offerings such as hotels, bed and breakfasts, and hostels. With Airbnb, the online marketplace and hospitality service that lists over 3 million accom-modation options in 65,000 cities in 191 countries around the world (Airbnb n.d.), the hosts set their rental prices and engage with consumers to the extent that they desire. Besides vacationers, others, such as David Roberts and his wife, Elaine Kuok, utilize Airbnb for their own ends. This couple wanted to explore and experience New York City better before purchasing a home, so they used Airbnb to live in a different NYC neighborhood each month of the year (Roberts 2015). Similar to Airbnb, Couchsurfing, helps vacationers con-nect with locals for the purpose of securing accommodation, but this organi-zation is a not-for-profit. Monetary transactions do not occur between the vacationer and the host; instead, the focus is on connecting with locals. There-fore, while they both offer accommodations that are alternatives to hotels, they utilize different understandings of what constitutes sharing and thus pro-vide users with different experiences. In a related matter, prior to leaving for vacation, consumers with dogs can connect with local pet sitters through platforms such as DogVacay to ensure that their friends are being cared for well. These examples present a small sample of current ventures that fall within the collaborative consumption-based sharing economy. While this account focuses on the user, the propagation of such options and the estimated growth projections of collaborative consumption-based initiatives indicate that, increasingly, consumers are opting to participate in this economy as producers, users, and perhaps both.

Despite its popularity, the state of the sharing economy is somewhat messy. Some, such as consumers who now have more convenient and perhaps more wallet-friendly options, and individual service providers that now have the opportunity to leverage their underutilized resources to earn additional income, benefit. Yet others, for example those in established industries such as employees of taxicab companies with whom sharing economy–based ventures such as Uber and Lyft compete, are negatively affected as their industry's competitive position is challenged by, and struggle to adapt to, the presence of these innovative businesses (see Chapter 12 by Ranchordás for an overview of tensions among sharing economy providers, public policy, and regulations). With this said, the reality is likely to be as clear-cut. Intuitively, as partaking in collaborative consumption-based offerings largely entail P2P transactions facilitated through a collaborative consumption platform that is somewhat removed, in certain instances, relative to established businesses, consumers may assume additional risks in engaging these services. In addition, service providers may be exploited, for instance, because the service facilitation companies or platforms retain a portion of the transaction fee. Therefore, while this space has developed tremendously, it is not without concerns. It comprises many forms of organizational models ranging from for-profits valued in the billions to nonprofits seeking ways to maintain their services, and the for-profits themselves are diverse in form and the extent to which they participate in the sharing experiences. Thus, while some laud the benefits of the sharing economy in terms of additional service options, convenience, additional income streams, and sustainability, others note that it simply encourages more consumption, forces providers and consumers to assume more risks, and ultimately exploits them. This compilation of writings is helpful in unpacking this space.

This book draws together the works of multiple researchers whose writings reflect different historical, national, and organizational contexts. For example, Findlay (Chapter 2) discusses how organizations in the sharing economy can learn from the experiences of cooperatives to avoid certain pitfalls including corporatizing pressures, while Lamberton (Chapter 10) examines how commercial sharing systems can be viable in current maturing marketplaces. The reader will note that the various authors' understanding of the sharing economy and collaborative consumption differs from one another. While some may take issue, this adds to the strength of the compilation because it provides insights into different ways of viewing this space, thereby adding richness to discussions to the various contentions surrounding the sharing economy.

The writings provide the reader with an understanding on multiple broad topics including what led to the development of the modern sharing economy (Chapter 3, Wolf and Ritz; Chapter 4, Hellwig, Sahakian, and Morhart), as well as the role of economics (Chapter 7, Teubner and Hawlitschek) and technology (Chapter 5, Harvey, Smith, and Golightly; Chapter 6 Kamilaris and Prenafeta-Boldú) in its development and continued growth. Over the past few years, the mainstream media has reported on the regulatory challenges faced by collaborative consumption platforms such as Uber and Airbnb as they spread to various locales in North America and around the world. Thus, in terms of G-2-P interactions, Chasin (Chapter 11) examines the case of how the city government officials in Seoul, South Korea, play an active role in facilitating the development of the sharing economy. The book also presents specific sharing and collaborative consumption experiences from a consumer perspective in different cultural contexts, for example, former East Germany (Chapter 3, Wolf and Ritz), New Zealand (Chapter 8, Philip, Ozanne, and Ballantine), and Sweden (Chapter 9, Albinsson and Perera). We, the editors, and the contributing authors created this book because we wanted to inspire more discussion and inspire solutions to challenges faced by various stakeholders involved in the sharing economy. In addition, given the range of topics covered, we hope these writings will provide the reader with new insights into the sharing economy and collaborative consumption, thereby inspiring ideas for practical applications, as well as future research.

References

Airbnb. n.d. "About Us." https://www.airbnb.ca/about/about-us?locale=en.

Bardhi, Fleura, and Giana M. Eckhardt. 2012. "Access-Based Consumption: The Case of Car Sharing." *Journal of Consumer Research* 39 (December): 881–898.

Belk, Russell. 2014. "You Are What You Can Access: Sharing and Collaborative Consumption Online." *Journal of Business Research* 67 (8): 1595–1600.

Botsman, Rachel. 2011. "The Sharing Economy Lacks a Shared Definition." http://www.fastcoexist.com/3022028/the-sharing-economy-lacks-a-shared-definition.

Botsman, Rachel, and Roo Rogers. 2010. *What's Mine Is Yours. The Rise of Collaborative Consumption*. New York: HarperCollins.

Ertz, Myriam, Fabien Durif, and Manon Arcand. 2016. "Collaborative Consumption: Conceptual Snapshot at a Buzzword." *Journal of Entrepreneurship Education* 19 (2): 1–23.

Hamari, J., M. Sjöklint, and A. Ukkonen. 2016. "The Sharing Economy: Why People Participate in Collaborative Consumption." *Journal of the Association for Information Science and Technology* 67: 2047–2059. doi:10.1002/asi.23552.

Nielsen. 2014. "Global Consumers Embrace the Sharing Economy." May 28. http://www.nielsen.com/ca/en/press-room/2014/global-consumers-embrace-the-share-economy.html.

PwC. 2015. "The Sharing Economy." *Consumer Intelligence Series.* https://www.pwc.com/us/en/technology/publications/assets/pwc-consumer-intelligence-series-the-sharing-economy.pdf.

Roberts, David. 2015. "Our Year of Living Airbnb." *New York Times.* November 25. https://www.nytimes.com/2015/11/29/realestate/our-year-of-living-airbnb.html?_r=0.

Schor, Juliet. 2014. "Debating the Sharing Economy." Great Transition Initiative. October 1. http://www.greattransition.org/publication/debating-the-sharing-economy.

Schor, Juliet. 2015. "On the Sharing Economy, Getting Sharing Right." Contexts. February 23. https://contexts.org/articles/on-the-sharing-economy/#schor.

Steinmetz, Katy. 2016. "Sharing Economy's True Size Revealed in New Poll." *Time.* January 6. http://time.com/4169532/sharing-economy-poll/.

TaskRabbit. n.d. "The Convenient & Fast Way to Get Things Done around the House." https://www.taskrabbit.com/.

CHAPTER TWO

Precursors to the Sharing Economy: Cooperatives

Isobel M. Findlay

Introduction

In the context of ongoing financial, economic, and environmental crises, many herald the sharing economy or collaborative consumption (Botsman and Rogers 2010)—distinguished by Belk (2010, 2014) from both gift giving and market exchanges—as a game changer (Walsh 2011). "Mindful consumption" (Sheth, Sethia, and Srinivas 2011)—distinct from both the constrained consumption of the underprivileged and the conspicuous consumption of the privileged—is characterized as a novel, disruptive, and innovative response to overconsumption of goods and services and underutilization of assets and resources. It is promoted as empowering people to achieve sustainable futures, avoid the excesses of ownership that precipitated the crises, and even promote "the re-emergence of community" (Botsman and Rogers 2010), especially in the context of changed mind-sets and knowledgeable, responsible consumption (Albinsson and Perera 2012). Exploring a "plenitude economy," Schor (2011) remarks on a "wave of social innovation" associated with such radical rethinking of economic and social values, part of larger efforts to humanize the economy and enhance well-being (Birchall 2011; Haque 2011; Loxley 2007; McMurtry 2010; Mook, Quarter, and Ryan 2012; Porter and Kramer 2011; Restakis 2010; Schor 2010; Schwab 2011).

The "dark side" of the sharing economy (Malhotra and Van Alstyne 2014) has not gone unnoticed, however, in a fast-growing gray and academic literature underlining legal, regulatory, political, and other battles; increased precariousness and risk shifting (Kaine, Logue, and Josserand 2016; Scholz 2014, 2016; Torjman 2016); and exposing practices that avoid taxes and regulation and even risk "breaking the law" (Baker 2014). Eckhardt and Bardhi (2015) insist that it "isn't really a 'sharing' economy at all; it's an access economy," while Hamari, Sjöklint, and Ukkonen (2015, 1) identify an "attitude-behavior gap" in motivations to participate in collaborative consumption. Schneider (2014, 1) underlines the failed promise of "a liberating Internet" reduced to "the dominance of a few mega-companies" enclosing the commons "by tweaking terms of service, diluting privacy, or charging fees for essential features." They do so while monetizing "users' unpaid labor of friending and posting" and extracting "five to ten times more profit" from remaining employees.

Indeed, this literature has added to our vocabulary in exposing the "share-washing" of platforms and activities such as Airbnb, Getable, Sidecar, Lyft, Yardle, TaskRabbit, Facebook, Google, and Twitter. Each of these businesses is eager to draw on the symbolic capital of "sharing" while supporting rather than subverting market logic and "the growth juggernaut of the mainstream economy" (Kalamar 2013). While immensely profitable—Uber and Airbnb are among the most valuable private enterprises, according to CB Insights (2017)—their activities even prove less green and social than public relations would suggest: their much-hyped novelty and trendiness obscuring classist, racist assumptions about premodern legacies of sharing that ignore the daily importance of "non-digital sharing practices" for many including "the working-class, poor, and minority communities" as well as persistent discrimination along class, gender, and race lines (Schor 2014, 5–8).

Avoiding the extremes of much commentary, Schor (2014) offers nuanced readings of the phenomenon, negotiating claims and counterclaims; distinguishing the new from the not-so-new, large and small, neighborhood and national initiatives, profit and nonprofit market orientation and market structure; and identifying social movement opportunities to harness technologies to fairer, progressive sharing ends. Schor (2014, 3) notes that cooperatives are "the historic form" of asset sharing in the interest of production, and that there has been renewed interest in cooperatives. Kaine, Logue, and Josserand (2016) likewise discuss cooperatives—"at the interface of major technological, business and social trends: the sharing economy, social entrepreneurship, impact investing and social purpose spending"—as an ownership model responding to the "'uberisation' of work." For Schneider (2014, 2–7), the renewed interest in cooperatives makes sense when "ownership matters as much as ever. . . . Whoever owns the platforms that help us share decides who accumulates wealth from them, and how." Those interested in "genuine sharing" must then "embrace ownership—and, as they do, they're changing what owning means altogether."

It is "a different ownership model" that similarly drives Scholz's (2014, 1–6) interest in cooperatives as a fairer, "humane alternative to the free market model" or "platform capitalism" that "trains people to be followers" and involves "subcontracting and rental economies with big payouts going to small groups of people." Cooperatives, by contrast, "could help weave some ethical threads into the fabric of 21st century work." Instead of the unsustainable practices of "suck[ing] value out of your interactions with everyday objects, recruiting . . . informants for surveillance capitalism," while "unleashing a colossal union-busting machine" (2–3), Scholz (2016, 11) finds in "platform cooperativism" some answers to "the old extractive model" in "reinvigorate[d] solidarity, change[d] ownership, and . . . democratic governance." Schor (2014) also begins to sketch out how cooperatives and the solidarity sector more generally might help the sharing economy avoid co-optation to monopoly interests, increase participation, and help redistribute wealth through "user-governed or cooperatively owned" platforms. Embedded in the right "political, regulatory, and social contexts," and enjoying "cross-fertilization" with other social movements, the sharing economy might avoid the commodifying, concentrating, and corporatizing pressures (Schor 2014, 11–12).

With a special emphasis on the Canadian experience, this chapter builds on these suggestions, reframing issues while taking back cooperative history and identity from corporate appropriations and distortions to rekindle cooperative memory; reanimate the seven principles; and promote economic, environmental, and cultural democracy. In the process it unpacks the dominant fictions of economic modernity that have brought us to the current tipping point and sacrificed alternative models and principles in the process.

Hidden History/Hidden Curriculum

Crises are the result of powerful discourses, institutions, meaning making, and material practices—as well as "functional stupidity" (Alvesson and Spicer 2012, 1194), or an unwillingness or incapacity to reflect critically on dominant terms or assumptions—that maintain the status quo and still keep cooperative forms of ownership largely invisible in business school curricula and in mass media (Findlay 2012; Shaw 2012). They are equally invisible in economics texts (Kalmi 2007; Quarter et al. 2002) and economics journals invested in "a neo-classical monoculture" (Webster et al. 2012). For all the postmodern claims about the end of history and the nation state, and the triumph of the liberal subject (eclectic, consumerist, individualist), big stories by self-inflating authors continue to favor mainstream interests and reproduce inequalities, while mediating our understanding of "realities" and our capacities to act and intervene in globalizing changes (Findlay 2004). The "strong wind of 'market fundamentalism'"—or faith in unregulated markets as the solution to social and economic problems—"has blown from New York to Washington, deeply influencing the approach to economic policy around the world" (Borzaga and Galera 2012, 3)—"blowing old and new pollutants while whipping the elements into new threats to human structures, economic activity, and human life," intensifying precarity and pitting short-term extractive opportunity against long-term, cooperative policy (Findlay and Findlay 2013, 814). Proponents of market fundamentalism characterize climate change and ecological interests as impediments to economies and social justice as a luxury we can no longer afford. They reduce "the plurality of economic and entrepreneurial models to a single, reductive logic" and multiple bottom lines to "a single financial one." In the process they distract "attention from human responsibility for the economic meltdown" and either discount or appropriate "to their own competitive purposes cooperation and multiple bottom lines" (Findlay 2012, 2; on Walmart, e.g., see Monllos 2015).

A key instrument in naturalizing and entrenching these "strong winds" and big stories is the so-called hidden curriculum (Jackson 1968; Margolis 2001), or what Smith (1990) calls "relations of ruling." This invisible infrastructure within educational institutions teaches dominant norms and values without ever acknowledging its biases. It appears so natural as to remain powerfully hidden in plain view despite being outed almost 50 years ago. And the mythical liberal sovereign subject, a rights bearer purportedly unmarked by gender, race, or class, continues to maintain the status quo (and the racial hierarchies on which it depends) despite learning across the disciplines about changing, adaptable human behavior, and economic choices (Schor 2010; Schulte-Tenckhoff 2015). The hidden curriculum similarly keeps hidden the holistic thinking of Indigenous peoples who respect the vitality, equality, and interdependence of all (human and nonhuman alike) and live in harmony with "All our relations," or *miyowicehtowin*—having or possessing good relations, the laws concerning good relations (Cardinal and Hildebrandt 2000, 14–16). It keeps hidden the ways that such thinking might yield new forms of sustainability by recognizing the full range of relations on which we depend (Findlay and Findlay 2012, 2013).

It is ironic that the hidden curriculum has for so long actively supported ignorance in the interests of domination and exploitation (Sullivan and Tuana 2007), while marginalizing knowledges and resources so critical to sustainable communities and economies. Globalizing modernity's wasteful ways fragmenting, individualizing, and privatizing knowledges and relegating some knowledges to the dustbin of history have been well documented by Bauman (2004). Such waste persists even as in 2012 there were three times more cooperative members than individual shareholders worldwide: 328 million direct shareholders compared with 1 billion member owners of cooperatives with a value of over US$1.6 trillion (Mayo 2012a); and even as Indigenous peoples representing only 4% of the world's population preserve 60% of its linguistic and biodiversity (Lertzman and Vredenburg 2005).

In resisting domination, exclusion, and exploitation in 19th-century Britain, new communications, communities, and identities produced alternative public spheres, including the cooperative movement committed to an educational project for the common good. As "school[s] for citizenship" (Ekelund 1987, 40)—or, for John Stuart Mill, "school[s] of the social sympathies and the practical intelligence" (quoted in Ekelund 1987, 55)—and key institutions for supporting and sustaining communities, cooperatives have much in common yet underused solidarity with Indigenous communities. If they are considered in educational and other settings, they are associated with the past or with the persistence of the curiously unmodern (Findlay 2003). And courts have compounded those difficulties in the case of Indigenous communities (Henderson, Benson, and Findlay 2000); in the case of cooperatives, courts have sided with corporatism, individual rights, and elite democracy over cooperative commitments to collective rights and democratic structure (Apland and Axworthy 1990; Axworthy 1990; Ish 1981, 1995). As habituated as cooperators are to the glib dismissal of mainstream institutions, Indigenous peoples turned to the United Nations for recognition of their rights and knowledges. Retrieving their role as "the teaching civilization" (Henderson 2008, 48), they challenged market logic and Eurocentric thinking that promotes European ways to the exclusion of other ways of knowing and being (Battiste and Henderson 2000; Henderson 2008). They did so while shifting "frames of understanding" to "knowledge ecologies" committed to "diversity as enrichment, people before profits, and sustainable practices rooted in land, language, and collective rights and responsibilities" (Findlay and Findlay 2012, 40).

Multiple histories of cooperation and cooperatives can take us in the urgent directions of economic, environmental, and cultural democracy; sharing for sustainability; and productive interdependency—the sort of social movement synergies invoked by Schor (2014). Such sharing would be a valuable corrective to the illusory individualism and Schumpeterian (1947) "creative destruction" that need retrieving from the reductive free market triumphalism of Schumpeter's disciples (Findlay and Findlay 2013). Through the related lenses of cooperative enterprise and of cooperation as a social, economic, and environmental value, one can better measure mainstream neoliberal exceptionalism in Canada (and beyond) and the ways in which too many policy makers and commentators continue to construct cooperatives as outmoded and uncompetitive, useful only for local treatment of the wounds and abrasions that selectively accompany the robust operations of "the" global market (Findlay and Findlay 2012, 2013; Webster et al. 2012).

On the basis of this unmasking and supplementation, I make a positive case for cooperatives in Canada as "*both* preservative *and* innovative," and not reducible to "the preservation/innovation binary" so dear to Schumpeter's less-thoughtful disciples. Cooperatives have preserved innovation, collective empowerment, and democratic practice "whose time has come with the current legitimation crisis" (Findlay and Findlay 2013, 818). And they have done so in a new wave of cooperative enterprises—in housing, culture, fishing, local foods, health, and platform cooperativism (Schneider 2014; Scholz 2014, 2016)—in the interests of a "generative economy" (Great Transition Initiative 2012). Cooperative adaptability and resilience is connected to cooperative enterprise and Indigenous innovation collaborating on pluralizing and humanizing the economy and multiplying cooperative histories, showing the persistent value of democratic mutualism to sustainable economies.

Reclaiming Cooperative History and Identity

If the history of cooperation and cooperatives has been deliberately or concertedly obscured by the dominant narrative of Western economic progress, that narrative is increasingly exposed for its narrow economic rationality, its naturalizing of the market and homo economicus (Findlay and Findlay 2013; Nowak 2012; Polanyi 1944; Schulte-Tenckhoff 2015). Cooperation has been not exceptional but foundational in the history of evolution (Nowak 2012). Socially embedded and culturally specific cooperative and competitive behaviors are a part of Western economic rationality that is different from but not superior to other societies invested in kinship relations, for instance. Neoclassical economic theory's principles of scarcity and profit maximization, similarly, are neither natural nor universal and are rejected by Amartya Sen, who characterized "*purely* economic man" as "indeed close to being a social moron" (cited in Schulte-Tenckhoff 2015, 31).

Working to uncover the hidden history of cooperation, cooperative movements, and communalism in America, Curl (2012) reshapes understanding of the role of cooperatives and economic democracy for social justice in diverse communities and for recapturing the commons from centuries of enclosure, commodification, and privatization. In *Collective Courage,* Gordon Nembhard (2014, 86, 25) traces links between cooperatives and the civil rights movement from the 1700s, rekindling cooperative memories and W.E.B. Du Bois's "intelligent cooperation" wherever she spoke, inquired, or presented, and retelling the story of African American history "through the lens of the Black cooperative movement" that engaged and nurtured black political and economic leadership. She makes clear that black cooperatives matter.

Among the diverse histories of cooperation and cooperatives worldwide, the Rochdale "myth" has proved especially powerful, its meaning contested, constructed, and reconstructed in the name of "participation and social change" (Fairbairn 1994, 1). Rochdale and its social movement partners and precedents—Owenism, Chartism, trade unionism, and the women's movement, including the Women's Co-operative Guild (Fairbairn 1994; Find-lay and Findlay 2012; Woodin 2012)—have inspired cooperators who "devel-oped, re-interpreted and adapted [values and principles] to meet diverse challenges and opportunities" (Webster et al. 2012, 4). Cooperatives are them-selves creatures and challengers of globalizing modernity and industrializa-tion's colonial and domestic axes. The legacy of legal and institutional forms available to and adapted by cooperators in the 1840s has given rise to conflicts and contradictions in the movement (Fairbairn et al. 1990).

In responding to politically unfettered market forces and the disastrous socioeconomic consequences of industrializing globalization for ordinary people, the Rochdale Pioneers sought answers through mutual self-help to the immediate needs of members but also "as soon as practicable, . . . to arrange the powers of production, distribution, education, and government, or in other words to establish a self-supporting home colony of united interests, or assist other Societies in establishing such colonies" (1844 Statute of Rochdale Pioneers, cited in Fairbairn 1994, 5). Theirs was an incisive politics with a "force and directness" very different from "the vague generalities and hack-neyed phrases" of the typical Member of Parliament (stonemason, cited by Woodin 2012, 81). Theirs was a commitment to shared risks and rewards, to people before profits, and to a set of business practices and principles "em-phasizing quality, honesty, market prices, cash trading . . . democratic gover-nance, provision of education and information to members" (Fairbairn 1994, 18–19). In their efforts to enact a social economy and creative strategies of survival, we can find hope in the current juncture. Committed to the common good, cooperators were intent on "making capital into a hired servant of theirs rather than their continuing as hired servants of capital," while seeking new terms and forms of association to capture new meanings for mainstream con-cepts of public goods. For influential cooperator George Jacob Holyoake and others, association was "a moral art as well as a new form of economy" (Yeo 1988, 2–3).

When the first International Cooperative Congress met in London in 1895, the British dominated the meeting, resolving that the purpose of the Interna-tional Co-operative Alliance was to "promote co-operation and profit-sharing" (Fairbairn 1994, 22), purposes and principles regularly revised thereafter un-til the 1995 Statement on Co-operative Identity defining cooperatives as "an autonomous association of persons united voluntarily to meet their common economic, social, and cultural needs and aspirations through a jointly-owned and democratically-controlled enterprise" (cited in International Co-operative Alliance (ICA) 2016).

Promoting cooperative or "owner responsibility" that marries economic and social models and values (Gould 2012, cited in Findlay and Findlay 2013, 810) long before the corporate world discovered corporate social responsibil-ity, cooperatives "pursued goals such as community capacity building, environmental sustainability, and local employment, including good governance practices" (Findlay 2012, 1), highlighted in the seven cooperative principles (ICA 2016):

- Voluntary and open membership
- Democratic member control
- Member economic participation
- Autonomy and independence
- Education, training, and information
- Cooperation among cooperatives
- Concern for community

Although work remains to be done to document more thoroughly and appropriately the cooperative difference and advantage (Brown and Novkovic 2015), events and publications of the UN International Year did much to shed light on co-op contributions to "poverty reduction, employment generation and social integration," and "to furthering socioeconomic development" (United Nations 2016). And the cooperative record on resilience and sustainability has been remarkable. Birchall and Hammond Ketilson (2009), for instance, have traced the growth of worker cooperatives and the overall resilience of cooperatives during times of crisis, including the banking sector (representing 177 million members in the World Council of Credit Unions and another 500 million in the International Raiffeisen Union), in sharp contrast to the private banking sector's massive bailouts. The seven principles and policy goals of financial inclusion and employment creation go some way to explaining this resilience. In their study of cooperative resilience, Myers, Maddocks, and Beecher (2012, 320) stress closeness, community links, accessibility, and attention to locality, which shape superior risk assessment. But they also caution that cooperatives cannot rest on their laurels—"trust, transparency and commitment to values-led business"—but must constantly review and renew for sustainable futures. If cooperatives have proved more stable and secure than other business types, they also offer decent work and in Arctic Canada "form the backbone of the local economy," with the year 2008 "a banner year" for the 31 cooperatives in Arctic Cooperatives Limited (ACL) (Birchall and Hammond Ketilson 2009, 31). Similarly, Keng (2014) has underlined the value of worker cooperatives in his calculation that if Apple were a worker cooperative, all employees would earn $403K!

It is this principled form of enterprise with its commitment to education and the welfare of the broader community that explains the resurgence of interest in cooperatives despite or perhaps because of "the hegemony of the investor-led business model in economic and business studies" (Webster et al.

2012, 4). Such a business monoculture purveyed as the only and natural way of doing business leaves many craving alternatives without adequate knowledge and tools to reimagine possibilities (Findlay 2004). But the histories of diverse cooperative systems have much to tell about the thriving of cooperatives in different sociocultural conditions. In the case of 19th-century Italian cooperatives, for example, different religious, intellectual, and political traditions with a shared commitment to "community happiness" contributed levels of trust and consensus to cooperative development. "In fact," Battilani (2012, 169) argues, "the expansion of an enterprise based on the principles of solidarity and the promotion of the well-being of its members, required a cultural framework in which solidarity was a recognised value, and in which the principle of community happiness countered the mere pursuit of individual gain or utility." In the per capita expenditure on welfare, Battilani finds a valuable indicator of "an institutional fabric and of a deep-rooted culture of community happiness." Similarly, across the world, cooperatives have flourished where they find common cause with traditional values and resilient social movements, as they have in Latin America (Lacey 2012). Klein (2014), for instance, has documented the worker takeover of abandoned factories in the wake of the 2001 Argentinian economic crisis; most of the worker-run cooperatives continue to thrive. Indeed, it is often among social movement "sisters" of the cooperative movement that "the next generation of co-operative innovators" emerges (Mayo 2012b, 351).

Unlike Italian Marxist Gramsci's "traditional intellectual" whose distance, disinterest, and detachment are the markers and modalities of effective commentary, cooperative intellectuals—"connected, committed, collaborative"—bring "to bear situated knowledge of multiple realities," sustaining cooperative development by connecting with community aspirations, powers, and human and other resources (Findlay 2004, 160). The cooperative intellectual builds on the legacy of Gramsci's "organic intellectual" whose "general practical activity" is "perpetually innovating the physical and social world, [and becoming] a new and integral conception of the world" (1971, 9). Operating in multiple locations, cooperative intellectuals renegotiate center/periphery relations, for instance, to galvanize the social intelligence "rooted in communities and their ecologies" for "community education and action, and for interrelationships that sustain enterprise." While such cooperative "sharing" of the power to define what counts can be crucial, we must likewise address cooperative roles in "a colonial past and ongoing present" (Findlay 2004, 160; Findlay and Findlay 2012). For that decolonizing work, we need those cooperative intellectuals committed to changing how we operate inside and outside the academy and in the cooperative movement. And that means listening attentively to cooperative members and managers, and to the elders, storytellers, professional, practicing, and academic teachers (Indigenous and non-Indigenous) (Findlay 2004; Findlay and Findlay 2012).

Pluralizing and Humanizing the Economy: Convergent Paths in Solidarity

Societies and their institutions require open, dynamic, and exemplary systems to facilitate new ways of thinking and doing (Findlay 2012). The multiple histories of cooperatives remind us of the extent to which those histories are embedded in larger sociocultural, economic, and political processes from which cooperatives have drawn strength and resilience. If cooperatives today are finding new opportunity in car, bike, and tool sharing, for example, they are also finding new energies, enterprise, and understandings in alternative traditions and knowledges so often demonized, disdained, or discarded by the mainstream. For example, the knowledges of Indigenous cooperatives and communities that were long discounted by self-serving experts justifying colonial dispossession and exploitation are now renewing cooperatives in Canada and around the world. In the cooperative form, Indigenous communities are finding capacities to revitalize entrepreneurship and resist neocolonial incursions, "bridging the traditional and social economies to achieve a common vision of a healthy, sustainable community" (Findlay 2012, 2; 2014; Findlay, Ray, and Basualdo 2011; Findlay and Wuttunee 2007).

Arctic Co-operatives Limited

In resisting the impact of succeeding waves of globalization, colonial and neocolonial law and policy, and the impoverishment of communities, Inuit (and Dene and Métis in the North) embarked on a journey to self-determination that involved links to other circumpolar communities and organizations, women's associations, and the cooperative movement in which they found something like their own "sharing culture" (ACL 2016). They established individual cooperatives in the 1950s and 1960s based on traditional cultural and economic practices (e.g., arts and crafts, fishing, fur harvesting). The cooperative model proved "the best way" to meet their goals to develop their own services, keep profits in the community, and employ their own people. Soon they were multiplying the purposes (retail stores, hotels, post offices, freight and fuel, transportation and construction, cable television, Internet services, real estate, etc.) and forming cooperative federations, including ACL incorporated in 1972 (ACL 2016). As one board member described it, they created ACL "so that whenever one co-op or co-ops are having problems they help each other" (cited in Findlay 2014, 50). Leadership training in their local cooperatives yielded benefits beyond the cooperative: more than half of the members of the Nunavut legislature have had such training, for example (Hammond Ketilson and MacPherson 2001). The Inuit connection with the land is profound. One Inuk, for instance, has said that Nunavut means, for those with a deep understanding of the Inuktitut language, "We share in this together, unconditionally" (cited in Findlay 2014, 47). They are also more than willing to share what they have achieved within and beyond their communities. In advertisements for Inns North owned and operated by ACL, they replay and revise old colonial terms when they invite visitors: "Discover the real Arctic with us. . . . We know the North and we are delighted to share our knowledge with you" (cited in Findlay 2014, 46).

In the case of Koomiut Co-operative in Kugaaruk in the central Arctic—accessible only by air (or sea for a couple of months a year)—the co-op is at the heart of the community. It is where community members gather, where they are served in their own language, where they can find the products and services they request at prices they trust (though very high compared to southern Canada because of high transportation costs), and where they can cash checks in the absence of banking facilities. The co-op supports community events, offers training and education, and is a source of great pride in what the community has achieved with its co-op, which is "much more than a business" and an important symbol of community ownership and control (cited in Findlay 2014, 52). Cooperative membership represents close to 99% of the population, and a large, engaged audience can be counted on at annual general meetings.

Having "a voice" is an important part of the meaning of co-op membership, and annual meetings often produce new ideas. Co-op members guard their membership against attempts by the corporate Northern Store to gain a foothold in the community, voting "no" and insisting they "want to help the co-op, we want to help the people" (cited in Findlay 2014, 54). And the elders are vital stewards of traditional cultural knowledge and also help develop new initiatives such as tourism with their promotion of kayak building. Innovation comes as a result of and not at the expense of Inuit knowledge and experience in land-based practices. Their enterprises, like the communities themselves, are constantly renegotiating colonial boxes and boundaries that presumed to define the world and circumscribe their efforts. The vigor of their co-ops and communities owes much to the collective intelligence of key players interrupting the privileges and priorities of center–margin relations and insisting on their commitment to and relationship with the land and their obligation to the creator for the plenty that sustains them. If controlling their own destiny is critical and their achievements are remarkable (ACL is one of the largest co-op federations in Canada), members do not rest on their laurels. They know well that ongoing support, especially among the youth, cannot be presumed and that the onus is on them to powerfully communicate (including in educational curricula) the value and meaning of the co-op.

Dene members of Great Bear Co-operative established in 1963 in Deline, Northwest Territories, similarly value the co-op for its contributions to cultural events and sports teams, board and staff training, building infrastructure such as telecommunications, and engaging the youth. They also understand the co-op is "not just a store"; it is "a community thing" and their version of self-government, which is why they consider it so important to maintain co-op values that they see as "work[ing] well together with Aboriginal values." They are also clear that the so-called hidden curriculum needs to be addressed in the messages sent about who or what matters in communities: "School should teach about co-ops. In a kindergarten class, there was a big lesson plan where all the examples were based on the Northern Store. . . . The co-op should be substituted for that" (cited in Findlay and Wuttunee 2007, 13–14).

ACL members teach us to find strength in networks, to diversify to meet member needs, to make the co-op the social and cultural center, to promote education, and to consolidate connection to place. Their teaching also "breathes a new pluralistic meaning into multiple bottom lines," stretching cooperative terms of engagement from independence to interdependence and reimagining the seventh cooperative principle—concern for community—to include the land and all that it sustains and is sustained by. Adopting and adapting the cooperative form, ACL members have faced many barriers and "natural obstacles," but they "have worked together with one voice, and have built a very impressive network of community-owned and -controlled enterprises. They have become a model for Aboriginal development in Canada" (then ACL president Bill Lyall, cited in Findlay 2014, 57–58).

The Northern Saskatchewan Trappers Association Co-operative

In the interests of its own decolonizing vision, the Northern Saskatchewan Trappers Association Co-operative (NSTAC) in Northern Saskatchewan aimed to reinvent itself and engage youth by incorporating as a nonprofit community development cooperative in 2007. The process of reinvention led the NSTAC to recall and retell its own history, remembering its own customary co-operative practices that taught "people their place in the world," their relation to all creatures, "their roles and responsibilities," what they could and could not do, and how to live harmoniously and sustainably. In retelling the story of trapping as a whole way of life, they underlined its meaning for justice, education, science, health, land management, as well as economic initiative. They "redefined trapping not as a quaint legacy of the past, but as an invaluable activity expressing the values of both the ongoing and revitalizing traditional economy and the social economy," offering alternative models putting people before profits; autonomous management, inclusion, and democratic participation; and sustainable environments and livelihoods (Findlay and Findlay 2013, 819; Findlay, Ray, and Basualdo 2011).

In challenging "the uncooperative economy" and trapping's association with "inhumane traps and Western patterns of conspicuous consumption," like ACL, the NSTAC gained a renewed sense of legitimacy in new solidarities with the cooperative movement and a shared history of principled practice. It breathed new meaning into multiple bottom lines, replenishing the economic with the ecological and stimulating cooperative cultural memory in resistance to the economic reductionism of capitalist competition. It encourages us "to think about and act on their interdependencies, recognize shared interest in change, and see in trapping new opportunities for the revitalization of cultural life and customary practices" (Findlay and Findlay 2013, 819). The NSTAC shows what Indigenous values and practices can mean for cooperative futures and for understanding cooperative resilience in responding to the hostility and amnesia of dominant discourses and globalizing forces. Neither co-ops nor Indigenous communities are frozen in time; cooperatives can be a powerful meeting place for intergenerational and intercultural dialogue and community learning. Cooperatives can accommodate "tradition and/as innovation in forms of therapeutic and ecological enterprise where young adults can themselves become trappers and educators rather than the ones trapped in the alienating individualism required and rewarded in so many mainstream Canadian institutions" (Findlay and Findlay 2013, 819).

Conclusion

Cooperative intellectuals ask us to remember our histories and responsibilities for a colonial encounter that cost Indigenous peoples dearly and also to learn from a history of interdependency nourished by sharing, respect, responsible use, and good government entailed in relational understandings of humans and their environment—"All my relations." The hope is that we can learn together and learn from one another to resist past paternalisms and redefine the latest version of the cutting edge, exposing the slipperiness of language used to promote as social innovation in "new" market behavior what is really profit-seeking for the few, promoting short-term extractive opportunity while intensifying precarity and lowering and offloading labor costs to the many. Then we might replay the incisive politics and "moral art" of Rochdale to produce a sustainable knowledge economy in the interests of community happiness and common goods—a social economy that truly shares without exploiting and commodifying Indigenous or other knowledges in the one-way "sharing" of predatory colonialism and capitalism. Then we might remedy discursive and democratic deficits, rename co-operatively the terms we live by, and renew shared stories and symbols that will fire the cooperative imagination and redefine the sharing economy.

Both ACL and the NSTAC are exemplary in their commitment to reimagining our futures together and refusing the dominant market mind-set that would make some co-operatives forget the cooperative difference and democratizing commitments. Learning from their examples, pluralizing and humanizing the economy in solidarity, we might better redefine the sharing economy, building on local knowledge and practice and on the territory marked by a history of cooperative activity that needs to become better known in mainstream institutions. Then Du Boisian "intelligent cooperation" might help us recast current crises as opportunities to take back our power to define the sharing or collaborative economy and to contest economic, social, cultural, and other monopolies. In a set of respectful emergent practices, we might expose and to some extent expunge the ultra-individualism and conspiratorial collectivism on which colonialism and neocolonialism so heavily depend and which they so ruthlessly defend.

Acknowledgments

I gratefully acknowledge funding from the Social Sciences and Humanities Research Council for my research with Arctic Co-operatives Limited (Co-operative Membership and Globalization: Creating Social Cohesion through Market Relations; principal investigator Brett Fairbairn) and for research with the NSTAC (Linking, Learning, Leveraging: Social Enterprises, Knowledgeable Economies, and Sustainable Communities, Regional Node of the Social Economy; principal investigator Lou Hammond Ketilson).

References

Albinsson, Pia A., and B. Yasanthi Perera. 2012. "Alternative Marketplaces in the 21st Century: Building Community through Sharing Events." *Journal of Consumer Behaviour* 11: 303–315.

Alvesson, Mats, and André Spicer. 2012. "A Stupidity-Based Theory of Organizations." *Journal of Management Studies* 49 (7): 1194–1220.

Apland, Lars, and Christopher S. Axworthy. 1990. "Collective and Individual Rights in Canada: A Legal Perspective on Co-operatives." In *Co-operative Organizations and Canadian Society: Popular Institutions and the Dilemmas of Change,* edited by Murray Fulton. 184–231. Toronto: University of Toronto Press.

Arctic Co-operatives Limited (ACL). 2016. "History." http://www.arcticco-op.com/about-acl-history.htm.

Axworthy, Christopher S. 1990. "Myth and Reality in Co-operative Organizations: Members, Directors, Employees, and Managers." In *Co-operative Organizations and Canadian Society: Popular Institutions and the Dilemmas of Change,* edited by Murray Fulton. 39–60. Toronto: University of Toronto Press.

Baker, Dean. 2014. "Don't Buy the 'Sharing Economy' Hype: Airbnb and Uber Are Facilitating Ripoffs." *The Guardian.* May 27. https://www.theguardian.com/commentisfree/2014/may/27/airbnb-uber-taxes-regulation.

Battilani, Patrizia. 2012. "The Creation of New Entities: Stakeholders and Shareholders in Nineteenth-Century Italian Co-operatives." In *The Hidden*

Alternative: Co-operative Values, Past, Present and Future, edited by Anthony Webster, Alyson Brown, David Stewart, John K. Walton, and Linda Shaw. 157–176. Manchester: Manchester University Press; New York: United Nations University Press.

Battiste, Marie, and James Youngblood Henderson. 2000. *Protecting Indigenous Knowledge and Heritage: A Global Challenge.* Saskatoon, SK: Purich.

Bauman, Zygmunt. 2004. *Wasted Lives: Modernity and Its Outcasts.* Cambridge, UK: Polity Press.

Belk, Russell. 2010. "Sharing." *Journal of Consumer Research* 36: 715–734.

Belk, Russell. 2014. "You Are What You Can Access: Sharing and Collaborative Consumption Online." *Journal of Business Research* 67: 1595–1600. doi. org/10.1016/jbusres.2013.10.001.

Birchall, Johnston. 2011. *People-Centred Businesses: Co-operatives, Mutuals and the Idea of Membership.* London: Palgrave Macmillan.

Birchall, Johnston, and Lou Hammond Ketilson. 2009. *Resilience of the Co-operative Business Model in Times of Crisis.* Geneva: International Labour Organization, Sustainable Enterprise Programme.

Borzaga, Carlo, and Giulia Galera. 2012. "Promoting the Understanding of Co-operatives for a Better World: EURICSE's Contribution to the International Year of Cooperatives." http://www.euricse.eu/wp-content/uploads/2015/03/promoting-the-understanting-of-cooperatives-for-a-better-world-full.pdf.

Botsman, Rachel, and Roo Rogers. 2010. *What's Mine Is Yours: The Rise of Collaborative Consumption.* New York: HarperCollins.

Brown, Leslie, and Sonja Novkovic. 2015. "Introduction." In *Co-operatives for Sustainable Communities: Tools to Measure Co-operative Impact and Performance,* edited by Leslie Brown, Chiara Carini, Jessica Gordon Nembhard, Lou Hammond Ketilson, Elizabeth Hicks, John McNamara, Sonja Novkovic, Daphne Rixon, and Richard Simmons. 3–16. Ottawa: Co-operatives and Mutuals Canada; Saskatoon, SK: Centre for the Study of Co-operatives.

Cardinal, Harold, and Walter Hildebrandt. 2000. *Treaty Elders of Saskatchewan: Our Dream Is That Our Peoples Will One Day Be Clearly Recognized as Nations.* Calgary: University of Calgary Press.

CB Insights. 2017. "The Unicorn List: Current Private Companies Valued at $1 B and Above." April 2, 2017. https://www.cbinsights.com/research-unicorn-companies.

Curl, John. 2012. *For All the People: Uncovering the Hidden History of Cooperation, Cooperative Movements, and Communalism in America.* Foreword by Ishmael Reed. 2nd ed. Oakland, CA: PM Press.

Eckhardt, Giana M., and Fleura Bardhi. 2015. "The Sharing Economy Isn't about Sharing at All." *Harvard Business Review.* January 28. https://hbr.org/2015/01/the-sharing-economy-isnt-about-sharing-at-all.

Ekelund, F. A. 1987. *The Property of the Common: Justifying Co-operative Activity.* Occasional Paper 7.02. Saskatoon, SK: Centre for the Study of Co-operatives, University of Saskatchewan.

Fairbairn, Brett. 1994. "The Meaning of Rochdale: The Rochdale Pioneers and the Co-operative Principles." Occasional Paper Series. Centre for the Study of Co-operatives. University of Saskatchewan, Saskatoon, Saskatchewan. http://usaskstudies.coop/documents/occasional-papers/Meaning%20of%20Rochdale.pdf.

Fairbairn, Brett, Christopher S. Axworthy, Murray Fulton, Lou Hammond Ketilson, and David Laycock. 1990. "Co-operative Institutions: Five Disciplinary Perspectives." In *Co-operative Organizations and Canadian Society: Popular Institutions and the Dilemmas of Change,* edited by Murray Fulton. 13–38. Toronto: University of Toronto Press.

Findlay, Isobel M. 2003. "Making a Co-operative Turn: Renegotiating Culture-State Relationships." In *Disability Studies & Indigenous Studies,* edited by James Gifford and Gabrielle Zezulka-Mailloux. 7–30. Edmonton: CRC Humanities Studio.

Findlay, Isobel M. 2004. "Remapping Co-operative Studies: Re-imagining Postcolonial Co-operative Futures." In *Co-operative Membership and Globalization,* edited by Brett Fairbairn and Nora Russell. 145–164. Saskatoon, SK: Centre for the Study of Co-operatives, University of Saskatchewan.

Findlay, Isobel M. 2012. "Back to the Future? Rebuilding Sustainable Economies and Communities." *Journal of Business and Financial Affairs* 1 (1): 106–107. doi:10.4172.bfsa.1000e106.

Findlay, Isobel M. 2014. "'Nuna Is My Body': What Northerners Can Teach about Social Cohesion." In *Co-operative Canada: Empowering Communities and Sustainable Businesses,* edited by Brett Fairbairn and Nora Russell. 41–65. Vancouver: University of British Columbia Press.

Findlay, Isobel M., and Len Findlay. 2012. "A New Opportunity for Co-operative Education: Linking and Learning with the Indigenous Humanities." In *New Opportunities for Co-operatives: New Opportunities for People—Proceedings of the 2012 ICA Global Research Conference, 24–27 August 2011, Mikkeli, Finland,* edited by Johanna Heiskanen, Hagen Henrÿ, Pekka Hytinkoski, and Tapani Köppä. 39–50. Helsinki: University of Helsinki Ruralia Institute.

Findlay, Isobel M., and Len Findlay. 2013. "Co-operatives: After the Crisis and beyond the Binaries." In *Genossenschaften im Fokus einer neuen Wirtschaftspolitik [Cooperatives in the Focus of a New Economic Policy]. 2012 XVII International Conference on Cooperative Studies,* Association of Cooperative Research Institutes, University of Vienna, edited by Johann Brazda, Markus Dellinger, and Dietmar Rößl (Hg.). 809–820. Vienna: LIT Verlag AG.

Findlay, Isobel M., Clifford Ray, and Maria Basualdo. 2011. "Research as Engagement: Rebuilding the Knowledge Economy of the Northern Saskatchewan Trappers Association Co-operative." In *Community-University*

Partnerships: Reflections on the Canadian Social Economy Experience, edited by Peter V. Hall and Ian MacPherson. 141–158. Victoria: University of Victoria.

Findlay, Isobel, and Wanda Wuttunee. 2007. "Aboriginal Women's Community Economic Development: Measuring and Promoting Success." *IRPP Choices* 13 (4): 1–26.

Gordon Nembhard, Jessica. 2014. *Collective Courage: A History of African American Cooperative Economic Thought and Practice.* University Park: Pennsylvania State University Press.

Gramsci, Antonio. 1971. "The Intellectuals." In *Selections from the Prison Notebooks,* edited by Quinton Hoare and Geoffrey Nowell Smith. 5–23. New York: International Publishers.

Great Transition Initiative. 2012, December. "The Architecture of Enterprise: Redesigning Ownership for a Great Transition." http://www.gtinitiative .org/documents/IssuePerspectives/GTI-Perspectives-Architecture_of_ Enterprise.pdf.

Hamari, Juho, Mimmi Sjöklint, and Antti Ukkonen. 2015. "The Sharing Economy: Why People Participate in Collaborative Consumption." *Journal of the Association for Information Science and Technology* 67 (9): 2047–2059. doi:10.1002/asi.23552.

Hammond Ketilson, Lou, and Ian MacPherson. 2001. *A Report on Aboriginal Co-operatives in Canada: Current Situation and Potential for Growth.* Saskatoon, SK: Centre for the Study of Co-operatives, University of Saskatchewan.

Haque, Umair. 2011. *The New Capitalist Manifesto: Building a Disruptively Better Business.* Boston, MA: Harvard Business School Publishing.

Henderson, James (Sakej) Youngblood. 2008. *Indigenous Diplomacy and the Rights of Peoples: Achieving UN Recognition.* Saskatoon, SK: Purich.

Henderson, James (Sakej) Youngblood, Marjorie L. Benson, and Isobel M. Findlay. 2000. *Aboriginal Tenure in the Constitution of Canada.* Scarborough, ON: Carswell.

International Co-operative Alliance. 2016. "Co-operative Identity, Values, and Principles." https://ica.coop/en/whats-co-op/co-operative-identity-values-principles.

Ish, Daniel. 1981. *The Law of Canadian Co-operatives.* Toronto: Carswell.

Ish, Daniel. 1995. "Co-operative Communities and Democratic Institutions." In *Realizing Community: Multidisciplinary Perspectives,* edited by L.L.M. Findlay and Isobel M. Findlay. 63–85. Saskatoon, SK: Humanities Research Unit and Centre for the Study of Co-operatives.

Jackson, Philip N. 1968. *Life in Classrooms.* New York: Holt, Rinehart, and Winston.

Kaine, Sarah, Danielle Logue, and Emmanuel Josserand. 2016. "The 'Uberisation' of Work Is Driving People to Co-operatives." *The Conversation.* September 27. http://theconversation.com/the-uberisation-of-work-is-driving-people-to-co-operatives-65333.

Kalamar, Anthony. 2013. "Sharewashing Is the New Greenwashing." *OpEdNews.* May 13. http://www.opednews.com/articles/Sharewashing-is-the-New-Gr-by-Anthony-Kalamar-130513-834.html.

Kalmi, P. 2007. "The Disappearance of Cooperatives from Economics Textbooks." *Cambridge Journal of Economics* 31 (4): 625–647.

Keng, Cameron. 2014. "If Apple Were a Worker Cooperative, Each Employee Would Earn at Least $403K." *Forbes.* December 18. http://www.forbes.com/sites/cameronkeng/2014/12/18/if-apple-was-a-worker-cooperative-each-employee-would-earn-at-least-403k/#2b0de95056cc.

Klein, Naomi. 2014. *This Changes Everything: Capitalism vs the Climate.* New York: Simon and Schuster.

Lacey, Samantha. 2012. "Beyond a Fair Price." In *The Hidden Alternative: Co-operative Values, Past, Present and Future,* edited by Anthony Webster, Alyson Brown, David Stewart, John K. Walton, and Linda Shaw. 96–114. Manchester: Manchester University Press; New York: United Nations University Press.

Lertzman, David A., and Harrie Vredenburg. 2005. "Indigenous Peoples, Resource Extraction and Sustainable Development: An Ethical Approach." *Journal of Business Ethics* 56: 239–254.

Loxley, John, ed. 2007. *Transforming and Reforming Capitalism: Towards a Theory of Community Economic Development.* Halifax: Fernwood Publishing.

Malhotra, Arvind, and Marshall Van Alstyne. 2014. "The Dark Side of the Sharing Economy . . . and How to Lighten It." *Communications of the ACM* 57 (11): 24–27. doi:0.1145/2668893.

Margolis, Eric, ed. 2001. *The Hidden Curriculum in Higher Education.* New York: Routledge.

Mayo, Ed. 2012a. *Global Business Ownership 2012: Members and Shareholders across the World.* Manchester: Co-operatives UK. https://www.uk.coop/sites/default/files/uploads/attachments/member_shares.pdf.

Mayo, Ed. 2012b. "The Hidden Alternative: Conclusion." In *The Hidden Alternative: Co-operative Values, Past, Present and Future,* edited by Anthony Webster, Alyson Brown, David Stewart, John K. Walton, and Linda Shaw. 347–353. Manchester: Manchester University Press; New York: United Nations University Press.

McMurtry, J. J., ed. 2010. *Living Economics: Canadian Perspectives on the Social Economy, Co-operatives, and Community Economic Development.* Toronto: Emond Montgomery Publications Limited.

Monllos, Kristina. 2015. "Is Walmart Trying to Brand Itself as Socially Conscious? The Value-Focused Chain Seems to Embrace Corporate Responsibility." *Adweek.* May 29. http://www.adweek.com/news/advertising-branding/walmart-trying-brand-itself-socially-conscious-165034.

Mook, Laurie, Jack Quarter, and Sherida Ryan, ed. 2012. *Businesses with a Difference: Balancing the Social and the Economic.* Toronto: University of Toronto Press.

Myers, Jan, John Maddocks, and James Beecher. 2012. "Resting on Laurels? Examining the Resilience of Co-operative Values in Times of Calm and Crisis." In *The Hidden Alternative: Co-operative Values, Past, Present and Future,* edited by Anthony Webster, Alyson Brown, David Stewart, John K. Walton, and Linda Shaw. 306–326. Manchester: Manchester University Press; New York: United Nations University Press.

Nowak, Martin A. 2012. "Why We Help: The Evolution of Cooperation." *Scientific American* 307 (1): 34–39.

Polanyi, Karl. 1944. *The Great Transformation: The Political and Economic Origins of Our Time.* New York: Beacon Press.

Porter, Michael E., and Mark R. Kramer. 2011. "Shared Value: How to Reinvent Capitalism and Unleash a Wave of Innovation and Growth." *Harvard Business Review* 89 (1–2): 63–77.

Quarter, Jack, Laurie Mook, and Betty Jane Richmond. 2002. *What Counts: Social Accounting for Nonprofits and Co-operatives.* Upper Saddle River, NJ: Prentice Hall.

Restakis, John. 2010. *Humanizing the Economy: Co-operatives in the Age of Capital.* Gabriola Island, BC: New Society Publishers.

Schneider, Nathan. 2014. "Owning Is the New Sharing." Shareable. December 21. http://www.shareable.net/blog/owning-is-the-new-sharing.

Scholz, Trevor. 2014. "Platform Cooperativism vs. the Sharing Economy." December 5. https://medium.com/@trebors/platform-cooperativism-vs-the-sharing-economy-2ea737f1b5ad#.jx1gykxhr.

Scholz, Trevor. 2016. "Platform Cooperativism: Challenging the Corporate Sharing Economy." Rosa Luxemburg Stiftung New York Office. http://www.rosalux-nyc.org/wp-content/files_mf/scholz_platformcoop_5.9.2016.pdf.

Schor, Juliet. 2010. "The Principles of Plenitude." *Minding Nature* 3 (2). http://www.humansandnature.org/august-2010-vol-3-no-2.

Schor, Juliet. 2011. "A Plenitude Economy." https://www.newdream.org/programs/redefining-the-dream/plenitude.

Schor, Juliet. 2014. "Debating the Sharing Economy." Great Transition Initiative. October. http://www.greattransition.org/publication/debating-the-sharing-economy.

Schulte-Tenckhoff, Isabelle. 2015. "Homo Cooperans: Lessons from Anthropology." In *Customizing a Patchwork Quilt: Consolidating Co-operative Studies within the University World. In Memoriam Professor Ian MacPherson,* edited by Hagen Henrÿ, Pekka Hytinkoski, and Tytti Klén. 27–33. Helsinki: University of Helsinki Ruralia Institute.

Schumpeter, J. A. 1947. *Capitalism, Socialism and Democracy.* 3rd ed. New York: Harper Torchbooks.

Schwab, K. 2012. "The Great Transformation: Shaping New Models." World Economic Forum 2012. http://apki.net/wp-content/uploads/2012/06/World-Economic-Forum-Annual-Meeting-2012-The-Great-Transformation.pdf.

Shaw, Linda. 2012. "International Perspectives on Co-operative Education." In *The Hidden Alternative: Co-operative Values, Past, Present and Future,* edited by Anthony Webster, Alyson Brown, David Stewart, John K. Walton, and Linda Shaw. 59–77. Manchester: Manchester University Press; New York: United Nations University Press.

Sheth, Jagdish N., N. K. Sethia, and Shanthi J. Srinivas. 2011. "Mindful Consumption: A Customer-Centric Approach to Sustainability." *Journal of the Academy of Marketing Science* 39: 21–39. doi:10.1007/s11747-010-0216-3.

Smith, Dorothy E. 1990. *Texts, Facts, and Femininity: Exploring the Relations of Ruling.* London: Routledge.

Sullivan, Shannon, and Nancy Tuana, ed. 2007. *Race and Epistemologies of Ignorance.* Albany: State University of New York Press.

Torjman, Sherri. 2016. "Here's the Downside of the Sharing Economy." *Globe and Mail.* June 13: B4. https://beta.theglobeandmail.com/report-on-business/rob-commentary/heres-the-downside-to-the-sharing-economy/article30408140/?ref=http://www.theglobeandmail.com

United Nations. 2016. "International Year of Co-operatives." http://social.un.org/coopsyear/.

Walsh, Bryan. 2011. "10 Ideas That Will Change the World." *Time* magazine. March 17. http://content.time.com/time/specials/packages/article/0,28804,2059521_2059717_2059710,00.html.

Webster, Anthony, Linda Shaw, David Stewart, John K. Walton, and Alyson Brown. 2012. "The Hidden Alternative?" In *The Hidden Alternative: Co-operative Values, Past, Present and Future,* edited by Anthony Webster, Alyson Brown, David Stewart, John K. Walton, and Linda Shaw. 1–15. Manchester: Manchester University Press; New York: United Nations University Press.

Woodin, Tom. 2012. "Co-operative Education in Britain during the Nineteenth and Early Twentieth Centuries: Context, Identity, and Learning." In *The Hidden Alternative: Co-operative Values, Past, Present and Future,* edited by Anthony Webster, Alyson Brown, David Stewart, John K. Walton, and Linda Shaw. 78–95. Manchester: Manchester University Press; New York: United Nations University Press.

Yeo, Stephen, ed. 1988. *New Views of Co-operation.* History Workshop Series. London and New York: Routledge.

CHAPTER THREE

When Sharing Was a Necessity: A Historical Perspective of Collaborative Consumption in East Germany

Marco Wolf and Wendy Ritz

Coming together is a beginning; keeping together is progress; working together is success.

—Henry Ford

Introduction

The allure of today's sharing systems is characterized by the presence of perceived product scarcity, minimized cost, and maximized benefit to consumers (Lamberton and Rose 2012). Societal *successes* derived from the shared economy are often overshadowed by commercialization and economic benefits (Matzler, Veider, and Kathan 2015). Pulitzer Prize–winning author Jared Diamond (2005) identified a five-point checklist that identifies the success or failure of a society; these include the following:

- Consumption and replenishment of environmental resources by humans
- Changes in climates that impact humans

- Attacks from enemies
- Friendliness of neighbors
- Response by (collaboration of) the community to solve resource issues

Since its introduction in the early 2000s, the sharing economy is often mentioned in conjunction with peer-to-peer or consumer-regulated marketplaces such as eBay, Uber, and Airbnb conveying a perception that the sharing economy is a recent phenomenon born by savvy entrepreneurs who discovered an opportunity to profit. But the motivation for sharing in an economy is often rooted in problems caused by a push for modern consumption, a consumption that is independent, free, and full of choices. Sharing between people is not new by any means, but what drives its popularity has its foundation in recognition of elements such as resource scarcity and environmental concerns, socioeconomic changes, and entrepreneurial opportunities to capitalize on behavioral trends (Belk 2014; Möhlmann 2015).

Few business-related studies have their focus set on dates prior to the millennium, giving the impression that collaborative consumption is a novel concept of Western origin: the importance of social cohesion and sustainability (Bijl 2011), the imperceptible change to a more sustainable society and functional economy (Stahel 2005), and the likelihood of businesses to share (Cho et al. 1998), though what might be novel is the capacity to organize, commercialize, and capitalize on the shared economy by using modern communication tools, the Internet, and innovative spirit. Our chapter attempts to show that the concept of the sharing economy is not recent or Western but has its roots in consumer-driven solutions to a variety of problems. By understanding the circumstances under which sharing takes place, marketers can identify and anticipate future sharing solutions in a variety of conditions. Maintaining a historical perspective should strengthen the importance of higher-order success indicators for peer-to-peer sharing programs such as longer product life cycles, sustainability, and societal success. Whereas recent sharing models appear to fill the void in a social drift between producers and consumers, the sharing economy may also be part of a solution in resource-restricted markets aiding in raising living standards when goods and resources are not readily available. Twenty-five years ago, sharing itself had been practiced as an absolute necessity by East Germans for several decades prior to the fall of the wall, not only sharing of products, raw materials, and services but, more important, communities collaborating to solve the problem of a lack of resource availability (Albinsson, Wolf, and Kopf 2010).

One might wonder why we bring back the long-forgotten issue of formerly divided Germany and what it has to do with the new economic and social movement of sharing. The importance of learning about historical events for the benefit of understanding the future was pointed out by Sir Winston Churchill's quote: "The farther back you can look, the farther forward you are likely to see." One such historic event we consider important is the illustration of scarcity and community-grown solutions in East Germany between August 1961 and 1989 during which the Berlin wall was built and torn down. We must review the unique environmental conditions that served as incubators for communal goods and services of past times to realize the growth potential for new industries and brands to improve the quality of life and societal conditions overall.

Today's digital networks can serve to inform consumer utilities (costs of ownership vs sharing) and/or function as a channel by which marketers can manipulate the perception of perceived scarcity risk for products and services (Lamberton and Rose 2012). The utility associated with sharing or renting products or services as opposed to ownership is that individuals have experiences they could not otherwise afford. Research by Möhlmann (2015) found that utility, trust, and familiarity had positive effects on satisfaction with the choice to share. Managers of non-sharing businesses should use these insights to adapt to collaborative consumer behavior (Belk 2010; Botsman and Rogers 2010).

The perceived lack of resources and risk of scarcity are motivators for collaborative consumption behaviors (Lamberton and Rose 2012). Understanding the propensity for participation in a sharing economy from both a consumer-centric and company-centric perspective is necessary. And to look at how this can be done, we look back in time to the former East Germany. In socialist market systems, resources were scarce and consumers did not have many choices in product offerings. To cope with these deficiencies, consumers developed strategies that involved innovative use and reuse of what was available to develop their own products and extend product life cycles. Support for determinants of collaborative consumption suggests the congregation supports either resources scarcity or one's self-centered need for cost benefits (Möhlmann 2015; Sheth, Sethia, and Srinivas 2011).

To draw useful inferences between East German sharing practices and behaviors, we must be aware that sharing resources is often mentioned in the same vein as consuming responsibly (Botsman and Rogers 2010). The problems of overconsumption, environmental degradation, and depletion of resources have initiated research focused around sustainable consumption. The premise of sustainable consumption seeks to address the negative impacts of dominating consumption patterns in affluent countries and their need to substantially reduce their consumption to achieve sustainability (Schrader and Thorgersen 2011). This macro objective can be achieved by distributing responsibilities to both companies and consumers. On the consumer side, two perspectives promise success. First, consumers can choose environment-friendly products and consume the "green" products the marketplace provides (Moisander 2007). The second perspective is that consumers can consume less or even refrain from consumption altogether. These perspectives entail a moral obligation and personal commitment to downscaling their consumption to reduce or eliminate negative effects on people and the environment. The principle of the sharing economy is to consume surplus or unused goods that otherwise would go to waste. Sharing does not necessarily limit or reduce consumption but in fact is a substitute for ownership. Marketing research has categorized this behavior as anti-consumption, made up of consumers who avoid consuming products and brands. Motivation to opt out of consumption may also stem from self-interest and personal well-being (Black and Cherrier 2010). Those who voluntarily free themselves of unnecessary consumption fall into the category of voluntary simplifiers. They freely choose a frugal and anti-consumer lifestyle that features low resource use and environmental impact but are not necessarily motivated by environmental factors (Black and Cherrier 2010).

The Political and Cultural Background for Consumption in East Germany

Germany's tumultuous past presents an intriguing case for historians and consumer behaviorists alike. First one country, then divided for three decades, then reunited again, Germany's emotional struggles have left traces in consumption patterns still detectable today. Let us look back for a moment to understand why one Germany developed a different set of skills, behaviors, and coping mechanisms than the other Germany. Following the end of World War II in May 1945, the Potsdam Conference regulated the governance of occupied zones in Germany. The territories in the east of Germany should be controlled by the Soviet Union and those in the west by the United States, the United Kingdom, and France. With the Soviets in the east and the Allied Western forces occupying the west, the sectors were soon to drift apart in their economic development, altering socioeconomic circumstances and even more so everyday consumer culture. West Germany, predominantly supported by the United States, quickly rebuilt infrastructure and realized prosperous growth with abundant consumer choices. East Germany experienced a recovery at a much slower rate. The reluctant recovery in the east was due to the Soviets' much greater use of industrial disassembly for reparation payments. Cold War tension added additional burden to the east when Western Allies stopped their reparation contributions to the Soviet Union in 1947. Soviet leadership shifted reparation accountability to the German Democratic Republic (GDR), resulting in the largest war reparation contribution ever demanded in the 20th century. In 1948, the Marshall Plan later incorporated West Germany accelerating economic development, which resulted in a widening of the socioeconomic gap between the two German states.

The increasing economic hardship continued in the centrally planned system and resulted in continuous material shortages for East Germans lasting until 1989. For nearly 40 years, the East German people endured societal isolation, limited resources, and an inadequate distribution of goods, which necessitated the development of a community-based skillset dependent on sharing rather than owning. The government's socialist ideology dictated a move from private property to a people-owned infrastructure (Volks Eigener Betrieb [VEB]). One answer to less private property yet continuous economic growth was the agricultural co-op Maschienen Traktoren Station. It represents a government approach to increase economic efficiency by organizing sharing of agricultural machines, tractors, and specialized labor. But informal approaches to sharing were also widely spread throughout the population, yet surprisingly efficient. East Germans called the network "Vitamin B," B standing for *Beziehungen* (*Beziehungen* = Connection). As Vitamin B is necessary for the human body to function, Vitamin (B)*eziehungen* was necessary to raise one's standard of living and to ensure the success of a society.

Predating access to Internet sharing platforms, East Germans organized sharing communities to solve problems that are now considered solutions to many of the challenges of modern consumption. In what follows, we take a closer look at how East Germans coped with market deficiencies and assumed roles that compare to newly trending concepts of sustainable consumption and sharing. We show how material deficiencies in the GDR's planned economy were bridged by individuals' innovative approaches to preserve, use, and reuse of materials to achieve cocreated value. Coupled with individual effort to circumvent the systems shortcomings, government infrastructure supported the trend to consume sustainably for years to come. The collaboration of the community served to solve resource deficits and strengthen the communal bonds.

Methodology

The fall of the wall in 1989, the reunification of East and West Germany, the conversion of the currency from east to west Mark, and dramatic change of the marketplace caused a plethora of consumer emotions and change in consumption patterns, patterns that were interesting to the authors and valuable to the field of marketing (Albinsson, Wolf, and Kopf 2010). To study the complexity of external factors on East German consumers during the market adjustment period, the first author, who was also a participant in the East German culture for nearly 20 years, conducted a series of interviews: 12 informal interviews and 20 formal in-depth interviews. All interviews were digitally recorded and transcribed verbatim immediately after each interview. The author who is bilingual in German and English translated the transcripts resulting in 300 single-spaced pages of qualitative data. Prior to gathering qualitative data, we developed interview guidelines addressing a broad array of sociocultural events dating from prior to the fall of the wall to more recent happenings. The enormous depth of the data provided rich detail about changes in consumption patterns and intensity but also about individual consumer practices more common in the east than west. Constant shortages of consumer goods provided the foundation for exploring consumer strategies to solve and circumvent such economic challenges. A first indication of economic sharing activities was reported during occurrences of extreme togetherness among East Germans. The initial informal interviews confirmed the common practice of forming communities among neighbors to overcome challenges. Challenges existed countrywide; thus, the sense to support one another did, in fact, extend to an overall attitude in all citizens. As part of a larger study on consumption patterns in transitional economies, we gathered many individual accounts of East Germans supporting one another through sharing and collaboration. What was immediately apparent was the hospitality and eagerness with which interview participants invited us and shared stories and experiences about the challenging nature of the limited resources in the east. All but 2 of the 20 formal participants were strangers to the researchers and generated through word of mouth and the snowball method. We found evidence of sharing behavior among our informants but only used the most interesting excerpts in this chapter to indicate the nature sharing behaviors in the east. Exact pseudonyms referenced in this chapter were also referenced in a larger study on anti-consumption in East Germany (Albinsson, Wolf, and Kopf 2010). The stories we collected included intimate and moving accounts involving themselves, loved ones, friends, and neighbors, lasting 60–120 minutes. During the data collection, we were given pictures, were allowed to take as many pictures ourselves, met relatives of participants, and were given product demonstrations, each of which had its own story, all of which accumulated to a rich set of cultural descriptions.

Findings

Marke Eigenbau—Do-It-Yourself but Together

The GDR economy was plagued by a constant unavailability of things, where "things" include a broad array from household goods to transportation and from entertainment to luxury goods. A typical GDR example was that what was not available in retail markets was constructed, redesigned, or sometimes invented. Through public exhibitions, the GDR government exposed the people to new consumer goods from all over the globe (Deutsche Welle 2016). The annual Meister der Messe von Morgen (MMM) was a government-organized competitive trade show focused on engendering consumer solutions, where the GDR presented a colorful palette of consumer goods to people from all over the world. GDR citizens were also invited to view the newest consumer innovations. However, outside the trade show doors was a stark contrast as citizens experienced daily shortages of basic market offerings.

Though the annual MMM trade show ignited the entrepreneurial spirit of many, the results were the creation of *homegrown* or cottage industries based on innovation and self-creations to fill the void of consumer products and services (Albinsson, Wolf, and Kopf 2010; Friebe and Ramge 2008).

Maintaining a comfortable standard of living became challenging and required spirit and ingenuity that resulted in strategies to circumvent the marketplace or fill the void of missing market options in self-effort. This practice opened the door to creative solutions that often were executed with the input of many. Decades of inefficient government distribution of consumer goods trained East Germans to become efficient in collecting and reusing products in innovative ways. Translated, this means that one rarely disposed of anything even when the product no longer served its intended purpose. Eventually, outserved goods were reintegrated to form new products. Frugality and ingenuity became national values, and the productive ownership and creation of things was elevated to a virtue. Scarcity was a challenge to the industriousness of a culture that prided itself on its engineering and scientific ability.

Marke Eigenbau describes the homegrown status of a product solution, which is like the Western concept of do-it-yourself (DIY). Similar to DIY, Marke Eigenbau is motivated by economic and marketplace factors such as lack of product availability, economic constraints, shortage of products, or lack of access to products (Wolf and McQuitty 2011), though Marke Eigenbau, as practiced in East Germany, differed from modern DIY in that products were usually assembled from an assortment of available raw materials and often involved the challenge of finding the materials necessary to even begin the project. Home improvement markets existed but were reflective of the overall economic conditions inclusive of empty shelves, lack of tools, and specialized services. East Germans had no choice but to accept the challenge and transform the environment of economic inadequacies into a bountiful sharing culture.

A unique property of Marke Eigenbau is its communal nature. An emerging theme of our interviews was community contribution to the development of an individual's brand. As much as individuals would claim the self-made nature of their product solutions, they also included the fact that many of the solutions were informed or supported by others. Sharing physical and idea resources in times of need cut across various consumer strategies (Albinsson, Wolf, and Kopf 2010). Particularly interesting was how individual projects developed a communal characteristic, with individuals collaborating efforts and sharing benefits. One informant, Peter, told us about an interesting neighborhood project to build an oversized antenna. What was motivated by the desire to receive an enhanced selection of televised programming by one person became a neighborhood project with shared benefits for all participating parties. The idea was to build an antenna high enough to receive an unconstrained TV signal and ultimately add channels, mostly Western, to the two channels of East German television. However, the size of the project presented an enormous challenge.

> The remote living situation only gave us bad TV reception and satellite dishes did not exist for us. To build an antenna of the size to receive decent TV channels was too expensive for just one person. I remember, one neighbor got really excited when I mentioned the idea. He immediately said "I know where we can get a large commercial electric pole." Not only this, he knew others that could transport it which was a huge operation. So, we got started and more neighbors joined the project to overhaul the pole. One allowed us to use their unutilized property to build it on including a large concrete foundation. We had five household contributing in different ways. (Peter)

This verbatim describes a larger community–shared project and indicates that Marke Eigenbau went beyond the individual to become a shared experience. Sharing was the only alternative to ownership or, better, non-ownership. Accomplishments such as the neighborhood TV antenna illustrates how the group worked together in overcoming limitations. Peter reported that the stakes of ownership of the antenna project were never discussed. The parties participated each to their capacity. All decisions were solely verbal agreements regulating community contributions to a somewhat equal share in either labor, material, property (land for placement), or financial contribution, yet ownership stakes were never assigned or discussed. The antenna project may well be viewed in light of East Germany's philosophy of people-owned property (VEB), where individuals are mainly interested in reaping the benefits of working together and less interested in personal ownership. Assigning stakes of ownership to participants was deemed pointless, as the project benefited the community in its entirety.

A slightly different story was unveiled by Michael. Michael told us about his house project that quickly became a neighbor-supported project where neighbors would trade each other's skills.

> I could do a lot of things myself, but there were things I could not do. So, we took advantage of what we know and shared out experiences and skills. Zachow (my neighbor) was good with electric, my neighbor across was a mechanic and I did well with concrete. What started out friendly neighborhood help ended as a friendship. (Michael)

The resource-distributing authority in East Germany may have welcomed the trend for self-help and encouraged consumers' self-initiatives to fill market voids, but Marke Eigenbau practices also celebrated customization by the innovator through reflections on building moments and expressions of personalized design. One such example of personal ingenuity applying to a common consumer problem was the home-built lawn mower (see Figure 3.1). All designs were exceptionally unique, simple, and extremely durable. Most common designs employed a platform usually made from scrap sheet metal, a motor from an outserved washing machine, wheels (often from a stroller or similar device), and a handle.

Figure 3.1 Lawn mower with repurposed motor
Source: Marco Wolf (2010).

All parts welded and assembled together provided a sturdy design that served East German homeowners long after the reunification. During in-depth interviews with creators, people proudly presented their inventions and shared the processes, including planning steps, information and material gathering, and the manufacturing stage. Again, while individuals' self-initiative was involved, one did not create the entire device alone. Ideas were gathered and shared between parties, including family, friends, and neighbors, or "over-the-fence" observations. Norbert stated the following.

> It was more the need to solve a problem. One used whatever sources available to build something to solve problems. Lawn mowers were one of a kind and each and everyone looked different even though they all had to fulfill the exact same purpose. When I built mine, I went around in the neighborhood and looked at some examples. Then it was just a matter what parts I could get. (Norbert)

Design information was shared openly between interested parties as a form of open source, promoting universal access to product designs and blueprints for subsequent improvement by anyone, and to convey something about the inventors and their networks. People we spoke with carried a tremendous sense of pride about their Marke Eigenbau, almost feeling relieved that someone wanted to access stored information. Every detail, every function, and every imaginable reason for the design was explained. Interviewees stated that while they received design ideas from others, they adjusted the designs depending on available resources and special applications. This is reflected by Norbert's continuing comment:

> Some mowers I looked at were pretty hideous but some others were nifty creations. One could tell someone put a lot of thought into it. It also

depends a bit of the parts used because they almost always were unique depending what access to material one had. (Norbert)

One of our most interesting informants (Heinz) presented an abundance of useful devices ranging from a mini tractor to an outdoor shower with solar water heater. Heinz also modified the lawn mower from a traditional four-wheel to a two-wheel design (see Figure 3.2). When asked, Heinz reasoned his design with improved maneuverability for hard-to-access places such as between hedges, between trees, and in corners. However, Heinz did not keep his designs secret; he loved sharing his ideas with others and even codesigning a tobacco-harvesting machine with the neighbor for his small field operation. He also told us with a smile that anybody sharing their ideas is a little bit interested in reserving bragging rights.

Figure 3.2 Zero-turn ratio lawn mower
Source: Marco Wolf (2010).

When Heinz heard of our interest in his ingenuity, he prepared for his fleet of Marke Eigenbau devices to be captured on camera and explained in detail. Part of Heinz's fleet were a mini tractor (see Figure 3.3), multiple log splitters (see Figure 3.4), lawn mowers, and a meat smoker, all of which were operational. Peter introduced an interesting innovation. As Peter built a house for his family in the country, he required machines to complete the construction. One device that interested us was a heavy-duty circular saw (see Figure 3.5) that appeared to be crossbred with a wheelbarrow. He explained that he would often find himself

Figure 3.3 Heinz tractor
Source: Marco Wolf (2010).

working alone after work and moving a traditional saw requires two people. The handles on one side and the wheel on the other would enable him to move the saw around the construction site by himself. Our participants emphasized the notion of the communal effort it took to accomplish most things in East Germany. Heinz said he traded parts with others to complete his machines, and Peter said he captured the images and parts for a wheelbarrow/saw combo from his brother in law. Heinz further made an impactful statement:

Figure 3.4 Tiller
Source: Marco Wolf (2010).

> There is no point in reinventing the wheel. I don't hide my things from others. And it is alright if someone else wants to use it. (Heinz)

Whether Heinz's attitude to sharing his ideas and equipment with others resulted from difficult experiences in a scarce resource-constraint society or his closeness to others in his small town is unclear, but we gathered that others valued his innovative spirit. Previous research has confirmed the overall community benefited from the products and ideas generated by Heinz (Seshadri 2013). Heinz is repeatedly asked to ride

Figure 3.5 Table saw
Source: Marco Wolf (2010).

his machines in parades celebrating town anniversaries.

Today, the Internet is a catalyst for the proliferation of sharing information, products, and services within communities (Belk 2014; Lamberton and Rose 2012 Matzler et al. 2015). It seems difficult to imagine that effective sharing of information could predate the Internet, but according to McLaren and Agyeman (2015), environments are conducive to becoming sharing communities in densely populated and highly networked places where demographic, economic, and cultural forces bring people together. During pre-Internet East Germany, meeting places were provided by the fence between neighbors (strangely serving as a unifier, not a separator), the neighborhood side street, or the local pub. A combination of ingenuity and communal spirit brought problem solvers together who informally shared their ideas and designs. Similar to open-source software development, individuals who found ways to improve their products would integrate these improvements and share the knowledge with others who encountered similar problems (Sowe, Stamelos, and Angelis 2008).

Friebe and Ramge (2008) describe the revival process in their book *Marke Eigenbau—Revolt of the Masses against Mass Production*. Here they focus on the concept of the consumer's response to market saturation, undifferentiated solutions, and growing skepticism about globalization. It appears that Marke Eigenbau has been repositioned as a "self-brand" alternative economy, globally intertwined yet "flying under the radar." The new Marke Eigenbau appears to have more in common with a resistance movement rather than a new paradigm of mass production. Contrary to its East German self, the self-made alternative is now aiming at market-controlling brands and the destructive side of mass production such as exploitation of low-wage countries, sweatshops, and global corporatism.

From Sustainability to Shareware

What makes Marke Eigenbau special is that it remains a "creeping" campaign. It possesses the characteristics of an underground movement: decentralized, flexible, self-empowered, and full of spirit; characteristics its global incumbents have traded for profits at some point. The passion put forth in the new Marke Eigenbau is spreading to cities in Germany, Europe, and globally, where young organizers and DIYers form altruistic organizations to repair, improve, and innovate products and solutions for everyday problems (Friebe and Ramge 2008). Their goal is to educate others on materials and practices and share of knowledge of the lost art of crafting and individualism through sharing true innovation and reuse of resources. An example is the Dutch nonprofit organization Repair Café, which was created out of frustration of short product life cycle and the excessive disposal of anything that essentially could be repaired. The first Repair Café was organized in 2009, and since 2011 the nonprofit organization offers professional repair support all over the Netherlands and other countries (www.repaircafe.org). The café is organized around a like-minded community, but not everybody coming to the café needs to repair something. The café also aims for visitors to just come and watch, offer, learn, or pass on new practical skills. In congruence with Marke Eigenbau's sneaking character, the Repair Café may be a disguised disciple with a serious agenda. The focus is not to repair one's TV, bike, or CD player but rather to secure past practices, share knowledge, and convert consumers for awareness of overconsumption and global degradation (McGrane 2012). Within its self-made effort, the environmental achievements of the café are impressive. In 2015, the Repair Café idea spread throughout 24 countries and accumulated to 200,000 repairs (about 70% of all items were repairable), meaning that 200,000 items did not end up in a landfill. In terms of CO_2 emissions, the three years during which the Repair Café has gained serious momentum, 400,000 kilograms of CO_2 emissions was extinguished. These powerful results are practical evidence to Möhlmann's (2015) theorized drivers of collaborative consumption which gain significant relevancy when they are practiced as a community.

Preceding the Repair Café, the desire for improved socioeconomic communities led East Germans to form close bonds and work toward homemade solutions. Included in the sharing was an informal knowledge base of individuals who had specialized skills that could add value by assisting in constructing or testing projects. These exchanges of information, skills, materials, and connections rarely resulted in monetary transactions and instead were reciprocated with similar courtesy. Research has shown that the perceived risk of scarcity will lead to hoarding behavior (McKinnon, Smith, and Hunt 1985). There was an abundance of objects available for exchanges as East Germans discarded very little; even broken or damaged items were kept for spare parts or were repurposed. For example, a broken washing machine offered an elector motor (see Figure 3.6) that could be reused in a circular saw, lawn mower, or cement mixer (see Figure 3.7). An outserved vehicle rim commonly became a hose stand (see Figure 3.8); the speakers from old TV sets or radios were installed in cars (a radio in a vehicle was considered a luxury item). The examples seem endless, and the underlying theme was to collect everything. While East Germans did not purposefully aim at minimizing consumption, practicing Marke Eigenbau resulted in a very efficient system for minimizing waste, reusing, and repairing.

Given our focus on East Germany's early attempts to resource conservation and waste reduction, we might ask if East Germans continue to make the most use of goods or if this is a lost art.

Today, 25 years after the reunification, Marke Eigenbau is destined to be revived. During the influx of new and "colorful" products during

Figure 3.6 Spare parts for repurposing
Source: Marco Wolf (2010).

Figure 3.7 Cement mixer
Source: Marco Wolf (2010).

Figure 3.8 Hose stand
Source: Marco Wolf (2010).

East Germany's transition to a market economy, Marke Eigenbau became stigmatized as improvised or second-choice solution for people who had little opportunity to partake in modern consumption. The results were West-ern—Western in a sense that East Germans abandoned their Marke Eigenbau efforts to delve into a new consumer world with no restrictions. Overcoming between-generation uncoolness, the outgoing generation practiced Marke Eigenbau to enhance consumption in contrast to the millennial generation who are utilizing its properties to demote consumption altogether.

Collaboration and Co-creation

The Trabant (automobile produced from 1957 to 1990 by former East German manufacturer, HQM Sachsenring GmbH) became known as a global symbol of economic stagnancy and frequently served as an object of satire in East and West. Since its manufacturing in 1964 the Trabant saw few changes and improvements within its 30 years of production. However, Trabi (term of endearment German people use when referring to the car) cherished their possession and the German people liked the simplistic vehicle for its ability to be easily fixed and maintained.

The Trabant signifies a special situation which made us consider this example in this chapter. Over nearly 20 years, it has served as a sharing platform for information about improvements and self-designed upgrades. Figures 3.9 and 3.10 represent the car that even as a "deluxe" version could be considered a bare-bone vehicle without "bells and whistles." Like with no other East German product the Trabant took center stage for gathering enthusiasts' ideas for improving a car that hasn't changed in 20 years.

In practice, individuals who were finally able to acquire a new Trabant would soon set out to add on improvements to their vehicles in self-effort. Given that the vast majority would own such vehicles, information of such improvement could be gathered with little effort. Rainer, a physician, called the Trabi a "technical masterpiece" fitting well with the overall material scarcity within the market. He also stated the following:

> The main point was that it had to last. The Trabi had a reputation to develop rust on the bottom, so I used construction tar to paint the bottom and fill tar into the hollow spaces of the frame as well. Conserving the car was common practice among owners I frequently talked with, just the material used depended on what each had available. But it seems obvious that pooling together things more would be better off. Somebody had a welding machine, somebody else had tar, steel, or other useful things. Rather than just improving your car, one could help out one or two more. (Rainer)

Jan, a retail manager, told us that he learned as a new Trabi owner the items he should always carry with him in case of a technical problem. He shared that the car would leave him stranded occasionally, but help was never far. And it was through those instances where he learned to keep a stash of necessary parts in his trunk.

> Given the car was so simple, I was told by other owners to always carry spark plugs, a distributor cab, an ignition, and for long trips a starter. It seems everyone had a little bag in the trunk with the necessities including tape and rope to fix a broken muffler. I later got better with my car and added a few things here and there, including damming the walls and car ceiling from noise. Another trick I learned from other Trabi drivers. (Jan)

Information for Trabi improvements was omnipresent in the home environment, at work, or on vacation. Special was the sharing of the information each owner had acquired at some point of driving his or her Trabant. Information even developed in one's own time and effort was not viewed as proprietary and freely given away at the right occasions (Friebe and Ramge 2008). Similar to an open-source cooperation where those who provide a base product/idea ask others to use, improve, and share the knowledge of their efforts to benefit all users, information on Trabant's improvements was treated as free shareware. Access to information had become a success factor in socialist Germany and was graded on the bases of two general conditions: East Germany's ideology of private property reduction and its awareness of others facing similar problems with products (Deutsche Welle 2016). The benefit of

Figure 3.9 Trabant by HQM Sachsenring GmbH
Source: Marco Wolfe (2010).

Figure 3.10 Trabant motor
Source: Marco Wolfe (2010).

nonproprietary information lies in the speed of dissemination, ultimately resulting in an improved product much faster.

In addition, the network created to facilitate the sharing of information had an interesting, encompassing side effect; it pushed consumers into a collective awareness and subliminal learning to consume sustainably, an outcome that caused challenges for many consumer-centric economies.

One important element in consuming sustainably is reducing waste. As the communist economy was not dictated by market forces, the communist leadership continued to face the dilemma of measuring up to the promise of continuously improving living conditions for its citizens (Deutsche Welle 2016). An economic system built on disposal and new acquisition was deemed inefficient by the GDR's resource-burdened government. Therefore, the centralized government commonly required minimum life cycles from manufactures for consumer goods (e.g., a minimum life of 25 years for refrigerators and washing machines). Consumer products manufactured in East Germany, therefore, achieved much higher levels of reparability and lifetime when compared with products manufactured in countries absent of governmental product life mandates.

East Germans demanded economic change and freedom of consumption in the years leading up to the fall of the wall. However, many assumed the positive forces of market capitalism would simply replace the shortcomings of communist rule and add further to the achievements of the GDR. Many, however, were rather disappointed by the quality of products the new system provided and began longing for a past time when products would last. East Germans viewed West German disposal practices as extremely wasteful and questioned the logic of such consumer-oriented system (Albinsson, Wolf, and Kopf 2010).

This frustration did not go unnoticed by political party representatives. According to the article by Die Welt (Fuest 2013), the left spectrum party Die Linke proposed legislation to mandate a minimum product life for cars and electronics. Under the title "Ressourcenschutz durch Vorgabe einer Mindest-nutzdauer für Technische Produkte" ("Resource Protection through Minimum Lifetime Requirements for Technology Products") the proposal specifies a minimum lifetime of five years for vehicles and three years for electronic goods. The issues associated with shorter lifecycles and repair-unfriendly electronic devices have caught public attention (Bulow 1986; Choi 1994; Waldman 1993). Consumers have increasingly voiced frustration with manufacturers designing products with a built-in expiration date (also known as planned obsolescence). Electronic equipment that have come under scrutiny include printers with determined page count and smartphones and tablets whose batteries cannot easily be changed or whose software is incompatible with older models of tablets. Consumers have become aware that this practice adds to landfills and could be avoided. Firms that practice market orientation would be wise to not only listen to consumers' desire for new product designs and functions but also acknowledge the growing concerns of short lifecycle and disposal practices.

Discussion

Recent discussions have highlighted Marke Eigenbau as a movement against mass production with which individual DIYers cater to current demand in niche markets (Friebe and Ramge 2008). It may be a stretch to predict sharing's future based on 28 years of East German Marke Eigenbau, from a period that poses little apparent relevancy. However, by examining the conditions under which Marke Eigenbau emerged, we gain access to sharing practices at a time when sharing was perceived anything but fashionable. The unique socioeconomic setting in which Marke Eigenbau began provides insight into the factors influencing the propensity for individuals to participate in today's sharing systems.

Our chapter outlines layers of collaboration incorporating three forces that drive sharing: cost, scarcity, and a sense of community. In the most basic form, collaborative consumption is an alternative to ownership, providing cost-related benefits through group discounts, warehouse memberships, and lowered transaction costs (Agyeman, McLaren, and Schaefer-Borrego 2013; Hamari, Sjöklint, and Ukkonen 2015; Lamberton and Rose 2012), and the ability to save money (Belk 2007). One Marke Eigenbau example illustrated how an individually planned project to build an oversized antenna quickly became a neighborhood project, with each party sharing the enormous cost of the venture. The result was a product that benefited those who contributed without defining ownership rules. Twenty-five years after idling in the shadows of satellite dishes, the antenna was finally taken down and the steel donated to a local soccer club. No contributor expected to gain or has gained from the donation, Birgit, one of members of the "Antenna task force," stated in a follow-up interview. The intangible remnants hint toward a time when community projects were undertaken for sharing cost, contributing resources, and, to some degree, selfless acts of benefiting others. Marke Eigenbau, as described here, depended on sharing tangible and intangible resources when material and information were scarce. Sharing access to material and knowledge among individuals allowed the creation of networks and communities who then conquered day-to-day problems in a collective effort. As a result, it would seem that these collaborators contributed to the community through improved sustainability processes and community accountability that comes from a greater sense of connectedness.

One shortcoming of today's collaborative consumption economy is in the motivation and goals that drive the movement. While financial potential for collaborative consumption often receives more attention than the actual impact of reduction in consumption, the sharing culture turns into yet "another way of doing business." We would like to believe, that once upon a time, popular and widely used sharing platforms were started with great altruistic enthusiasm, but the current sharing infrastructure seems to challenge this ideal.

Our chapter indicates the importance of selflessness and reduced significance of a central Internet body organizing sharing activities. This seems to contradict modern assumptions of a successful sharing system, which in most instances have morphed into profit-oriented Internet entities. Most popular examples are Uber and Airbnb, both of which began as altruistic sharing platforms but are now valued at $50 and $25 billion, respectively. What started out as sharing for all the reasons that made sharing the new "it" in saving resources and sustainability may have turned into nothing but a new way to redistribute resources via electronically connected users. Airbnb began its services as an organization platform to offer value in the form of connecting those that offer a place to "crash" for the night and those that want to "crash" for the night. While financial compensation may be part of the equation, owners and renters may also value sociocultural benefits of tapping into the true living culture of owners in the area, away from sterile all-look-alike hotel chains. Property owners convert inner-city flats and condos into Airbnb rentals offering few unique experiences, with little feeling of sharing anything for the landlord never to be seen. Both Airbnb and Uber now face regulatory challenges by governments that simply no longer accept their altruistic claims and, thus, must face the business regulatory environment (Coldwell 2014).

Our chapter highlights the customary community experience linked with Marke Eigenbau through which the East German society may have received its stability and constancy in a deteriorating political system. *Friendliness of neighbors* is viewed as one driver of societal success (Diamond 2005), and Marke Eigenbau provided the catalyst in which individuals interact, learn, and appreciate one another. The strength of a community network facilitates outreach to new members. Homogeneity of the member's environment facilitated Marke Eigenbau. Those who sought increased living standards were anxious to share their projects and encourage conversation in the quest to solve problems. Today's peer-to-peer, online community members can be overcritical and disparaging, although counterintuitive to strict social entities, contributing to a more transparent and diverse group (Närvänen, Kartasenpää, and Kussela 2013).

In this regard, we seek to learn from the East Germans and explore how choosing to hold onto products longer, to possibly repurpose, or to share products may be the best possible way to create a sustainable economy. Although some countries and governmental agencies are advocating for more sustainable consumption, actual policy making and regulations are lagging behind what the *Brundtland Report: Our Common Future (WCED 1987)* visualized would be in effect by now in terms of sustainable development (Peattie and Peattie 2009). Although its ideas have been widely discussed by businesses and government alike, critics claim that talking is not enough. In response, many consumer segments have started to implement (and returned to) more responsible consumption decisions in terms of upcycling, recycling, and voluntary simplicity. It is yet to be determined if these consumer efforts are enough to make a real and lasting impact.

As marketers, it is vital to study consumption trends to gain a deeper understanding of how and where to respond to consumer needs and wants. Through the personal stories shared during our in-depth interviews, we can ascertain current sharing motivations, such as individuals perceiving high utility in repurposing old material possessions. Peattie and Peattie (2009) pointed out that meaningful progress toward sustainability can only be made by introducing more radical solutions to consumers, marketers, and policy makers. However, the current sociopolitical landscape does not support radical solutions, which arguably could be a reason that successful ideas of sharing enter the field under altruistic ideals only to become profit-centered businesses. It seems clear from our research in East Germany that individuals are wired to share, and if given the opportunity and a reason, consumption patterns can change in favor of reduced consumption, recycling, and an overall sustainable behavior.

References

Agyeman, Julian, Duncan McLaren, and Adrianne Schaefer-Borrego. 2013. "Sharing Cities." *Friends of the Earth Briefing*, 1–32. https://www.foe .co.uk/sites/default/files/downloads/agyeman_sharing_cities.pdf.

Albinsson, Pia, Marco Wolf, and Dennis Kopf. 2010. "Anti-Consumption in East Germany: Consumer Resistance to Hyperconsumption." *Journal of Consumer Behavior* 9 (6): 412–425.

Belk, Russell. 2007. "Why Not Share Rather Than Own?" *The Annals of the American Academy of Political and Social Science* 611 (1): 126–140.

Belk, Russell. 2010. "Sharing." *Journal of Consumer Research* 36: 715–734.

Belk, Russell. 2014. "You Are What You Can Access: Sharing and Collaborative Consumption Online." *Journal of Business Research* 67 (8): 1595–1600.

Bijl, Rob. 2011. "Never Waste a Good Crisis: Towards Social Sustainable Development." *Social Indicators Research* 102 (1): 157–168.

Black, Ian R., and Helene Cherrier. 2010. "Anti-Consumption as Part of Living a Sustainable Lifestyle: Daily Practices, Contextual Motivations and Subjective Values." *Journal of Consumer Behaviour* 9 (9/10): 437–453.

Botsman, Rachel, and Roo Rogers. 2010. *Whats Mine Is Yours: The Rise of Collaborative Consumption*. New York: HarperCollins.

Bulow, Jeremy. 1986. "An Economic Theory of Planned Obsolescence." *The Quarterly Journal of Economic* 101 (4): 729–749.

Cho, Min Je, Chea Ryeon Woo, Hyung Rim, Soon Goo Hong, Kang Bae Lee, and Su Jin Park. 1998. "Business Model for the Sharing Economy between Enterprises." *Advances in Economics, Law and Political Sciences* 6: 181–189.

Choi, Jay Pil. 1994. "Network Externality, Compatibility Choice, and Planned Obsolescence." *The Journal of Industrial Economics* June (1): 167–182.

Coldwell, Will. 2014. "AirBnB Legal Troubles: What Are the Issues?" *The Guardian* (online). https://www.theguardian.com/travel/2014/jul/08/AirBnB-legal-troubles-what-are-the-issues.

Deutsche Welle. 2016. "Marke Eigenbau: Do It Yourself-Design." http://www.dw.com/de/marke-eigenbau-do-it-yourself-design/a-36451213.

Diamond, Jared. 2005. *Collapse: How Societies Choose to Fail or Succeed*. London, UK: Penguin Publishing.

Friebe, Holm, and Thomas Ramge. 2008. *Marke Eigenbau: Der Aufstand der Massen Gegen die Massenproduktion* [*Marke Eigenbau—Revolt of the Masses against Mass Production*]. Frankfurt/Main: Campus Verlag.

Fuest, B. 2013. Gesetz soll Geräten lange Lebensdauer Vorschreiben, *Die Welt*. April 22.

Hamari, Juho, Mimmi Sjöklint, and Antti Ukkonen. 2015. "The Sharing Economy: Why People Participate in Collaborative Consumption." *Journal of the Association for Information Science and Technology* 67 (9): 2047–2059.

Lamberton, Cait Poyner, and Randall L. Rose. 2012. "When Is Ours Better Than Mine? A Framework for Understanding and Altering Participation in Commercial Sharing Systems." *Journal of Marketing* 76 (4): 109–125.

Matzler, Kurt, Viktoria Veider, and Wolfgang Kathan. 2015. "Adapting to the Sharing Economy." *MIT Sloan Management Review* 56 (2): 71–77.

McGrane, Sally. 2012. "An Effort to Bury a Throwaway Culture One Repair at a Time." *New York Times* (online). http://www.nytimes.com/2012/05/09/world/europe/amsterdam-tries-to-change-culture-with-repair-cafes.html.

McKinnon, Gary, Milton E. Smith, and Keith H. Hunt. 1985. "Hoarding Behavior among Consumers: Conceptualization and Marketing Implications." *Journal of the Academy of Marketing Science* 13 (1): 340–351.

McLaren, Duncan, and Julian Agyeman. 2015. *Sharing Cities: A Case for Truly Smart and Sustainable Cities.* Cambridge: MIT Press.

Möhlmann, Mareike. 2015. "Collaborative Consumption: Determinants of Satisfaction and the Likelihood of Using a Sharing Economy Option Again." *Journal of Consumer Behavior* 14 (3): 193–207.

Moisander, Johanna. 2007. "Motivational Complexity of Green Consumerism." *International Journal of Consumer Studies* 31 (4): 404–409.

Närvänen, Elina, Elina Kartasenpää, and Hannu Kussela. 2013. "Online Lifestyle Consumption Dynamics: A Practice-Based Analysis." *Journal of Consumer Behavior* 12 (5): 358–369.

Peattie, Ken, and Peattie Sue. 2009. "Social Marketing: A Pathway to Consumption Reduction?" *Journal of Business Research* 62: 260–268.

Repaircafe.org. 2016. "Repair Cafe." https://repaircafe.org/en/.

Schrader, Ulf, and John Thorgersen. 2011. "Putting Sustainable Consumption into Practice." *Journal of Consumer Policy* 34: 3–8.

Seshadri, Sudhi. 2013. "The Sustainability Syndicate: Shared Responsibility in a Trans-Organizational Business Model." *Industrial Marketing Management* 42 (5): 765–772.

Sheth, Jagdish, Nirmal Sethia, and Shanthi Srinivas. 2011. "Mindful Consumption: A Customer-Centric Approach to Sustainability." *Journal of the Academy of Marketing Science* 39 (1): 21–39.

Sowe, Sulayman K., Ioannis Stamelos, and Lefteris Angelis. 2008. "Understanding Knowledge Sharing Activities in Free/Open Source Software Projects: An Empirical Study." *Journal of Systems and Software* 81 (3): 431–446.

Stahel, Walter, R. 2005. "The Functional Economy: Cultural and Organizational Change." *International Journal of Performability Engineering* 1 (2): 121–130.

Waldman, Michael. 1993. "A New Perspective on Planned Obsolescence." *The Quarterly Journal of Economics* 108 (1): 273–283.

Wolf, Marco, and Shaun McQuitty. 2011. "Understanding the Do-It-Yourself Consumer: DIY Motivations and Outcomes." *Academy of Marketing Science Review* 1 (3–4): 154–170.

CHAPTER FOUR

Societal Factors and the Emergence of the Sharing Economy

Katharina Hellwig, Marlyne Sahakian,
and Felicitas Morhart

Since *Time* magazine nominated sharing as "one of 10 ideas that would change the world" (Walsh 2011), it was clear that what is now commonly known as the sharing economy would become more than a niche trend. Summarized under different labels such as "collaborative consumption" (Botsman and Rogers 2010), "sharing economy" (Sacks 2011), "the mesh" (Gansky 2010), or "peer-to-peer economy" (Chase 2015), the term is mostly used to describe technologically mediated peer-to-peer exchanges that reinvent modes of consumption, such as sharing, bartering, and lending. Even if estimates of future potential and current size of the sharing market vary due to the fuzzy definition of the term, the sharing economy, estimated to represent $335 billion in revenue worldwide by 2025, is still considered to be a serious game changer for the world's consumption and production patterns (PwC 2013).

Given the increasing threats that overconsumption poses, not only to the environment but also to individuals' economic and psychological well-being in many developed nations (Arrow et al. 2004; Kasser 2003; Sheth, Sethia, and Srinivas 2011), exploring the ideas and the roots that underlie some of the innovative sharing economy consumption practices, which challenge the "business of usual" form of corporate capitalism, is an important academic endeavor. In times of economic hardship, different societies have demonstrated resilience by creating alternatives to redress economic and social instability. In 19th-century Europe, when early forms of industrialization were leading to unprecedented levels of urban poverty, cooperatives and associations were created as "the first line of defence" (Lewis 1997, in Laville 2011) to protect workers from private interests. As a reaction to the tightening of credit following the Great Depression, Swiss entrepreneurs created the WIR (acronym for Wirtschafts-Ring, which is German for "economic cycle," while "wir" translates to "we") system, a complementary currency that continues to be exchanged to this day—particularly when Swiss francs are in short supply (Sahakian 2014). In Argentina, following the collapse of the national economy in the late 1990s, several complementary currencies involving an extensive *Red de Trueque* or barter network emerged and were sustained for over a decade (Sahakian 2014). Barter systems in Greece have also emerged in recent years as a response to the economic crises of the late 2000s (Chatzidakis, Maclaran, and Bradshaw 2012; Poggioli 2011). While different regions of the world have experienced recurring economic crises over the past decades, deeper issues also prevail. These include widening inequalities, the loss of biodiversity, the anthropogenic altering of carbon and nitrogen cycles (Ayres, Schlesinger, and Socolow 1994), and the collapse of community in certain contexts (Putnam 2000)—all pointing to an "unsustainable global system" (Worldwatch Institute 2015).

The notion of "sustainable development" is an appropriate starting point for grappling with the various societal factors that operate at a macro-level and relate to how individuals participate in the sharing economy and indeed shape its practices. As put forward in the Brundtland report (WCED 1987), sustainable development is an attempt to integrate economic, environmental, and social concerns under a new paradigm. We contend that the failure of this paradigm toward creating more environmentally sound and socially just societies has left in its wake a vacuum with a slew of terms emerging to fill this void from the people-first or human economy (Hart, Laville, and Cattani 2010; Ransom and Baird 2010) to the new economy (Schor and Thompson 2014), the green economy (UNEP 2011), diverse economies (Gibson-Graham 2006, 2008), and variations on the circular economy (Ellen MacArthur Foundation 2013; Yuan, Bi, and Moriguichi 2006) to which the sharing economy can be added. Yet the sharing economy is more than a result of a failed paradigm: it is also a catch-all phrase, much like "sustainability," that can become a depository for all sorts of frustrations about the dominant capitalist system. Currently, the sharing economy is often positioned in the headlines as breeding business practices that are marginally illegal, support tax fraud, and undermine workers' rights and social security (Cagle 2014; Morozov 2013). This criticism most commonly refers to the brands of the sharing economy that are most successful by traditional capitalist standards. Although the most popular brands such as Uber and Airbnb (based on platform-mediated P2P marketplaces), or Zipcar (access to company-owned assets), feature fundamentally different business models, a commonality is that they use the principles of the sharing economy for maximizing the profits of their shareholders, thus following the rules of what Schor (2014) has labeled "business as usual." But there is also the hope that the sharing economy represents a quest for a new ideology (Schor and Thompson 2014), which might lead to "joint (psychological) ownership and pro-social intentions" of resources (Belk 2010), or "sharing in solidarity" (Sahakian and Servet 2016).

While the sharing economy has been greatly facilitated through technological advances (addressed in Chapters 5 and 6 of this volume), this chapter focuses on other societal factors, which we define as a series of interrelated trends that shape and are shaped by international policies and national regulations, social norms, and collective conventions. Every day, these macro-level societal factors influence, and are influenced by, people, thereby shaping an understanding of their dual role as citizens and as consumers in an increasingly global society. We propose to engage with two levels of analysis: macro-level societal factors that have laid the groundwork for the emergence of the sharing economy and a more micro-level understanding of how and in what way people engage with and in turn shape the sharing economy. We begin the first section of this chapter with a bird's-eye view of how recurring economic crises and growing environmental awareness, coupled with major societal shifts, have facilitated the emergence of the sharing economy characterized by alternative forms of production, consumption, and financing. We link this macro-level and historic analysis to how the sharing economy is playing out today, from a bottom-up perspective. In the second section, we illustrate our key points through vignettes, drawing mostly from examples of how the sharing economy is playing out in Switzerland where the research team is located. Vignettes are commonly used in social sciences research to highlight situations and structures that reference the most relevant points in the analysis of social contexts (Hughes 1998).

Macro-Level Analysis of Societal Trends Shaping the Sharing Economy

Three interrelated factors—ecological, economic, and sociocultural—which, we contend, have laid the groundwork for the emergence of and interest in the sharing economy will be discussed in this section.

Ecological Factors

To begin with ecological factors, the link between environmental degradation and the unequal distribution of wealth first emerged at the UN Conference on the Human Environment that took place in Stockholm in 1972. Many consider this conference as signifying the birth of the environmental movement at an institutional and international level. In the same year, the Meadows report

(Meadows et al. 1972) by prominent MIT researchers insisted on "the limits of growth" in relation to environmental resources—particularly nonrenewable resources such as fossil fuels. As if on cue, in 1973, the world experienced its first oil crisis resulting in an ever-increasing concern about the access to an unevenly distributed, nonrenewable resource on which most economic activity depends. This was a time of raising awareness about environmental problems, such as acid rain and ozone depletion, that were increasingly global in scale. If Earth Day in 1970 mobilized millions of Americans, by 1990 hundreds of millions of global citizens from over 140 countries participated in the event (McNeill 2000), thus making environmentalism a worldwide movement.

A decade after the Stockholm report and despite growing awareness, the United Nations recognized that the issues raised in 1972 had not been addressed—and, in fact, many had been exacerbated. As it was in the common interest of all nations to establish policies addressing these concerns, the World Commission on Environment and Development (WCED) was convened by the United Nations in 1983, under the auspices of Dr. Gro Harlem Brundtland, to independently tackle these issues in earnest. What emerged was the now-famous Our Common Future report (commonly known as the Brundtland report), which placed an emphasis on three pillars of development—economic, environmental, and social—with sustainability achieved at the intersection of these three spheres (WCED 1987). The report fails, however, to place these spheres in any kind of hierarchical relation: economic activities were not submitted to biophysical limits, for example (Daly 1977; Georgescu-Roegen 1971); nor were they seen as embedded in social relations and institutional arrangements (Polanyi 2001/1944). In the Our Common Future report, economic growth is uniquely positioned among the three pillars as a panacea for development ails. In addition to faith in the dominant, market-driven economic paradigm, the Brundtland report ushered in an era of technological optimism (Chertow 2001) whereby technological fixes would address major environmental problems. In the coming years and in the policy discourse, greater efficiency, rather than sufficiency, was touted as the solution to overconsumption (Fuchs and Lorek 2005). Perhaps thanks to the reinforcement of business as usual, the notion of sustainability became a paradigm that could be picked up by a diverse set of actors but with varying interpretations. Sustainability may have served to further enforce, rather than challenge, what authors have called "growthmania mentality" (Daly 1974), a "growth fetish" (McNeill 2000) or "growth addiction" (van Griethuysen 2010), despite ever-rising environmental concerns and inequalities.

Economic Factors

Fast forward to the 1990s, which ushered in an era of recurring financial crises and economic recession across Asia, Latin America, Europe, and North America. By this stage, there is growing evidence that any achievements in efficiency have been largely compensated by growth in absolute consumption (Greening, Greene, and Difgli 2000), leading to the definition of weak versus strong sustainable consumption (Fuchs and Lorek 2005). In 1997, countries negotiated the Kyoto Protocol to set binding targets toward reducing greenhouse gas emissions, yet maintaining a market-based mechanism that would prove ultimately ineffective in achieving overall reductions. Participants at the first World Social Forum in Porto Alegre in 2001 declared that "another world is possible," calling for an economic paradigm shift in this new world order. The social economy is rekindled, a notion that predates environmental concerns: starting in the 19th century, in a period of rapid industrialization, people-driven innovations emerged as a way to protect workers from the ravages of unchecked capitalism. In his analysis of this period, Polanyi states that "to the bewilderment of thinking minds, unheard-of-wealth turned out to be inseparable from unheard-of-poverty" (Polanyi 2001/1944, 102)—a statement that could very well be echoed today by the Occupy Wall Street Movement and its popular slogan "We are the 99%." What has emerged, since the 1990s, is a renewed interest in what is being termed the "social *and solidarity* economy" (SSE),[1] which is being interpreted in different ways across the world (Fraisse 2003). Adding "solidarity" to the social economy was a way to differentiate this economy from what had been termed the "third sector," or an economy based on nonprofits and charitable organizations that have been positioned in response to market and state failures. Rather, the SSE is a plural economy that could potentially transform the value system that guides a market- or redistribution-based economy, respectively, in relation to the private and public spheres.

Although the concept of an SSE predates the interest in a sharing economy, the SSE failed to capture imagination in the same way as the sharing economy, most likely because it is a less-flexible term: people are given primacy over the accumulation of profit, thus making it a more political interpretation of the economy. By the 2000s, when the sharing economy began to emerge as a concept and practice, financial crises became the norm rather than the exception—involving major financial institutions on the brink of collapse, the bursting of the housing bubble in the United States, the European sovereign-debt crisis, all of which have repercussions at a global scale. While sharing out of economic need, in dire straits, has existed throughout time, the sharing economy is conceived as moving beyond this type of activity to include sharing in solidarity, based on an identification of common needs and shared resources (Belk 2010; Sahakian 2016; Sahakian and Servet 2016).

Sociocultural Factors

What we have described earlier are the ecological and economic factors that have contributed to the interest in the sharing economy. Yet we contend that the conjoint ecological, social, and economic crises that many highly developed capitalist economies are facing are also occurring over a period of neoliberalism coupled with a late modernist consumer culture, shaping the way people understand themselves as global citizens. First, the individual has been positioned as being central to change, in an agency-based model, which emphasizes individual behavior over social or institutional change (Giesler and Veresiu 2014). This has led to what authors have called the over-individualization of environmental responsibility (e.g., Maniates 2001) and the notion that choice is limited to consumption, rather than seeing consumers as citizens and actors toward social change (e.g., Zacaï and Haynes 2008). Second, most highly developed nations are in a state of what has been labeled "liquid modernity." The term that has been coined by sociologist Zygmunt Bauman (2000) refers to the instability or "liquidity" of social relationships and orientations that challenge traditional networks of support such as the family, neighborhoods, the workplace, and the church. Global nomadism plays a crucial role in the idea of liquid modernity, where people tend to frequently change not only domiciles, jobs, and occupations but also partners and social networks, and increasingly even deeply rooted convictions, values, or sexual orientation (Bauman 2000, 2007). In his discussion of liquid modernity, Bauman emphasizes the new burden of responsibility that the replacement of traditional patterns by self-chosen ones places on the individual, resulting in an overt emphasis on the agency of the individual as responsible consumer, or what Giesler and Veresiu (2014, 842) have labeled the "neoliberal mythology of shared responsibility." According to this neoliberalism narrative, individuals as consumers are responsible not only for their own happiness and well-being but also for the well-being of society and the planet—putting individual responsible consumption at the fore of transforming the world toward the better.

We suggest that it is, in particular, the reliance on such agency-based model of change, placing people at the center of transformation, which drives the fast and wide adoption of the sharing economy. Statements like Gabriel Metcalf's (2015) and Rachel Botsman's (in an interview with Gardner 2012) claim that the sharing economy will lead to a "new democracy" in which consumers are ascribed agency over a broad range of possible developments that resonate well with the idealistic narratives of late modern consumer culture that employs the consumer as moral subject. Rather than seeking top-down institutional and social change, the starting point and locus of change in the sharing economy is the individual itself. Consumption trends such as short-term commitments and flexibility, but also the strong need for self-representation, link the needs of the late modern consumer with the liquid and individual-centered business models that dominate the sharing economy. Consider, for example, the broad domain of access-based consumption (Bardhi and Eckhardt 2012) or the multitude of platforms that employ the language of micro-entrepreneurism such as Etsy or Airbnb (further discussed in Chapter 8 of this volume).

Even if its interplay of social, technological, and legal advancements might, and indeed has started to, challenge traditional capitalist social structures in the long term, the sharing economy does not represent a primarily political attempt to shake the very foundations of corporate capitalism, but rather one that is driven by consumer needs and wants.

The next section of this chapter focuses on the different consumer motives and consumption needs that prevail in the sharing economy and discusses how these sometimes-conflicting needs have been shaped by but also shape the macro-factors outlined earlier.

Micro-Level Analysis: How People Relate to the Sharing Economy

VIGNETTE: SEGMENTING THE SHARING MARKET IN SWITZERLAND

There seems to be little homogeneity when it comes to consumers' motivation to participate in the sharing economy. In our own research (Hellwig et al. 2015), we worked with a market research company to explore different "sharing types" that consumers can be grouped into. We discovered three segments—in addition to one segment of "sharing opponents" who simply show no interest in sharing as an alternative mode of consumption. The "sharing pragmatists" are not very emotional about the act of sharing and consider sharing as a matter of fair resource distribution within a social entity such as a family or a flatshare. The "sharing normatives" denote a group of consumers engaging in sharing practices mainly for reasons of social recognition, such as being known as a generous person and being needed by others. The "sharing idealists" are intrinsically driven and engage in sharing out of enjoyment of the community bonds and sociality that can be created. Maria, clearly a member of this group, says, "For me, it [sharing] has to do with benevolence, with affection, with giving to each other."

Interestingly, none of these segments turns out to engage in sharing practices for mainly economic reasons. This finding is certainly Switzerland-specific and reflects the above-average wealth of Switzerland and its citizens and the constant low rate of unemployment compared to other countries in this world.

Much of the future of the sharing economy depends on consumers' motivation to participate in it. Inasmuch as the notion of the sharing economy lumps together different forms of ventures, it subsumes at least as many consumer needs that are being addressed by these ventures. Some of these needs and wants are clearly utilitarian, while others are driven by primary social or environmental goals. We suggest that the rapid adoption of the sharing economy is driven by its positioning as the new sustainability that allows different consumer subsegments to pursue their needs in parallel under the umbrella term of the sharing economy.

At least four different motivations for consumers to participate in the sharing economy can be identified, each of them rooted in the changing economic, environmental, and sociocultural conditions that were discussed in the previous section. Together, these consumer motivations shape the value proposition of the sharing economy. Depending on the dominance of either of these consumer motivations, the sharing economy will be more or less able to respond to the plea of sustainable development.

The first two motivations are of economic character. According to the recent global "consumer sentiment" survey by McKinsey & Company (Magni, Martinez, and Motiwala 2016), with 44% of consumers "increasingly looking for ways to save money" (this number goes up to more than 70% in countries like Brazil and South Africa), consumers are becoming more thrifty. Consumers' increasing caution in spending is put into perspective, with more than 50% being worried about job loss in their household in the coming year and with more than 25% living paycheck to paycheck. For many consumers, the economic downturn is an everyday reality, and personal financial strain looms constantly. To these consumers, the sharing economy has much to offer.

On the spending side, individuals can save money on their daily consumption by postponing big purchases (e.g., a car) and replacing them with access-based consumption offering the same value-in-use but for less money (e.g., Zipcar). Furthermore, nonmonetary sharing systems such as food sharing (e.g., foodsharing.de) or hospitality networks (e.g., Couchsurfing) offer thrifty consumers ways to obtain material or immaterial value by means of their sweat equity instead of financial resources (e.g., picking up surplus food at supermarkets to be entitled to benefit from it) (Gollnhofer, Hellwig, and Morhart 2016).

On the income side, some consumers hope to improve their assets by turning their own idle capacities into market offerings and become micro-entrepreneurs such as in the case of Airbnb, Elance, TaskRabbit, or Uber. During our engagement with the sharing economy, we observed an increasing number of individuals for whom incomes from sharing economy activities constitute a substantial part of their livelihood. This might, however, also lead to questionable situations such as the fact that a considerable number of Airbnb users now are dependent on regularly renting out parts of their homes to Airbnb guests in order to afford their rent. As part of our research projects for which we have studied Airbnb hosts over a period of more than three years, we encountered several Airbnb hosts who obviously could not afford the places that they lived in by means of their regular jobs. Consider the example of Lola, who works as a yoga teacher in New York and hosted one of the authors for three nights in her small but perfectly located apartment in SoHo (see Vignette: Hosting out of Necessity).

VIGNETTE: HOSTING OUT OF NECESSITY

When Lola opened the door I immediately realized that she was suffering from a very bad cold. Wrapped in a thick cardigan and scarf, she welcomed me and guided me through her cramped apartment into her—obviously only—bedroom. Despite being sick, she insisted that I sleep in her bed and bedroom and that she sleep on an air mattress on the floor in her small living room that also served as the kitchen. I had feelings of guilt and compassion, mixed with wanting the service I had paid for and a latent fear of her passing her cold on to me. From talking to her over a cup of tea later that afternoon, the mixed blessings of Airbnb to her became very apparent. On the one hand, when she gave up her corporate career for the sake of becoming a yoga teacher, Airbnb allowed to her to keep her SoHo apartment despite exorbitant rental price. On the other hand, she became so dependent on Airbnb that she refrained from canceling reservations out of fear of financial losses and bad reviews despite putting her own well-being and health at risk. As I left, she was already on the phone with the next guest—her apartment was booked out for the entire week.

Source: Field notes from an Airbnb stay in New York City in December 2014.

The case of Airbnb is also an interesting example of how consumer behavior in the sharing economy has wider influence on the social context. The fast adoption of Airbnb has a demonstrable impact on rental prices. In cities like New York City or Munich, where housing is a rare and valuable resource, the usage of private property to house travelers is fueling already exorbitant rental costs. This pushes municipalities to intervene and regulate this newly emerging market by implementing new laws or enforcing existing ones (Huet 2014; Müller 2016).

A third motivation to participate in the sharing economy is being ideal-driven. Idealism can relate both to environmental concerns and to concerns of increasing social instability and social isolation that are linked to liquid modernity. For both cases, the sharing economy offers a variety of examples showcasing how individuals try to resolve respective issues by means of consumption. In contrast to many sustainability initiatives of previous decades discussed earlier, the sharing economy employs a variety of appeals to utopian ideals of a more economically, socially, and environmentally just world in which the human being is placed at the center of societal transformation.

Consider, for example, Rachel Botsman's (2012) claim to "re-establish humanity" in the economy by creating "marketplaces built on human relationships rather than empty transactions" that "empower people to make meaningful connections." Such declarations to change corporate capitalism toward a more humane, social, and compassionate economy resonate well with the "sharing" label that has asserted itself as an eponym for a rather diverse assemblage of ideas, hopes, and different business models.

In consumer research, the notion of sharing has a tradition of being constructed as a dramaturgic opposition to the hard logics of (corporate) capitalism and hyper-consumption that blend in a series of (anti) consumption trends, such as consumer resistance (see Fournier 1998 and Peñaloza and Price 1993 for an overview), consumer activism (Kozinets and Handelman 2004), and attempts to fortify the role of community (see, e.g., Muniz Jr. and O'Guinn 2001; Schau, Muniz Jr., and Arnould 2009; Thompson and Coskuner-Balli 2007) and authenticity (Gilmore and Pine 2007; Grayson and Martinec 2004; Potter 2010) in consumption. In several empirical studies, acts of what is perceived and described as sharing have been found to be in direct discursive contrast to the logic of capitalism and the market. For example, in their study on the participants of swap/gift and alternative market events, Albinsson and Perera (2012) found that participants construct their sharing practice as a protest against "hyper-consumption" in an increasingly "marketized" society. Similarly, Ozanne and Ballantine's (2010) toy library users see their toy-sharing practices as acts of anti-consumption. The essence of how sharing is constructed in opposition to capitalist marketplace logics is perhaps most striking in Kozinets's (2002) ethnography of the Burning Man festival as a week-long attempt of consumers to escape the capitalist market. As Kozinets (2002) puts it, the ideal market is closely associated to what Tönnies (1887/1957) called a "Gesellschaft" type of social network in the sense that it provides more formal contracted and socially distant relationships that occur for the sake of economic transactions (Weber 1978/1922; Williamson 1975). Sharing, in contrast, is much closer to Tönnies's conceptualization of "Gemeinschaft" in which a community of individuals is united by a common higher goal and mutual appreciation and affection, resulting in a climate of "caring and sharing" for others, nature, and oneself. Advocates of the sharing economy suggest that, thanks to the connective power of technology, the ideal of such a sharing and caring Gemeinschaft type of economy is now becoming realistic at a global scale (Botsman and Rogers 2010; Gansky 2010; Rifkin 2009; Sacks 2011).

Although it is very clear that many of the heterogeneous practices and business within the sharing economy do not live up to these idealistic promises, the idea of sharing implies the promise to replace the hegemonic social order of capitalism by a more socially and personally fulfilling economic environment. These ideals become especially visible in light of the criticism that has lately accumulated against the business practices of the sharing economy. Accusations of rampant neoliberalism, the undermining of workers' rights and social security, or the diminution of quality of life by drastically increasing rental prices (e.g., Bardhi and Eckhardt 2015; Cagle 2014; Morozov 2013; see Belk 2017 for a comprehensive review of sharing economy criticism) hit the core of the sharing economy because they fundamentally challenge the hopes of a more humane and egalitarian economy (Botsman and Rogers 2010; Rifkin 2009; Seibel 2015).

While research oftentimes indicates how little such idealism actually translates into consumption practices, the sharing economy caters to the increasing willingness of mainstream consumers to do good—if it is not at their own expense in terms of higher prices or less convenience. Many consumers are willing to embrace sharing offers when they simultaneously offer a good consciousness on top of superior value for money. A good example of this is the Mobility car-sharing service in Switzerland, which offers multimodal transportation options—linking cars to public transport and shared bicycles—at a more favorable cost to consumers, as opposed to car ownership (see Vignette: Mobility—Car-Sharing in Switzerland).

VIGNETTE: MOBILITY—CAR-SHARING IN SWITZERLAND

Based in Lucerne and founded in 2007, the "Mobility" cooperative is the main car-sharing service in Switzerland and, in its active encouragement of public transport, it very much presents a worldwide best practice. At the onset, the public rail system joined forces with Mobility to increase transport options from car to rail with the goal of reducing private car transport on longer routes. Today, Mobility offers a multimodal transport proposition through Swiss Pass, linking car-sharing to trains to public bikes. According to Sonia Roos, head of sustainability for strategic projects,[2] the key factors to the success of Mobility are convenience and cost: the Mobility fleet is densely located across cities in Switzerland, with parking spaces at all major transit hubs, and using Mobility is generally cheaper than car ownership. Approximately 120,000 people used Mobility services in 2014, or 7.4% more than that in the previous year. Based on a 2013 Mobility study, one shared vehicle replaces nine privately owned vehicles; without Mobility, 22% of their users would buy a car today. Yet car-sharing increases private transport mileage (vs public transport, biking or walking) and could incite people to become first-time car owners. According to Roos, this "rebound effect"[3] could be abated through more positive effects, such as Mobility users giving up their second car or privileging rail over cars

> *for longer distances. A distinction could be made between sufficiency, which would entail less car usage overall, and efficiency, or linking car-sharing to public transport, as is the case with Mobility services.*
>
> Source: Interview by Marlyne Sahakian with Sonia Roos, head of Strategic Projects, Mobility, on July 21, 2015.

At the same time, consumers who go beyond the "eco mainstream" and belong to the group of "believers" in self-transcendent values of universalism and benevolence (Schwartz 1992) find in the sharing economy a playing field to advance the idea of sociality and environmental conservation. Those mission-driven needs are best catered to by mostly nonmonetary sharing models devoted to closed-loop consumption (e.g., swaps) and idle capacity usage to save resources (e.g., toy libraries), and social gatherings (e.g., MamaBake). Especially the small-scale and oftentimes less publicly discussed platforms of the sharing economy offer a substantial potential to translate idealism into practice by merging it with convenience. Consider the example of Pumpipumpe, a neighborhood sharing platform operating in Switzerland, Germany, and Austria (see Vignette: Pumpipumpe).

VIGNETTE: PUMPIPUMPE

Initiated by Lisa Ochsenbein and Ivan Mele in 2012, Pumpipumpe is a sharing platform that works at the level of neighborhoods by using the mailbox as a personal space and communication tool. Users can order a series of pumpipumpe, which visually represent the different household items (e.g., drill, ladder, books, toys) that they are willing to share, and place these stickers in a visible public space on their mailbox. Although how much sharing is taking place is difficult to gauge, more than 15,000 households in Switzerland, Germany, and Austria have ordered these stickers. Recently, Pumpipumpe launched an online map that allows people to view approximately 7,000 addresses where objects are available for sharing. Ochsenbein envisions an online application for identifying different available items but also stresses the importance of our "real, live network," recognizing the interest in being connected to people around the world through a digital network but also that "the actual network around us is really underdeveloped."

Source: Interview by Marlyne Sahakian with Lisa Ochsenbein, cofounder and president of Pumpipumpe, on July 23, 2015.

And finally, one important motivation to participate in the sharing economy is a lifestyle choice. Since the release of Tim Ferriss's (2007) best seller *The 4-Hour Workweek*, a frugal lifestyle—at least in terms of possessions—is a new form of luxury. According to Ferriss (2007, 7), "The New Rich (NR) are those who abandon the deferred-life plan and create luxury lifestyles in the present using the currency of the New Rich: time and mobility." What Ferriss refers to is a growing consumer elite of "global nomads" (Bardhi, Eckhardt, and Arnould 2012) to whom many possessions are a heavy burden and stumbling block to their otherwise-flexible and light lives. Global nomadism, a phenomenon of the globalized world, entails constant border-crossing and multidirectional flow of people. In this increasingly liquid world, the value of immateriality supersedes consumers' previous attachment to "stuff," that is, global consumers increasingly develop liquid relationships to possessions (Bardhi, Eckhardt, and Arnould 2012; Baumann 2007). As global nomads belong to the top of the consumer pyramid in terms of financial resources and status, their intentionally immaterial lifestyle might redefine previous notions of social status. The liquid lifestyle of the "New Rich" (as Ferriss calls them) offers a new version of an aspirational lifestyle in a globalized world and hence provides an example to many other consumers who prefer *smart* (i.e., mobility-liberating; low maintenance) consumption over *hard* (i.e., mobility-constraining; high maintenance) consumption. Many offers of the sharing economy exquisitely cater to this new need of consuming in a smart, light, and flexible way. This is especially so of access-based consumption and co-ownership offers that provide access to capital-intensive items from cars (Zipcar) to luxury watches (Eleven James) and luxury yachts (Smartyacht).

The multitude of consumer motivations to engage in the sharing economy unearth the inherent tension between the mode of "being consumer" and the mode of "being citizen." Economic and lifestyle motivations can especially produce adversarial effects with regard to more ecologically and socially driven motivations, such as in the case of Mobility and Couchsurfing where competitively priced (or even nonmonetary) sharing offers might engender an increase in individuals' personal ecological footprint (through increased driven and flown mileage). Likewise, lifestyle motivations in order to differentiate oneself through a "smarter" way of consumption cement only existing social strata instead of bringing society together. Whether the sharing economy will become a lasting game changer depends on participants' ability to pursue their own motivation without hurting the goals of other participants. One such avenue would be to give preference to the notion of sufficiency over efficiency in one's economically driven, utilitarian pursuits when sharing.

Concluding Discussion—Where Did the Sharing Economy Come from, and Where Is It Heading?

The sharing economy presents an opportunity: it is heralded for its disruptive potential toward a new economic paradigm, but it yet also runs the risk of becoming a catch-all phrase which includes a range of activities from business as usual to new forms of consumption and production. One major takeaway from our analysis is that the sharing economy is built on several factors that have lastingly influenced how it has developed and how it is perceived and enacted by businesses and individuals. Many of the frustrations with the current capitalist system of production and consumption but also the disappointments with earlier attempts to curtail the outgrowths of this system flow together in the vessel of the sharing economy. This has translated into an assemblage of very different goals and motivations that drive consumer behavior in the sharing economy as well as to many different new business models and circuits of commerce (Schor 2014). In this way, the sharing economy shows a strong resemblance to the notion of sustainability, an equally blurry concept. In this chapter, we demonstrated how macroeconomic factors—including a series of economic, sociocultural, and ecological factors—have created public interest in the emergence of a sharing economy. These macro-level forces are influenced by, and in turn influence, individuals, which is why we find it pertinent to focus on how people understand their role in this increasingly global society. We point to how neoliberalism coupled with liquid modernity has positioned the individual as a central agent for change, giving rise to an agency-based model of sharing between individuals. While sharing can be motivated by individuals' economic needs, it can also be an intentional expression of lifestyle. The question remains whether people in a liquid consumer culture will consume more smartly—that is, more efficient—or whether they will consume more "sufficiently."

In many cases, media are shaping perceptions around the sharing economy. Much of the current media as well as scholarly discourse on the sharing economy focuses on those elements that are fairly easy to reconcile with the principles and ideals of the capitalist system, or, as Schor puts it, is "highly integrated into existing economic interests" (Schor 2014, 4). The usage of idle capacity by sharing existing private or pooled resources is without doubt smart and efficient and, as demonstrated by Uber, Zipcar, or Airbnb, it allows for high economic profits. But they paint neither a holistic picture nor one that is just in terms of the sharing economy and its potential. Here we see strong similarities between the sharing economy and the emphasis on "organic" or "green" consumption in the sustainability discussion. While the latter undoubtedly constitutes an important part of the sustainability movement, it represents a small fraction of it regardless of the fact that it has wrongly been turned into its poster children. Rather than focusing on headlines about sharing giants such as Uber and Airbnb, more attention should be placed on lesser-known sharing initiatives taking place on a more local scale. Even if these entities may not be as big and profitable as Uber or Airbnb, and hence not as successful by classical capitalist standards, especially those "high-touch" local sharing economy initiatives have substantial disruptive potential, because they uphold the ideals and energy for societal change.

Ultimately, if we continue the comparison between the notions of the sharing economy and sustainability, there is an opportunity to learn from the past: what was missing from the sustainable development paradigm was a clear sense of priorities, whereby biophysical limits and social equity should have prevailed over capitalistic economic development. The sharing economy offers a concrete opportunity to tackle questions of social change in earnest, but for this to take place people involved in the sharing economy must come to understand their role not only as individuals and consumers but also as social actors and citizens. Sharing out of economic dire straits has always taken place and will continue: if we want the sharing economy to do more than this, version 2.0 must engage with social change.

Notes

1. The SSE is generally defined as an economy that seeks to foster solidarity by placing more importance on people than on the accumulation of capital or profit. The goal is to place "service to its members or to the community ahead of profit; autonomous management; a democratic decision-making process; the primacy of people and work over capital in the distribution of revenues" (Defourny, Develtere, and Fonteneau 2000, 30). In the European context, there is an emphasis on the "democratization" of the economy based on the participatory engagement of all citizens (Defourny and Develtere 1999; Fraisse, Guérin, and Laville 2007; Jean-Louis 2011; Laville 2003). In the United States, the SSE aims toward the systemic transformation of the economy as a whole, across "all of the diverse ways that human communities meet their needs and create livelihoods together" (Miller 2001 in Kawano, Masterson, and Teller-Elsberg 2009, 30), including the private and public sectors, and as part of a "counter-hegemonic political economy" (Satgar 2014) or postcapitalist agenda (Kawano 2013).

2. Interview between Marlyne Sahakian and Sonia Roos, head of Strategic Projects, Mobility, on July 21, 2015, on the phone between Geneva and Lucerne.

3. "Rebound effect" is a term used to explain how efficiency measures can be lower than anticipated or even negative (also called "backfire"), when overall consumption is increased, see, for example, Hertwich (2005).

References

Albinsson, Pia A., and Yasanthi B. Perera. 2012. "Alternative Marketplaces in the 21st Century: Building Community through Sharing Events." *Journal of Consumer Behaviour* 11 (4): 303–315.

Arrow, Kenneth, Partha Dasgupta, Lawrence Goulder, Gretchen Daily, Paul Ehrlich, Geoffrey Heal, Simon Levin, Karl-Göran Mäler, Stephen Schneider, David Starrett, and Brian Walker. 2004. "Are We Consuming Too Much?" *The Journal of Economic Perspectives* 18 (3): 147–172.

Ayres, Robert U., William H. Schlesinger, and Robert H. Socolow. 1994. "Human Impacts on the Carbon and Nitrogen Cycles." In *Industrial Ecology and Global Change*, edited by R. H. Socolow, C. Andrews, R. Berkhout, and V. Thomas. 121–155. New York: Cambridge University Press.

Bardhi, Fleura, and Giana M. Eckhardt. 2012. "Access-Based Consumption: The Case of Car Sharing." *Journal of Consumer Research* 39 (4): 1–18.

Bardhi, Fleura, and Giana M. Eckhardt. 2015. "The Sharing Economy Isn't about Sharing at All." *Harvard Business Review*. January 28. https://hbr .org/2015/01/the-sharing-economy-isnt-about-sharing-at-all.

Bardhi, Fleura, Giana M. Eckhardt, and Eric J. Arnould. 2012. "Liquid Relationship to Possessions." *Journal of Consumer Research* 39 (3): 510–529.

Bauman, Zygmunt. 2000. *Liquid Modernity*. Cambridge: Polity.

Bauman, Zygmunt. 2007. *Liquid Times: Living in an Age of Uncertainty*. Cambridge: Polity.

Belk, Russell W. 2010. "Sharing." *Journal of Consumer Research* 36 (5): 715–734.

Belk, Russell W. 2017. "Sharing, Materialism, and Design for Sustainability." In *Routledge Handbook of Sustainable Product Design,* edited by Jonathan Chapman, 160–173. London: Routledge.

Botsman, Rachel. 2012. "The Currency of the New Economy Is Trust." TED Talk. https://www.youtube.com/watch?v=kTqgiF4HmgQ.

Botsman, Rachel, and Roo Rogers. 2010. *What's Mine Is Yours: The Rise of Collaborative Consumption*. New York: HarperCollins.

Cagle, Susie. 2014. "The Case against Sharing." *Medium*. May 27. https://medium. com/the-nib/the-case-against-sharing-9ea5ba3d216d.

Chase, Robin. 2015. *Peers Inc: How People and Platforms Are Inventing the Collaborative Economy and Reinventing Capitalism*. New York: PublicAffairs.

Chatzidakis, Andreas, Pauline Maclaran, and Alan Bradshaw. 2012. "Heterotopian Space and the Utopics of Ethical and Green Consumption." *Journal of Marketing Management* 28 (3–4): 494–515.

Chertow, M. 2001. "The IPAT Equation and Its Variants: Changing Views of Technology and Environmental Impact." *Journal of Industrial Ecology* 4: 13–29.

Daly, Herman E. 1974. "Steady-State Economics versus Growthmania: A Critique of the Orthodox Conceptions of Growth, Wants, Scarcity, and Efficiency." *Policy Sciences* 5 (2): 149–167.

Daly, Herman E. 1977. *Steady-State Economics: The Economics of Biophysical Equilibrium and Moral Growth*. San Francisco, CA: W. H. Freeman and Company.

Defourny, Jacques, and Patrick Develtere. 1999. *Origines et contours de l'économie sociale au nord et au sud. L'économie sociale au Nord et au Sud* [Origins and Contours of the Social Economy in the North and South. The Social Economy in the North and South]. Brussels: De Boeck Université, 25–50.

Defourny, Jacques, Patrick Develtere, and Bénédicte Fonteneau. 2000. *Social Economy North and South*. Leuven; Liège: HIVA and Centre d'Economie Sociale.

Ellen MacArthur Foundation. 2013. "Towards the Circular Economy: Economic and Business Rationale for an Accelerated Transition." http://www.ellenmacarthurfoundation.org/circular-economy/circular-economy/towards-the-circular-economy.

Ferriss, Timothy. 2011. *The 4-Hour Work Week: Escape the 9–5, Live Anywhere and Join the New Rich*. New York: Random House.

Fournier, Susan. 1998. "Special Session Summary Consumer Resistance: Societal Motivations, Consumer Manifestations, and Implications in the Marketing Domain." In *NA—Advances in Consumer Research*, volume 25, edited by Joseph W. Alba and J. Wesley Hutchinson. 88–90. Provo, UT: Association for Consumer Research.

Fraisse, Laurent. 2003. "Quels projets politiques pour l'économie solidaire?" ["What Political Projects for the Solidarity Economy?"]. *Cultures en mouvement [Cultures in Movement]* 62 (4): 36–39.

Fraisse, Laurent, Isabelle Guérin, and Jean-Louis Laville. 2007. "Economie Solidaire: Des Initiatives Locales à l'action Publique. Introduction" ["Solidarity Economy: From local initiatives to public action. Introduction"]. *Revue Tiers Monde* 190: 245–253.

Fuchs, Doris A., and Sylvia Lorek. 2005. "Sustainable Consumption Governance: A History of Promises and Failures." *Journal of Consumer Policy* 28: 261–288.

Gansky, Lisa. 2010. *The Mesh: Why the Future of Business Is Sharing*. New York: Portfolio.

Gardner, Jasmine. 2012 "The Sharer Barer: Rachel Botsman on the New Democracy." *Evening Standard*. June 27. http://www.standard.co.uk/lifestyle/london-life/the-sharer-barer-rachel-botsman-on-the-new-democracy-8676228.html.

Georgescu-Roegen, Nicholas. 1971. *The Entropy Law and the Economic Process*. Cambridge, MA: Harvard University Press.

Gibson-Graham, J. K. 2006. *A Postcapitalist Politics*. Minneapolis: University of Minnesota Press.

Gibson-Graham, J. K. 2008. "Diverse Economies: Performative Practices for 'Other Worlds.'" *Progress in Human Geography* 32 (5): 613–632.

Giesler, Markus, and Ela Veresiu. 2014. "Creating the Responsible Consumer: Moralistic Governance Regimes and Consumer Subjectivity." *Journal of Consumer Research* 41 (3): 840–857.

Gilmore, James H., and B. Joseph Pine. 2007. *Authenticity: What Consumers Really Want*. Boston, MA: Harvard Business School Press.

Gollnhofer, Johanna F., Katharina Hellwig, and Felicitas Morhart. 2016. "Fair Is Good but What Is Fair? Negotiations of Distributive Justice in an Emerging Non-Monetary Sharing Model." *Journal of the Association for Consumer Research* 1 (2): 226–245.

Grayson, Kent, and Radan Martinec. 2004. "Consumer Perceptions of Iconicity and Indexicality and Their Influence on Assessments of Authentic Market Offerings." *Journal of Consumer Research* 31 (2): 296–312.

Greening, Lorna A., David L. Greene, and Carmen Difglio. 2000. "Energy Efficiency and Consumption—The Rebound Effect—A Survey." *Energy Policy* 28: 389–401.

Hart, Keith, Jean-Louis Laville, and Antonio David Cattani, eds. 2010. *The Human Economy: A Citizen's Guide.* Cambridge, UK, and Malden, MA: Polity Press.

Hellwig, Katharina, Felicitas Morhart, Florent Girardin, and Mirjam Hauser. 2015. "Exploring Different Types of Sharing: A Proposed Segmentation of the Market for 'Sharing' Businesses." *Psychology & Marketing* 32 (9): 891–906.

Hertwich, Edgar G. 2005. "Consumption and the Rebound Effect: An Industrial Ecology Perspective." *Journal of Industrial Ecology* 9 (1–2): 85–98.

Huet, Ellen. 2014. "New York Slams Airbnb, Says Most of Its Rentals Are Illegal." *Forbes.* October 16. http://www.forbes.com/sites/ellenhuet/2014/10/16/new-york-slams-airbnb-says-most-of-its-rentals-are-illegal/.

Hughes, Rhidian. 1998. "Considering the Vignette Technique and Its Application to a Study of Drug Injecting and HIV Risk and Safer Behaviour." *Sociology of Health & Illness* 20 (3): 381–400.

Jean-Louis, Laville. ed. 2011. *L'économie solidaire, Les Essentiels d'Hermès* [*The Solidarity Economy, The Hermes Essentials*]. Paris: CNRS Editions.

Kasser, Tim. 2003. *The High Price of Materialism.* London: MIT Press.

Kawano, Emily. 2013. "Social Solidarity Economy: Toward Convergence across Continental Divides." *News & Views.* February 26. http://www.unrisd.org/unrisd/website/newsview.nsf/%28httpNews%29/F1E9214CF8EA21A8C1257B1E003B4F65?OpenDocument.

Kawano, Emily, Thomas N. Masterson, and Jonathan Teller-Elsberg. 2009. *Solidarity Economy I: Building Alternatives for People and Planet.* Amherst, MA: Center for Popular Economics.

Kozinets, Robert V. 2002. "Can Consumers Escape the Market? Emancipatory Illuminations from Burning Man." *Journal of Consumer Research* 29 (1): 20–38.

Kozinets, Robert V., and Jay M. Handelman. 2004. "Adversaries of Consumption: Consumer Movements, Activism, and Ideology." *Journal of Consumer Research* 31 (3): 691–704. doi:10.1086/425104.

Laville, Jean-Louis. 2003. "A New European Socioeconomic Perspective." *Review of Social Economy* 61 (3): 389–405.

Laville, Jean-Louis. 2011. "What Is the Third Sector? From the Non-Profit Sector to the Social and Solidarity Economy: Theoretical Debates and European Reality." EMES European Research Network Working Paper 11/01.

Lowen, Mark. 2012. "Greece Bartering System Popular in Volos." http://www.bbc.com/news/world-europe-17680904.

Magni, Max, Anne Martinez, and Rukhshana Motiwala. 2016. "Saving, Scrimping, and . . . Splurging? New Insights into Consumer Behavior." McKinsey Global Consumer Sentiment Survey. http://www.mckinsey.com/industries/consumer-packaged-goods/our-insights/saving-scrimping-and-splurging-new-insights-into-consumer-behavior.

Maniates, Michael F. 2001. "Individualization: Plant a Tree, Buy a Bike, Save the World?" *Global Environmental Politics* 1 (3): 31–52.

McNeill, J. R. 2000. *Something New under the Sun: An Environmental History of the Twentieth Century.* New York: W. W. Norton.

Meadows, Donella H., Dennis L. Meadows, Jørgen Randers, and William W. I. Behrens. 1972. *The Limits to Growth.* London: Earth Island; Compton Printing Ltd.

Metcalf, Gabriel. 2015. *Democratic by Design: How Carsharing, Co-ops, and Community Land Trusts Are Reinventing America.* New York: St. Martin's Press.

Miller, Daniel. 2001. *Volume I: Theory and Issues in the Study of Consumption. Consumption: Critical Concepts in the Social Sciences.* London; New York: Routledge.

Morozov, Evgeny. 2013. "The 'Sharing Economy' Undermines Workers' Rights." *Financial Times.* October 14. https://www.ft.com/content/92c3021c-34c2-11e3-8148-00144feab7de.

Müller, Benedikt. 2016. "Zu viele Ferienwohnungen, kein Platz für Mieter." Süddeutsche Zeitung [Too Many Vacation Rentals, No Place for Tenants]. April 16. http://www.sueddeutsche.de/wirtschaft/airbnb-in-staedten-vermietung-von-ferienwohnungen-laeuft-aus-dem-ruder-1.2954475.

Muniz, Albert M., Jr., and Thomas C. O'Guinn. 2001. "Brand Community." *Journal of Consumer Research* 27 (4): 412–432.

Ozanne, Lucie K., and Paul W. Ballantine. 2010. "Sharing as a Form of Anti-Consumption? An Examination of Toy Library Users." *Journal of Consumer Behaviour* 9 (6): 485–498.

Peñaloza, Lisa, and Linda L. Price. 1993. "Consumer Resistance: A Conceptual Overview." In *NA—Advances in Consumer Research,* volume 20, edited by Leigh McAlister and Michael L. Rothschild. 123–128. Provo, UT: Association for Consumer Research.

Poggioli, Sylvia. 2011. "Modern Greeks Return to Ancient System of Barter." http://www.npr.org/2011/11/29/142908549/modern-greeks-return-to-ancient-system-of-barter.

Polanyi, Karl. 2001/1944. *The Great Transformation: The Political and Economic Origins of Our Time.* Boston, MA: Beacon Press.

Potter, Andrew. 2010. *The Authenticity Hoax: How We Get Lost Finding Ourselves.* New York: HarperCollins.

Putnam, Robert D. 2000. *Bowling Alone: The Collapse and Revival of American Community.* New York: Simon and Schuster.

PwC. 2013. "The Sharing Economy—Sizing the Revenue Opportunity." http://www.pwc.co.uk/issues/megatrends/collisions/sharingeconomy/the-sharing-economy-sizing-the-revenue-opportunity.html.

Ransom, David, and Vanessa Baird. 2010. *People First Economics.* Oxford, UK: New Internationalist Publications.

Rifkin, Jeremy. 2009. *The Empathic Civilization: The Race to Global Consciousness in a World in Crisis.* New York: Tarcher.

Sacks, Danielle. 2011. "The Sharing Economy." *FastCompany* magazine. April 18. www.fastcompany.com/magazine/155/the-sharing-economy.html.

Sahakian, Marlyne. 2014. "Complementary Currencies, What Opportunities for Sustainable Consumption in Times of Crisis and Beyond?" *Sustainability: Science, Practice, & Policy* 10 (1): 4–13.

Sahakian, Marlyne. 2016. "The Social and Solidarity Economy: Why Is It Relevant to Industrial Ecology?" In *Taking Stock of Industrial Ecology,* edited by Roland Clift and Angela Druckman. 205–227. Wiesbaden: Springer.

Sahakian, Marlyne, and Jean-Michel Servet. 2016. "Separating the Wheat from the Chaff: Sharing versus Self-Interest in Crowdfunding." In *Strategic Approaches to Successful Crowdfunding,* edited by Djamchid Assadi 295–313. Hershey, PA: IGI Global.

Satgar, Vishwas. 2014. *The Solidarity Economy Alternative: Emerging Theory and Practice.* Pietermaritzburg, South Africa: University of KwaZulu-Natal Press.

Schau, Hope Jensen, Albert M. Muniz, Jr., and Eric J. Arnould. 2009. "How Brand Community Practices Create Value." *Journal of Marketing* 73 (5): 30–51.

Schor, Juliet B. 2014. "Debating the Sharing Economy." http://www.greattransition.org/publication/debating-the-sharing-economy.

Schor, Juliet B., Connor Fitzmaurice, Lindsey B. Carfagna, Will Attwood-Charles, and Emilie Dubois Poteat. 2016. "Paradoxes of Openness and Distinction in the Sharing Economy." *Poetics* 54: 66–81.

Schor, Juliet B., and C. J. Thompson. 2014. *Sustainable Lifestyles and the Quest for Plenitude Case Studies of the New Economy.* New Haven, CT: Yale University Press.

Schwartz, Shalom H. 1992. "Universals in the Content and Structure of Values: Theoretical Advances and Empirical Tests in 20 Countries." *Advances in Experimental Social Psychology* 25 (1): 1–65.

Seibel, Steffen Jan. 2015. "Ich Zahle Mit Meiner Persönlichkeit" [I Pay with My Personality"]. *ZEITmagazin.* July 28. http://www.zeit.de/zeit-magazin/leben/2015-07/share-economy-kapitalismus-social-economy.

Sheth, Jagdish N., Nirmal K. Sethia, and Shanthi Srinivas. 2011. "Mindful Consumption: A Customer-Centric Approach to Sustainability." *Journal of the Academy of Marketing Science.* 39 (1): 21–39.

Thompson, Craig J., and Gokcen Coskuner-Balli. 2007. "Countervailing Market Responses to Corporate Co-optation and the Ideological Recruitment of Consumption Communities." *Journal of Consumer Research* 34 (2): 135–152.

Tönnies, Ferdinand. 1957/1887. *Gemeinschaft und Gesellschaft,* translated by Charles P. Loomis. East Lansing: Michigan State University Press.

UNEP. 2011. "Green Economy Report. Part II—Investing in Energy and Resource Efficiency: Cities." United Nations Environment Programme.

van Griethuysen, Pascal. 2010. "Why Are We Growth-Addicted? The Hard Way toward Degrowth in the Involutionary Western Development Path." *Journal of Cleaner Production* 18 (6): 590–595.

Walsh, Bryan. 2011. "10 Ideas That Will Change the World." *Time* magazine. March 17. www.time.com/time/specials/packages/article/0,28804,2059521_2059717_2059710,00.html.

WCED. 1987. *Our Common Future*. New York; Oxford: The World Commission on Environment and Development.

Weber, Max. 1978/1922. *Economy and Society: An Outline of Interpretive Sociology*. Berkeley: University of California Press.

Williamson, Oliver E. 1975. *Markets and Hierarchies: Antitrust Analysis and Implications*. New York: The Free Press.

Worldwatch Institute. 2015. *State of the World 2015: Confronting Hidden Threats to Sustainability*. Washington, DC: Island Press.

Yuan, Z., J. Bi, and Y. Moriguichi. 2006. "The Circular Economy: A New Development Strategy in China." *Journal of Industrial Ecology*. 10 (1–2): 4–8.

Zacaï, Edwin, and Isabelle Haynes, eds. 2008. *La société de consommation face aux défis écologiques. Problèmes politiques et sociaux* [*The Consumer Society and the Ecological Challenges. Political and Social Problems*]. Paris, France: La documentation Française.

PART 2

Technology: A Facilitator of Modern-Day Sharing

CHAPTER FIVE

Online Technology as a Driver of Sharing

John Harvey, Andrew Smith,
and David Golightly

What We Talk about When We Talk about "Sharing"

From childhood, we share toys, food, time, and space. Indeed, from nursery to nursing home, we hear the *sharing is caring* mantra. To care we *must* share, right? Sharing is a learned behavior. Sharing is the foundation on which social relations are built. Economic relations of mutuality are often described as being "base" or more provocatively "baseline communism" (Graeber 2011; Gudeman 2008). There can be no freedom to exchange goods without a rudimentary understanding of the social rules of appropriation and expropriation. To share is to *be* social, for there can be no society, nor institution of even elementary form, without a repository of goods that remain common.

Since the 1990s, a number of capabilities and applications have arrived (see Table 5.1), which have either driven new forms of sharing or have modified the manner or scale of preexisting forms of sharing. In some cases, these are technical capabilities that have underpinned the online experience (e.g., the introduction of the web) or delivered online technology at a scale where access is cheap and resources are limitless (e.g., the introduction of Amazon cloud services, the widespread introduction of fast broadband). Other developments have introduced specific applications that have broken traditional commercial models (e.g., eBay, Napster) or have introduced the types of human–computer interaction conventions that offer individuals and

Table 5.1 Technology Capabilities and Relevance to Sharing

Innovation	Date	Implication for Sharing
World Wide Web	Formal specification of www—1990; launch of JavaScript—1995	Lightweight, accessible platform for presentation and exchange of content, functionality, and media
Web-based consumer commerce	Launch of Amazon—1994; launch of eBay—1995	Decentralized, peer-to-peer commerce (eBay); introduction of reputation, trust, and recommendation metaphors, which are now widely used
Free consumer e-mail	Launch of Hotmail—1996	Cheap, flexible means for online communication for all
Peer-to-peer sharing	Launch of Napster—1999; launch of Wikipedia—2001	Platforms for distributing media content and information within peer-based communities
Security	Current version of HTTPS specified—2000	High levels of security leading to widespread trust in Internet commerce (in terms of both exchange of money and security around personal information)
3G phone network	First UK 3G service launched—2003	Fast access to Internet content on the move
Social media	First full public access to Facebook—2006	Means of communication; platform for ad hoc and informal groups; establishing online profiles and presence with potential for reputation and trust
Cloud storage and services	Launch of Amazon web services—2006	Cheap, high volume provision of complex functionality and vast, low-cost storage
High-speed home broadband	Over 50% UK homes access high-speed broadband—2007	Widespread access at speeds that make viable all forms of casual and home use to all. Erosion of "digital divide"
Multifunction mobile device	Launch of iPhone—2007; launch of android devices—2008	Allows access to all of the above on the move, at point of need and context aware (e.g., location-based functionality)

organizations to have an online presence, history, and reputation (e.g., Amazon reviews, Facebook profiles). Critically, it is this combination of low-cost and high-performance online technology, coupled with rich functionality and strong usability, which has made new forms of exchange or commerce available to the majority of the population. The culmination is the smartphone, offering all of the aforementioned features but also being on the move while being context aware. This means services (and people) can be accessed anywhere, supplemented, or contextualized by the user's location and availability, and contextualized to the user's histories, preference, and needs.

As these new capabilities have grown in availability and acceptance, there has been a widespread rethinking of resource sharing and its potential to change the social and even political order.

This has led to the popularization of the term "sharing economy." The term refers to a loosely defined group of organizations that develop Internet-enabled services. These organizations often encourage peer-to-peer interaction either online or offline. In the media coverage, one can find examples of the catch-all term "sharing economy" being used liberally to refer to people lending, borrowing, loaning, renting, giving, and sharing their belongings. Academic research is similarly conflicted over definitional terms; indeed, there has been a flurry of typologies and taxonomies attempting to account for the wide variety of emerging services (e.g., Breitsohl et al. 2015; Bucher, Fieseler, and Lutz 2016; Hellwig et al. 2015; Lamberton and Rose 2012; Scaraboto 2015; Schor and Fitzmaurice 2015; Watkins, Denegri-Knott, and Molesworth 2016).

Typically, the services referred to earlier provide a platform for people to interact on rather than actually selling directly to consumers. The services are highly decentralized insofar as they do not own the objects that circulate but instead enable transactions between people. Websites and applications provide a means for people to browse or search a database and subsequently interact with other people rather than the organization itself. We contend that two distinct forms of organizations are regularly conflated; this conflation has profound implications for the analysis of any such service:

(1) The first category is what we, and others, have referred to elsewhere as "prosocial exchange systems," wherein people circulate goods without the need for financial remuneration. These systems are perhaps best conceptualized as a tool to help people share or give away objects.

(2) The second category of organization encourages collaborative forms of consumption that are monetized. They emphasize access to property rights rather than ownership, but the organizations and indeed the people using their services are at least to some extent motivated by financial returns. An example is the commercial "ridesharing" application Uber (see, e.g., Glöss, McGregor, and Brown 2016). If these organizations are encouraging sharing, it is as Belk argues "pseudo-sharing" (2014a, 1596).

At face value, both types of organizations are creating something novel. Their marketing campaigns often stress positive social consequences, boast of stimulating local economies, and highlight a reduction in the need to produce goods that are harmful to the environment. The sharing economy has received an enormous amount of attention from across the political spectrum despite the fluid, indistinct, and problematic nature of the term.

Depending on one's preferred definition of the word "economy," the phrase "sharing economy" is either a tautology or an oxymoron. The etymology of the word "economy" has two root words: *oiko* (house) and *nomos* (rule or law). In Aristotle's *Politics,* economics meant the art of household management, or, in other words, how families share resources. Various 20th-century economists (Hayek 1982; von Mises 1949) opposed this definition because, for them, the central aim of economics was to gain a scientific understanding of the interplay between all decision makers in society, not just to analyze individual households. Hayek (1982, 108) proposed the word "catallaxy" as an alternative (derived from the Greek verb *katallatein*). His definition meant not only to change or exchange but also to receive a person into favor or debt. It therefore refers to the order brought about by the mutual adjustment of many individual economies in a market. This higher-level definition is the meaning that most economists already give to the word "economy."

The dissection of a misnomer is not the focus of this chapter, but we do try to maintain some semantic discipline by directing attention specifically at research into nonmonetary forms of economics (type 1 as identified earlier), such as giving and sharing, and how the web is reshaping these practices. The word "sharing" is used liberally, but the definitions of sharing commonly attributed to the word often conflate or ignore distinct social arrangements, which we suggest should be the starting point for any analysis into the role of technology in sharing.

Anthropological Accounts of Giving and Sharing

If we cannot give evil, how can we give good? (Caille 2010, 182)

Anthropological records are replete with colorful accounts of giving, sharing, nonmonetary economics, and associated tales of morality. This is particularly true for historical records of cultures without explicit forms of quantitative currency. The names of these economic arrangements are no less diverse, famously including such customs, rituals, and exchange systems as "Potlatch" from the indigenous peoples of northwest Canada, the Maori "Koha," and "Moka" and "Kula ring" of Papua New Guinea. To help distinguish the motivations of people involved in computer-mediated nonmonetary initiatives, it is worth examining the motivations previously identified in the anthropological records. These examples include indirect trade between communities

(Malinowski 1992/1922), political sacrifice (Sahlins 1963), seasonal ceremonies (Boas 1896; Kan 1986), intracommunity gifting (Weinberger and Wallendorf 2011), matrimonial rituals (Valeri 1994), cosmological sacrifice (Hubert and Mauss 1964; Van der Leeuw 1938), bribery (Torsello 2011), digital file sharing (Giesler 2003, 2006), and physical body part donations, for example, organs and blood (Lock 2002). There are hundreds, if not thousands, of other examples of giving and sharing in the literature, but the examples shown here serve as a demonstration of the enormous scope of gift giving and sharing across cultures. Anthropologists often describe sharing as a one-way economic transfer rather than an exchange (Hunt 2000), but within the consumer behavior literature sharing has sometimes been subsumed by research that perceives gift giving as a form of reciprocal behavior (e.g., Sherry 1983). Some have also conceived these ostensibly one-way economic transfers as a form of "generalized" reciprocity between kin (Sahlins 1972). Altruistic sharing and its theoretical opposite "negative reciprocity" (e.g., theft) are described as special types of reciprocity, distinct from the balanced reciprocity of exchange.

In the consumer behavior literature, Belk (2010) offers a prototypical account of sharing alongside giving and exchange. A range of characteristics, counterindications, and exceptions delineate sharing as a distinct form of human interaction. The result is that Belk's prototypical categories are polythetic or "fuzzy" (see Needham 1975). Consequently, when new computer-mediated giving and sharing practices are analyzed, indications and counterindications can appear between the three forms, such that it is difficult to describe practices without resorting to "hybridization" of terms (see, e.g., Dobscha and Arsel 2011; Harvey, Smith, and Golightly 2014a). Similarly, Kennedy (2016) suggests three questions can help distinguish sharing from giving and exchange: (1) expectation of reciprocity, (2) expectation of compensation, and (3) transfer of ownership.

Classification becomes harder after a closer look at the analytical categories used; these often presuppose conflicting epistemological and ontological positions (Arnould and Rose 2016). Some economists (e.g., Musgrave 1959; Ostrom 2003; Samuelson 1954) suggest that there are various types of goods; each type, respectively, determines the potential property rights that people can appropriate. Two factors precede property rights: (1) whether or not a person can *exclude* a good from another person and (2) whether one person interacting with the good *subtracts* from the possibility that another person can replicate the interaction. In this account, sharing implies a logical division or coextension of an object, whether tangible or intangible, abstract or experiential. In contrast, anthropologists (e.g., Busse 2013; Verdery and Humphrey 2004) have drawn attention to the limits of analytical categories such as *personhood, property,* and *social relations.* A range of consumer behavior researchers have also drawn attention to goods being inherently ambiguous categories because of ephemerality, or as a consequence of tensions in social relations, such as during interpersonal borrowing (Denegri-Knot and Parsons 2014; Jenkins et al. 2014; Slater 2014). As technologies such as the Internet mediate access to an increasing number of goods, it becomes harder to delimit the social and technical entities that make sharing possible. Indeed, as the cognitive anthropologist Hutchins (2010, 706) notes, "Every boundary placement makes some things easy to see, and others impossible to see."

Once motivation is taken into account, the analytical categories become blurred further still. Benkler (2004) suggests that sharing is prosocial but, for the sake of analysis here, it seems unnecessary to impose an extra altruist/ egoist criterion. Multiple researchers have examined the motivations people have for participating in the sharing economy, including thriftiness, enjoyment, sustainability, or postcapitalist politics (Hamari, Sjöklint, and Ukkonen 2015; Hawlitschek, Teubner, and Gimpel 2016). However, for the purpose of the case studies reviewed in this chapter, it would be arbitrary and potentially misleading to suggest such diverse ideological or circumstantial motivations are essential for participation.

Before exchange-based economies became the norm, sharing was the predominate form of resource distribution (Graeber 2011). Exchange is predicated on debt. Without a sense of otherness between two parties, a reciprocal obligation would cease to exist. Therefore, to conceive of sharing as a form of reciprocity emphasizes a consequentialist mode of thought and removes the potential to critically interpret it as a type of noncommittal behavior. Similarly, the concept of generalized reciprocity does not adequately account for the "free rider" problem (known as "phenotypic defectors" in evolutionary biology—see Sherratt and Roberts 2001) in which people with access to a shared resource may consume more than they contribute. There may even be instances in which sharing occurs freely with people who simply cannot contribute due to inability, for example, children or elders who are physically incapable or ill. We suggest that within every heterogeneous population asymmetrical relations exist, which are likely to deny reciprocity. Sharing and exchange are two separate modes of property transfer, each entailing a specific moral basis (Woodburn 1998). Despite this distinction, it is clear that acts of sharing often possess the potential to become reciprocal obligations. The eventual outcome of two-way transfer thus appears to be a form of exchange and raises significant theoretical and practical issues. People involved in sharing may revise their needs and decide that a previous act of sharing may be best maintained as a form of exchange. A giver may revoke access to a resource in favor of exchange, or a receiver may opt out of sharing due to the moral imperative associated with consumption. Even with protracted ethnographic research, there may be instances in which it is impossible to note how personal motivations regarding resource consumption change over extended time frames. It is therefore potentially difficult to observe whether balanced reciprocity, akin to exchange, will emerge. If within a communal context it is

possible to observe an offer made (that is not premised on or causally connected to a balancing transfer), it is still near-impossible to establish clear
demarcation of whether a transfer is one way or reciprocal.

The diversity of available records raises some important questions: is sharing cooperative or competitive, benevolent or malevolent, altruistic and egoistic, persons or things? The answer to these questions, as in most
anthropological research, is complex and highly nuanced. The assumption
that sharing is simply prosocial with an implicit a priori altruistic motivation
is short sighted. This is contentious because a definition of sharing that fails to
recognize the potential for egoistic participation in sharing is incomplete.
Rather than focus on the possibility of altruism in exchange, Hunt (2000) suggests that an emic stance is needed to determine how both the giver and
receiver view the transfer and if they recognize the need to provide an appropriate form of reciprocity. Widlock (2004) suggests that instead of emphasiz-
ing the longitudinal potential for balance, it is more pragmatic to evaluate
whether sharing is an act *for its own sake*. This is similar to the so-called autotelic giving interpreted by Giesler (2003) when describing "gifting as participation" in the digital music file-sharing service Napster. Sharing thus occurs
as an expressive behavior, done for the experience of belonging. It is not the
"sharing out" that is typically associated with reciprocal arrangements between
dyads. Sharing here is a form of "sharing in"—a means of extending the potential benefits of a resource to others unconditionally (Belk 2010). Widlock
(2004, 62) notes:

> Sharing can be initiated both by the giver and by the receiver; demand
> sharing is a common and accepted practice. Even more frequent among
> hunters and gatherers is sharing that does not involve any transfer from
> A to B but in which A and B help themselves to x or y.

Sharing can also involve indirect transfer through an intermediary where
every attempt is made to emphasize that sharing happens for the sake of sharing, of sustenance or participation. In contrast, accumulation and exchange
are done for the sake of something else, an instrumental purpose, in order to
achieve something in the future or to even out (or surpass) something from
the past.

Ambiguity in epistemic categories means it is difficult to analyze compre-
hensively the way technology influences the wide variety of existing sharing
practices. Any starting point can seem potentially compromised by failing to
account for the different ways that people think of themselves and the relations they have with objects. We contend that websites and applications are
not passive tools in the relationship between people sharing objects. The
capacity of tools to capture and externalize human intentions is what makes
sharing such a problematic concept. Recent approaches to socio-materiality

argue that technology itself possesses intentionality or agency (e.g., Actor-Network Theory—Latour 2005; Material Engagement Theory—Malafouris 2013). We do not make such a claim, but we do nonetheless accept that only through material objects do humans come to have agency in the world. Technology influences resource sharing either by mediating dialogue between humans directly or by externalizing and managing the rules of sharing initiatives, such that interpersonal dialogue is not a prerequisite (examples of both of these forms are discussed at length in the following section). This distinction is important because it allows for a contrast to be drawn between sharing that occurs through technology with the implicit approval of people, or by comparison technology can be used to mediate dialogue, such that conditional relationships premised on sharing can emerge. As Wittel suggests, "Whereas the sharing of material things produces the social (as a consequence), the sharing of immaterial things is social in the first place" (Wittel 2011, 5).

Technology as a Means to Understand Forms of Sharing

If, as John (2013) notes, sharing is fundamental and constitutive of the web, it is because the term has become so detached from a referent that it is now a free-floating signifier. Belk (2014b) suggests that it is possible to distinguish between sharing and pseudo-sharing in Web 2.0 services. Examples of pseudo-sharing include long-term renting and leasing, short-term rental, online sites "sharing" your data with others, and online-facilitated barter economics. By contrast, the examples of genuine sharing described by Belk include the intentional sharing of online ephemera, online-facilitated offline sharing, peer-to-peer online sharing, and online-facilitated hospitality. To help illustrate the typology described in the previous section, the following sections draw on empirical examples from each of Belk's sharing categories in order to demonstrate how web technology helps to mediate each of the forms of sharing. These categories are by no means comprehensive but serve as a starting point for reviewing literature. A systematic approach to reviewing literature in this area is difficult due to the relatively broad nature of a topic spread across numerous disciplines. Consequently, we have included illustrative empirical and exploratory studies from consumer research, marketing, human–computer interaction, and tourism research.

By pairing a basic understanding of motivation (being either autotelic and an end in itself or instrumental toward some further goal) with an understanding of how people interact with property (either through interpersonal negotiation or directly through technology itself), it is possible to think of how an individual can be involved in sharing through different forms. The following typology, inspired by Holt's (1995) analysis of consumption, presents some of the potential interactions. It serves as a means to distinguish

Table 5.2 A Typology of Computer-Mediated Sharing

		Motivation for Sharing	
		Instrumental	Autotelic
Locus of interaction	**Human– computer**	Vicarious sharing	Participatory sharing
	Human–human	Allegiance sharing	Playful sharing

between forms of sharing by considering the nature of the relationship and the object shared regardless of form, whether it is a tangible consumer good, digital artifact, or an experience. The typology entails four metaphors, which include *participatory sharing*—a means of extending the self through a good without forming an explicit interpersonal relationship; *vicarious sharing*— sharing of a common good with an instrumental purpose despite a lack of explicit interpersonal relationships; *allegiance sharing*—interpersonal sharing focused on creating instrumental and reciprocal social arrangements; and, finally, sharing as *play*—an autotelic act of interpersonal sharing, done for the simple pleasure of belonging. We discuss each of these in the following section.

Allegiance Sharing

Allegiance sharing happens when people agree to an ongoing conditional relationship in relation to an object. Sharing in this sense takes on an instrumental purpose. Within the existing literature, the allegiance metaphor is particularly relevant where online interaction is a precursor to sharing offline. An example can be seen in the website Landshare, which encourages sharing of garden or allotment space between people who want to grow vegetables and people with spare growing space. Research examining this organization (Harvey, Smith, and Golightly 2014a; McArthur 2014) has found that relationships that form through this service tend to be long term, progressing through the growing seasons. The website provides a means to identify the geolocation of growing spaces on a digital map and to mediate dialogue between potential partners. It also offers a downloadable legal agreement that both participants can sign to formalize the agreement.

Sharing of a more formal nature is well established in many car-sharing arrangements around the world. This is reflected in the existing literature, which describes a broad continuum of websites that encourage forms of car-sharing and ridesharing for frequent and infrequent journeys (Bardhi and Eckhardt 2012; Bevan et al. 2013; Shaheen and Cohen 2013; Shaheen, Mallery, and Kingsley 2012). Examples range from fractional ownership of vehicles to peer-to-peer car-sharing. The huge variety of organizations in this area demonstrates how sharing practices become hybridized, providing indications and counterindications of Belk's sharing and exchange categories. As car-sharing relationships are often based on frequent repeated interactions, successful online services typically deploy a range of techniques in order to help sustain goodwill. These include responsive web designs for all devices, algorithmically matched user profiles, personalized trust and feedback review systems, and dispute resolution contact forms. However, a purely impartial, automated approach is rarely enough to cement the arrangement. The subtleties and specifics of each journey may be unique, even within established communities of lift sharing, and interpersonal communications are vital both to finesse the arrangements and to ensure trust between all parties (Brereton and Ghelewat 2010).

A similar sentiment is expressed in studies of shared domestic technology and airtime sharing, that is, a joint access to mobile phone connectivity (Brush and Inkpen 2007; Sambasivan and Cutrell 2012). These studies suggest that ongoing relationships that are not based on existing family relations or remuneration schemes rely on social negotiation. Multiple obligations overlap in order for shared access to work. Human–computer interaction designers can thus help to remove contention by personalizing the way that individuals interact with a device, for example, by including user profiles.

Allegiance sharing is also apparent in services that encourage shared access to human labor. "Time banking" is sometimes characterized as a form of exchange, but some research into time banking and skill sharing websites suggests that metaphors from banking and debt are often inappropriate in relation to this concept (Bellotti et al. 2014; Harvey 2016; Papaoikonomou and Valor 2016). While the relationships that emerge based on shared labor are often long term and conditional on prerequisites, they are not premised on debt or transferable obligations in practice. These relationships are likely to lead to an ongoing productive arrangement through joint participation, so the technology that mediates the relationship needs to encourage appropriate partner selection.

Playful Sharing

Central to this metaphor are the criteria that the technology enables human–human interaction and that these interactions do not entail reciprocal obligation. The people who participate in sharing through this form do so on an autotelic basis, typically for the simple and unconditional pleasure of expression. Intrinsic motivation is the driver for play and leads to the creation of serendipitous connections. The web "increases the ease with which we form friendships around common cultural interests and, at the same time, diminishes the bonding power of these experiences" (Parigi and State 2014, 166).

The playful metaphor, similar to allegiance, is apparent in numerous distinct instances; with technology mediating communication, many such cases encourage sharing offline. For example, Couchsurfing, the international accommodation sharing service, fits this description (Lauterbach et al. 2009; Molz 2013; Parigi et al. 2013). People who use the Couchsurfing service do not pay their accommodation hosts, nor are they obligated to reciprocate in kind. Instead, many participants have an imbalanced ledger in terms of how many people they host and how many times they are hosted; indeed, many people choose to perform only one side of the relationship. The purpose of the website is to make travel a social experience. The website serves as a tool to curate and manage personal identity so that people can list their languages, motivations, likes, and dislikes, in order to facilitate partner selection. After the accommodation sharing is finished, both participants have the opportunity to write public feedback about their experience. Subsequent participants can utilize this feedback to inform their own selection process.

Playful sharing is not restricted to temporary access rights being transferred but can also be seen in instances where the rights of absolute ownership are transferred. This is indicated in the work of a growing number of researchers who have examined the organizations Freecycle and Freegle, and the similar service Ecomodo (Arsel and Dobsha 2011; Foden 2015; Martin, Budd, and Upham 2015; Martin and Upham 2016; Piscicelli et al. 2015; Willer, Flynn, and Zak 2012). All of these services exist to help people dispose of, or reappropriate, objects, with the aim of reducing waste. Previous work suggests that disposal allows people to escape the tensions of gift economies where reciprocity is a condition of participation (Guillard and Del Bucchia 2012). In these instances, the interaction is autotelic and people are not bound by further obligations. The behavior these services encourage diverges from the prototypical forms identified by Belk, by providing indications and counterindications of both giving and sharing simultaneously. Their websites serve as a means of connecting people through the descriptions of items, rather than online personas, as is the case with Couchsurfing. The degree of anonymity afforded to people using the service may actually help to remove any sense of reciprocal obligation during participation. The listings focus on the object in question, its respective description, location, and temporal availability. The relationship is singular, with a likelihood that the participants may actually never meet online or offline ever again.

An analogue can be seen in the service Bookcrossing.com, an online service designed to encourage sharing of books across the world (Corciolani and Dalli 2014; Dalli and Corciolani 2008). The website provides unique-ID coding tools and database technology to track books as they move between owners. An emphasis on the life history of the books becomes the focus of the service rather than any sense of interpersonal balance. Bookcrossing (2016) describes its initial belief for starting the service as "books were more than just tangible objects, rather they possessed elements of emotional attachment and strong opinion; books were not only items collected and revered, but were intrinsically shared," and yet most books sit on a shelf for most of their existence. The web offers a means to help liberate these underutilized resources, for the simple purpose of shared enjoyment.

Vicarious Sharing

The web runs on open standards that allow multiple types of software to communicate. Globally accepted agreements have allowed for a high degree of standardization that reduces participation costs and helps encourage further innovation (see the World Wide Web Consortium's defence of standardization) (W3.org 2016). This dedication to sharing technology for the sake of an instrumental social purpose is central to the existence of the web itself, but it is also a key feature of many popular services online. We describe this sharing as vicarious, insofar as the interaction with a shared good occurs through human–computer interaction but without interpersonal dialogue.

Sharing freely available *open-source* software and source code has allowed developers to interact vicariously with the aim of a sublimated social goal. Social negotiation is not required to participate in sharing because the design of the technology accords to specific protocols. The best example of this is the freely available Linux computer operating systems that support a large number of online services (Hemetsberger and Reinhardt 2009). Linux, by offering the software free through General Public License, shares a wide range of property rights, including the rights to run, study, copy, or distribute the program to other people, with everybody. Although the developers and end users are not bound by reciprocal agreements, they do share an ongoing instrumental purpose of opposing proprietary software.

This model is also visible in websites such as Wikipedia, a form of commons-*based peer production* (Benkler 2006). Sharing here is sharing for all, by default, without negotiation. The overarching aim of Wikipedia is to provide accessible knowledge for everyone; thus, sharing serves an instrumental political purpose. Digital goods provide an ideal means for vicarious sharing because they are not subject to subtractability and excludability in the same way as physical goods. Multiple computers can simultaneously gain access to the same files without diminishing the quality of the experience as with physical goods. As Benkler (2006, 121) notes, "By lowering the capital costs required for effective individual action, these technologies have allowed various provisioning problems to be structured in forms amenable to decentralised production based on social relations, rather than through markets or hierarchies." This capacity of sharing to subvert the market is not without consequence, as Giesler's work (2003, 2006) on digital file-sharing services such as Napster indicates. Sharing does not necessarily assume some prosocial end; indeed, providing access to a freely available digital good can create a parasitic relationship between new practices and the market. This is perhaps particularly true for digital resources such as music and video files; replication of these is easy.

Participatory Sharing

Sharing through participation is a metaphor for autotelic interaction with a common object, done without interpersonal negotiation. The fact that the interaction occurs without the moral invocation of reciprocity suggests that the behavior is based on a virtue ethic. Many examples fall under the description of "prosocial interaction design" (see Harvey, Golightly, and Smith 2014b). Work in this field attempts to understand and then enable the disenfranchised of society through informed design. Research in this area reveals examples of location-based information systems to help tackle food poverty and food insecurity, identify leftover food waste, and share wild food foraging locations (Chamberlain and Griffiths 2013; Codagnone et al. 2016; Dombrowski et al. 2013). Similarly, the literature describes how many researchers and activists have designed forms of human–computer interaction with the explicit aim of encouraging people to share skills, resources, and time particularly with vulnerable people. Examples include systems that encourage donations to homeless shelters and crowd-sourced knowledge contributions in the aftermath of natural disasters (Starbird 2013; Starbird and Palen 2011). Clearly, these arrangements are not based in any sense of reciprocal obligation. Autotelic reasoning motivates this interaction, typically to help improve the material status of people in unfortunate circumstances.

Citizen science projects are another example of labor and knowledge sharing where the emphasis is on participation. Citizen science is research conducted, in whole or part, by amateur or nonprofessional participants, typically generated through crowd-sourcing techniques. The volunteers in these arrangements are often unfamiliar with each other but, nonetheless, participate in sharing because of a common interest. These projects often contain huge datasets that are categorized through volunteered information. Examples vary dramatically in their objectives and respective scientific disciplines, from ornithology to biology to astronomy—from classifying organisms and ecosystems here on earth to identifying features on the surface of other planets (Bonney et al. 2009; Silvertown 2009; Simpson, Page, and De Roure 2014). These projects are typically time dependent and require a sufficient number of contributions before the project is complete, but they are not based on an ongoing obligation between the chief scientists and/or any of the volunteers. The motivations to explore, to learn, or to inform drive participation, so education is an end in itself.

The Implications of the Typology

Since the beginning of the web, principles of decentralization and sharing have been crucial. As Tim Berners-Lee (1998) suggested:

> The dream behind the Web is of a common information space in which we communicate by sharing information. Its universality is essential: the fact that a hypertext link can point to anything, be it personal, local or global, be it draft or highly polished.

The typology provided in the previous section offers a basic characterization of resource sharing from the perspective of the individual, but anthropologists regularly stress the importance of examining the broader social context in which behavior occurs. Sharing always involves more than one person. Durkheim (1982/1895) and Mauss argued that economic acts should be examined in the context of broader social practices such that they can be understood as "total social facts." To understand economic behavior, it is essential to first gain an understanding of how a culture conceptualizes religion, kin, gender, politics, and the whole gamut of social experience. The sharing economy has come under scrutiny from policy makers across the world, but academic attention is at present lacking cultural breadth. A recent report for the European Commission suggests much of the literature relates specifically to the United States. Indeed, in a comprehensive literature review of 140 sources, only 20 focused on countries within Europe (see Codagnone, Biagi, and Abadie 2016, 8). Mauss noted that a broad range of nonmonetary economic institutions share similar features, including

> the so to speak voluntary character of these total services, apparently free and disinterested but nevertheless constrained and self-interested. Almost always such services have taken the form of the gift, the present generously given even when, in the gesture accompanying the transaction, there is only a polite fiction, formalism, and social deceit, and when really there is obligation and economic self-interest. (1967/1925, 4)

This epistemological position stresses that any analysis of economic behavior at face value will invariably be reductive and may therefore actually mask the real motivation for acting. Ironically, this position led to Mauss's work spawning utilitarian interpretations of the gift, despite arguing specifically against the dominance of utilitarian thought (see Douglas 1990). Indeed, ever since the publication of *The Gift,* the use and abuse of Maussian thought has come to characterize the split between perspectives in economic anthropology. Whether or not a polite fiction of formalism is present in all social life is central to a dispute that has dogged economics for the past 150 years. We believe that to explain sharing fully, social structure must be recognized as having causal efficacy in human interaction. Elder-Vass (2015) has suggested that both anthropologists and economists have denied the role of agency or have reinforced utilitarian perspectives that ignore social structure. Consequently, both forms of analysis tend to reduce the motivation of people giving and sharing to one of "exchangeism." We believe that the "positional giving" Elder-Vass describes offers an interesting alternative approach insofar as it recognizes the significance of social position regardless of which sharing initiative is being examined. Indeed, in recent research into how people use a prosocial exchange system in England, we found that people are more likely to perform distinct roles as either initiators or recipients in sharing relationships rather than both (see Harvey 2016). Age, gender, occupation, education, and wealth inequality underpin differences in social position that create the possibility for unreciprocated transfers of property rights. For example, ridesharing is often motivated because one party does not have access to a vehicle and therefore by default is unable to reciprocate. In such cases, other forms of compensation may be offered (e.g., sharing petrol costs, Christmas gifts, baking a cake—see Golightly et al. 2010).

Dredge and Gyimóthy (2015) illustrate the wide variety of banal names associated and sometimes used interchangeably with the sharing economy through a chronological literature review of academic research (they found 17 different names!). Admittedly, we may have added to the list of verbiage in the course of our own endeavors, but it is imperative that policy makers do not conflate organizations that enable nonmonetary forms of sharing with those that encourage renting. We suggest that an industrial standard would help to classify the organizations for the purpose of macroeconomic analysis and legislation. A recent independent review for the UK government (Wosskow 2014) called for the creation of a form of quality certification. Indeed, responsible sharing platforms that meet a minimum standard may achieve such certification. The suggested criteria to adjudicate responsible sharing practices include avenues for dispute resolution, respecting data privacy, insurance for users, providing users with legal compliance information, and ensuring user reviews are unbiased. We believe these criteria are worthwhile standards that should be implemented but would add that any such certification should be sufficiently nuanced to recognize two types of organizations—prosocial exchange and pseudo-sharing. There are clear moral differences in how users of these systems act, and these variations are likely to increase in number during the coming decade.

Sharing and pseudo-sharing organizations use both technology and the web to challenge historical forms of ownership. This reorientation of the relationship between enterprise and the individual is not a negative prospect in itself unless and until one associates it with a model that belies the decentralization of production. Centralized ownership and decentralized production can result only in further economic inequality. These organizations may create new possibilities for consumption, but they stultify any potential to reduce asymmetries of wealth. The pseudo-sharing economy shifts the focus of economic life from the exchange of goods to the monetization of peer-to-peer service. This would not be such a grim prospect if the majority controlled corporate ownership and executive decision making. The reality is that many of the commercially successful organizations of the present day are simply capitalism supercharged—sharing is not their goal. It is ironic that the few that skim profits from the transactions of the many have appropriated the language of "sharing," so often used to represent the ultimate goal of economic mutuality by communists and anarchists. The amount of research into innovative new initiatives of genuine sharing represents only a fraction of literature describing the so-called sharing economy.

References

Arnould, E., and A. Rose. 2016. "Mutuality: Critique and Substitute for Belk's Sharing." *Marketing Theory* 16: 1–25.

Arsel, Z., and S. Dobsha. 2011. "Hybrid Pro-Social Exchange Systems: The Case of Freecycle." *Advances in Consumer Research* 39: 66–67.

Bardhi, F., and G. Eckhardt. 2012. "Access Based Consumption: The Case of Car Sharing." *Journal of Consumer Research* 39: 881–898.

Belk, R. 2010. "Sharing." *Journal of Consumer Research* 365: 715–734.

Belk, R. 2014a. "You Are What You Can Access: Sharing and Collaborative Consumption Online." *Journal of Business Research* 67 (8): 1595–1600.

Belk, R. 2014b. "Sharing versus Pseudo-Sharing in Web 2.0." *The Anthropologist* 18 (1): 7–23.

Bellotti, V., S. Cambridge, K. Hoy, P. Shih, L. Handalian, K. Han, and J. Carrol. 2014. "Towards Community-Centered Support for Peer-to-Peer Service Exchange." *Proceedings of the 32nd Annual ACM Conference on Human Factors in Computing Systems—CHI '14.* 2975–2984. New York: ACM Press.

Benkler, Y. 2004. "Sharing Nicely: On Shareable Goods and the Emergence of Sharing as a Modality of Economic Production." *Yale Law Journal* 114: 273–358.

Benkler, Y. 2006. *The Wealth of Networks: How Social Production Transforms Markets and Freedoms.* New Haven, CT: Yale University Press.

Berners-Lee, T. 1998. "The World Wide Web: A Very Short Personal History." https://www.w3.org/People/Berners-Lee/ShortHistory.html.

Bevan, C., L. Emanuel, J. Padget, J. Swart, J. Powell, and S. Basurra. 2013. "Factors in the Emergence and Sustainability of Self-Regulation." AISB Convention. Social Coordination: Principles, Artefacts and Theories. Exeter, UK.

Boas, F. 1896. "The Indians of British Columbia." *Journal of the American Geographical Society* 28: 229–243.

Bonney, R., C. Cooper, J. Dickinson, S. Kelling, T. Phillips, K. Rosenberg, and J. Shirk. 2009. "Citizen Science: A Developing Tool for Expanding Science Knowledge and Scientific Literacy." *BioScience* 59: 977–984.

Bookcrossing. 2016. "Bookcrossing—About Page." http://www.bookcrossing.com/about.

Breitsohl, J., W. H. Kunz, and D. Dowell. 2015. "Does the Host Match the Content? A Taxonomical Update on Online Consumption Communities." *Journal of Marketing Management* 31 (9–10): 1040–1064.

Brereton, M., and S. Ghelewat. 2010. "Designing for Participant in Local Social Ridesharing Networks—Grass Roots Prototyping of IT Systems." *Proceedings of PDC '10*, Sydney, Australia.

Brush, A. J., and K. M. Inkpen. 2007. "Yours, Mine and Ours? Sharing and Use of Technology in Domestic Environments." In Proceedings of Ubicomp '07, Innsbruck, Austria, pp. 109–126.

Bucher, E., C. Fieseler, and C. Lutz. 2016. "What's Mine Is Yours (for a Nominal Fee)—Exploring the Spectrum of Utilitarian to Altruistic Motives for Internet-Mediated Sharing." *Computers in Human Behavior* 62: 316–326.

Busse, M. W. 2013. "Property." In *A Handbook of Economic Anthropology,* edited by J. Carrier. 111–127. Cheltenham, UK: Edward Elgar.

Caille, A. 2010. "Gift." In *The Human Economy*, edited by K. Hart, J. V. Laville, and A. D. Cattani. 180–186. Cambridge: Polity.

Chamberlain, A., and C. Griffiths. 2013. "Taste and Place: Design, HCI, Location and Food." *Proceedings of the 5th International Workshop on Multimedia for Cooking and Eating Activities*, Barcelona, Spain, pp. 57–62.

Codagnone, C., F. Biagi, and F. Abadie. 2016. *The Passions and the Interests: Unpacking the Sharing Economy.* Institute for Prospective Technological Studies, JRC Science for Policy Report. EUR 27914 EN, doi:10.2791/474555

Corciolani, M., and D. Dalli. 2014. "Gift-Giving, Sharing and Commodity Exchange at Bookcrossing.com: New Insights from a Qualitative Analysis." *Management Decision* 52 (4): 755–776.

Dalli, D., and M. Corciolani. 2008. "Releasing Books into the Wild. Communal Gift Giving at Bookcrossing.Com." In *NA—Advances in Consumer Research*, volume 35, edited by Angela Y. Lee and Dilip Soman. Duluth, MN: Association for Consumer Research. http://acrwebsite.org/volumes/13346/volumes/v35/NA-35.

Denegri-Knot, J., and E. Parsons. 2014. "Disordering Things." *Journal of Consumer Behaviour* 13 (2): 89–98.

Dobscha, S., and Z. Arsel. 2011. "Hybrid Prosocial Exchange Systems: The Case of Freecycle." Presented at the ACR's Association of Consumer Research, St. Louis, Missouri.

Dombrowski, L., J. R. Brubaker, S. H. Hirano, M. Mazmanian, and G. R. Hayes. 2013. "It Takes a Network to Get Dinner." *Proceedings of UbiComp '13*, Zurich, Switzerland, pp. 519–528. ACM Press.

Douglas, M. 1990. "Foreword: No Free Gifts." In *The Gift*, edited by M. Mauss. ix–xxiii. London; New York: Routledge.

Dredge, D., and S. Gyimóthy. 2015. "The Collaborative Economy and Tourism: Critical Perspectives, Questionable Claims and Silenced Voices." *Tourism Recreation Research* 40 (3): 286–302.

Durkheim, E. 1982/1895. *The Rules of Sociological Method and Selected Texts on Sociology and Its Method,* edited by Steven Lukes. New York: Free Press.

Elder-Vass, D. 2015. "Free Gifts and Positional Gifts: Beyond Exchangeism." *European Journal of Social Theory* 18 (4): 451–468.

Foden, M. 2015. "Saving Time, Saving Money, Saving the Planet, 'One Gift at a Time': A Practice-Centred Exploration of Free Online Reuse Exchange." *Ephemera* 15 (1): 41–65.

Giesler, M. 2003. "An Anthropology of File Sharing." *Advances in Consumer Research* 30: 273–279.

Giesler, M. 2006. "Consumer Gift Systems." *Journal of Consumer Research* 33 (2): 283–290.

Glöss, M., M. McGregor, and B. Brown. 2016. "Designing for Labour: Uber and the On-Demand Mobile Workforce." In *Proceedings of 2016 CHI Conference on Human Factors in Computing Systems,* pp. 1632–1643.

Golightly, D., S. Sharples, A. Irune, C. Leygue, J. Cranwell, and C. O'Malley. 2010. "User and Organisational Needs for Ad-Hoc Ride Sharing." *Proceedings of Digital Futures Conference,* Nottingham, UK. https://www.researchgate.net/publication/304202976_User_and_organisational_needs_for_ad-hoc_car_sharing.

Graeber, D. 2011. *Debt: The First 5,000 Years.* New York: Melville House.

Gudeman, S. 2008. *Economy's Tension: The Dialectics of Community and Markets.* Oxford: Berghahn Books.

Guillard, V., and C. Del Bucchia. 2012. "When Online Recycling Enables Givers to Escape the Tensions of the Gift Economy." *Research in Consumer Behavior* 14: 47–65.

Hamari, J., M. Sjöklint, and A. Ukkonen. 2015. "The Sharing Economy: Why People Participate in Collaborative Consumption." *Journal of the Association for Information Science and Technology* 67: 2047–2059. doi:10.1002/asi.23552.

Harvey, J. 2016. "An Economic Anthropology of Computer-Mediated Non-Monetary Exchange in England." PhD Thesis, University of Nottingham. http://eprints.nottingham.ac.uk/id/eprint/35266.

Harvey, J., A. Smith, and D. Golightly. 2014a. "Giving and Sharing in the Computer-Mediated Economy." *Journal of Consumer Behaviour* 16: 363–371. doi: 10.1002/cb.1499.

Harvey, J., D. Golightly, and A. Smith. 2014b. "HCI as a Means to Prosociality in the Economy." *Proceedings of the SIGCHI Conference on Human Factors in Computing Systems (CHI '14).* 2955–2964. New York: ACM.

Hawlitschek, F., T. Teubner, and H. Gimpel. 2016. "Understanding the Sharing Economy—Drivers and Impediments for Participation in Peer-to-Peer Rental." *Proceedings of the 49th Hawaii International Conference on System Sciences (HICSS),* Koloa, HI, USA, pp. 4782–4791.

Hayek, F. A. 1982. *Law, Legislation and Liberty*. London: Routledge.

Hellwig, K., F. Morhart, F. Girardin, and M. Hauser. 2015. "Exploring Different Types of Sharing: A Proposed Segmentation of the Market for 'Sharing' Businesses." *Psychology & Marketing* 32 (9): 891–906.

Hemetsberger, A., and C. Reinhardt. 2009. "Collective Development in Open-Source Communities: An Activity Theoretical Perspective on Successful Online Collaboration." *Organization Studies* 30 (9): 987–1008.

Holt, D. B. 1995. "How Consumers Consume: A Typology of Consumption Practices." *The Journal of Consumer Research* 22 (1): 1–16.

Hubert, H., and M. Mauss. 1964. *Sacrifice: Its Nature and Function*. London: Cohen & West.

Hunt, R. 2000. "Forager Food Sharing Economy: Transfers and Exchanges." In *The Social Economy of Sharing. Resource Allocation and Modern Hunter-Gatherers*, edited by G. Wenzel, G. Hovesrud-Broda, and N. Kishigami. 7–26. Osaka: National Museum of Ethnology.

Hutchins, E. 2010. "Cognitive Ecology." *Topics in Cognitive Science* 2: 705–715.

Jenkins, R., M. Molesworth, and R. Scullion. 2014 "The Messy Social Lives of Objects: Inter-Personal Borrowing and the Ambiguity of Possession and Ownership." *Journal of Consumer Behaviour* 13: 131–139. doi:10.1002/cb.1469.

John, N. A. 2013. "Sharing and Web 2.0: The Emergence of a Keyword." *New Media & Society* 15 (2): 167–182.

Kan, S. 1986. "The 19th-Century Tlingit Potlatch: A New Perspective." *American Ethnologist* 13: 191–212.

Kennedy, J. 2016. "Conceptual Boundaries of Sharing." *Information, Communication & Society* 19 (4): 461–474.

Lamberton, C. P., and R. L. Rose. 2012. "When Is Ours Better Than Mine? A Framework for Understanding and Altering Participation in Commercial Sharing Systems." *Journal of Marketing* 76 (4): 109–125.

Latour, B. 2005. *Reassembling the Social: An Introduction to Actor Network-Theory*. Oxford: Oxford University Press.

Lauterbach, D., H. Truong, T. Shah, and L. Adamic. 2009. "Surfing a Web of Trust: Reputation and Reciprocity on Couchsurfing." *Proceedings of the 2009 International Conference on Computational Science and Engineering*, Vancouver, Canada, volume 4, pp. 346–353.

Lock, M. 2002. *Twice Dead: Organ Transplants and the Reinvention of Death*. California Series in Public Anthropology, no. 1. Berkeley; Los Angeles: University of California Press.

Malafouris, L. 2013. *How Things Shape the Mind: A Theory of Material Engagement*. Cambridge: MIT Press.

Malinowski, B. 1992/1922. *Argonauts of the Western Pacific*. London: Routledge and Kegan Paul.

Martin, C. J., L. Budd, and P. Upham. 2015. "Commercial Orientation in Grassroots Social Innovation: Insights from the Sharing Economy." *Ecological Economics* 118: 240–251.

Martin, C. J., and P. Upham. 2016. "Grassroots Social Innovation and the Mobil-
    isation of Values in Collaborative Consumption: A Conceptual Model."
    Journal of Cleaner Production 134: 204–213.

Mauss, M. 1967/1925. *The Gift: Forms and Functions of Exchange in Archaic Societ-
    ies,* edited by I. Cunnison. New York: Norton.

McArthur, E. 2014. "Many-to-Many Exchange without Money: Why People
    Share Their Resources." *Consumption Markets & Culture* 18 (3): 239–256.

Molz, J. 2013. "Social Networking Technologies and the Moral Economy of
    Alternative Tourism: The Case of Couchsurfing.org." *Annals of Tourism
    Research* 43: 210–230.

Musgrave, R. A. 1959. *The Theory of Public Finance.* New York: McGraw-Hill.

Needham, R. 1975. "Polythetic Classification: Convergence and Consequences."
    Man 10: 349–369.

Ostrom, E. 2003. "How Types of Goods and Property Rights Jointly Affect Col-
    lective Action." *Journal of Theoretical Politics* 15 (3): 239–270.

Papaoikonomou, E., and C. Valor. 2016. "Exploring Commitment in Peer-to-Peer
    Exchanges: The Case of Timebanks." *Journal of Marketing Management* 32:
    13–14, 1333–1358, doi: 10.1080/0267257X.2016.1177578.

Parigi, P., and B. State. 2014. "Disenchanting the World: The Impact of Technol-
    ogy on Relationships." In *Social Informatics,* volume 8851, edited by L.
    Aiello and D. McFarland. 166–182. Springer International Publishing.

Parigi, P., B. State, D. Dakhlallah, R. Corten, K. Cook, et al. 2013. "A Community
    of Strangers: The Dis-Embedding of Social Ties." *PLoS ONE* 8(7).

Piscicelli, L., T. Cooper, and T. Fisher. 2015. "The Role of Values in Collaborative
    Consumption: Insights from a Product-Service System for Lending and
    Borrowing in the UK." *Journal of Cleaner Production* 97: 21–29, https://doi.
    org/10.1016/j.jclepro.2014.07.032.

Sahlins, M. 1963. "Poor Man, Rich Man, Big Man, Chief. Political Types in Mela-
    nesia and Polynesia." *Comparative Studies in Society and History* 5:
    285–300.

Sahlins, M. 1972. *Stone Age Economics.* Chicago: Aldine-Atherton.

Sambasivan, N., and E. Cutrell. 2012. "Understanding Negotiation in Airtime
    Sharing in Low-Income Microenterprises." *Proceedings of the SIGCHI Con-
    ference on Human Factors in Computing Systems (CHI '12).* 791–800. New
    York: ACM.

Samuelson, P. 1954. "The Pure Theory of Public Expenditure." *Review of Econom-
    ics and Expenditure* 36 (November): 387–389.

Scaraboto, D. 2015. "Selling, Sharing, and Everything In Between: The Hybrid
    Economies of Collaborative Networks." *Journal of Consumer Research* 42
    (1): 152–176.

Schor, J., and C. Fitzmaurice. 2015. "Collaborating and Connecting: The Emer-
    gence of the Sharing Economy." In *Handbook of Research on Sustainable
    Consumption,* edited by Lucia Reisch and John Thogersen. 410–425.
    Cheltenham, UK: Edward Elgar.

Shaheen, S. A., and A. P. Cohen 2013. "Carsharing and Personal Vehicle Services: Worldwide Market Developments and Emerging Trends." *International Journal of Sustainable Transportation* 7 (1): 5–34.

Shaheen, S. A., M. A. Mallery, and K. J. Kingsley. 2012. "Personal Vehicle Sharing Services in North America." *Research in Transportation Business and Management* 3: 71–81.

Sherratt, T. N., and G. Roberts. 2001. "The Role of Phenotypic Defectors in Stabilizing Reciprocal Altruism." *Behavioral Ecology* 12: 313–317.

Sherry, J. F. 1983. "Gift Giving in Anthropological Perspective." *The Journal of Consumer Research* 10 (2): 157–168.

Silvertown, J. 2009. "A New Dawn for Citizen Science." *Trends in Ecology and Evolution* 1118: 1–5.

Simpson, R., K. R. Page, and D. De Roure. 2014. "Zooniverse: Observing the World's Largest Citizen Science Platform." *Proceedings of the Companion Publication of the 23rd International Conference on World Wide Web*, Seoul, Korea, pp. 1049–1054.

Slater, D. 2014. "Ambiguous Goods and Nebulous Things." *Journal of Consumer Behaviour* 13: 99–107.

Starbird, K. 2013. "Delivering Patients to Sacré Coeur: Collective Intelligence in Digital Volunteer Communities." In *Proceedings of the SIGCHI Conference on Human Factors in Computing Systems (CHI '13).* 801–810. New York: ACM.

Starbird, K., and L. Palen. 2011. "'Voluntweeters': Selforganizing by Digital Volunteers in Times of Crisis." In *Proceedings of the SIGCHI Conference on Human Factors in Computing Systems (CHI '11).* 1071–1080. New York: ACM.

Torsello, D. 2011. "The Ethnography of Corruption: Research Themes in Political Anthropology." QoG Working Paper Series, The Quality of Government. Institute., University of. Gothenburg, March.

Valeri, V. 1994. "Buying Women but Not Selling Them: Gift and Commodity Exchange in Huaulu Alliance." *Man* 29: 1–24.

Van der Leeuw, G. 1938. *Religion in Essence and Manifestation.* London: Allen and Unwin.

Verdery, K., and C. Humphrey. 2004. *Property in Question: Value Transformation in the Global Economy.* Oxford; New York: Berg Press.

von Mises, L. 1949. *Human Action: A Treatise on Economics.* New York: The Foundation for Economic Education.

Watkins, R., J. Denegri-Knott, and M. Molesworth. 2016. "The Relationship between Ownership and Possession: Observations from the Context of Digital Virtual Goods." *Journal of Marketing Management* 32: 44–70.

Weinberger, M. F., and M. Wallendorf. 2011. "Intracommunity Gifting at the Intersection of Contemporary Moral and Market Economies." *Journal of Consumer Research* 39: 74–92.

Widlock, T. 2004. "Sharing by Default: Outline of an Anthropology of Virtue." *Anthropological Theory* 4 (1): 53–70.

Willer, R., F. J. Flynn, and S. Zak. 2012. "Structure, Identity, and Solidarity: A Comparative Field Study of Generalized and Direct Exchange." *Administrative Science Quarterly* 57 (1): 119–155.

Wittel, A. 2011. "Qualities of Sharing and Their Transformations in the Digital Age." *International Review of Information Ethics* 15 (9): 3–8.

Woodburn, J. 1998. "'Sharing Is Not a Form of Exchange': An Analysis of Property-Sharing in Immediate-Return Hunter-Gatherer Societies." In *Property Relations: Renewing the Anthropological Tradition*, edited by C. M. Hann. 48–63. Cambridge: Cambridge University Press.

Wosskow, D. 2014. *Unlocking the Sharing Economy. An Independent Review.* London: UK Department for Business, Innovation and Skills. https://www .gov.uk/government/uploads/system/uploads/attachment_data/file/ 378291/bis-14-1227-unlocking-the-sharing-economy-an-independent review.pdf

W3.org. 2016. "World Wide Web Consortium—Mission." https://www.w3.org/ Consortium/mission#vision.

CHAPTER SIX

Mapping the Collaborative Economy Landscape and Its Relationship with Information and Communication Technologies

Andreas Kamilaris and Francesc X. Prenafeta-Boldú

Introduction

A variety of factors have led to a rise in the popularity of the collaborative economy (CE) practice, encouraging numerous successful initiatives (mostly) in developed countries. The CE, also known as sharing economy, is defined as a peer-to-peer-based sharing of access to goods and services (Belk 2014a; Owyang, Tran, and Silva 2013; Schor et al. 2016) characterized by complex interactions among peers who collaborate to achieve certain socioeconomic goals (Thomas, Price, and Schau 2013). It is a new socioeconomic practice in which traditional sharing, bartering, lending, trading, renting, and swapping are redefined through technology and peer communities (Albinsson and Perera 2012; Hamari, Sjöklint, and Ukkonen 2015; Van de Glind 2013) forming platform-enabled consumer ecosystems (Choudary, Van Alstyne, and Parker

2016; Möhlmann 2015) that evolve into systems of collaborative consumption (Botsman and Rogers 2010).

Many believe that CE will redefine the buyer–seller relationship in that it constitutes a natural evolution of social business (Owyang, Tran, and Silva 2013; Rifkin 2014). This leads to the emergence of collaborative consumer–producer networks, a hybrid economy with hybrid modes of exchange (Scaraboto 2015), where circulation enables the systemic creation of value by connecting networked participants (Figueiredo and Scaraboto 2016). CE is highly related to the concept of circular economy (Ghisellini, Cialani, and Ulgiati 2016), which emphasizes in recycling and reusing of products and raw materials.

Some established companies, such as Toyota, NBC, and Enterprise, have joined this movement to avoid the risk of being excluded by customers who connect to each other (Enterprise CarShare 2012). Indeed, CE is rising in popularity and becoming better established: U.S. companies operating in this domain employ approximately 60,000 employees and are valued at US$17 billion (CrowdExpert.com 2016; Owyang and VBProfiles 2015). Projections indicate that the total value of CE transactions in Europe could reach 570 billion EUR by 2025 from 28 billion today (PwC 2015).

The projected growth of this sector is attributed to increasing support from citizens stemming from enjoyment of the offerings, economic gains, personal reputation, social acceptance, and sustainability (Hamari, Sjöklint, and Ukkonen 2015; Wasko and Faraj 2005). Since in CE markets people act not only as consumers but also as micro-entrepreneurs (Owyang 2014), CE has risen in popularity, with consumers seeking less-expensive ways to cover their needs. Citizens who saw their income decrease due to the financial crisis took the opportunity to sell products/services to other people through online websites and mobile applications, thus earning extra money. This peer-to-peer manner of exploiting goods and services resulted in recognizing more the usability of a product or service than its ownership (Bardhi and Eckhardt 2012; Botsman and Rogers 2010).

In addition, with increasing urbanization, leading people to compete for space and resources, sharing may be the best action in many cases (Benkler 2004; Finley 2013). Moreover, advances in information and communication technologies (ICT), including richer online experience, more trust in online financial transactions, availability of broadband Internet access from mobile phones, rise of social media, and use of smartphones as multi-sensor powerful computing devices, have enabled larger adoption of CE-based practices across the world (Rifkin 2014). The actual sharing and collaboration in CE relies heavily on social dynamics (Benkler 2004; Figueiredo and Scaraboto 2016; Scaraboto 2015) that are made possible through these ICT advancements in recent years (Wiertz and de Ruyter 2007). This observed conjuncture between the establishment of the digital era and the rise of CE practice has motivated this study that examines the relationship, and correlation, between CE and ICT, focusing on how ICT has influenced, or been utilized in, recent CE practices.

Existing literature has examined sharing in Web 2.0 (Belk 2014a), the business implications of online collaborative consumption (Belk 2014b), reasons for online participation (Hamari, Sjöklint, and Ukkonen 2015), impact of online social dynamics (Wiertz and de Ruyter 2007), motivations for online information sharing (Nov 2007; Nov, Naaman, and Ye 2010; Wasko and Faraj 2005), legal aspects in online sharing (Manner, Siniketo, and Polland 2009), trust in online collaborative consumption (Keymolen 2013), and e-commerce (McKnight, Choudhury, and Kacmar 2002). However, the literature does not provide an elaborate mapping, or even an exploration, of the CE's most well-known initiatives based on their use of ICT for operational purposes.

This chapter aims to fill this gap by exploring how the most high-impact CE initiatives utilize ICT and how these technologies reduce the barriers of wide adoption facilitating operation and success of these ventures. This effort is of particular interest from socioeconomic and environmental perspectives (Belk 2014b; EU Environment 2013), as most of these initiatives operate sustainably, and promote concepts of community spirit, (pseudo-)sharing, and reuse (Belk 2014a; Benkler 2004; Hamari, Sjöklint, and Ukkonen 2015), although some misuse, dangers, and challenges do exist as well (Martin 2016; Schor et al. 2016). This knowledge is expected to help future CE entrepreneurs and practitioners to better exploit ICT technology, avoid common mistakes, and follow best design elements that have been used in popular initiatives. It will also be useful for researchers and policy makers to understand the trends of CE in the future, in relation to the projected future of ICT.

Methodology

The methodology of this survey involved three steps:

1. Collection of CE-relevant initiatives
2. Clustering of related work
3. Analysis of each cluster

In the first step, a keyword-based search was conducted using popular web search engines (e.g., Bing, Yahoo!, and Google). The keywords utilized were "collaborative economy," "sharing economy," "sharing goods," "sharing services," "peer-to-peer sharing," and combinations of these terms. This approach resulted in the identification of many initiatives with a web presence, as well as articles and papers which listed and reviewed relevant companies and organizations (DGRV 2015; Owyang, Tran, and Silva 2013). By focusing only on initiatives that used ICT in their operations, the sample was curtailed to 156 initiatives, which engaged in both monetary and nonmonetary exchanges (Albinsson and Perera 2012).

In the second step, the initiatives were categorized according to their area of application/operation and type of goods or services being shared, exchanged, borrowed, or used. This resulted in 6 broad categories, which were then sub-divided into 14 subcategories. These (sub)categories were selected by the authors based on the list of recorded initiatives, and they seem to cover the whole spectrum of ICT-enabled CE companies and initiatives.

In the final step, each category was examined separately, and each initiative was analyzed using the following questions:

1. Has CE practice been successful in this category?
2. Has it been popular and widely adopted by its targeted audience?
3. What are the barriers for wider adoption?
4. Which type of ICT has been used and how?
5. What have been the points of success?
6. What have been the failure factors?
7. Are there any design elements (focusing on ICT) that make it more success-ful/engaging to its user community?

To answer these seven questions, two parallel approaches were followed.

Questions were directly posed to people involved (CEOs, managers), and the authors attempted to answer the questions based on their review of reports and news articles about each initiative. The authors contacted the managers or CEOs of each of the 156 initiatives. To increase their honesty, full anonymity was promised, as well as discretion regarding any private data they might share. Twenty eight responses were received (17.9% response rate), with at least one response from each of the six categories as defined earlier. Of these 28 responses, 19 were from the initiatives' CEOs/managers (67.8%) and nine (32.2%) from other employees. The rest of this survey is based on the authors' research of publicly available information regarding the initiatives in the sample.

A Review of Collaborative Economy Initiatives

The CE ecosystem is illustrated in Figure 6.1. In the following subsections, the 14 subcategories are described. In addition, each subsection includes an example, comprising two hypothetical characters—Alice (as consumer) and Bob (as producer of some transaction/exchange), of how CE works in this particular domain. In some examples, Bob serves as friend/consultant to Alice and helps her with her task/issue.

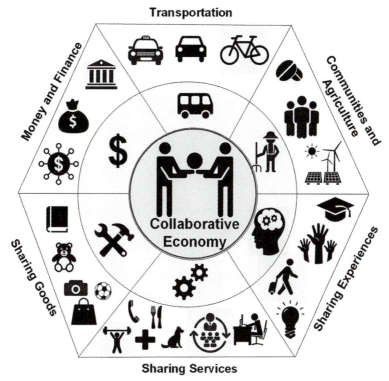

Figure 6.1 The ecosystem of CE

Money and Finance

This category represents initiatives related to money and finance such as crowdfunding and banking.

Crowdfunding

Crowdfunding, which raised US$34 billion in 2015 (CrowdExpert.com 2016), entails funding projects or ventures through raising monetary contributions from the public (Share 2013). Examples of initiatives that fund creative projects based on online platforms are Indiegogo, Ulule, and the popular Kickstarter. Similar initiatives focusing on funding related to the environment and, in particular, sustainable energy are supported by Abundance Generation, TRINE, and Green Crowding.

Crowdfunding that targets renewable energy projects are facilitated by Citizenergy, Lumo, and Lendosphere. Joukon Voima is a marketplace for connecting projects related to sustainable consumption and energy production with willing funders. Neighborly is a crowdfunding site that facilitates people investing in local civic projects that they care about, thus creating new options for communities to approach capital formation. Finally, funding bodies that directly invest in funding sustainable projects include Heinrich Böll Foundation and United Nations Development Programme.

Example: Alice aims to develop a technological product that allows mobile phones to charge through cycling from the energy produced by the bike's movement. She needs funding to develop this project, and Bob suggests that she utilize Kickstarter to describe her idea and invite micro-investors to fund it, in exchange for the promise to gift them the product when it is developed.

Banking

Ethical banks, an alternative to mainstream banks, do not regard profit as their overriding objective; they are concerned about the social and environmental impact of their investments and loans (Move Your Money UK 2016). Often, multiple private investors are involved in raising capital for these initiatives. Examples include Triodos Bank (multi-European), EBanka (Croatia), Banca Etica (Italy), and La Nef (France). Moreover, Charity Bank (United Kingdom), which has lent more than GBP 250 million to charities and social enterprises since 2002, has a mission to help charities and social enterprises. The federation of the aforementioned banks is the European Federation of Ethical and Alternative Banks.

Example: Alice wants to provide a loan for an environmental project that will benefit her community: the creation of recycling stations where people can dispose of organic waste. She contacts Bob, who works in an ethical bank that funds environment-friendly projects from funding garnered from citizens who assign the bank the responsibility to invest other peers' green action projects. Alice convinces Bob about her project's potential for having a positive environmental impact, so the bank decides to fund her work.

Finance

This subcategory also comprises initiatives dealing with alternative forms of financing, the so-called social lending. The Crowdfunding Academy provides advice on how to prepare successful funding campaigns. Tilt builds software that makes pooling resources easier and at minimal or no risk, as it matches borrowers and investors based on particular characteristics. The Lending Club and Zopa Bank are online marketplaces that connect borrowers and private investors. Such platforms transform the banking system toward more affordable credit that provides savings to borrowers in the form of lower rates as well as more rewarding experiences to investors in the form of solid returns.

Example: Alice wants to borrow a small amount of money to buy a new laptop for her daughter who recently entered university. However, she wants to avoid banks that charge high interests, so she uses Tilt, which matches her request with Bob who is a micro-investor. They agree on the exact amount, the payback period, and the interest rate. Thus, they both profit from the transaction: Alice from the lower interest rate relative to that offered by banks and Bob from the higher rate received compared to that for investing his money at a bank through a fixed-term deposit.

Transportation

The transportation category relates to ridesharing between individuals, as well as sharing taxies, bicycles, or even information about the availability of parking spots.

Car-Sharing

Uber, one of the most famous platforms for peer-to-peer car-sharing, has experienced much publicity recently due to conflicts between its providers and professional taxi drivers (*The Telegraph* 2016). Through Uber, individuals can use their car to provide taxi service and earn revenues, or they can utilize providers' vehicles for transportation for a fee in lieu of taxis. Similar to Uber, Lyft and Getaround are transportation services that match users' current location with local drivers in the vicinity to obtain service within minutes. Drive-MyCar offers similar services in Australia, SnappCar in the Netherlands, and Autonetzer in Germany. FlightCar allows people who park their vehicles at the airport during trips to rent them out to other traveling members.

Furthermore, sharing knowledge about parking spots is useful when driving a car. Park Circa and JustPark connect people who have empty parking spaces during a set time with people that need them. MonkeyParking encourages users to list available spots they encounter as they go about their business. ParkOnMyDrive allows those who have empty driveways and garages to rent this space to motorists.

Example: Alice wants to take a taxi to go to a party. She uses Uber through her smartphone to locate a nearby Uber taxi. In order to do so, she checks the profile of the driver, Bob, including other travelers' ratings to examine how safely he drives and how polite he is with the customers. As she is happy with Bob's profile, Alice books the taxi, and she is informed of its location in real time including its distance from her current location. Bob drives Alice safely to her destination, and she pays a smaller amount compared to if she had used a regular taxi service.

Bike and Ridesharing

Bike sharing entails renting a bike from a company or from peers. Company-based initiatives include Velib (France), Bixi (Canada), BCycle (United States), and Call-A-Bike (Germany). Peer-based initiatives include Spinlister and SocialBicycles that offer online platforms that support transactions between people who want to rent bikes and people who want to share their bikes and earn some money while doing so. In a similar vein, Boatbound facilitates boat sharing, and OpenAirplane involves the renting of aircrafts.

In terms of ridesharing, Zimride is a platform designed for companies and universities, which saves employees' time and money while helping them to become acquainted with their coworkers and simultaneously relieving parking congestion. Nuride rewards users with restaurant coupons, discounts, and tickets to shows and attractions when they walk, bike, or take public transportation, and helps them locate carpool or commute buddies. Carma promotes carpooling, thereby aspiring to transform wasted parking lot hours into dynamic mobility services responding to people's transportation needs. Finally, BlaBlaCar and Taxistop promise trusted ridesharing by connecting people who need to travel with drivers who have empty seats.

Example: Alice wants to visit her grandparents who live in another city. To save money, she uses BlaBlaCar to locate drivers who plan to perform the same trip. She locates Bob, who is traveling the same route on the same day. His overall feedback by other travelers is positive, so Alice contacts him through her smartphone, pays his fee with her visa card, and reserves a seat in Bob's car.

Communities and Agriculture

This category includes cooperatives and communities whose goal is to become socially, economically, and ecologically sustainable.

Agriculture

The agricultural sector is famous for its many cooperatives and coalitions around the world. These cooperatives involve collaboration between operators in the production chain, single selling brand, and exporting operations, in order to exchange goods, know-how, and technology, as well as provide financing. A popular cooperative is Coop de France, which represents smaller cooperatives and hundreds of other organizations, while Vignerons coop is a French cooperative for wine producers. In addition, La Terra e il Cielo is an organic farming cooperative in Italy, Milcobel is a cooperative of dairy farmers in Belgium, and Bios Coop is a cooperative nonprofit supermarket, selling goods produced by more than 400 producers in Northern Greece.

Skills Framework for the Information Age (SFIA) is a global organization with 100,000 members in 160 countries, promoting cultural, environmental, and social goals built around the rights of high-quality food security and biodiversity protection. Finally, seed-sharing communities, which promote the cultivation of organic, non-GMO crops, include Seed Savers Exchange (North

America), Seed Saver Foundation (Australia), and Let's Liberate Diversity network (Europe).

Example: Alice recently became a farmer, producing organic apples and vegetables, in Italy, To reduce her costs on distribution of goods and avoid the hassle of dealing with wholesalers, she joined La Terra e il Cielo where her friend Bob is also a member. She realizes that, through the cooperative, she can exchange know-how with other farmers and share agricultural tools/machinery, thereby reducing her overall costs. At the same time, the cooperative protects and supports the community's rights and farmers' interests.

Renewable Energy

Energy cooperatives constitute projects locally owned by public or private entities who utilize renewable energy to decrease the energy costs of their local communities, and reduce dependency on the utility grid. An example is Som Energia, which manages community projects involving renewable energy production, mostly related to photovoltaics. Similarly, De Windvogel (the Netherlands) focuses on wind turbines and Coopernico (Portugal) claims to have supported 217 projects up to now. Moreover, Solar Century (UK) encourages communities to pool investment to fund their own solar farms. Finally, Trade Unions for Energy Democracy is a global initiative aspiring to advance democratic energy direction, promoting solutions to climate crisis and energy poverty.

Example: Alice is the president of a local community in Portugal that wants to switch to photovoltaics to cover the energy needs of its members. The community decides to fund the project with money coming from its members, with the promise that members who invest more will have priority over their energy needs, while any profits from selling excess energy back to the grid will be used to pay back their members through time. Alice listens to the suggestion of Bob, another community member, to collaborate with Coopernico to realize the project. Coopernico deals with legal and technical aspects, and the project is implemented.

Eco-communities

Eco-communities are committed to ecological and socioeconomic sustainability of their members and of the physical environment (L.O.V.E. Production 2015). Global Ecovillage Network is a network of sustainable communities bridging different cultures and countries, serving as an umbrella organization for eco-villages, transition town initiatives, and ecologically minded individuals. An example of an eco-village is Findhorn, which serves as a tangible demonstration of the links between spiritual, social, ecological, and economic aspects of life. Transition Towns (Transition Towns 2006), community-organized social innovations present in 44 countries, attempt to build local resilience to climate change and economic crisis. Time banking (Seyfang 2004; Time Banks 2006) is a value-based mechanism for reciprocal service exchange, focusing on the contributions everyone can make to meeting needs within a local community. Unit of exchange is simply the hours spent giving/receiving service. It counts 40,000 members in 587 communities. Finally, ToolzDO is a social platform for connecting neighbors to their local community to strengthen community life.

Example: Alice is the manager of a transition town in New York. Bob, a member who is an agricultural scientist by profession, proposes to develop a project on urban agriculture. Alice and the other members are excited, and the agreement is that members who have backyard space will grow organic vegetables, which they would then exchange and share with the other community members. This project helps members to learn and appreciate farming and get access to organic, healthier food, as well as increase community spirit.

Sharing Experiences

The most recreational form of CE is that of sharing experiences with peers in the form of education, know-how, and best practices and volunteering for good causes, as well as tourism services including ecotourism.

Education and Knowledge

Here, we can observe communities and online platforms for education and skill sharing, and schools with anthropocentric and sustainable educational goals. Edufire is a distance education platform for teaching and learning. Brooklyn Skillshare consists of community-based learning events. Grassroots Economic Organizing is a collective of educators and grassroots activists promoting an economy based on democratic participation and community ownership.

Online education includes popular examples such as Moodle, Udemy, and Coursera that offer courses from statistics to astronomy, and from yoga to photography. Kaggle runs programming contests to crowdsource machine learning solutions, giving prizes to the best ones.

Schools with alternative learning approaches include Steiner Waldorf (Ireland and the United Kingdom), which helps students to choose and realize their individual paths through life as adults, and Findhorn Foundation College (Scotland), which engages participants in transformative education for personal empowerment through offering holistic education for sustainable living. DESIS is a network of labs, based in design schools, promoting and supporting sustainable change. Gaia Education supports communities to replace input-intensive agriculture with new food systems, focusing on well-being and resilience.

Example: Alice is a passionate violin player living in Brooklyn. She wants to create a neoclassical metal-style band playing metal songs through classical music.

Through Brooklyn Skillshare she meets Bob, a talented cellist, and teaches him about the concept she has in mind. They form an alternative band that eventually meets great success in Brooklyn and beyond.

Volunteering

Volunteering services ask for labor in exchange for accommodation, education, entertainment, and skills. Modern volunteerism goes beyond traditional forms of charity, involving activism and participation in actions, demonstrations, and initiatives dealing with well-being, justice, sustainability, solidarity, and so on.

HelpX is an online listing of farm and home stays, hostels, and sailing boats, where the owners invite volunteer helpers to stay for a short term in exchange for food and accommodation. Similarly, WWOOF links volunteers with organic farms and growers. LeftoverSwap and Copia deal with peer-based donations of excess food, handling the process of food distribution and enabling peers to receive tax deductions reducing disposal costs.

Example: Alice aims to learn about organic farming through volunteerism. She uses HelpX to get in touch with Bob, who runs an organic farm producing dairy products. Bob agrees to host Alice at his farm for two weeks, offering her food and accommodation, while Alice assists in the farm's daily operations.

Travel and Tourism

Alternative models of tourism can support and promote sustainable development (Dredge and Gyimóthy 2015). Initiatives include sharing space and accommodation and tourist guide services performed by locals, as well as ecotourism in sustainable communities and organic farms.

In accommodation sharing, the most popular are Airbnb and Couchsurfing. Statistics indicate that CE now accounts for approximately 40% of the overall world accommodation market (Berlin 2014). Regarding vacation rental marketplaces, worth mentioning are Pillow, HomeAway, FlipKey, and Flatbook.

Le Mat plans travel itineraries to help users discover new places and spend time with social entrepreneurs. Rent-A-Guide offers more than 5,600 tours in 81 counties. Shiroube not only offers guides but sorts them out according to interests as well. Viator and Vayable have a large repository of travel guides, their reviews, portfolios, and descriptions. Finally, Jib.li uses social network-like connections to match those with unused allowances with others on the same flight looking to avoid such charges.

Example: Alice wants to travel to Thailand and experience the Asian culture. As she does not have a large budget for the trip, she uses Couchsurfing to locate Bob, a host who lives in Bangkok, who agrees to accommodate her during her trip. During her stay in Bangkok, Alice uses Vayable to find a low-cost travel guide.

Sharing Services

Sharing services, which span a variety of industries, relate to both individuals and companies (Belk 2014a).

Personal

Personal services are provided to individuals on a sharing and/or peer-to-peer basis. Nanny in The Clouds enables parents to find out whether there will be registered nannies traveling on their flight who are willing to provide childcare services for a pre-negotiated fee. Based on the customer's schedule, Heal makes it easy and affordable to see a doctor at home. Wello, conducted over live video, is like working out with a personal trainer in a gym or attending a group fitness class at a studio.

GetMaid offers eco-friendly green cleaning services with discounted pricing. Guevara, which offers lower-cost driving insurance to groups of people, allows users to save up to 50% when claims are kept low. RentAFriend provides "friends" for hire, for example, to attend social events, act as tourist guides, and teach new skills/hobbies, or just for companionship. TaskRabbit, Handy, Zaarly, and AtYourService are platforms connecting people to safe and reliable services from professionals at reasonable costs.

Moreover, related to food, EatWith and HomeDine are about sharing meals with other community members. Through Feastly, passionate chefs connect with adventurous eaters. Fon asks you to allow others to access your home Wi-Fi network in exchange for getting free WiFi at any of the 8M worldwide hotspots in Fon's network. Focusing on pets, DogVacay helps to find *pet sitters* when traveling, while Rover is a platform that allows users to find local dog sitters in over 10,000 cities.

Finally, urban logistic on-demand delivery platforms including Postmates and Deliv connect customers with local couriers who purchase and deliver goods anywhere in the city. Instacard and Deliveroo, which deliver food and grocery goods, offer similar services. Finally, with Sidecar, individuals use their cars for on-demand delivery of various products.

Example: Alice plans a trip to her parents who live in another country. Due to high charges of air carriers, she cannot take her dog with her. Therefore, she uses DogVacay to find a pet sitter to take care of her dog during the trip. She locates Bob, who has an excellent profile based on positive comments from the community about his pet sitting services. Bob charges a reasonable fee and takes care of Alice's pet as she visits her parents without any worries about her dog's safety and well-being.

Enterprise

Enterprise services are provided to companies on a sharing basis. Desks Near Me, Desksurfing, PivotDesk, and Spaceout help to find or rent out storage, office, parking, rural, or commercial space, converting extra or unused space into a regular income. FLOOW2 and Getable are sharing marketplaces for business equipment and services, such as cars, meeting rooms, specialists, and machinery. Cohealo deals with sharing of medical equipment across facilities. Yard Club facilitates the renting of agricultural machinery among peers.

Outsourcing is a practice used by some companies to reduce costs, and it entails transferring portions of work to outside suppliers. HourlyNerd, UpWork, and Freelancer are online platforms that instantly connect users with the world's smartest experts at a fraction of the price. Crowdflower focuses on data analysis jobs and Amazon Mechanical Turk on human intelligence tasks.

Moreover, TechShop is a community of inventors that facilitates access to tools, software, and space. StudioMates is a collaborative workspace of designers and developers. Finally, Coloft and Impact Hub are communities of entrepreneurs that share their knowledge and collaborate in open-work environments.

Example: Alice runs a start-up company offering data analysis services to insurance companies. As her company is still young, she tries to keep her running costs low and uses Desksurfing to locate similar companies that want to share workspace to reduce their costs. She agrees with Bob to share a common office, and they keep their expenses low by equally splitting monthly rent and utility fees.

Sharing Goods

Sharing goods entails the exchange of products among peers: those who do not need products anymore share them with those in need of them. The transaction is usually performed for free or for a price that is much lower relative to buying the product brand new. Exchange is for short periods (rent) or forever (sale).

Popular marketplaces, such as eBay and Etsy, which facilitate billions of annual transactions, support millions of buyers and sellers. One of the most "traditional" product types exchanged are books. Chegg, BookRenter, and Zookal, which focus on higher education, rent textbooks for a fraction of the cost of the bookstore (claiming savings up to 90%). CampusBookRentals, which offers free shipping, supports over 1 million students across 6,000 campuses.

Regarding toys, Pley is a toy rental company that allows unlimited exchanges from a large collection of toys. babyPlays sells second-hand toys after an elaborate sanitization process at a much lower price.

Related to fashion, Poshmark is a peer-based marketplace for clothing items. Through Rent the Runway and Fashion Hire, customers can rent clothes on a monthly membership basis. Bag Borrow or Steal is an online platform for people to borrow, sell, or rent handbags.

Neighborrow and frents facilitate renting items between friends and neighbors, for free or at low prices. Friends with Things and Streetbank promote borrowing or sharing things between neighbors, supporting the sharing of skills, expertise, and local knowledge. Yerdle promotes swap of stuff using *Yerdle Dollars* (during swap) for the purchase of new goods. Finally, Garage Sale Trail, which organizes garage sale events, is a people-powered reuse movement.

Example: Alice wants to buy some toys for her baby but realizes that toys have a short life cycle since children get bored fast. She decides to buy second-hand toys from babyPlays. At the same time, Bob sells his child's old toys to babyPlays. These toys, after being sanitized, become available for Alice to purchase.

ICT-Based Analysis

In this section, each (sub)category is analyzed to address the research questions listed in section Methodology. Table 6.1 lists our findings for each subcategory. The first column contains the research questions, and the remaining columns provide the results per subcategory. In the first two questions, a Likert scale[1] was followed, and the findings are based on the 28 responses of the CEOs/managers/employees of the CE initiatives. The possible bias in these first two questions is acknowledged by the authors.

As Table 6.1 indicates, the most successful CE approaches seem to be in car-sharing (e.g., Uber, Getaround), travel, and tourism (e.g., Couchsurfing, Airbnb), as well as in agricultural cooperatives (e.g., Coop de France, Vignerons). The least successful ones are in banking and finance, as they are still in their infancy. Most popular and widely adopted are initiatives related to crowdfunding (e.g., Indiegogo, Kickstarter), car-sharing, enterprise services (e.g., Desksurfing, Freelancer), agriculture, travel, and tourism, while the least popular are those in renewable energy, eco-communities, banking and finance, and volunteering. Sharing goods has been widely adopted only by a few initiatives (e.g., eBay, Etsy, CampusBookRentals), while many approaches did not scale at large (e.g., frents, Neighborrow, Yerdle).

Barriers and Reasons for Success or Failure

Barriers for wider adoption differ per category; however, issues of trust (Owyang, Tran, and Silva 2013), privacy, and unfamiliarity with the concept of sharing (Belk 2014a) are common obstacles, similar to the findings of Möhlmann (2015). In money and finance, legal issues (e.g., policies, protocols, privacy) seem to be important barriers (Manner, Siniketo, and Polland 2009), while competition with conventional banks is difficult. Ethical banks and crowdfunding campaigns lack experience in effective marketing strategies and high-valued customer services. Particularly with crowdfunding, investors sometimes do not understand precisely their return on investment (ROI).

Lack of convenience is a barrier in transportation (i.e., time consuming, not convenient pickup points), eco-communities (i.e., limited access to facilities, no availability of certain services), and sharing of goods (i.e., time needed for the agreement with the seller, time and cost of purchase/delivery or product not as expected), while better recognition, motives, and incentives are required in agriculture (i.e., explain potential benefits to farmers to join a cooperative), eco-communities (i.e., difficult to live for a long time, especially as the member gets older and needs access to health services or cannot contribute much to the community), education (i.e., companies and universities not recognizing online courses), volunteering (i.e., the effort of the person does not have any recognition besides personal satisfaction and skills acquired), and enterprise services (i.e., no incentives for medium-to-large companies to share resources with other institutes or use outsourcing).

On sharing goods, indirect costs involved (i.e., product shipping, guarantees), especially for low-cost products, are core barriers for revenue growth. Further, new forms of cooperatives in agriculture and renewable energy still need to publish proof of concept success stories and solid ROI estimations (e.g., Coopernico). Finally, general barriers involve regulatory issues (e.g., gray zones for taxation) and vested interests (e.g., taxi drivers demonstrating against Uber [*The Telegraph* 2016]).

Success points facilitating CE initiatives to flourish involve lower cost of product purchased (e.g., second-hand toys, books) or service used (e.g., outsourcing tasks to freelancers), common use of resources (e.g., goods, services, community-produced energy, shared office space), connection to nature (e.g., eco-communities, volunteerism), community spirit (e.g., agricultural cooperatives, eco-communities, renewable energy projects), and personal satisfaction for being sustainable and preserving the environment (e.g., crowdfunding, eco-communities, volunteering). Moreover, convenience and personalization are positive factors used in education/knowledge (e.g., attend the course during free time, select from a wider range of courses and difficulty levels) and in sharing services (e.g., choose a professional based on people's feedback and service provider's online profile and availability). Specifically in crowdfunding, rapid fund-raising and access to high-tech products constitute engaging elements (e.g., Indiegogo, Kickstarter), while ethical banking counts on ethics and transparency (e.g., Triodos, Banka Etica). Finally, CE-based financing promises lower lending rates and solid investor returns (e.g., Lending Club, Zopa Bank).

Table 6.1 Analysis of Collaborative Economy per Category

Category	Money and Finance			Transportation		Communities and Agriculture			Sharing Experiences			Sharing Services		Goods
Question/Subcategory	Crowd funding	Banking	Finance	Car-Sharing	Bike/Ride Share	Agriculture	Renewable Energy	Eco-communities	Education Knowledge	Volunteering	Travel Tourism	Sharing Personal Services	Enterprise Services	Sharing Goods
Has CE been successful?	Much	Little	Little	Very much	Much	Very much	Much	Aver age	Average	Aver age	Very much	Aver age	Much	Much
Popular and widely adopted?	Very much	Little	Little	Very much	Average	Very much	Little	Little	Average	Little	Very much	Aver age	Very much	Much
Barriers for wider adoption?	Policies, protocols, ROI, trust, marketing strategies, customer services, competition with conventional banks, unfamiliarity			Trust, convenience, privacy, personalization, unfamiliarity		Policies, motives, incentives, trust, proof of concept, ROI, unfamiliarity		Convenience, public services, work	Recognition, incentives, trust, unfamiliarity	Incentives, trust	Trust, unfamiliarity	Trust, unfamiliarity	Incentives, trust, unfamiliarity	Convenience, trust, indirect costs
Success points?	Fast and easier fund-raising, high-tech products involved, ethics, transparency, lower rates, solid returns			Lower cost, friendly to the environment		Robust processes and sales, lower costs, reliability, reputation, friendly to the environment, sustainable, personal satisfaction, connection to nature, community spirit, sustainability			Low cost, targeted, personalized education and experiences, sustainability, personal satisfaction, connection to nature, convenience			Lower cost, convenience, personalization, community spirit		Lower cost
Failure factors?	Overambitious projects, campaigns that did not deliver their products, payment issues (crowdfunding), no reputation and trust, limited deposits' insurance (banking)			Fear of strangers, privacy, convenience, small market		Lack of good coordination, clear policies, motives, and trust. ROI not well defined			Degree recognition, limited business opportunities	Gap between offer and demand, reliability, trust, small market		Lack of reputation and trust, small market		Inconvenience, indirect costs, small market

ICT used?	Web apps, social media	Web apps	Web apps, mobile apps	Website	Website, social media	Website, social media	Web apps, mobile apps, social media	Web apps, e-markets, mobile apps, social media	Web apps, e-markets	Web apps, e-markets, mobile apps, social media
Successful and engaging design elements?	Cool videos for high-tech products and community building (crowdfunding); personal stories of sustainability, transparency, ethics, good causes, promotion building of community spirit (banking and finance)	Reputation systems, user profiling, personalized services, social networking features, community building	Success stories of cooperatives and eco-communities, community spirit, environmental awareness campaigns, community building	Promoting alternative curriculums, distant learning, remote courses, social networking features, personalization		Photos and videos of the accommodation, venue, location, events, and operations involved, community building, reputation systems, privacy		Personalization, short self-explanatory animated videos, social networking features, user profiling		Success stories, guarantees and free shipping, privacy, user profiling, reputation systems, community building

The earlier findings are in line with related works (Albinsson and Perera 2012; Hamari, Sjöklint, and Ukkonen 2015; Möhlmann 2015), suggesting that people participate in CE because of sustainability, enjoyment of the activity, and sense of community as well as economic gains. Sense of community has been identified in related work also as an important driver of participation (especially) in nonmonetary-based CE initiatives (Albinsson and Perera 2012).

Reasons for failure include privacy, convenience and trust, and lack of reputation and reliability. Crowdfunding sometimes fails because of overambitious projects, while car-sharing approaches face people's fear of strangers. In agricultural and renewable energy coops, it has been observed that lack of good coordination, clear policies, and motives is an open issue, while education efforts suffer from limited-degree recognition and poor business opportunities for graduates. Small market is a failure factor in transportation-based initiatives, volunteering, travel and tourism, and sharing services and goods. Related work (Tussyadiah 2015) reveals lack of trust, lack of efficacy with regard to technology, and lack of economic benefits as barriers in CE-based transportation, factors that agree with our findings. In all cases, radical innovations may have too much of a distance from the status quo and thus fail to align and expand (e.g., banking, finance), while many efforts suffer from a lack of window of opportunity and misconception around the presence of a true user need, which they try to address collaboratively (especially in sharing services and goods) (Gauthey 2014).

ICT Used

Focusing on ICT used, most (with the exception of initiatives from agriculture, renewable energy, and eco-communities, which mainly use common websites) have grown by employing web and mobile apps. The three aforementioned subcategories can also benefit by using ICT, which could be harnessed to reduce some of the barriers for wider adoption, such as better presentation of success stories; more interactive demonstration of ROI estimations and proof of concept; and stronger, more connected, and resilient agricultural collectives.

For the remaining subcategories, Web 2.0 has been the dominant platform, while mobile apps have been employed in transportation, travel, and tourism, and in sharing personal services/goods. Mobile apps are useful when people need to use services while commuting or on the go, outside home/work, for example to book a taxi (transportation), scroll across accommodation options for their weekend getaway (travel and tourism), find someone to take care of their pet (sharing personal services), or rent tools for home repairs at lower price (sharing goods). E-markets are used for sharing of goods and services (Hamari, Sjöklint, and Ukkonen 2015; Wang and Zhang 2012), where transactions are performed on a peer-to-peer basis through web interfaces (Einav, Farronato, and Levin 2016).

Finally, many initiatives from various subcategories relied on online social media (e.g., Facebook, Twitter) for community building and news/stories sharing, especially those related to crowdfunding, renewable energy, eco-communities, education and knowledge, volunteering, travel and tourism, sharing personal services and goods. Online social media offer an easy way to reach the masses and acquire new members, followers, and supporters.

Discussion

CE is an upcoming trend (CrowdExpert.com 2016; Owyang and VBProfiles 2015; PwC 2015; Schor et al. 2016). Peer-to-peer communities from the most well-known (e.g., Airbnb and Uber) to small-scale local networks for exchanging food or tools, with origins and growth stemming from the tech-driven culture of Silicon Valley, are the new "hot thing" (Hamari, Sjöklint, and Ukkonen 2015). Yet this trend has not yet been widely adopted in all commercial areas, being a niche whose development is promising and gradually increasing, but also still uncertain with risks and challenges (Rifkin 2014).

Technologies, Similarities, and Challenges

Sharing of experiences constitutes one of the most widely adopted CE areas, largely developed by means of Web 2.0 and mobile applications. Through web portals, users are encouraged to produce and consume rich content, and share experiences and ideas. Blogs, collaborative platforms, discussion forums, online communities, and chat rooms offer to users the opportunity to become creators and editors. These online spaces create new opportunities for alternative, faster, and targeted learning experience through collaboration, sharing, and interaction. Apart from knowledge, benefits of CE platforms include multicultural interactions, acceptance of and influence from different religions, cultures and ideas, increase of self-esteem and responsibility, positive psychology, and acquisition of various personal skills such as organization and innovation potential. This sharing of knowledge and experiences is booming in education and knowledge, volunteering, and travel and tourism, with popular examples including TripAdvisor (for travelers), StackOverflow (for computer programmers), Moodle (open-source learning platform for students), Ask.com (for the general public), and, of course, Wikipedia (open online encyclopedia).

The content produced and shared by the users has large impact on the operations, popularity, and user engagement with the CE initiatives. The most successful, profitable, and popular initiatives understand this impact, maintaining an e-business model adapted to the needs of their community (Belk 2014a) (e.g., TripAdvisor, HelpX).

Seeking for similarities among popular initiatives, all combine trust, respect of privacy, lower costs in comparison to conventional approaches, convenience (or avoidance of lack of it), feelings of personal satisfaction, sustainability, and bulletproof success stories (Hamari, Sjöklint, and Ukkonen 2015). Botsman claims that "trust will become the currency of the new economy" (Botsman and Rogers 2010). CE is not expected to lead to interpersonal trust (e.g., interaction between peers) but technology itself will shape and build these trust relationships, and this is a challenge for CE (Keymolen 2013). In other words, "Online trust is not just about you and me, but about you, me and the system that brings us together." For example, a company may safeguard its online community by proactively monitoring the platform to catch fraud and other malicious actions, or have clear resolution processes, such as the measures taken by Airbnb and eBay (McKnight, Choudhury, and Kacmar 2002). On the other hand, all failed initiatives lack some of the aforementioned qualities, or the society and markets are not yet ready for them, or even their target groups are not large enough for satisfactory profits. Other reasons for failure include mistrust in Internet transactions (McKnight, Choudhury, and Kacmar 2002) and lack of knowledge of who is responsible in case a problem arises (European Commission 2016).

Reputation is a crucial element for building trust, as the examples of large, successful platforms such as Airbnb (Finley 2013) indicate. For the Airbnb case, an emergent philosophy regarding the development of trust within the platform is highlighted, in a "the more information, the better" approach. This information includes the hosts' rating by other users, their response rates, verified e-mails and telephone numbers. This information, together with texting, creates trusting relationships between guests and hosts. It is also important to note the concept of the *electronic word of mouth* (eWOM) (Hennig-Thurau et al. 2004), where users and consumers seek for comments, feedback, and ratings from other users before purchasing something or using some service. Positive eWOM helps a company to build trust and good reputation.

A challenge of future ICT-based CE initiatives in building trust is to leverage an individual's digital footprint to build a portable, trustworthy reputation (Finley 2013). TrustCloud, using a point system to score individual buyers and sellers online, is a leader among this trend of reputation-oriented start-ups. It is based on the principle that if someone has a good reputation in apartment renting, he or she is likely to be a reliable provider of other services too (Kolodny 2012).

Design Elements

Some general successful design elements and guidelines adopted in current CE-based initiatives (recommended also for future initiatives) have been listed in Table 6.2. It is useful to determine which elements of the ICT employed

Table 6.2 Successful Design Elements in Collaborative Economy

No.	Design Element	Subcategories
1.	Video describing a high-tech product/service in less than five minutes	Crowdfunding
2.	Photos and videos describing goods, services, location, events, and operations	Volunteering, travel and tourism, sharing services and goods
3.	Narratives of success stories	Crowdfunding, banking, finance, agriculture, renewable energy, eco-communities, sharing goods
4.	Promotion of community spirit	Banking, finance, agriculture, renewable energy, eco-communities
5.	Community building	Crowdfunding, car-sharing, bike/ride share, agriculture, renewable energy, eco-communities, volunteering, travel and tourism, sharing goods
6.	Environmental awareness campaigns	Agriculture, renewable energy, eco-communities
7.	Social networking features	Car-sharing, bike/ride share, education and knowledge, sharing services
8.	Privacy features	Volunteering, travel and tourism, sharing goods
9.	User profiling	Car-sharing, bike/ride share, sharing services and goods
10.	Personalized services and recommendations	Car-sharing, bike/ride share, sharing services
11.	Reputation-based systems (crowd feedback/ratings)	Car-sharing, bike/ride share, volunteering, travel and tourism, sharing goods
12.	Mashups of information together with interactive geospatial maps	Car-sharing, bike/ride share, volunteering, travel and tourism, sharing personal services, sharing goods
13.	Distant learning and remote education, promotion of alternative curriculum	Education and knowledge

proved to be successful for building user communities, adding more members, customers, and users, or increasing profit.

Different subcategories have different *winning* design characteristics. These characteristics aim to address or mitigate barriers for adoption, as identified in Table 6.1, especially privacy (e.g., privacy features), personalization (e.g., personalized services, user profiling), and trust (e.g., reputation-based systems, user profiling, success stories, photo/video descriptions).

Community building is crucial in various initiatives (e.g., in crowdfunding, transportation, sharing services and goods) for the creation of value (Cova 1997), since a critical mass of users is required for them to operate (Keymolen 2013). This community building is facilitated by social networking features, promotion of community spirit, environmental awareness campaigns, and, most important, common socioeconomic interests (e.g., eco-communities and renewable energy projects). Research indicates that networks of possibly heterogeneous actors tend to preserve their continuity when community members depend on each other for social and economic resources (Thomas, Price, and Schau 2013). This could explain the resilience and long-lasting operation of agricultural collectives.

It is noted that community-building practices in CE have been inspired by successful gamification-based methods used generally in community-driven web platforms (Michael and Chen 2005), with examples including badges and points (e.g., TripAdvisor—travel and tourism), discounts (e.g., BlaBlaCar—car-sharing), certificates (e.g., Moodle—education and knowledge), gifts (e.g., Kickstarter—crowdfunding), and virtual money (e.g., Time Banks—eco-communities), as well as recognition, thanksgiving (e.g., Indiegogo—crowdfunding), and user ranking (e.g., Kaggle—education and knowledge).

Initiatives in agriculture, crowdfunding, banking, renewable energy, and eco-communities pay much attention to success stories and environmental awareness campaigns to convince potential members and customers. Crowdfunding provides a suggested roadmap to follow, in order to achieve a successful campaign, while Indiegogo provides a complete guide to successful crowdfunding (Indiegogo 2016). Distance learning has become established as the mainstream channel of collaborative education. Moreover, interactive geospatial maps are used to visualize real-time information to the users, such as the closest bike rental place or most convenient getaway for the weekend, while car-sharing platforms suggest similar routes and schedules with other people.

Specifically related to mobile apps, users have high expectations for the following: elegance, stability, usability, quality and accuracy of content, security, performance of operation, interoperability with other apps and systems, privacy of user information, and pricing (Gray 2015). Designers of CE-based mobile apps need to carefully consider these aspects to increase users' satisfaction, participation, and engagement.

Projections for the Future

It is not easy to predict the future of CE, but its impact on economy is already large (CrowdExpert.com 2016; Owyang and VBProfiles 2015; PwC 2015). Figure 6.2 illustrates a timeline comprising the year each of the 156 identified initiatives was founded, together with important advancements in ICT. Without surprise, most of the initiatives were founded after 2005, when Web 2.0 and online social media became available, and the large majority appeared after 2007, when smartphones (iPhone, Android, etc.) accompanied by low-cost broadband Internet access entered the market.

Some particular categories (e.g., sharing experiences, services and goods, transportation, crowdfunding) have benefited most from ICT to inspire novel initiatives. In traditional categories (e.g., ethical banks, finance, eco-communities, and agriculture), initiatives that existed before this ICT evolution significantly improved their services/operations by exploiting ICT, especially in terms of community building. Hence, it is evident from Figure 6.2 that ICT has been a large driver of the CE practice globally.

New ICT innovations could inspire even more CE-based initiatives. In projecting the evolution of ICT in the next 10 years, and how this can influence the future of CE, the following possible scenarios are posited:

- *Internet of Things* (IoT) (Mattern and Floerkemeier 2010) becomes a reality, which means that physical devices become connected to the Internet. In this way, transactions for sharing of goods and things can become much more reliable and trustworthy, while new CE-based initiatives would

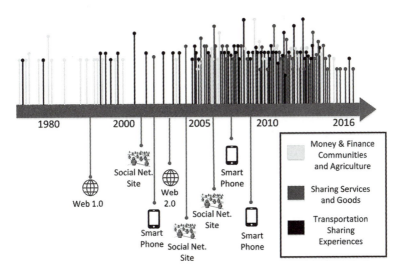

Figure 6.2 Collaborative economy initiatives in relation to ICT evolution

become smart enough to propose things needed for or missing from one's home; hence, personalization would be highly increased (Rifkin 2014). For example, IoT sensors in one's smart fridge could sense absence of some vegetables and connect the user with a local producer of organic goods or place an order for vegetables automatically. Easier and seamless discovery of things would enhance existing sharing initiatives, for example, some user could get notified while walking in the city that in less than 200 meters there is a useful service or needed tool. Ridesharing (see section Bike and Ridesharing) could benefit from more information over the journey's cost, according to weather conditions, existing petrol price, current traffic, and so on. This cost could be shared with the driver and the passenger(s) to aid them is negotiating a fairer price.

- *Web of Things* (WoT) (Kamilaris, Trifa, and Pitsillides 2011b) becomes enabled on top of IoT, thus allowing people to share real-world devices and their services through the web, monitoring in real time and automating their smart homes (Kamilaris, Trifa, and Pitsillides 2011a), or becoming more engaged with their smart city (Kamilaris, Iannarilli, et al. 2011). For example, agriculture (see section Agriculture) could benefit from web platforms that provide fast alerts and notifications to farmers when a form of pest is detected on crops or some disease on the animals (Kamilaris et al. 2016). The data gathered through web-enabled sensors could be reported real time to a web platform where community farmers are subscribed for relevant local events.

- Rising popularity and adoption of *alternative currencies* such as Bitcoin (Bitcoin Project 2007) and Litecoins (Litecoin Project 2011) could affect CE initiatives to adopt these currencies for payments. Alternative currencies could help avoid some barriers such as the dependency on conventional payment systems, regulatory and legal issues, and privacy concerns. More powerful smartphones could perform encrypted cryptocurrency transactions on the go. Another alternative currency could be *time banks* (Seyfang 2004; Time Banks 2006), using time as a unit of local currency, where community members give and receive help in exchange for time credits. For example, eco-communities (see section Eco-communities) could adopt some alternative currency in order to form more resilient micro-societies that are not dependent on their country's economy and tax system.

- More penetration of *online social media* to CE. Having access to people's online profiles and visibility to their preferences, views, and interests (respecting what they wish to keep private) allows trust between peers to be developed more easily, personalized services to thrive, and user communities to grow more resiliently and organically, forming islands of similar-minded people. For example, people who want to volunteer (see section Volunteering) could be directed only to those causes with high positive feedback from others, or to those undertaken by peers having similar visions and ideologies, activities, or online contacts.

- The introduction of the *semantic web* (Berners-Lee et al. 2001) (or Web 3.0 as referred) is expected to bring more semantics and better annotations of data on the web, thus allowing for easier integration among online data sources. This would enhance the services offered by various initiatives as they could seamlessly harness other online (real-time) sources of information. For example, tourism services (see section Travel and Tourism) could harness well-described open data in order to suggest future destinations based on current levels of safety and potential dangers, weather forecasting, organization of local events, celebrations, and so on, taking into account, among others, the user's profile and preferences, budget available, and previous trips performed.

- *Predictive intelligence* is a method of delivering unique experiences to each individual, enabling CE-based initiatives to observe their users' behavior, and—with every action taken—to build a profile of users' preferences for delivering better content. This relates, of course, to personalization (mentioned in the previous scenarios), but it is a much stronger concept, as it anticipates users' intents, providing more unique recommendations and driving key business results. It can combine advances in IoT/WoT, online social media, and semantic web to achieve this. For example, in platforms providing educational services and online courses (see section Education and Knowledge), the system could monitor the actions of the user on the platform (e.g., clicks, time spent at each course/activity/exercise, current performance) to adapt the learning experience to his or her needs, level of expertise, capabilities, and so on.

- *Big data analysis* (Labrinidis and Jagadish 2012) for identification of higher-quality services to use, lower-cost and more convenient products to purchase, suitable places to visit and experiences to gain, better recommendations for shared investments, and more precise ROI estimations. For example, CE enterprise sharing services (see section Enterprise) would be improved by analyzing large-scale data coming from a large variety of different, possibly heterogeneous sources, in order to match companies with similar goals and aims, identifying and suggesting win-win opportunities that could relate to improvement of production, more productivity, reduction of costs, higher-quality research and development, minimization of financial and technical risks, and so on.

- More *secure and private communication protocols* on the Internet/web are expected to increase trust and reliability of online (micro-)transactions, and this is expected to help CE to grow even faster, overcoming barriers of convenience, trust, and unfamiliarity. For example, this will influence primarily initiatives for sharing goods (see section Sharing Goods) and services (see section Sharing Services), as it would encourage peers to sell or rent their unneeded tools and stuff or offer their services easier to other interested people.

- *Collaborative commerce* (Thuraisingham et al. 2002), as a strategy for the next stage of electronic business evolution, could be harnessed by CE initiatives to create, manage, and use data in a shared environment to design, build, and support better collaborative products and services. A global public collaborative e-marketplace could be developed, based on open principles, which would give rise (together with big data analysis) to improved "CE-relevant inventory" visibility, event notification, and performance measurement, as well as real-time decision making, recommendations, and analytics. For example, this would benefit money and finance (see section Money and Finance), since investors will be matched more effectively with borrowers, while the potential risks and dangers will be reduced, and transparency and visibility will be increased.

• In more *futuristic* scenarios, CE could involve sharing drone- and robot-based services, community-owned solar-powered cars, synthetic organs (Colton 1995), or even realities and conscious experiences of people's minds available as shared virtual reality information. For example, sharing drones and robots between farmers would be very beneficial in agriculture for improving productivity and enabling precision agriculture (Zhang and Kovacs 2012), while community-owned cars could serve as low-cost services for citizens in car-sharing scenarios (see section Car-Sharing). The cost could be reduced even further when autonomous cars and the concept of *Internet of Vehicles* become mainstream (Gerla et al. 2014), possibly replacing traditional taxi services.

Conclusion

In this chapter, we offer an overview of the CE identifying and listing popular initiatives from all over the world. By examining the initiatives' relationship with ICT, and discussing successful practices and failures, best design elements involved, and obstacles for wider adoption, we try to predict the future of CE, in parallel with the projected future of ICT.

Several conclusions can be drawn from this chapter. CE has penetrated into numerous aspects of people's everyday lives and business operations, and this survey mapped the CE initiatives collected into 6 main categories and 14 subcategories. Most successful CE practices exploit ICT, especially by means of web applications, mobile apps, and online social networking, for user interaction and community building. Future creators and designers of novel CE initiatives need to carefully study the successful points or reasons for failure of previous and present CE efforts. They need to adopt the positive strategies and overcome common barriers such as policy and privacy issues, user unfamiliarity, and reduced trust. Trust is definitely the most important characteristic of successful initiatives (Botsman and Rogers 2010) and needs to be supported inherently by the systems involved (Keymolen 2013). Some general design elements seem to be well-accepted by user communities, constituting important characteristics that lead to user engagement, active participation, and overall satisfaction. Finally, this chapter has listed some promising ICT innovations that could disrupt the CE landscape, creating more targeted and personalized, secure, intelligent, efficient, resourceful, and trustful peer-to-peer services. IoT, predictive intelligence, and big data analysis could be game-changing technologies in the next 5–10 years.

It is apparent that CE offers solutions in almost every possible aspect where human (and machine?) interaction is involved. Aspects not discussed in this survey which constitute potential sources of inspiration for future CE-based start-ups include sharing of natural resources (e.g., water, energy, and land), financial risks, and business opportunities. Particularly for agriculture and farming, there are still large opportunities for sharing of water, fertilizers, pesticides, crops, machinery, and land and even data. Sharing of energy is in its infancy and can become a reality through distributed generation of electricity and micro-grids (Kamilaris et al. 2017; Smallwood 2002).

An important question would be how CE initiatives could adapt to the future needs of people and societies. A challenge would be on collaborating together offering better services to their users, or acting as mediators/brokers, combining services for higher-quality user experience. For example, a marketplace for sharing car services could communicate with a marketplace about sharing car parts, providing an augmented service of car repair based on cheap, second-hand parts from local users. Education-based shared platforms could collaborate with volunteering organizations and renewable energy projects, matching volunteers who wish to become educated on renewable energy by offering some labor service to these organizations and projects. The performance of students could decide their acceptance opportunities at these organizations/projects, offering recognition to their learning efforts. Current examples include Tripping and VRBO, which operate as vacation rental intermediary services.

Summing up, it is becoming evident that ICT, especially Web 2.0 and mobile apps, is accelerating the advancement of the CE, changing people's mind-sets from possession to (pseudo-)sharing, toward common profit (Belk 2014a; Botsman and Rogers 2010). As Rifkin points out (Rifkin 2014), ICT together with IoT, which connects everything and everyone as a new technology platform, is leading us to an era of nearly free goods and services, where the inherent entrepreneurial dynamism of CE-based markets could change forever the global economy and "business as usual" practices. In parallel with this trend however, the big stake is whether and how the sharing economy niche could be steered toward a pathway aligned with a transition to sustainability (Martin 2016; Schor et al. 2016). It is in our hands to guide this growing CE force, empowered through ICT, as a driver of change toward a sustainable future for humanity and our planet.

Acknowledgment

This research has been supported by the P-SPHERE project, which has received funding from the European Union's Horizon 2020 research and innovation program under the Marie Skodowska-Curie grant agreement no. 665919.

Note

1. 1: Not at all, 2: Little, 3: Average, 4: Much, 5: Very much.

References

Albinsson, Pia A., and B. Yasanthi Perera. 2012. "Alternative Marketplaces in the 21st Century: Building Community through Sharing Events." *Journal of Consumer Behaviour* 11 (4): 303–315.

Bardhi, Fleura, and Giana M. Eckhardt. 2012. "Access-Based Consumption: The Case of Car Sharing." *Journal of Consumer Research* 39 (4): 881–898.

Belk, Russell. 2014a. "Sharing versus Pseudo-Sharing in Web 2.0." *The Anthropologist* 18 (1): 7–23.

Belk, Russell. 2014b. "You Are What You Can Access: Sharing and Collaborative Consumption Online." *Journal of Business Research* 67 (8): 1595–1600.

Benkler, Yochai. 2004. "Sharing Nicely: On Shareable Goods and the Emergence of Sharing as a Modality of Economic Production." *Yale Law Journal* 1: 273–358.

Berlin, ITB. 2014. "ITB World Travel Trends Report 2014/2015." Messe Berlin GmbH, Berlin.

Berners-Lee, Tim, James Hendler, and Ora Lassila. 2001. "The Semantic Web." *Scientific American* 284 (5): 28–37.

Bitcoin Project. 2007. "Bitcoin." https://bitcoin.org/en/.

Botsman, Rachel, and Roo Rogers. 2010. *What's Mine Is Yours. The Rise of Collaborative Consumption.* New York: HarperCollins.

Choudary, Sangeet Paul, Marshall W. Van Alstyne, and Geoffrey G. Parker. 2016. *Platform Revolution: How Networked Markets Are Transforming the Economy—And How to Make Them Work for You.* New York: W. W. Norton.

Colton, Clark K. 1995. "Implantable Bio-Hybrid Artificial Organs." *Cell Transplantation* 4 (4): 415–436.

Cova, Bernard. 1997. "Community and Consumption: Towards a Definition of the Linking Value of Product or Services." *European Journal of Marketing* 31 (3/4): 297–316.

CrowdExpert.com. 2016. "Crowdfunding Industry Statistics 2015 2016." http://crowdexpert.com/crowdfunding-industry-statistics/.

DGRV. 2015. "Facts and Figures—Cooperative Banks, Commodity and Service Cooperatives." https://www.dgrv.de/en/cooperatives/$file/Facts_and_Figures.pdf.

Dredge, Dianne, and Szilvia Gyimóthy. 2015. "The Collaborative Economy and Tourism: Critical Perspectives, Questionable Claims and Silenced Voices." *Tourism Recreation Research* 40 (3): 286–302.

Einav, Liran, Chiara Farronato, and Jonathan Levin. 2016. "Peer-to-Peer Markets." *Annual Review of Economics* 8: 615–635.

Enterprise CarShare. 2012. "Hourly Car Rental and Car Sharing." https://www.enterprisecarshare.com.

EU Environment. 2013. "New Research Indicates Sharing Economy Is Gaining in Importance." EU Environment Online Resource Efficiency Platform. http://ec.europa.eu/environment/resource_efficiency/documents/erep_manifesto_and_policy_recommendations_31-03-2014.pdf.

European Commission. 2016. "The Use of Collaborative Platforms." http://ec.europa.eu/COMMFrontOffice/publicopinion/index.cfm/Survey/getSurveyDetail/instruments/FLASH/surveyKy/2112.

Figueiredo, Bernardo, and Daiane Scaraboto. 2016. "The Systemic Creation of Value through Circulation in Collaborative Consumer Networks." *Journal of Consumer Research* 43 (4): 509–533.

Finley, Katie. 2013. "Trust in the Sharing Economy: An Exploratory Study." Centre for Cultural Policy Studies, University of Warwick, Coventry, United Kingdom.

Gauthey, Marc-Arthur. 2014. "Why the Majority of Sharing Economy Startups Will Fail." http://magazine.ouishare.net/2014/11/why-the-majority-of-sharing-economy-start-ups-will-fail/.

Gerla, Mario, Eun-Kyu Lee, Giovanni Pau, and Uichin Lee. 2014. "Internet of Vehicles: From Intelligent Grid to Autonomous Cars and Vehicular Clouds." *2014 IEEE World Forum on Internet of Things (WF-IoT)*. IEEE, Seoul, South Korea, pp. 241–246.

Ghisellini, Patrizia, Catia Cialani, and Sergio Ulgiati. 2016. "A Review on Circular Economy: The Expected Transition to a Balanced Interplay of Environmental and Economic Systems." *Journal of Cleaner Production* 114: 11–32.

Gray, Ben. 2015. "Applause: Rating the Best Apps in the Sharing Economy." ARC 360 Report. http://go.applause.com/rs/539-CKP-074/images/ARC-The-Best-Sharing-Economy-Apps-2015.pdf.

Hamari, Juho, Mimmi Sjöklint, and Antti Ukkonen. 2016. "The Sharing Economy: Why People Participate in Collaborative Consumption." *Journal of the Association for Information Science and Technology* 67 (9): 2047–2059.

Hennig-Thurau, Thorsten, Kevin P. Gwinner, Gianfranco Walsh, and Dwayne D. Gremler. 2004. "Electronic Word-of-Mouth via Consumer-Opinion Platforms: What Motivates Consumers to Articulate Themselves on the Internet?" *Journal of Interactive Marketing* 18 (1): 38–52.

Indiegogo. 2016. "Indiegogo Crowdfunding Field Guide." https://learn.indi egogo.com/marketing-crowdfunding-field-guide-a/.

Kamilaris, Andreas, Feng Gao, Francesc X. Prenafeta-Boldú, and Muhammad Intizar Ali. 2016, December. "Agri-IoT: A Semantic Framework for Internet of Things-Enabled Smart Farming Applications." *IEEE World Forum on Internet of Things (WF-IoT)*. IEEE, Reston, VA.

Kamilaris, Andreas, Nicolas Iannarilli, Vlad Trifa, and Andreas Pitsillides. 2011, November. "Bridging the Mobile Web and the Web of Things in Urban Environments." *First International Workshop the Urban Internet of Things (Urban IOT 2010)*. Tokyo, Japan.

Kamilaris, Andreas, Andreas Kartakoullis, and Francesc X. Prenafeta-Boldú. 2017, December. "A Review on the Practice of Big Data Analysis in Agriculture." *Computers and Electronics in Agriculture International Journal* 143: 23–37.

Kamilaris, Andreas, Vlad Trifa, and Andreas Pitsillides. 2011a, May. "HomeWeb: An Application Framework for Web-Based Smart Homes." *18th International Conference on Telecommunications (ICT)*, Ayia Napa, Cyprus.

Kamilaris, Andreas, Vlad Trifa, and Andreas Pitsillides. 2011b. "The Smart Home Meets the Web of Things." *International Journal of Ad Hoc and Ubiquitous Computing (IJAHUC)* 7 (3): 145–154.

Keymolen, Esther. 2013. "Trust and Technology in Collaborative Consumption. Why It Is Not Just about You and Me." *Bridging Distances in Technology and Regulation*, 135–150.

Kolodny, Lora. 2012. "With Angel Support, TrustCloud Rates How People Do Business Online." *The Wall Street Journal*. https://www.wsj.com/articles/ DJFVW00020120628e86sb04gv.

Labrinidis, Alexandros, and Hosagrahar V. Jagadish. 2012. "Challenges and Opportunities with Big Data." *Proceedings of the VLDB Endowment* 5 (12): 2032–2033.

Litecoin Project. 2011. "Litecoins." https://litecoin.org/.

L.O.V.E. Production. 2015. "Ecovillages and Communities." http://newwe.jimdo .com/about-1/ecovillages/.

Manner, Mikko, Topi Siniketo, and Ulrika Polland. 2009. "The Pirate Bay Ruling—When the Fun and Games End." *Entertainment Law Review* 20 (6): 197–205.

Martin, Chris J. 2016. "The Sharing Economy: A Pathway to Sustainability or a Nightmarish Form of Neoliberal Capitalism?" *Ecological Economics* 121: 149–159.

Mattern, Friedemann, and Christian Floerkemeier. 2010. "From the Internet of Computers to the Internet of Things." *From Active Data Management to Event-Based Systems and More*, edited by Kai Sachs, Ilia Petrov, and Pablo Guerrero. 242–259. New York: Springer.

McKnight, D. Harrison, Vivek Choudhury, and Charles Kacmar. 2002. "Developing and Validating Trust Measures for e-Commerce: An Integrative Typology." *Information Systems Research* 13 (3): 334–359.

Michael, David R., and Sandra L. Chen. 2005. *Serious Games: Games That Educate, Train, and Inform*. Cincinnati, OH: Muska & Lipman/Premier-Trade.

Möhlmann, Mareike. 2015. "Collaborative Consumption: Determinants of Satisfaction and the Likelihood of Using a Sharing Economy Option Again." *Journal of Consumer Behaviour* 14 (3): 193–207.

Move Your Money UK. 2016. "Ethical Banks." http://moveyourmoney.org. uk/institution-types/ethical-banks/.

Nov, Oded. 2007. "What Motivates Wikipedians?" *Communications of the ACM* 50 (11): 60–64.

Nov, Oded, Mor Naaman, and Chen Ye. 2010. "Analysis of Participation in an Online Photo-Sharing Community: A Multidimensional Perspective." *Journal of the American Society for Information Science and Technology* 61 (3): 555–566.

Owyang, Jeremiah. 2014. "Crowdcompanies." http://crowdcompanies.com/.

Owyang, Jeremiah, Christine Tran, and Chris Silva. 2013. "The Collaborative Economy." *Altimeter.* http://www.slideshare.net/Altimeter/the-collaborative-economy.

Owyang, Jeremiah and VBProfiles. 2015. "Meet the Interactive Collaborative Economy Landscape." http://pages.vbprofiles.com/Collaborativeeconomy.

PwC. 2015, April. "The Sharing Economy." Technical Report, Consumer Intelligence Series.

Rifkin, Jeremy. 2014. *The Zero Marginal Cost Society: The Internet of Things, the Collaborative Commons, and the Eclipse of Capitalism.* London: Palgrave Macmillan.

Scaraboto, Daiane. 2015. "Selling, Sharing, and Everything in Between: The Hybrid Economies of Collaborative Networks." *Journal of Consumer Research* 42 (1): 152–176.

Schor, Juliet. 2016. "Debating the Sharing Economy." *Journal of Self-Governance and Management Economics* 4 (3): 7–22.

Seyfang, Gill. 2004. "Time Banks: Rewarding Community Self-Help in the Inner City?" *Community Development Journal* 39 (1): 62–71.

Share, City Car. 2013. *Working the Crowd: A Short Guide to Crowdfunding and How It Can Work for You.* London: Nesta.

Smallwood, Cameron L. 2002. "Distributed Generation in Autonomous and Non-Autonomous Micro Grids." *IEEE Rural Electric Power Conference.* IEEE, D1–D6.

The Telegraph. 2016. "Anti-Uber Protests around the World." http://www.tele graph.co.uk/technology/picture-galleries/11902080/Anti-Uber-protests-around-the-world-in-pictures.html.

Thomas, Tandy Chalmers, Linda L. Price, and Hope Jensen Schau. 2013. "When Differences Unite: Resource Dependence in Heterogeneous Consumption Communities." *Journal of Consumer Research* 39 (5): 1010–1033.

Thuraisingham, Bhavani, Amar Gupta, Elisa Bertino, and Elena Ferrari. 2002. "Collaborative Commerce and Knowledge Management." *Knowledge and Process Management* 9 (1): 43–53.

Time Banks. 2006. Time-based currency. https://www.hourworld.org/.

Transition Towns. 2006. Transition Network. http://www.transitionus.org/transition-towns.

Tussyadiah, Iis P. 2015. "An Exploratory Study on Drivers and Deterrents of Collaborative Consumption in Travel." In *Information and Communication Technologies in Tourism 2015.* 817–830. Cham: Springer.

Van de Glind, P. B. 2013. "The Consumer Potential of Collaborative Consumption: Identifying the Motives of Dutch Collaborative Consumers and Measuring the Consumer Potential of Collaborative Consumption within the Municipality of Amsterdam." Master's thesis.

Wang, Chingning, and Ping Zhang. 2012. "The Evolution of Social Commerce: The People, Management, Technology, and Information Dimensions." *Communications of the Association for Information Systems* 31 (5): 1–23.

Wasko, Molly McLure, and Samer Faraj. 2005. "Why Should I Share? Examining Social Capital and Knowledge Contribution in Electronic Networks of Practice." *MIS Quarterly* 29(1): 35–57.

Wiertz, Caroline, and Ko de Ruyter. 2007. "Beyond the Call of Duty: Why Customers Contribute to Firm-Hosted Commercial Online Communities." *Organization Studies* 28 (3): 347–376.

Zhang, Chunhua, and John M. Kovacs. 2012. "The Application of Small Unmanned Aerial Systems for Precision Agriculture: A Review." *Precision Agriculture* 13 (6): 693–712.

CHAPTER SEVEN

The Economics of Peer-to-Peer Online Sharing

Timm Teubner and Florian Hawlitschek

Today's e-commerce landscape has experienced the development of novel markets. While e-commerce was predominantly characterized by business-to-consumer (B2C) structures in the past (Gefen and Straub 2004), today an ever-growing variety of consumer-to-consumer platforms (C2C, often "peer-to-peer" [P2P]) enable resource exchange among private individuals (Sundararajan 2014). Several forms of private resource provision and consumption—casually often referred to as "sharing"—have moved from offline to online environments. This shift, among other reasons, has laid the ground for what made headlines as the sharing economy.[1] Sharing resources, however, is not a new idea. Quite the contrary, it is probably as old as mankind itself (Sahlins 1974). Also in pre-Internet industrial societies, people were able to lease, rent, re-sell, borrow, and share. Chan and Shaheen (2012, 97), for instance, trace back ridesharing to its early advents during World War II, where the government prompted "four workers to share a ride in one car to conserve rubber for the war effort," and dramatically called on the citizens' duties, stating "when you ride alone you ride with Hitler" (poster by Weimer Pursell 1943). The customer approach and the language used have changed since then. Today, car-sharing and ridesharing platforms emphasize not only cost and resource savings but also a variety of further aspects like social experience or hedonic value (Hawlitschek, Teubner, and Gimpel 2016).

Cooperatives, flea markets and garage sales, commercial ridesharing bureaus, bulletin boards, and so on existed long before the advent of the

Internet. However, the scope, pace, and virtually frictionless operability of today's peer-to-peer online economy are unprecedented. The substantial reduction of search and transaction costs has unleashed a vast body of resources, previously lying dormant in our prosperous societies' cubbyholes.

The list of "sharable" products and services includes apartments (Airbnb, Homestay), vehicles (Turo, Drivy, Camplify), rides (Zimride, BlaBlaCar), parking space (Parknow), and tools and appliances (Zilok) (see Slee 2016, Stephany 2015, and Sundararajan 2016 for more comprehensive overviews). Making resources available to others usually enables higher utilization through shared consumption and use patterns. Thus, these large-scale, peer-to-peer networks often promise a more social, sustainable, varied, convenient, anti-capitalistic, or inexpensive alternative to other traditional means of consumption (Belk 2007; Leismann et al. 2013; Matzner, Chasin, and Todenhöfer 2015), whereas the set of individual user motives for and against partaking includes many further aspects (Hawlitschek, Teubner, and Gimpel 2016). Yet with respect to other factors, peer-to-peer sharing can also appear unfavorable compared to traditional modes of consumption. This may be due to a lack of trust, efficacy, or economic benefits (Tussyadiah 2015), or may be grounded in effort expectancy, resource unavailability (Lamberton and Rose 2012), or privacy concerns (Acquisti, Brandimarte, and Loewenstein 2015; Teubner and Flath 2016).

The range of existing platforms illustrates that the sharing economy has also shifted goods and services into the realm of P2P markets, which we probably would not have expected to see. Beyond objects like vacation homes, which have been brokered between individuals offline already, today even hand bags, clothing, and pets can be exchanged from peer to peer (Torregrossa 2014). Some regard this as the dawn of a "Zero Marginal Cost Society" (Rifkin 2014). The poster child players of this sharing economy have well understood to market themselves on the wave toward a novel, more sustainable, social, personal, local, or ethical mode of consumption. It is unlikely, however, that creating a better world reflects their—or their investors'—single or core purpose. Likewise, they provide business opportunities for micro-entrepreneurs and participate in each of their transactions in the form of a substantial commission (Malhotra and Van Alstyne 2014). Dörr et al. (2016) point out that the current appeal of the sharing economy may, in fact, root in a deeper, societal desire for a different way of life: natural, sustainable, independent, connected, to name just a few catchwords. In that sense, the 1970s' oil crisis and the Limits of Growth debate issued by the Club of Rome, a global think tank focusing on the environment, economy, and climate change, have laid the ground for the sharing economy's current popularity and success. From this point of view, the sharing economy's fascination may be understood as a counterreaction to modern industrial processes, characterized by abundance, anonymity, division of labor, large corporations and chains, low-cost/

low-quality products, and the alienation from manufacturing processes. Against this backdrop, many concepts in the sharing economy appear to represent a better, even more human market principle for many.

It is almost ironic that the most successful and most frequently referenced examples are highly commercialized and profit-oriented platforms such as Airbnb, Uber, or eBay. In particular, matchmaker business models are often regarded as a template for successful peer-to-peer mediation (Mullins 2014). In a working paper, Horton and Zeckhauser (2016) used Google's auto-complete function as a source of market sentiment to survey what users search for online. Entering the partial query "Airbnb for . . ." triggered telling auto-completions such as cars, office space, food, parking, boats, bikes, and even dogs. This suggests a marked readiness, both to supply and to consume via P2P platforms.

A strong indication of the sharing economy's success is the publicly expressed discontent of industry incumbents such as hotel chains, car rental companies, or taxi service operators.[2] This has already shed light on some unarguably outdated regulation schemes (Koopman, Mitchell, and Thierer 2014), as, for instance, local knowledge tests for taxi drivers in times of Global Positioning System navigation. But sharing practices have also raised questions about social security. Morozov (2012) pointed out that risks are shifted unilaterally toward workers, while platforms conceive themselves as mere brokers with no further due responsibility. In addition, the rich supply cumulated by online platforms in combination with total transparency and comparability can lead to fierce competition and pricing, and the narrative of the "empowered micro entrepreneur" in reality becomes "a race to the bottom" (Avital et al. 2015). Morozov (2013) deemed this as a form of "neo-liberalism on steroids," commercializing aspects previously beyond the scope of the market. *The Economist*[3] foresaw this societal shift as early as in 2013, stating that "on the Internet, *everything* is for hire" (emphasis mine).

Over the past years, sharing economy platforms have experienced tremendous economic growth and increasing attention in both the academic and popular press. Despite its side effects such as legal and regulatory concerns (Hartl, Hofmann, and Kirchler 2015) and discrimination (Edelman and Luca 2014; Edelman, Luca, and Svirsky 2017), sharing economy platforms attract a wide range of users (Hellwig et al. 2015) and have established themselves as an alternative to traditional business models (Cusumano 2015; Guttentag 2015). Many studies on the sharing economy focus on shared mobility services (e.g., Cohen and Kietzmann 2014; Shaheen, Mallery, and Kingsley 2012; Teubner and Flath 2015) and accommodation sharing (e.g., Ikkala and Lampinen 2015; Karlsson, Kemperman, and Dolnicar 2017; Tussyadiah 2016). The motives to engage in P2P sharing are manifold, including economic, sustainability-related, social, and anti-capitalistic motives (Edbring et al. 2016; Hawlitschek, Teubner, and Gimpel 2016).

Despite the varying orientations and strategies of different platforms, most of them share several key factors. Many successful platforms rely on transactional standards and designs, that is, they resemble each other in terms of look and feel, and how transactions are guided (Kulp and Kool 2015). First, their business is conducted online, typically based on web services and mobile applications. Thus, besides societal reasons, the current popularity of shared consumption patterns is inevitably linked to the omnipresence, ease of use, and general acceptance of web services—and hence to e-commerce practices, web design patterns, online trust and verification mechanisms, and privacy concerns. In this part, we consider the question of what are the specific aspects of "sharing online" that make platforms like Airbnb and its fellows so successful in many domains. As we will outline, the P2P online economy encounters some recurring obstacles and issues, and similar patterns and practices have emerged, differentiating current platforms from their predecessors and counterparts from the offline world.

We structure this work as follows. After sketching out a rough demarcation of what we refer to as the P2P online sharing economy in the first part, we illustrate how network effects and decreasing transaction costs shape such two-sided markets. We then consider how, beyond this, information technology and systems create additional value within sharing applications. Next, we take a closer look at the recurring and central theme of trust—and how as well as by which tools it is commonly addressed. Finally, we sketch out some thoughts regarding the emerging and multilayered subject of privacy.

The P2P Online Sharing Economy

To pin down our understanding of the "P2P online sharing economy," we propose a set of characteristic properties, which we elaborate on in the following. To this end, it is fertile to approach the *sharing economy* from its very literal building blocks—"sharing" and "economy."

Extended Use Patterns

First, the notion of *sharing* has experienced a remarkable transformation in its linguistic history. In the 16th century it was used in the sense of splitting something into pieces, just like soil is torn by a plough*share* (John 2013, 114). This entails that sharing does not necessarily imply efficiency or utility gains, as it constitutes a zero-sum game. Other meanings of sharing include the distributive idea of "having something in common," or co-usage—just as in sharing a belief or sharing a room. In particular, the latter, that is, sharing tangible objects, describes the logic of today's sharing economies well. In contrast to its primordial meaning, it explicitly does not constitute a zero-sum game, since it yields higher utilization than individual use, and thus potentially higher efficiency and welfare. Besides these connotations of sharing, the term has also gained a communicational meaning since the 1930s, like in *sharing thoughts, emotions*—or stories and photos on Facebook today (John 2012). The boundaries blur when considering concepts such as knowledge sharing (Wang and Noe 2010).

Pure services (e.g., taxi rides) or intangible products (e.g., music files) usually lack the property of nonutilized or underutilized resources. Withal, this property also distinguishes services like Uber (driver effectively works as a chauffeur) from ridesharing (driver travels from A to B anyway). In this sense, Uber drivers offer a service while ridesharing drivers offer a spare resource, namely available seats on a given ride. Moreover, copying a digital resource (e.g., file sharing) does not increase the utilization of the original resource per se but creates a completely new instance, which then can be used by others. We deliberately distinguish this special property of digital goods from our notion of P2P sharing. Note, however, that it may well apply to other digital resources, that is, if proper copy protection is in place and the possibility and legal rights to access can be transferred (e.g., conceivable for e-books, shared Netflix accounts, or digital assets with blockchain-based proof of ownership).

A viable proxy for "extended use patterns" is the condition that two or more individuals use a resource where the (original) owner is among those users. This deliberately includes extended use patterns *with* a transfer of ownership. Renting out a room (which is usually used by the inhabitants) meets this criterion, whereas buying an apartment with the purpose to rent it out on Airbnb does not. Selling one's old MTB on eBay is an example of extended use patterns with a transfer of ownership, whereas manufacturing and selling handicraft art on Etsy[4] again violates the contemplated condition. Platforms like Etsy (resources primarily produced for the purpose of professional sale or rental) certainly constitute P2P economies, simply not P2P *sharing* economies in the aforementioned sense.

Economic Compensation

Second, *Meriam-Webster* dictionary defines an economy as "the process or system by which goods and services are produced, sold, and bought in a country or region." An economy thus involves the usage of money or a surrogate currency. Free-of-charge offers like in gifting or lending platforms are hence out of the scope of our definition of economic P2P sharing. The same usually applies for community-based networks (e.g., Couchsurfing). Beyond concepts such as eBay, an increasing share of the economic literature today explicitly considers peer-to-peer rental as a core concept of sharing economy platforms (Hawlitschek, Teubner, and Gimpel 2016; Tussyadiah and Pesonen 2016).

P2P Resource Transfer

Third, we focus on P2P networks in which resources are transferred from one private party (provider) to another (consumer). P2P here refers to both "peer-to-peer" and "private-to-private," explicitly excluding pooled (and usually professionally managed) resources like in car-sharing programs (Shaheen and Cohen 2013). Moreover, forms of collaborative consumption, for instance, buying and drinking a pitcher of beer with friends (Belk 2014) or buyers' clubs, as frequently formed for acquiring and maintaining high-value assets (e.g., sporting aircrafts or boats), are also beyond the scope of our delimitation of P2P online sharing. Transferring a resource implies some degree of tangibility, in particular with regard to legal ownership and exclusivity of access. It may be transferred temporary (e.g., rental) or permanently (e.g., selling).

Casualness of Use

Finally, a characteristic property of the novel P2P online sharing economy is its short-term and repeated nature. Transactions are typically executed frequently with alternating partners. This property does not often apply to platforms for (re-)selling assets such as apartments and cars (e.g., Realtor.com, Immoscout.com, Autotrader.com, AutoScout24.com). Here, resources are typically not sold or rented casually to mitigate underutilization but rather for long-term replacement or capital yield. The casualness-of-use condition hence comprises en passant transactions, excluding major "once-in-a-lifetime" events.

Who Shares?

To better understand the current success of P2P platforms, it is important to highlight that, beyond technological advances, societal transformation processes are also at play. While access (as compared to ownership) was traditionally attributed lower social status (Ozanne and Ballantine 2010), the picture has fundamentally changed. Collaborative and minimalistic lifestyles have gained popularity—particularly among generation Y (Möhlmann 2015)—and represent a novel form of conspicuous consumption, and independence, sometimes referred to as *digital nomadism* (Hart 2015). Without doubt, shared consumption patterns have the potential to contribute to a more sustainable use of resources, especially in urban areas. Here, high financial, timely, and spatial stress (e.g., exorbitant rents, congestion, and scarcity of parking space) intersect with short distances, high density of like-minded people, and thus rich supply and demand to tap into. In other words, sharing in metropolitan areas is both indicated *and* particularly easy. People in such areas are prevalently young, well educated, and technology savvy—and so are typical sharing economy users (Frick, Hauser, and Gürtler 2013; PwC 2015). These digital natives use Internet and mobile technology naturally and encounter low mental and technical entry barriers. Moreover, they are attuned to the very idea of interacting and trusting online. In the following, we therefore outline the—in our view—most typical and online-specific features in view of the P2P sharing economy, namely, transaction costs, network effects, and digital added-value, as well as trust and privacy concerns.

Transaction Costs and Network Effects

The global sharing economy is growing rapidly. PricewaterhouseCoopers (PwC) estimated the potential value of the five main sharing economy sectors (including peer-to-peer finance, online staffing, peer-to-peer accommodation, and car-sharing, as well as music and video streaming) by 2025 to be US$335 billion with annual growth rates of up to 25%.[5] Comparable to file sharing in the early 2000s (Aigrain 2012), the sharing economy's shift from a niche to a global phenomenon was, and is, driven by the widespread and inexpensive availability of Internet technology. The Internet has changed the game of sharing economy services due to at least two reasons.

First, search and transaction costs have vanished. Purchasing second-hand goods, a shared ride, or accommodation is as easy as a few mouse clicks. Also advertising one's spare goods involves little effort and is usually free of (upfront) costs, since most platforms charge only transaction-based commissions. Second, this ease of use draws in and connects a myriad of users, formerly separated by time and/or space. Surpassing critical mass is crucial for P2P sharing platforms, representing two-sided marketplaces with direct cross-side network effects (Eisenmann, Parker, and Van Alstyne 2006). Both demand and supply are dispersed across private individuals. Hence, both sides benefit from additional users on the respective *opposite* market side.

In the following, we sketch out a simple model of a two-sided market with cross-side network effects, in which the suppliers, for example, the hosts on Airbnb or the drivers on BlaBlaCar, determine the price of a homogeneous good. This reasoning differentiates the economic mechanisms of platforms such as Airbnb from most of the literature on two-sided markets, where the main focus was "to address how the intermediary (or 'the platform') sets prices for both sides of the market simultaneously" (Rysman 2009, 141). Analogous to traditional products with network effects, for example, the fax machine (Easley and Kleinberg 2010), the mutual interdependencies across the market sides can be represented by the supply and demand functions $S(d)$ and $D(s)$, where $S(d)$ depicts the number of suppliers in the market, given an expected market size of d demanders. Analogously, $D(s)$ depicts the number of demanders, given an expected number of s suppliers. We assume that for both D(s) and S(d) there exist thresholds for s and d, below which the number of users on the respective other market is negligible. Above these thresholds, S(d) and D(s) increase concavely, that is, at decreasing growth rate. Naturally, threshold values and growth rates may differ, but the general assumptions of thresholds and concavity are readily justified for either side. First, assuming a very limited number of suppliers, demanders are simply too unlikely to find a suitable match. Moreover, for too few demanders, there is no way for suppliers to break even, and thus even small market entry costs prove prohibitive for participation. Second, concavity emerges from the existence of natural constraints. At some point, ever-increasing numbers of demanders (assuming a fixed price level) will surpass the supply side's capacity to serve them. Vice versa, ever-increasing supply will, at some point, generate only little or no effective additional choice.

Beyond supply and demand in two-sided platforms, models of P2P sharing economy platforms need to consider pricing. Much of the literature on two-sided markets has addressed the platforms' pricing strategies, that is how to charge provisions or fixed fees from one, the other, or both market sides, as well as platform competition (Rochet and Tirole 2003). Much of this literature considered online advertisement and credit card businesses, where it is usually assumed that transactions between end users do not involve payments (Rochet and Tirole 2004). Against the backdrop of P2P sharing of tangible resources, it appears worthwhile to also take a closer look at product pricing. For the sake of simplicity, we abstain from platform fees entirely. A common and important characteristic of P2P sharing platforms is that suppliers set product prices themselves, individually, and (mostly) uncontrolled by the platform.[6] We assume product and cost homogeneity on the platform, and hence a uniform price level. Admittedly, for platforms like Airbnb, this represents an overly stark simplification, acknowledging that there exist offers for houseboats, castles, and tree houses. For ridesharing in contrast, the different rides from city A to city B do not differ all that much. Now, given an established price p, it is straightforward to assume that a higher price level will yield more supply for some fixed level of demand. Some additional suppliers will now find it worthwhile to enter the market, as there is more to earn than before. Likewise, a lower price will drive some suppliers out of the market. The same reasoning (with opposite signs) applies for the demand side. Here, ceteris paribus, higher prices yield lower demand, whereas lower prices yield higher demand. These comparative statics are depicted in the main diagram of Figure 7.1.

The market reaches an equilibrium state where the mutual best responses of supply and demand intersect, formally represented by $D(s) = d$ and $S(d) = s$, or simply $D(s) = S'(s)$. Obviously, there may exist multiple equilibria. Given our conceptualization, the origin $(0, 0)$ always represents an equilibrium.

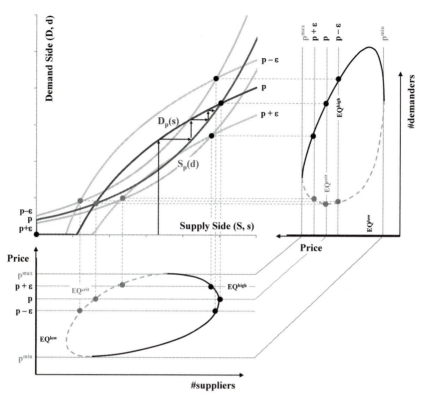

Figure 7.1 Prices in two-sided platforms

Furthermore, given the described curvature, there may exist an intermediate price range with two additional intersection points. The lower of these equilibria is critical, that is, unstable against even small disturbances of either market side into any direction. For such disturbances, D(s) and S(d) will converge toward either the low (0, 0) or the high equilibrium. This convergence dynamic is similar to that of other (one-sided) markets with network effects (Easley and Kleinberg 2010). The high-equilibria states are robust against disturbances and hence stable. Mapping these stable equilibria onto demand/price and supply/price charts yields elliptic shapes, where the right edge represents stable and the left edge the critical equilibria (Figure 7.1).

Assuming that the high-equilibrium state is reached, that is, the platform manages to surpass critical supply and demand, we now consider the suppliers' pricing decisions. By setting a price, the supply side implicitly determines the number of suppliers and demanders, where their calculus is as follows. A supplier maximizes her individual profit and knows that she will have to share the total of D demanders among all S suppliers. Assuming costs of c for one unit of supply, she hence maximizes the product of D/S-ratio and price-cost margin $D^*(p)/S^*(p)(p—c)$ with respect to p. As seen for revenue optimality in other cases (Voigt and Hinz 2015), this does not necessarily result in equal-sized market sides, that is, numbers of suppliers and demanders.

The result of this process depends on the specific shapes of D(s), S(d), and the magnitude of c. While a detailed formal analysis is out of scope here, this simple model yet allows for some valuable inferences. There are scenarios, for instance, in which suppliers will cut prices as much as possible. Below some price level, lowering prices pushes some suppliers out of the market and simultaneously increases demand, based on the price elasticities described earlier. This increases an individual supplier's demand share both by increasing the nominator and by decreasing the denominator of the aforementioned fraction. At some point however, due to a lack of sufficient supply—and *despite* decreasing prices—the number of demanders will also drop but still improve the situation for the suppliers. This counterintuitive observation may eventually result in market inefficiency and certainly does not match the platform's best interest since there exist states with higher prices *and* more supply *and* more demand. Platform managers should hence act to prevent such supply-side-driven market contraction. A variety of arrangements are conceivable. Platforms can set defaults and upper/lower bounds for pricing, such as practiced by BlaBlaCar. Pricing recommendations and analytical tools are possible too (Edelman and Luca 2014). Other measures like deliberately reducing market transparency or the demand side's price elasticity appear less suited or much harder to achieve. More promising, platforms can try to reduce *perceived* competition on the supply side, hence calling on a supplier's myopic tendency to charge higher prices. Moreover, platforms can reduce *actual* competition, for example, by allowing for horizontal and/or vertical product differentiation. Airbnb's "Superhost" and "business-travel-ready" badges can be seen as attempts in this regard. Thus, beyond mere technical facilitation, P2P online platforms can (and must) offer some added-value to the sharing economy, where means for product differentiation and pricing are central, as we have seen. In the following, we further explore how digital added-value may be created.

Beyond Facilitation: Digital Added-Value and Secondary Services

A major advantage of online-mediated services is immediacy. Compared to advertisements in catalogues or on bulletin boards, it is directly visible whether a certain accommodation or ride is still available or already booked, avoiding unnecessary requests. Moreover, given that all parties provide the necessary data (e.g., credit card accounts), immediate booking and payment are enabled, saving time and reducing organizational overhead and uncertainty. For transactions with in-person encounters, the payment process can be shifted to the background decently, avoiding awkward situations, in particular when the atmosphere among the peers is cordial. Furthermore, automated payment processes have a very practical effect in that they avoid issues with cash transactions, including providing change, as is often the case with ridesharing.

Moreover, online sharing and information systems allow for an enhancement of sharing services, for instance, based on social media, location-based, traffic, weather, or other real-time data—or by recombination of existing resources, for example, multi-hop ridesharing (Teubner and Flath 2015). Moreover, platforms can generate novel insights based on transaction-based and user data, which, in turn, enable recommender systems (Adomavicius and Tuzhilin 2005), assisted pricing tools (Airbnb), and more apposite ad campaigns. The common business model is to charge a fraction of the payments between supplier and consumer. For obvious reasons, this works best for high-value commodities such as apartments, cars, and boats, or high-value equipment—and when the platform can offer additional services, which make it inconvenient or risky to circumvent its booking process (secure and convenient billing, insurances, etc.). Since this is vital for a platform's commercial success, added-value and secondary services should be of high priority to P2P platform operators.

The Currency of Online Sharing: Trust

Like sharing itself, the P2P online sharing economy is built on trust (Belk 2010). Trust is a multifaceted and complex construct—often hard to pin down (Keen et al. 1999). Not only the media (e.g., Ufford 2015) but also business consultancies regard trust as crucial for the sharing economy: "To share is to trust. That, in a nutshell, is the fundamental principle" (Freese and Schönberg 2014). Botsman (2012) considers trust as the sharing economy's currency. In addition, PwC (2015) concluded, "convenience and cost-savings are beacons, but what ultimately keeps this economy spinning—and growing—is trust."

Whereas e-vendors face the challenge of winning and maintaining their customers' trust (Gefen 2000; Tamjidyamcholo et al. 2013), C2C platforms, beyond that, must also consider trust *among* their users. Whether or not customers are willing to auction off or bid for products (Teubner, Adam, and Riordan 2015), offer or seek a shared ride (Teubner and Flath 2015), temporarily rent out their apartment (Hawlitschek, Teubner, and Weinhardt 2016), or let others use their equipment (Hamari, Sjöklint, and Ukkonen 2016) will hence depend not only on the trustworthiness of the platform (e.g., data security, third-party advertisement) but also on the extent to which other users appear trustworthy (e.g., with regard to ability, integrity, and benevolence [Gefen, Benbasat, and Pavlou 2008]). Moreover, since a rented car, for instance, may break down, in many scenarios, the product itself is subject to trust considerations too. This is reflected in three distinct targets of trust in

P2P online sharing: trust toward peer, platform, and product—referred to as the "3P" (Hawlitschek, Teubner, and Weinhardt 2016). As suggested by Bardhi and Eckhardt (2012), it appears beneficial to further investigate the triadic constellation of consumer–consumer, consumer–marketer, and consumer–object relationships.

Hawlitschek, Teubner, and Gimpel (2016) found trust to be a relevant factor for participation in peer-to-peer rental. It is one if not the important driving factor for the long-term success of sharing platforms (Strader and Ramaswami 2002). Platform operators have established a plethora of design patterns and mechanisms to establish and maintain trust among their users, including verification mechanisms, mutual rating and review schemes, or insurances and web design techniques (Teubner 2014). From the user perspective, meaningful profiles and especially profile *photos* are a driver of trust and sharing behavior in P2P platforms (Karlsson, Kemperman, and Dolnicar 2017; Ma et al. 2017; Teubner et al. 2014). Beyond considering trusting beliefs, recent approaches have begun to assess trust in the sharing economy in terms of actual behavior, that is, based on experiments and behavioral evidence (Edelman, Luca, and Svirsky 2017; Hawlitschek, Teubner, Adam, et al. 2016).

Verification and Signaling

A commonly pursued approach is to offer ways for users to verify (i) their existence as actual human beings (as opposed to fake accounts) and (ii) their qualification in the given context, for example, as a driver in ridesharing. For this purpose, the platform serves as a mutually trusted party. Potential suppliers and consumers send a scan of their identification card to the platform, which verifies its authenticity and matches actual and user names. The same is possible for e-mail addresses and cell phone numbers, verified by clicking a link or confirming a sent password. Note that the actual information (ID number, e-mail address, phone number, etc.) is usually not displayed on the platform. A badge, however, indicates that it was provided and verified.

For special-purpose platforms, users may want to signal competence, for example, when seeking to rent a boat (boating certificate), or when offering a shared ride as driver (driver's license; "zero accidents in x years" statement issued by their insurance). Another possibility is social signaling. Based on social media integration, users can demonstrate their willingness to rely on their social environment as good repute. Likewise, it can be understood as an act of strategic self-commitment, increasing incurred social cost if a transaction partner raises complaints. Making malicious behavior costly for oneself ex ante signals a high willingness to behave benevolently. Moreover, a reasonable number of Facebook friends may casually be regarded as indication for not being a psychopath, for example, based on presumed popularity or attractiveness (Tong et al. 2008). Social media integration also taps into the trust potential of social similarity (McAllister 1995), for instance, when discovering shared interests or even common friends.

Another verification and—at the same time—quality management strategy is followed by Airbnb. Eligible hosts are offered a professional photographer service, free of charge. Airbnb's partner photographers visit the hosts, arrange rooms, and thereby make sure the apartments are presented in the best possible light. Such watermark-verified photos are trustworthy as they believably depict the actual apartment. Beyond credibility and increasing trust toward the product, this is likely to make advertisements more appealing, benefiting both hosts and platform.

Ratings and Reviews

Beyond verification and signaling, data on prior transactions and evaluations is informative and hence entails high trust-building potentials. Therefore, a common approach for establishing trust in P2P platforms is the use of reputation systems. Such systems allow for collecting, aggregating, and providing feedback on past user behavior (Resnick et al. 2000), typically based on five-star ratings on different aspects and text reviews. From a theoretical perspective, the effectiveness of this approach is grounded in social proof, stating that in situations of uncertainty, individuals derive behavioral cues from the previous actions of others (Cialdini and Garde 1987). Consequently, if aggregated feedback comprises credible information about the past behavior of other market participants, reputation systems can help establish trust toward potential interaction partners online (Fuller, Serva, and Benamati 2007).

With the rise of the sharing economy, the importance of online reputation systems has increased tremendously. Here, "reputation serves as the digital institution that protects buyers and prevents the market failure that economists and policy makers worry about" (Sundararajan 2012). From a customer's perspective, the decision of which host, guest, driver, passenger, seller, buyer, or lender to pick becomes much more informed when it is based on the aggregated experiences of many other users. We refer to Zervas, Proserpio, and Byers (2015) for a more comprehensive description of such processes.

One early and intensely investigated reputation system in C2C e-commerce was implemented by eBay (Dellarocas 2003). From the 2000s until today, much effort was put into understanding and improving such systems (Bolton, Katok, and Ockenfels 2004). One recent modification addresses collusive behavior (i.e., undesired reciprocity) in peer review processes (Bolton, Greiner, and Ockenfels 2013). To limit tit-for-tat and hence inflationary positive reviews, Airbnb switched from sequential to simultaneous reviews in July 2014 (Airbnb 2014; Zervas, Proserpio, and Byers 2015).

The importance of ratings and reviews becomes evident when considering the associated value as *reputation,* or *social capital* (Huang et al. 2017), which particularly applies to the sharing economy. The information enclosed in positive or negative ratings not only affects "soft" factors like loyalty, satisfaction, or peer trust (Bente, Baptist, and Leuschner 2012) but has also immediate ramifications for the involved parties. Host on Airbnb, for instance, capitalize a good reputation (i.e., positive reviews), either by demanding higher prices or by choosing guests more selectively, representing tangible economic value (Gutt and Herrmann 2015; Ikkala and Lampinen 2015). To demonstrate this, Teubner et al. (2016) consider the impact of average rating scores on prices, based on actual market data (Airbnb listings from Germany), including prices and a variety of control variables. Multivariate regression analysis reveals that higher average scores are indeed capitalized by *higher* prices. Sharing economy providers and consumers alike are hence compelled to actively manage their online reputation. Considering that single but particular negative reviews can have ruinous effects, and also that peer feedback can be very subjective, many platforms now allow for a response (Abramova et al. 2015). The latter authors found that different reasons of critique (self-inflicted or not) imply different best response strategies (e.g., confession, denial, apology, excuse).

Despite the success of reputation systems in P2P sharing, their effectiveness and informativeness have not remained uncontested. As discussed by Slee (2013) and Zervas, Proserpio, and Byers (2015), ratings on Airbnb (also compared to those of the same apartments on other platforms) are strikingly positive.[7] This, however, reduces the possibility to differentiate between different offers based on the review score. This "j-shaped" distribution of online reviews is not a new phenomenon and was already observed on Amazon.com (Hu, Zhang, and Pavlou 2009). The characteristic distribution of P2P ratings can be traced back to herding behavior (prior ratings subtly bias the evaluations of subsequent reviewers), underreporting of negative reviews (fear of retaliatory reviews), self-selection (higher a priori likelihood of satisfaction of users compared to nonusers), and strategic manipulations, for example, through bought reviews (Zervas, Proserpio, and Byers 2015). On Airbnb, as pointed out by Mulshine (2015), hosts get to see not only the reviews potential guests *received* but also those they *wrote*. Hence, guests may want to avoid providing (honest) critical feedback, because future hosts might be reluctant to rent to them, fearing they will receive an all-too-honest review, too (Mulshine 2015).

Insurances and Support

Another way to mitigate users' trust concerns is deliberately addressing worst-case scenarios and offering insurance and support for such cases. Airbnb, for instance, offers a $1,000,000 insurance for damages incurred by guests. It is argued, however, that, if needed, the platforms' guidelines make it difficult to obtain recovery (Hooshmand 2015). The ridesharing platform Carpooling.com even used to offer compensatory train tickets for passengers in case a driver canceled a ride on short notice or did not show up. In cooperation with the insurance company AXA, BlaBlaCar offers services such as roadside assistance, additional insurances, legal advice, and even return shipments of forgotten items.[8]

Web Design

Beyond such approaches toward engineering trust, there also lies a passive trust potential in a platform's appearance. Jones and Leonard (2008, 93) found that "a consumer's perceptions of that [web site's] quality can result in a feeling of trust about the owner of the site" and concluded that maintaining a high level of quality is crucial for C2C platforms. Joe Gebbia—cofounder of Airbnb—states to actively address trust issues by deliberate design choices, where "building the right amount of trust takes the right amount of disclosure." This is nudged by the size of text input forms to suggest the right length, and guiding prompts intended to encourage communication.[9]

Moreover, as indicated by Cyr, Head, and Larios et al. (2010), the choice of colors in online market platforms is relevant too and may even affect trusting and reciprocating behavior (Hawlitschek, Jansen, et al. 2016). Colors can induce specific perceptions of warmth since humans tend to associate different colors with different degrees of warmth (Fenko et al. 2009). Most studies agree on the general notion that blue is perceived as a cool color, while red is perceived as a warm color (Fenko et al. 2009). Remarkably, cold and warm temperatures affect the perception of interpersonal warmth and in turn trusting behavior (Kang et al. 2010; Williams and Bargh 2008). The effect of temperature priming on trust was found in Prisoner's Dilemma (Storey and Workman 2013) and trust game situations (Kang et al. 2010). Whether or not the evolution of Airbnb's logo is to be seen from a color-trust perspective remains unclear. Airbnb's blog[10] referred to the new color as one "which delivers the emotion and passion around the brand, without the aggression of pure red."

Many e-commerce vendors also rely on third-party certification to signal high service quality, reliability, and hence trustworthiness. A graphical seal on their website, as, for instance, the Trusted Shop Guarantee, often designates such certification.[11] The provider's promise is to approve high levels of data security, cost transparency, variety of payment options, adequate shipping, and a fair management of return shipments and cancellations. Plonka and Janik (2013) investigated users' gaze paths on apparel shopping websites containing such trust seals, employing eye-tracking devices. Rather than paying attention to the e-trust seal, however, users primarily looked at the face of the female model presenting the product, the brand logo, and the main text headings. In fact, the model's face was the *first* focal point of user attention, as humans "are social animals, . . . perfectly wired to automatically read the subtle social cues" (Plonka and Janik 2013).

User Representation

This paramount importance of faces as one type of pictorial stimuli leads us to one of the most commonly adopted elements for trust building in e-commerce: expressive user profiles and photos in particular. User representation draws on several streams of research. First, research on e-commerce and information systems has, starting from the early 2000s, extensively investigated how images and representations of humans in product websites affect shopping behavior. They were found to stimulate social presence, trust, and e-loyalty (Cyr et al. 2009; Hassanein and Head 2007). Perceived social presence, that is, "the degree of salience of the other person in the interaction and the consequent salience of the interpersonal relationships" (Short, Williams, and Christie 1976, 65), was identified as a central construct in this regard. It is increased by the presence of visual user representations and mediates their effect onto behavioral and trust dimensions. For the case of C2C platforms, however, only few studies considered the impact of providing actual user photos on sharing behavior (Bente, Baptist, and Leuschner 2012; Ert, Fleischer, and Magen 2016; Teubner et al. 2014)—but results are unambiguous: faces create trust. Many P2P platforms rely on this effect. Carpooling.com, for instance, literally reminded its users that "faces create trust" and prompted them to complete their profile accordingly.[12] Also Flinc.org asks its users to "upload a picture" and hence to "create trust." BlaBlaCar even offers a filter in its search to show ride offers only by drivers *with* a photo.

Second, user representation by avatars as an alternative to actual photos is also considered in a variety of domains, for example, in e-commerce, online gaming, and e-learning (Bente, Baptist, and Leuschner 2012; Blascovich et al. 2002; Lee, Kozar, and Larsen 2009; Nowak and Biocca 2003; Qiu and Benbasat 2005; Slater and Steed 2002). In particular, the emerging field of NeuroIS—using neuroimaging techniques—has revealed that almost any reasonable form of avatar faces (cartoon, animal, photorealistic, animated) is perceived very similar to actual human faces by the brain. In fact, the fusiform face area is activated not only for human but also for animal and cartoon faces (Kanwisher, McDermott, and Chun 1997; Tong et al. 2000). Things that look like faces are hence processed like faces by the brain, which appears reasonable from an evolutionary point of view, since for most of human history—without artificial images—everything that looked like a face in fact was a face. Moreover, even macaque monkeys have been found to exhibit specific brain cell activation when exposed to cartoon faces (Freiwald, Tsao, and Livingstone 2009). Such representations hence have the potential to convey the same positive effects (i.e., social presence, trust). Much of the research in this context considers behavior in hypothetical scenarios, whereas recent studies also use experimental, incentivized approaches and investigate user behavior in P2P scenarios (Teubner et al. 2013, 2014).

It can be assumed that the role of user representations in P2P platforms is more potent than that in traditional e-commerce, due to the fact that these pictures refer to actual human beings, as compared to human props for product advertisement (Teubner et al. 2014). Moreover, the effect is most likely stronger for P2P rental (e.g., Airbnb) than for selling (e.g., eBay), due to stronger social interaction among the peers. Thus, social and personal cues, and especially human faces, create trust as a prerequisite for peer interaction. Recent research is increasingly concerned with regulatory and other "dark sides" of the sharing economy (Malhotra and Van Alstyne 2014). Edelman and Luca (2014), for instance, suggested that there exist distinct race-based price differences on Airbnb (controlling for all other visible data on the platform). They concluded that profile pictures as a "seemingly-routine mechanism for building trust" entail important unintended consequences (2). Beyond being a potential source of discrimination, providing a photo of oneself immanently reduces anonymity and may hence give rise to privacy concerns, evoking discomfort or even discouraging registration and activity in the first place. We consider this flipside of the medal in the next section.

Privacy

Under the impression of the emerging technology of photography, Warren and Brandeis (1890, 193) defined privacy as "the right to be left alone." Today's Internet users have come a long way since then. They share personal information online quite permissively, knowingly or unknowingly, and for the case of social network sites (SNS) often with the emphatic desire *not* to be left alone, but to provoke feedback, the experience of emotional support (Koroleva et al. 2011), and connectedness (Krasnova, Veltri, and Günther 2012). Privacy in the sharing economy is fundamentally rooted in theories of privacy regulation, which define privacy as people's desire to determine "when, how, and to what extent information about them is communicated to others" (Westin 1967), or as the "selective control of access to the self" (Altman 1975, 24). P2P online platforms inherently create an audience for personal information. Moreover, the sharing economy has started to blur the lines between personal and commercial spheres (Sundararajan 2016). Seeking to offer personal economic assets online requires actively balancing economic aspiration (e.g., target group size) and individual privacy concerns, by choosing which information to disclose, to whom, and via which channel(s).

Once disclosed information on any platform can be (mis)used for economic and social discrimination, hidden influence and manipulation, coercion, or censorship (Acquisti, Brandimarte, and Loewenstein 2015). In particular, the aggregation of different information sources, for example, from SNS and C2C platforms, enables far-reaching inferences, exploitable for personalized advertising, behavior prediction, profiling, or the extraction of sensitive information like political views (Mitrou et al. 2014). In light of this relevance of privacy-related user behavior in online contexts and the associated technologies, "the information age has rendered information privacy a core topic in IS research" (Pavlou 2011, 977).

P2P sharing platforms are the most promising channels for advertising many types of personal assets. They put their users into a quite controversial position, requiring disclosure of personal data for providing information, marketing, or creating trust (Teubner 2014). Against this backdrop, personal information disclosure, economic considerations, and privacy concerns interact in manifold ways. "If this is the age of information, then privacy is the issue of our times" (Acquisti, Brandimarte, and Loewenstein 2015, 509). Despite the facilitation of economic peer-to-peer sharing, renting, and selling and the growing importance of C2C platforms (PwC 2015), there is a lack of understanding under which circumstances such advertisements are realized—and when they are not (Teubner and Flath 2016). Overall, the willingness to disclose and share intimate information appears to be on the decline (Acquisti, Brandimarte, and Loewenstein 2015). One may assume that this is due to perceptions of psychological privacy risks (Hauff, Veit, and Tuunainen 2015), emerging from the potential reach of online communication and the dramatic scale of some social media outrages in particular. However, any inhibiting concerns take a backseat in some of the most expansive communication channels such as platforms such as Airbnb. This notion is supported by research on concerns related to information disclosure in such platforms, following a curvilinear form in perceived communication reach (Teubner and Flath 2016). Potential concerns mitigated in small, secluded settings (intimacy) and on very broad platforms (anonymity). Platform operators should hence carefully consider whether to jeopardize their size-related anonymity advantage by creating close proximity to (less anonymous) social media channels.

Conclusion

The P2P online sharing economy has started to affect many domains of our daily lives, including retail, hospitality, mobility, work, and financial services. The extended use of underutilized assets seems to catch the spirit of our age. In this respect, the transition from *offline* to *online* represents a key driver of this development, marginalizing search and transaction costs, as well as enabling to surpass critical market size in two-sided economies. Moreover, the use of IT yields very direct advantages such as real-time information, use of location-based data, and convenience.

In online environments, however, there occur novel problems. For operators and users of platforms alike, trust plays a crucial role. Trust building in peer-to-peer online economies, however, is intricate. The terms and conditions simply differ to heirloom offline transactions, where people meet in person, shake hands, and remain personally accessible and accountable. As we have outlined, the designers and engineers of P2P platforms have developed means to establish trust among peers as well as toward platform and products, including verification and signaling, insurances, ratings and reviews, and meaningful user profiles.

Economic peer-to-peer interactions may be seen as a form of reconnection with and re-appreciation of underlying production processes of goods and services, but coincidentally also as a form of economization of civic life. In economics, markets are usually assumed to be inert, that is, not changing the meaning of the goods being exchanged. Platforms like Airbnb, in contrast, advertise in a value-laden way, claiming to broker *local, sustainable, social,* or *personal* products and services. This blurring of lines between the personal and economic spheres and the corresponding novel relationships among peers, platforms, and products give rise to new questions. Where one's friends in an online social network serve as a certification of credibility to potential interaction partners, they inevitably also become an asset. Moreover, P2P platforms extend market principles to domains formally out of the scope of commerce. Beyond this societal dimension, P2P economies also create issues and the need for trade-offs on an individual level, for example, with regard to privacy. The fate of sharing economy services but also broader societal developments will depend on how the outlined issues are addressed, but also on asking the right questions. The increasing orbit of the P2P online sharing economy will hence urge the need for answers from academic, practical, and regulatory perspectives.

Notes

1. Information systems (IS) research has considered the "sharing economy" mainly as an umbrella term covering phenomena such as "collaborative consumption" (Botsman and Rogers 2010), "access-based consumption" (Bardhi and Eckhardt 2012), or "commercial sharing systems" (Lamberton and Rose 2012).

2. http://business.time.com/2013/06/06/sharing-is-hard-legal-trouble-for-airbnb-relayrides-flightcar/; http://www.bloomberg.com/news/articles/2015-10-30/new-york-hotel-group-goes-on-offensive-against-airbnb-rentals; http://www.theguardian.com/technology/2016/feb/10/black-cab-drivers-uber-protest-london-traffic-standstill.

3. http://www.economist.com/news/leaders/21573104-internet-everything-hire-rise-sharing-economy.

4. "Etsy is a marketplace where people around the world connect, both online and offline, to make, sell and buy unique goods" (https://www.etsy.com/about/).

5. http://www.pwc.co.uk/issues/megatrends/collisions/sharingeconomy.html; http://www.forbes.com/sites/tomiogeron/2013/01/23/airbnb-and-the-unstoppable-rise-of-the-share-economy/#356d00b36790.

6. BlaBlaCar specifies an upper bound for prices, which drivers (i.e., the supply side) cannot exceed. Besides a certain degree of price predictability and stability, this most likely serves the purpose to render the users' activity noncommercial and hence avert legal issues and inconvenient regulation.

7. Zervas, Proserpio, and Byers's (2015) article on Airbnb pointedly reads: "Where Every Stay is Above Average."

8. https://www.blablacar.de/news/start-onlinezahlung-axa.

9. http://www.ted.com/talks/joe_gebbia_how_airbnb_designs_for_trust.

10. www.underconsideration.com/brandnew/archives/new_logo_and_identity_for_airbnb_by_designstudio.php.

11. http://www.trustedshops.com/.

12. http://www.mitfahrgelegenheit.de/news/viewNews/464.

References

Abramova, Olga, Tetiana Shavanova, Andrea Fuhrer, Hanna Krasnova, and Peter Buxmann. 2015. "Understanding the Sharing Economy: The Role of Response to Negative Reviews in the Peer-To-Peer Accommodation Sharing Network." *ECIS 2015 Proceedings*, Münster, Germany, pp. 1–16,.

Acquisti, A., L. Brandimarte, and G. Loewenstein. 2015. "Privacy and Human Behavior in the Age of Information." *Science* 347 (6221): 509–514.

Adomavicius, Gediminas, and Alexander Tuzhilin. 2005. "Toward the Next Generation of Recommender Systems: A Survey of the State-of-the-Art and Possible Extensions." *IEEE Transactions on Knowledge and Data Engineering* 17 (6): 734–749.

Aigrain, Philippe. 2012. *Sharing: Culture and the Economy in the Internet Age*. Amsterdam: Amsterdam University Press.

Airbnb. 2014. "Building Trust with a New Review System." *Airbnb*. http://blog.atairbnb.com/building-trust-new-review-system/.

Altman, Irwin. 1975. *The Environment and Social Behavior: Privacy, Personal Space, Territory, and Crowding*. Pacific Grove, CA: Brooks/Cole Publishing Company.

Andreas Kamilaris, Andreas Kartakoullis and Francesc X. Prenafeta-Boldú. A Review on the Practice of Big Data Analysis in Agriculture. Computers and Electronics in Agriculture International Journal, vol. 143, pp. 23–37, December 2017.

Avital, Michel, John M. Carroll, Anders Hjalmarsson, Natalia Levina, Arvind Malhotra, and Arun Sundararajan. 2015. "The Sharing Economy: Friend or Foe?" *ICIS 2015 Proceedings*, Fort Worth, USA, pp. 1–8.

Bardhi, Fleura, and Giana M. Eckhardt. 2012. "Access-Based Consumption: The Case of Car Sharing." *Journal of Consumer Research* 39 (4): 881–898.

Belk, Russell. 2007. "Why Not Share Rather Than Own?" *Annals of the American Academy of Political and Social Science* 611 (1): 126–140.

Belk, Russell. 2010. "Sharing." *Journal of Consumer Research* 36 (5): 715–734.

Belk, Russell. 2014. "You Are What You Can Access: Sharing and Collaborative Consumption Online." *Journal of Business Research* 67 (8): 1595–1600.

Bente, Gary, Odile Baptist, and Haug Leuschner. 2012. "To Buy or Not to Buy: Influence of Seller Photos and Reputation on Buyer Trust and Purchase Behavior." *International Journal of Human Computer Studies* 70 (1): 1–13.

Blascovich, Jim, Jack Loomis, Andrew C. Beall, Kimberly R. Swinth, Crystal L. Hoyt, and Jeremy N. Bailenson. 2002. "Immersive Virtual Environment Technology as a Methodological Tool for Social Psychology." *Psychological Inquiry* 13 (2): 103–124.

Bolton, Gary, Ben Greiner, and Axel Ockenfels. 2013. "Engineering Trust: Reciprocity in the Production of Reputation Information." *Management Science* 59 (2): 265–285.

Bolton, Gary E., Elena Katok, and Axel Ockenfels. 2004. "How Effective Are Electronic Reputation Mechanisms? An Experimental Investigation." *Management Science* 50 (11): 1587–1602.

Botsman, Rachel. 2012. "The Currency of the New Economy Is Trust." TED.com. https://www.ted.com/talks/rachel_botsman_the_currency_of_the_new_economy_is_trust.

Botsman, Rachel, and Roo Rogers. 2010. *What's Mine Is Yours: How Collaborative Consumption Is Changing the Way We Live*. London: Collins.

Chan, Nelson D., and Susan A. Shaheen. 2012. "Ridesharing in North America: Past, Present, and Future." *Transport Reviews* 32 (1): 93–112.

Cialdini, Robert B. 1987. *Influence: The Psychology of Persuasion*. New York: HarperCollins.

Cohen, Boyd, and Jan Kietzmann. 2014. "Ride On! Mobility Business Models for the Sharing Economy." *Organization & Environment* 27 (3): 279–296.

Cusumano, Michael A. 2015. "How Traditional Firms Must Compete in the Sharing Economy." *Communications of the ACM* 58 (1): 32–34.

Cyr, Dianne, Milena Head, and Hector Larios. 2010. "Colour Appeal in Website Design within and across Cultures: A Multi-Method Evaluation." *International Journal of Human Computer Studies* 68 (1–2): 1–21.

Cyr, Dianne, Milena Head, Hector Larios, and Bing Pan. 2009. "Exploring Human Images in Website Design: A Multi-Method Approach." *MIS Quarterly* 33 (3): 539–566.

Dellarocas, Chrysanthos. 2003. "The Digitization of Word of Mouth: Promise and Challenges of Online Feedback Mechanisms." *Management Science* 49 (10): 1407–1424.

Dörr, J., and Goldschmidt N. 2016. "Share Economy: Vom Wert Des Teilens." http://www.faz.net/aktuell/wirtschaft/share-economy-vom-wert-des-teilens-13990987.html.

Easley, David, and Jon Kleinberg. 2010. "Network Effects." In *Networks, Crowds, and Markets: Reasoning about a Highly Connected World*, edited by David Easley, and Jon Kleinberg. 509–542. Cambridge, MA: Cambridge University Press.

Edbring, Emma Gullstr, Matthias Lehner, Oksana Mont, and Emma Gullstrand Edbring. 2016. "Exploring Consumer Attitudes to Alternative Models of Consumption: Motivations and Barriers." *Journal of Cleaner Production* 123: 5–15.

Edelman, Benjamin G., and Michael Luca. 2014. "Digital Discrimination: The Case of Airbnb.com." Harvard Business School Working Paper.

Edelman, Benjamin G., Michael Luca, and Dan Svirsky. 2017. "Racial Discrimination in the Sharing Economy: Evidence from a Field Experiment." *American Economic Journal: Applied Economics* 9 (2): 1–22.

Eisenmann, Thomas, Geoffrey Parker, and Marshall W. Van Alstyne. 2006. "Strategies for Two-Sided Markets." *Harvard Business Review* 84 (10): 1–11.

Ert, Eyal, Aliza Fleischer, and Nathan Magen. 2016. "Trust and Reputation in the Sharing Economy: The Role of Personal Photos on Airbnb." *Tourism Management* 55: 62–73.

Fenko, Anna, Hendrik N. J. Schifferstein, Tse Chia Huang, and Paul Hekkert. 2009. "What Makes Products Fresh: The Smell or the Colour?" *Food Quality and Preference* 20 (5): 372–379.

Freese, Christian, and A. T. Schönberg. 2014. "Shared Mobility: How New Businesses Are Rewriting the Rules of the Private Transportation Game." https://www.wesrch.com/business/paper-details/pdf-BU1O8D9J4AACN-shared-mobility-how-new-businesses-are-rewriting-the-rules-of-the-private-transportation-game#page1.

Freiwald, Winrich A., Doris Y. Tsao, and Margaret S. Livingstone. 2009. "A Face Feature Space in the Macaque Temporal Lobe." *Nature Neuroscience* 12 (9): 1187–1196.

Frick, Karin, Mirjam Hauser, and Detlef Gürtler. 2013. "Sharity: Die Zukunft Des Teilens" ["Sharity: The Future of Sharing"], Gottlieb Duttweiler Institute, Switzerland.

Fuller, Mark A., Mark A. Serva, and John Benamati. 2007. "Seeing Is Believing: The Transitory Influence of Reputation Information on E-Commerce Trust and Decision Making." *Decision Sciences* 38 (4): 675–699.

Gefen, David. 2000. "E-Commerce: The Role of Familiarity and Trust." *Omega* 28 (6): 725–737.

Gefen, David, Izak Benbasat, and Paula Pavlou. 2008. "A Research Agenda for Trust in Online Environments." *Journal of Management Information Systems* 24 (4): 275–286.

Gefen, David, and Detmar W. Straub. 2004. "Consumer Trust in B2C E-Commerce and the Importance of Social Presence: Experiments in E-Products and E-Services." *Omega* 32 (6): 407–424.

Gutt, Dominik, and Philipp Herrmann. 2015. "Sharing Means Caring? Hosts' Price Reaction to Rating Visibility." *ECIS 2015 Proceedings*, Münster, Germany, pp. 1–13.

Guttentag, Daniel. 2015. "Airbnb: Disruptive Innovation and the Rise of an Informal Tourism Accommodation Sector." *Current Issues in Tourism* 18 (12): 1192–1217.

Hamari, Juho, Mimmi Sjöklint, and Antti Ukkonen. 2016. "The Sharing Economy: Why People Participate in Collaborative Consumption." *Journal of the Association for Information Science and Technology* 67 (9): 2047–2059.

Hart, Anna. 2015. "Living and Working in Paradise: The Rise of the 'Digital Nomad.'" http://www.telegraph.co.uk/news/features/11597145/Living-and-working-in-paradise-the-rise-of-the-digital-nomad.html.

Hartl, Barbara, Eva Hofmann, and Erich Kirchler. 2015. "Do We Need Rules for 'What's Mine Is Yours'? Governance in Collaborative Consumption Communities." *Journal of Business Research* 69 (8): 2756–2763.

Hassanein, Khaled, and Milena Head. 2007. "Manipulating Perceived Social Presence through the Web Interface and Its Impact on Attitude towards Online Shopping." *International Journal of Human-Computer Studies* 65 (8): 689–708.

Hauff, Sabrina, Daniel Veit, and Virpi Tuunainen. 2015. "Towards a Taxonomy of Perceived Consequences of Privacy-Invasive Practices." *ECIS 2015 Proceedings*, Münster, Germany, pp. 1–15.

Hawlitschek, Florian, Lars Erik Jansen, Ewa Lux, Timm Teubner, and Christof Weinhardt. 2016. "Colors and Trust: The Influence of User Interface Design on Trust and Reciprocity." *HICSS 2016 Proceedings*, Koloa, USA, pp. 590–599.

Hawlitschek, Florian, Timm Teubner, Marc T. P. Adam, Nils Borchers, Mareike Moehlmann, and Christof Weinhardt. 2016. "Trust in the Sharing Economy: An Experimental Framework." *ICIS 2016 Proceedings*, Dublin, Ireland, pp. 1–14.

Hawlitschek, Florian, Timm Teubner, and Henner Gimpel. 2016. "Understanding the Sharing Economy—Drivers and Impediments for Participation in Peer-to-Peer Rental." *HICSS 2016 Proceedings*, Koloa, USA, pp. 4782–4791.

Hawlitschek, Florian, Timm Teubner, and Christof Weinhardt. 2016. "Trust in the Sharing Economy." *Swiss Journal of Business Research and Practice* 70 (1): 26–44.

Hellwig, Katharina, Felicitas Morhart, Florent Girardin, and Mirjam Hauser. 2015. "Exploring Different Types of Sharing: A Proposed Segmentation of the Market for 'Sharing' Businesses." *Psychology & Marketing* 32 (9): 891–906.

Hooshmand, Mark. 2015. "The Risks of Being a Host in the Sharing-Economy: A Look at Short-Term Rentals and the Liability and Public-Policy Problems They Present." *Plaintiff* magazine. http://www.plaintiffmagazine.com/recent-issues/item/the-risks-of-being-a-host-in-the-sharing-economy.

Horton, John J., and Richard J. Zeckhauser. 2016. "Owning, Using and Renting: Some Simple Economics of the 'Sharing Economy.'" NBER Working Paper Series.

Hu, Nan, Jie Zhang, and Paul A. Pavlou. 2009. "Overcoming the J-Shaped Distribution of Product Reviews." *Communications of the ACM* 52 (10): 144–147.

Huang, Qian, Xiayu Chen, Carol Xiaojuan Ou, Robert M. Davison, and Zhongsheng Hua. 2017. "Understanding Buyers' Loyalty to a C$_2$C Platform: The Roles of Social Capital, Satisfaction and Perceived Effectiveness of E-Commerce Institutional Mechanisms." *Information Systems Journal* 27 (1): 91–119.

Ikkala, Tapio, and Airi Lampinen. 2015. "Monetizing Network Hospitality: Hospitality and Sociability in the Context of Airbnb." *CSCW'15 Proceedings*, Vancouver, Canada, pp. 1033–1044.

John, Nicholas A. 2012. "Sharing and Web 2.0: The Emergence of a Keyword." *New Media & Society* 15 (2): 167–182.

John, Nicholas A. 2013. "The Social Logics of Sharing." *The Communication Review* 16 (3): 113–131.

Jones, Kiku, and Lori N. K. Leonard. 2008. "Trust in Consumer-to-Consumer Electronic Commerce." *Information and Management* 45 (2): 88–95.

Kang, Ping, Mingxiang Liao, Michael R. Wester, J. Steven Leeder, and Robin E. Pearce. 2010. "NIH Public Access." *Ratio* 36 (3): 490–499.

Kanwisher, Nancy, Josh McDermott, and Marvin M. Chun. 1997. "The Fusiform Face Area: A Module in Human Extrastriate Cortex Specialized for Face Perception." *The Journal of Neuroscience* 17 (11): 4302–4311.

Karlsson, Logi, Astrid Kemperman, and Sara Dolnicar. 2017. "May I Sleep in Your Bed? Getting Permission to Book." *Annals of Tourism Research* 62: 1–12.

Keen, Peter, Graigg Ballance, Sally Chan, and Steve Schrump. 1999. *Electronic Commerce Relationships: Trust by Design.* Upper Saddle River, NJ: Prentice Hall PTR.

Koopman, Christopher, Matthew Mitchell, and Adam Thierer. 2014. "The Sharing Economy and Consumer Protection Regulation: The Case for Policy Change." *Journal of Business Entrepreneurship & Law* 8 (2): 529–545.

Koroleva, Ksenia, Franziska Brecht, Luise Goebel, and Monika Malinova. 2011. "'Generation Facebook'—A Cognitive Calculus Model of Teenage User Behavior on Social Network Sites." *AMCIS 2011 Proceedings*, Detroit, USA, pp. 1–8.

Krasnova, Hanna, Natasha F. Veltri, and Oliver Günther. 2012. "Self-Disclosure and Privacy Calculus on Social Networking Sites: The Role of Culture Intercultural Dynamics of Privacy Calculus." *Business and Information Systems Engineering* 4 (3): 127–135.

Kulp, Heather Scheiwe, and Amanda L. Kool. 2015. "You Help Me, He Helps You: Dispute Systems Design in the Sharing Economy." Washington University Working Paper.

Lamberton, Cait Poynor, and Randall L. Rose. 2012. "When Is Ours Better Than Mine? A Framework for Understanding and Altering Participation in Commercial Sharing Systems." *Journal of Marketing* 76 (4): 109–125.

Lee, Younghwa, Kenneth A. Kozar, and Kai R. Larsen. 2009. "Avatar E-Mail versus Traditional E-Mail: Perceptual Difference and Media Selection Difference." *Decision Support Systems* 46 (2): 451–467.

Leismann, Kristin, Martina Schmitt, Holger Rohn, and Carolin Baedeker. 2013. "Collaborative Consumption: Towards a Resource-Saving Consumption Culture." *Resources* 2 (3): 184–203.

Ma, Xiao, Jeffrey T. Hancock, Kenneth Lim Mingjie, and Mor Naaman. 2017. "Self-Disclosure and Perceived Trustworthiness of Airbnb Host Profiles." *CSCW'17 Proceedings*, Portland, USA, pp. 1–13.

Malhotra, Arvind, and Marshall Van Alstyne. 2014. "The Dark Side of the Sharing Economy . . . and How to Lighten It." *Communications of the ACM* 57 (11): 24–27.

Matzner, Martin, Friedrich Chasin, and Lydia Todenhöfer. 2015. "To Share or Not to Share—Towards Understanding the Antecedents of Participation in IT-Enabled Sharing Services." *ECIS 2015 Proceedings*, Münster, Germany, pp. 1–13.

McAllister, Daniel J. 1995. "Affect- and Cognition-Based Trust as Foundations for Interpersonal Cooperation in Organizations." *The Academy of Management Journal* 38 (1): 24–59.

Mitrou, Lilian, Miltiadis Kandias, Vasilis Stavrou, and Dimitris Gritzalis. 2014. "Social Media Profiling: A Panopticon or Omniopticon Tool?" *Proceedings of the 6th Conference of the Surveillance Studies Network*, Barcelona, Spain, pp. 1–15.

Möhlmann, Mareike. 2015. "Collaborative Consumption: Determinants of Satisfaction and the Likelihood of Using a Sharing Economy Option Again." *Journal of Consumer Behaviour* 14 (3): 193–207.

Morozov, Evgeny. 2012. *The Net Delusion: The Dark Side of Internet Freedom*. New York City: PublicAffairs.

Morozov, Evgeny. 2013. "The 'Sharing Economy' Undermines Workers' Rights." *The Financial Times*. http://www.ft.com/cms/s/0/92c3021c-34c2-11e3-8148-00144feab7de.html#axzz428H0hF00.

Mullins, John. 2014. *The Customer-Funded Business: Start, Finance, or Grow Your Company with Your Customers' Cash*. Hoboken, NJ: John Wiley & Sons.

Mulshine, Molly. 2015. "After a Disappointing Airbnb Stay, I Realized There's a Major Flaw in the Review System." *Business Insider*. http://www.businessinsider.com/why-airbnb-reviews-are-a-problem-for-the-site-2015-6.

Nowak, Kristine L., and Frank Biocca. 2003. "The Effect of the Agency and Anthropomorphism on Users' Sense of Telepresence, Copresence, and Social Presence in Virtual Environments." *Presence: Teleoperators and Virtual Environments* 12 (5): 481–494.

Ozanne, Lucie K., and Paul W. Ballantine. 2010. "Sharing as a Form of Anti-Consumption? An Examination of Toy Library Users." *Journal of Consumer Behaviour* 9 (6): 485–498.

Pavlou, Paul A. 2011. "State of the Information Privacy Literature: Where Are We Now and Where Should We Go?" *MIS Quarterly* 35 (4): 977–988.

Plonka, Maciej, and Justyna Janik. 2013. "Context Matters." *Boxes and Arrows*. http://boxesandarrows.com/context-matters.

Pursell, Weimer. 1943. "When You Ride Alone You Ride with Hitler! Join a Car-Sharing Club TODAY!" Government Printing Office for the Office of Price Administration. https://de.wikipedia.org/wiki/Datei:Ride_with_hitler.jpg.

PwC. 2015. "The Sharing Economy—Consumer Intelligence Series." Price water house Coopers.

Qiu, Lingyun, and Izak Benbasat. 2005. "Online Consumer Trust and Live Help Interfaces: The Effects of Text-to-Speech Voice and Three-Dimensional Avatars." *International Journal of Human-Computer Interaction* 19 (1): 75–94.

Resnick, Paul, Ko Kuwabara, Richard Zeckhauser, and Eric Friedman. 2000. "Reputation Systems." *Communications of the ACM* 43 (12): 45–48.

Rifkin, Jeremy. 2014. *The Zero Marginal Cost Society: The Internet of Things, the Collaborative Commons, and the Eclipse of Capitalism.* London: Palgrave Macmillan.

Rochet, Jean-Charles, and Jean Tirole. 2003. "Platform Competition in Two-Sided Markets." *Journal of the European Economic Association* 1 (4): 990–1029.

Rochet, Jean-Charles, and Jean Tirole. 2004. "Two-Sided Markets: An Overview." Working Paper.

Rysman, Marc. 2009. "The Economics of Two-Sided Markets." *The Journal of Economic Perspectives* 23 (3): 125–143.

Sahlins, Marshall David. 1974. *Stone Age Economics,* volume 130. Piscataway, NJ: Transaction Publishers.

Shaheen, Susan A., and Adam P. Cohen. 2013. "Carsharing and Personal Vehicle Services: Worldwide Market Developments and Emerging Trends." *International Journal of Sustainable Transportation* 7 (1): 5–34.

Shaheen, Susan A., Mark A. Mallery, and Karla J. Kingsley. 2012. "Personal Vehicle Sharing Services in North America." *Research in Transportation Business and Management* 3: 71–81.

Short, John, Ederyn Williams, and Bruce Christie. 1976. *The Social Psychology of Telecommunications.* London: John Wiley & Sons Ltd.

Slater, Mel, and Anthony Steed. 2002. "Meeting People Virtually: Experiments in Shared Virtual Environments." In Ralph Schroeder, ed. *The Social Life of Avatars.* 146–171. London: Springer.

Slee, Tom. 2013. "Some Obvious Things about Internet Reputation Systems." Working Paper, 1–13.

Slee, Tom. 2016. *What's Yours Is Mine: Against the Sharing Economy.* London; New York: OR Books.

Stephany, Alex. 2015. *The Business of Sharing: Making It in the New Sharing Economy.* London: Palgrave Macmillan.

Storey, Simon, and Lance Workman. 2013. "The Effects of Temperature Priming on Cooperation in the Iterated Prisoner's Dilemma." *Evolutionary Psychology* 11 (1): 52–67.

Strader, Troy J., and Sridhar N. Ramaswami. 2002. "The Value of Seller Trustworthiness in C_2C Online Markets." *Communications of the ACM* 45 (12): 45–49.

Sundararajan, Arun. 2012. "Why the Government Doesn't Need to Regulate the Sharing Economy." *Wired.* http://www.wired.com/2012/10/from-airbnb-to-coursera-why-the-government-shouldnt-regulate-the-sharing-economy.

Sundararajan, Arun. 2014. "Peer-to-Peer Businesses and the Sharing (Collaborative) Economy: Overview, Economic Effects and Regulatory Issues." https://pdfs. semanticscholar.org/5898/c40a1b56bc38a91cd16b506c8d3475e2acea.pdf.

Sundararajan, Arun. 2016. *The Sharing Economy: The End of Employment and the Rise of Crowd-Based Capitalism.* Cambridge, MA: MIT Press.

Tamjidyamcholo, Alireza, Mohd Sapiyan Bin Baba, Hamed Tamjid, and Rahmatollah Gholipour. 2013. "Information Security—Professional Perceptions of Knowledge-Sharing Intention under Self-Efficacy, Trust, Reciprocity, and Shared-Language." *Computers and Education* 68: 223–232.

Teubner, Timm. 2014. "Thoughts on the Sharing Economy." *Proceedings of the International Conference on E-Commerce*, Lisbon, Portugal, pp. 322–326.

Teubner, Timm, Marc T. P. Adam, Sonia Camacho, and Khaled Hassanein. 2014. "Understanding Resource Sharing in C_2C Platforms: The Role of Picture Humanization." *ACIS 2014 Proceedings*, Auckland, New Zealand, pp. 1–10.

Teubner, Timm, Marc T. P. Adam, and Ryan Riordan. 2015. "The Impact of Computerized Agents on Immediate Emotions, Overall Arousal and Bidding Behavior in Electronic Auctions." *Journal of the Association for Information Systems* 16 (10): 838–879.

Teubner, Timm, and Christoph M. Flath. 2015. "The Economics of Multi-Hop Ride Sharing: Creating New Mobility Networks through IS." *Business and Information Systems Engineering* 57 (5): 311–324.

Teubner, Timm, and Christoph M. Flath. 2016. "Privacy in the Sharing Economy." Working Paper.

Teubner, Timm, Florian Hawlitschek, Marc T. P. Adam, and Christof Weinhardt. 2013. "Social Identity and Reciprocity in Online Gift Giving Networks." *HICSS 2013 Proceedings,* Wailea, USA, pp. 708–717.

Teubner, Timm, Norman Saade, Florian Hawlitschek, and Christof Weinhardt. 2016. "It's Only Pixels, Badges, and Stars: On the Economic Value of Reputation on Airbnb." *ACIS 2016 Proceedings*, Wollongong, Australia, pp. 1–11.

Tong, Frank, Ken Nakayama, Morris Moscovitch, Oren Weinrib, and Nancy Kanwisher. 2000. "Response Properties of the Human Fusiform Face Area." *Cognitive Neuropsychology* 17 (1–3): 257–280.

Tong, Stephanie Tom, Brandon Van Der Heide, Lindsey Langwell, and Joseph B. Walther. 2008. "Too Much of a Good Thing? The Relationship between Number of Friends and Interpersonal Impressions on Facebook." *Journal of Computer-Mediated Communication* 13 (3): 531–549.

Torregrossa, Marco. 2014. "The 'Crazy' Sharing Economy." http://de.slideshare. net/speed101/marco-torregrossasharingeconomyrotarybxl.

Tussyadiah, Iis P. 2015. "An Exploratory Study on Drivers and Deterrents of Collaborative Consumption in Travel." In *Information and Communication Technologies in Tourism*, edited by Iis Tussyadiah and Alessandro Inversini. 817–830. New York: Springer.

Tussyadiah, Iis P. 2016. "Factors of Satisfaction and Intention to Use Peer-to-Peer Accommodation." *International Journal of Hospitality Management* 55: 70–80.

Tussyadiah, Iis P., and Juho Pesonen. 2016. "Drivers and Barriers of Peer-to-Peer Accommodation Stay—An Exploratory Study with American and Finnish Travellers." *Current Issues in Tourism,* 1–18. http://www.tandfonline.com/doi/abs/10.1080/13683500.2016.1141180.

Ufford, Stephen. 2015. "The Future of the Sharing Economy Depends on Trust." *Forbes.* http://www.forbes.com/sites/theyec/2015/02/10/the-future-of-the-sharing-economy-depends-on-trust/#738f80b258ff.

Voigt, Sebastian, and Oliver Hinz. 2015. "Network Effects in Two-Sided Markets: Why a 50/50 User Split Is Not Necessarily Revenue Optimal." *Business Research* 8 (1): 139–170.

Wang, Sheng, and Raymond A. Noe. 2010. "Knowledge Sharing: A Review and Directions for Future Research." *Human Resource Management Review* 20 (2): 115–131.

Warren, Samuel D., and Louis D. Brandeis. 1890. "The Right to Privacy." *Harvard Law Review* 4 (5): 193–220.

Westin, Alan F. 1967. *Privacy and Freedom.* New York: Atheneum.

Williams, Lawrence E., and John A. Bargh. 2008. "Experiencing Physical Warmth Promotes Interpersonal Warmth." *Science* 322 (5901): 606–607.

Zervas, Georgios, Davide Proserpio, and John Byers. 2015. "A First Look at Online Reputation on Airbnb, Where Every Stay Is above Average." SSRN Working Paper 2554500.

PART 3

Collaborative Consumption: Peer-to-Peer Engagements in the Sharing Economy

The Rise and Fall of Peer-to-Peer Collaborative Consumption: A Perspective from Two Types of Collaborative Consumption Practices

Heather E. Philip, Lucie K. Ozanne,
and Paul W. Ballantine

Introduction

Six years ago, Rachel Botsman (2010) stood on the TEDxSydney stage and pointed out the wastefulness of owning a power drill. Saying it would only be used for 12–13 minutes in its entire lifetime, she asked the audience, "Why don't you rent the drill, or even better, rent out your own drill to other people and make money from it?" (10:30). Botsman's speech created a worldwide phenomenon of what Botsman and Rogers (2010, xiii) called "collaborative consumption" (CC), or "an unbounded marketplace for efficient peer-to-peer exchanges."

Recent research suggests that CC is primarily a technologically enabled phenomenon motivated by enjoyment of the activity, economic gain, and concern for environmental sustainability (Hamari, Sjöklint, and Ukkonen 2015). Looking at it broadly as a technological phenomenon, we define CC as the act and process of private individuals (i.e., peers) *providing* to others, and/or the act and process of *taking* something from other private individuals, as facilitated by an online network. These disposition and acquisition activities rest on a continuum of transfer durations, where individuals can provide their goods temporarily or permanently. Mechanisms for the exchange can also fall on a continuum of market-based mechanisms in which individuals provide to others for free, or for other goods or services, or for money. The latter two options are usually denoted as market-based exchanges, whereas the first is nonmarket-based.

The research in this chapter focuses on two CC types: peer-to-peer (P2P) renting and P2P swapping. These types were chosen because they have been sparingly explored in the literature as compared to more mainstream examples (e.g., Airbnb, Spinlister, Freecycle, and Uber) and because both practices can disrupt traditional forms of ownership (Nissanoff 2007).

The Emergence of Collaborative Consumption

In 2012, Sagar suggested that "globally there are 161 resource sharing partners (businesses) with a reach of over 60 million people in 147 countries" (2012, no pagination). Botsman and Rogers (2010) argued that four main drivers contribute to the expansion of second-hand exchange between peers: (1) cost consciousness and thrift leading to a wave of entrepreneurial and cost-saving activity, (2) waste aversion leading to increased concerns for the environment, (3) P2P technologies making it easier to connect and build trust with strangers, and (4) community values becoming more salient.

While Botsman and Roger's (2010) vision initiated interest and excitement leading to CC website development, many recent articles point to the fall of CC (Kessler 2015). For instance, a recent practitioner article suggested that developing successful CC businesses is difficult, as they "face a unique set of challenges . . . that in many ways represents a whole new era of doing business" (Anderson 2014, no pagination). In this review of 45 CC start-ups that have closed or experienced significant setbacks, Anderson (2014) suggests that the top five failure characteristics include lack of scale (or an inability to gain critical mass in both supply and demand), unclear value proposition, lack of product focus, insufficient funding, and regulatory challenges (Anderson 2014). Others have also suggested that a lack of

Table 8.1 Factors Contributing to the Rise and Fall of CC Websites

Motivating Factors—"The Rise of CC"	Inhibiting Factors—"The Fall of CC"
Cost consciousness	Lack of critical mass
Consumer empowerment	Lack of trust
Political concerns for environment/society	Lack of product focus
Community engagement	Unclear value proposition
Ability to build online trust	Not worth the effort
Enjoyment of the activity	Insufficient funding

specific product focus can hamper the success of CC businesses (Schwartz 2013). For instance, Makkonen (2014) suggests that many online P2P marketplaces struggle because they are not solving a real consumer problem, lack a specific product focus, and fail to raise sufficient venture capital. As Anderson (2014) explains, many start-ups in this space fail to clearly articulate and reinforce the necessity or need for their service. A survey of 383 participants (Campbell Mithun 2012) found that a lack of "value" ("not worth the effort"), followed by lack of trust, was one of the most significant barriers to participation. Reflecting on the suggestions posed in the literature, Table 8.1 provides a summary of the factors contributing to the growth and potential decline in CC.

P2P Online Renting

We define P2P renting as individual *providers* renting their items for an agreed rental fee and specified time period to rental *takers*.[1] P2P online renting allows private individuals to engage in the temporary disposition or acquisition of everyday items with peers via an online rental network (Philip, Ozanne, and Ballantine 2015). With the majority of research focusing on permanent disposition (Albinsson and Perera 2012), temporary disposition is often an overlooked aspect of consumer behavior. As argued by Sheth and Uslay (2007, 303), "The value creation paradigm encourages marketers to think of other types of value by reaching beyond value in exchange and even in use. For example, the long-neglected value in disposal." As research indicates that consumers rarely consider renting out or loaning their belongings compared to more permanent disposal options (Jacoby, Berning, and Dietvorst 1977), it is not surprising that temporary disposition has not been the focus of study. In addition, renters have often been perceived as flawed consumers (Cheshire, Walters, and Rosenblatt 2010).

Temporary acquisition is also an understudied topic in the literature compared to traditional ownership, but its occurrence surpasses that of temporary disposition because the act of renting and leasing is not as foreign to consumers as the idea of providing items to rent. Previous research has therefore explored various forms of commercial renting, where consumers rent from organizations. Durgee and O'Connor (1995) argue that the person–object relationship is altered when the object is rented. Their findings indicate that the behavior is a high-involvement transaction with low post-purchase dissonance and that it is preferred when the need is temporary. In addition, renting is an attractive option as renters exact greater wear and tear on rental goods.

In exploring consumer preference for renting, Moeller and Wittkowski (2010) find that non-ownership is negatively influenced by possession importance but positively influenced by consumers' trend and convenience orientation. In their study, consumer preference for renting also did not appear to be motivated by price consciousness or environmentalism. Contrary to these findings, Lawson (2011) reported that consumers' attitude toward renting was motivated by value seeking and environmentalism. In an examination of automobile leasing, Trocchia and Beatty (2003) find that desire for variety, simplified maintenance, and social approval motivate this behavior. Mont (2008) found that renting provides users access to higher-quality products as well as more object diversity. Finally, a survey of Ecomodo users (P2P renting website) found that 19% were mainly motivated to join to get more out of the things they own (Piscielli, Cooper, and Fisher 2015).

P2P Online Swapping

P2P online swapping is a type of redistribution market that allows consumers to engage in "the continuous replacement of our personal possessions" through collaboration with other consumers (Nissanoff 2007, 7). We define P2P online swapping as an exchange, mediated by technology, whereby one individual trades his or her physical possessions for the physical possessions of another individual. Swapping has usually been examined under the term "bartering," a moneyless market exchange (Dalton 1982). Unlike monetary exchange, where one of the traded objects (money) has no intrinsic value but is predetermined by a governmental authority as legal tender (Simmel 1978), the bartering economy involves exchange determined by a trader's interest in an object, where the traded object's value is incomparable and instead requires a "double coincidence of wants" (Jevons 1875). For example, a prospective provider of a drill who seeks a ladder needs to find not only a provider with a spare ladder but one who is also seeking a drill at that exact time. For this reason, direct bartering (Oh 1989; Rice 2003) is associated with inefficiency (e.g., Banerjee and Maskin 1996) as finding the needed trader and coming to an agreed-upon exchange can be difficult.

With online broker networks, potential barter customers are able to make their products and wants available across a greater number of interested parties by reducing the social and geographical distance between peers, thus facilitating the growth in barter trade (e.g., Rice 2003). However, as economic theory assumes consumers would rather trade for cash than for goods (Magenheim and Murrell 1988), swapping disposition, dismissed as unstructured and insignificant to the economy (e.g., Dalton 1982; Marvasti and Smyth 1998), has failed to be a central focus of consumer studies. Further, C2C bartering has often been seen as a recreational activity for hobbyists (e.g., trading collectibles such as beanie babies or Pokémon cards) rather than an alternative for traditional consumer acquisition or redistribution (Jowanza 2011).

In the past few years, however, studies of swapping between individual peers have been slowly appearing in the literature. For example, researchers have examined online bartering motivations (Lee, Chen, and Hung 2014), motivations for swapping clothing (Matthews and Hodge 2014), reciprocity within barter markets (Ye 2013), and online barter markets for books (Ye, Viswanathan, and Hann 2016). The coverage on this behavior still remains under-investigated in the literature. Further, researchers have ignored organically formed second-hand networks on P2P-created websites (e.g., Pinterest, Reddit, and Facebook) (Toivanen 2015), which is surprising given the vast number of online pages devoted to swapping exchange.

Research Questions

We examine these practices guided by two research questions: (1) What is the nature of the consumer experience derived from online P2P swapping and renting? and (2) What enabling factors may make these systems more effective and appealing? These questions were explored through in-depth online interviews with participants in these two online practices. In addition, we tracked businesses that facilitate these behaviors over a four-year period to better understand the factors that led to their success or failure. In the subsequent section, we begin with a discussion of our methods followed by our findings. Consistent with ethnographic research, the discussion of relevant literature is integrated with the findings.

Methods

As we were interested in the experiences of online P2P swapping and renting users in order to determine the factors that would impact participation in such practices, we were interested in interviewing anyone who had signed up on a P2P swapping or renting website. Purposive sampling was used in order to get a representative overview of three types of users: two-way users (takers and providers), one-way users (takers or providers), and nonusers (those who had not yet participated in a transaction but were members of a P2P rental or swapping website).

Due to the "grassroots" growing nature of these websites, some respondents were connected to the websites' business (e.g., interns, founders), but they also participated as users. These key informants were included in the chosen sample in order to provide a more in-depth understanding of an otherwise-underexplored practice, as the literature suggests they are more knowledgeable about target market behavior (Kumar, Stern, and Anderson 1993).

Data collection occurred from 2011 to 2014. Participants were directly recruited from swapping and renting websites using instant messaging, comment features, and community forums. Respondents from North America, Australia, New Zealand, and the United Kingdom were given a US$25 gift card (of their choice converted to the local currency) for their time. Users were interviewed over Skype using a semi-structured guide that asked about their motivations, experiences, and assumptions of the websites they were signed up to; interviews ranged between 30 and 120 minutes. The final transcripts (246 pages for swapping and 333 pages for renting) were subjected to data-driven thematic analysis (Braun and Clarke 2006) whereby common themes were identified by recurrence, forcefulness, and repetition (Keyton 2011; Owen 1984). Renting and swapping data was first analyzed separately and then mixed for a third round of theoretically driven comparison of motivations and challenges. Extant literature was also integrated into the findings as theoretical inspiration and to provide clarification.

In addition, in order to better understand the factors leading to the success/failure of online P2P renting and swapping businesses, 87 such businesses were tracked from 2011 to 2015. From an examination of their websites, we were able to categorize businesses based on a number of factors that were relevant for the study at hand, including renting or swapping, general or specific product category, type of governance, presence of a participant forum, and costs to users. Some of these factors were also rated on a five-item scale (Minimal, Poor, Sufficient, Good, and Excellent) based on whether the information was updated, was used by participants, was easy to understand, and/or had multiple features available. When this information was not easily available, the company was contacted to clarify and provide more complete information. As we conducted this process in 2011 and 2015, we were able to determine which businesses were still in operation, which had closed down or had no activity, and which had rebranded or changed the nature of their operations (e.g., shifting focus from P2P to B2C). Thus, we have data to provide clarity on the success of online P2P swapping and renting businesses both from tracking their businesses over time and from the perspective of users of their sites.

In our findings, we first discuss the nature of existing CC websites with our examination of P2P swapping and renting websites. We then discuss the experience described by swapping and renting participants from our qualitative interviews.

Findings

P2P Online Businesses

Of the 87 businesses we tracked, 62 were P2P renting websites and 25 were swapping websites. Most renting websites (62.9%) were broadly focused and allowed all types of products to be rented. However, since 2011 there has been an emergence of more focused rental websites promoting rental of specific products. Overall, renting websites were more likely to have a general product focus that allows all types of products to be rented, 62.9%, compared to swapping sites, 16%. In fact, the vast majority of swapping sites had a specific product focus (e.g., books, baby goods and toys, clothing, and media), 84%, compared to 35.5% for renting sites.

Over the four-year tracking period, a large number of both renting and swapping websites, 24% and 32%, respectively, ceased operation. In addition, 12.9% of renting websites were either acquired by other companies or rebranded. For the renting websites, those with a general product focus were more likely to have shut down in this time period, 80% compared to only 20% for those that had a specific product focus. Although a larger percentage of swapping websites that have shut down had a specific product focus, 62.5%, compared to 37.5% of those that have shut down with a general focus, only four of the swapping websites had a general product focus, and three of those have shut down, or 75%.

The vast majority of both renting and swapping websites had a governance policy (98.4% and 100%, respectively), which emphasized trust between users and clearly explained solutions for when something went wrong (e.g., swaplift, broken items). Also, a very large majority of the websites had a high level of user profile functionality, 96.8% and 92%, respectively. However, 64.5% of renting and 16% of swapping websites provided no user forums. With all websites, responsibilities for object curation fell on providers as they were expected to list descriptions of their items for prospective takers. Some websites offered a feature for would-be renters to post a request for items that they were interested in renting; however, at least 37% did not offer this option. We found 3% of websites also offered an option to post items to rent so that the fees would go to a chosen charity.

Shortly after finishing our qualitative data collection, we noticed a dramatic drop in active CC websites. By 2015, all eight of the rental websites and three of the six swapping websites from where respondents were interviewed shut down and/or were no longer active.

In addition to websites devoted to P2P renting, we found a few (less than 20) Facebook pages and online forums (e.g., Reddit) devoted to the facilitation of P2P renting between users. However, these did not appear to be heavily used. In contrast, we found over 100 actively used cases of Reddit, Facebook, and Pinterest pages as well as online forums fostering swapping of collectibles such as miniatures, games, music, movies, stamps, and postcards, as well as fashion items such as clothing, shoes, makeup, and nail polish.

P2P Online Participants

The final sample of 19 rental users came from 8 P2P renting websites. It was evenly split with 10 females and 9 males, and included an assortment of 13 ordinary informants (regular to irregular users and nonusers) and 6 key informants (3 founders and 3 interns). The final sample of 12 swapping users came from 6 swapping websites, had 11 females and 1 male, and included an assortment of 11 ordinary informants (regular to irregular users and nonusers) and 1 key informant (a moderator of the website). Using thematic analysis, we present our findings of the main motivating and challenging factors affecting involvement in swapping and renting websites as discussed by users.

Motivating Factors of Online P2P Swapping and Renting Involvement

Consumer Empowerment—"It Just Makes Sense"

Participants felt empowered by CC websites due to a number of benefits, which included economic cost and entrepreneurial considerations, reduction in the burdens and stress of access, ownership, and disposition. Respondents often echoed the phrase "it just makes sense" when describing their pragmatic desire to find more valuable and effective consumption alternatives.

Providers believed swapping and renting modes of disposition offered a viable way to capture their object's "redemption value"—the residual utility gained from disposition (Parasuraman and Grewal 2000). For example, Amanda liked swapping as opposed to selling second-hand because it felt like her "things [were] actually worth something instead of before when [she] didn't think they were worth anything," calling it "a new form of currency." Likewise, rental providers said they were able to get a lot more back for their item than if they had tried to sell it. For example, two-way rental user Charlotte said she successfully rented out her iPad for $30. Because this was only temporary, she could theoretically repeat the exchange and make far more than from selling it.

For acquisition, many takers were motivated to avoid the burdens of ownership (Moeller and Wittkowski 2010), such as the dissonance that might arise out of more permanent and traditional forms of acquisition (e.g., Denegri-Knott and Molesworth 2009a). Swapping and renting acquisition enabled takers to engage in product trial before committing to a high-involvement purchase (e.g., Lawson 2011; Ozanne and Ozanne 2011). For example, rental takers appreciated being able to use an iPad to test out its functionality, read an expensive textbook before deciding if it was worth the shelf space, and discover what to look for when buying a high-powered vacuum. These examples support Durgee and O'Connor's (1995) proposition that renting inspires consumer product exploration, Ozanne and Ozanne's (2011, 270) findings that patrons in toy libraries "could engage in limited trial of toys to determine if the toys were developmentally appropriate," and Lawson's (2011) discovery that renting before buying reduced dissonance avoidance for users of car-renting schemes.

Swapping was also seen as less stressful because takers could easily re-swap an item if they felt they made the wrong choice. For example, Joanna said she could easily "re-post it and re-trade it if it doesn't work out; you're not stuck with it," while Natalia said as someone who was unsure what "staples" or "favorites" to buy could inexpensively try out various cosmetic brands through swapping. This increased bravery "to try new styles and experiment more" was also found to be a motivating factor in recent research on clothes swapping and clothing libraries (Grimshorn and Jordan 2015, 40). Using swapping and renting to acquire objects thus empowered users to find ways of reducing traditional costs of acquisition, usage, and future disposition.

Political Concerns for Environment/Society—"A More Responsible Way to Live"

Botsman and Rogers (2010) argued that environmental concerns have become increasingly salient in consumer decision-making choices (e.g., Heinrichs 2013; Leonard 2010; Martenson 2011). Although this CC driver was also heavily discussed by respondents, our respondents showed a more passive concern about the environment and saw reduced waste as "an added bonus" to CC involvement.

Using the three Rs (Reduce, Reuse, Recycle), we found swapping respondents were mostly motivated to "Reuse" and "Recycle" through ethical *disposition* (i.e., providers, as simultaneous takers, perceived swapping disposition as environment-friendly compared to other types of disposition). For example, many respondents perceived swapping to be a more *environmentally* sustainable option than other disposition practices because as Kelly put it, "I'm at least helping not lead to so much waste," and Rose thought swapping was "a really cool concept" because instead of "wasting items," swapping involved "reusing items . . . and saving the environment."

Meanwhile, rental respondents were more motivated to "reduce" through ethical *acquisition* (i.e., rental takers perceived renting as more environment-friendly than buying something that wouldn't be used, while rental providers perceived their items being shared as helping prevent people from buying something new). For example, Earl, as a rental Taker, saw temporary access as "a more responsible way to live," while Desired Rental Taker, Anita, stressed that renting minimized "production in the embodied energy and carbon and all that sort of business," and "if people can share their things, then it should reduce the cost of manufacturing, and the cost to the planet."

Community Engagement—"I Think Just Meeting People Is a Healthy Thing to Do"

When discussing their favorite aspect of renting and swapping, many respondents pointed to their ability to build interpersonal connections. Rental respondents, who found themselves in an isolated social situation, appreciated face-to-face interaction with people in their community. For example, Leigh, a commuter who did not meet many people at university, found that renting her textbook out allowed her to meet someone new on campus. Swapping respondents also spoke of getting to interact with like-minded people. Amanda, for instance, stated she "really like[d] chatting with the girls there," and Joanna shared stories of her friendships with a select few people with whom she had "several successful swaps."

In addition, renting and swapping provided an outlet for generalized reciprocity and altruistic behavior, as many providers said they felt *altruistically gratified* to share their things which might be of high value to other people. This gratification was often increased by websites with low spatial and interpersonal anonymity, as many respondents appreciated the friendships and social contact they had gained through their participation. For example, Kelly echoed many respondents when she explained how swapping was more gratifying than other disposition options because she could "know where it's going."

Community engagement was also beneficial for acquisition, as many swapping takers appreciated that their formation of swapping friends often came with added extras, such as freebies, and a better experience through learning more about the product. Meanwhile, rental takers appreciated meeting their neighbors and talking about the rental object with an individual Provider. Bailey, a rental Taker, recalled traveling out of her usual route to rent an item from someone and recounted her appreciation about gaining personal insight into a new area.

These examples of users benefiting by making social connections are similar to the findings of Ozanne and Ballantine (2010) and Ozanne and Ozanne (2011), who found that families felt supported by other toy library members, and van de Glind's (2013) finding that CC websites can help those who have moved to a new city. Thus, the desire for community and social interaction within P2P models seemed to deviate from commercial access models, where Bardhi and Eckhardt (2012) found that consumers resisted the efforts of a car-sharing company to build a brand community. Further, the common overlap of swapping and renting respondents seeking interpersonal connections between users, and stories about objects, supports Appelgren and Bohlin's (2015, 152) claim that although different in character, various forms of second-hand exchange typically involve exchange that is "often richly socially embedded, involving verbal or written exchanges regarding the quality and history of the thing being sold, sometimes involving personal anecdotes as well as meetings between" Taker and Provider.

Ability to Build Online Trust—"You Can Learn How to Trust People"

Botsman and Rogers's suggestion that open governance features allow strangers to connect online and build trust was also agreed upon by many rental respondents, as none of them expressed concerns for betrayal aversion (e.g., Bohnet, Herrmann, and Zeckhauser 2010; Fehr and Fischbacher 2003) or being cheated by others. This may be because no rental respondents had heard or experienced first-hand negative reciprocity occurring in P2P renting.

Alternatively, many swapping respondents *had* heard about others being wronged and/or had been *personally* swaplifted and indicated a cautious distrust of other users. Their accounts echoed Natalia's belief that "when you swap with a stranger . . . you don't actually know that you will get something in return." Previous research has shown that people are less willing to trust after being exposed to unsuccessful interactions (e.g., Brehm and Rahn 1997), so this may be a reason why swapping respondents were more often concerned with being cheated than rental respondents.

However, almost all of the swapping respondents who had been swaplifted or betrayed still perceived their overall experiences as successful. This propensity to overlook tragedies of the swapping commons may be because most swapping users had repeat transactions with the same people (compared to P2P renting where a transaction was more often one-off and infrequent). Also, because interactions were more enduring, Corrine mirrored many respondents when she explained her aversion to leaving things on a negative note (in case of future interactions and swaps), saying, "We kept like messaging back and forth and we changed our negative [feedback] that we gave each other to positive tokens because we worked through it."

We now turn to the main challenges that impeded respondents from getting involved with P2P swapping and renting websites.

Challenges of Swapping and Renting Involvement

Lack of Sufficient Network Externalities—"I Can't Find What I'm Looking For" and Leaky User Retention—"Why Should I Jump through All the Hoops on the Site When I Can Do It Myself?"

For renting, as many authors discussed (Botsman and Rogers 2010; Makkonen 2014; Schwartz 2013), our interviews suggested that the ideal critical mass had never occurred because insufficient network externalities (e.g., Song and Walden 2007) often impeded users' participation. Rental users were particularly constrained; as aspiring rental providers complained that no one had yet requested their items, would-be rental takers were disappointed by the site's limited number of items available to rent nearby. As rental intern Leigh explains, "As long as people go to the website and don't find what they're looking for, then they're less inclined to add their items to the website, so it's kind of like a vicious cycle where the website comes to a standstill and stays that way as long as people aren't getting what they need from the site." Indeed, Leigh's comments were not inaccurate, as Murphy and Liao (2013) studied the motivations for reselling on eBay and found the "market efficiency" of high network externalities to be a major factor for choosing to sell online.

On the other hand, most swapping respondents were satisfied with the amount of listed objects and active exchange partners. However, due to the interpersonal closeness of swapping causing many people to accumulate swapping connections, a few respondents stopped using the website (to avoid hassle and/or fees) and contacted each other directly. For example, Kelly (as a swapping key informant) revealed in follow-up correspondence that she had stopped using the swapping websites and started a Facebook group with her favorite swapping users. Meanwhile, rental key informant Tara echoed the concerns of rental founders Lynne and Wade when she explained that her website's newsletters included want ads and contact information, which sometimes led some users to avoid the system. Thus, instances of "leaky user retention" were a challenge to the success of CC websites.

Risks of Usage—"What If . . .?"

Although users were satisfied with the current status quo for building trust, many were still concerned about risk (i.e., they feared having something go wrong out of bad luck or unforeseen circumstances). Providers were ultimately concerned about two types of risks: (1) individual risk—a fear of being cheated or wronged, such as a concern for the hidden action on the part of the Taker; and (2) social guilt risk—a fear of accidentally cheating the other exchange partner. For *individual risk*, swapping providers were mainly concerned with the potential theft of their object, while rental providers were concerned their object could be damaged or lost.

Meanwhile, *social guilt risk* was more prevalent for swapping providers who were concerned they would make a mistake with *object curation* (e.g., not disclosing faults with the object). Although rental providers also did not want to be seen making a mistake, this was not a common topic of concern for respondents—perhaps because they were providing something for temporary use and they felt mistakes could be rectified easily throughout the many interaction points between the Provider and Taker.

Individual risk occurred mostly for swapping takers, who were mainly concerned that the object had not been properly described. While most rental takers did not express any types of individual risks, there were cases where the rental takers said they were taking a risk that the Provider might back out of the exchange at the last minute and affect their plans.

Social guilt risk was more prevalent for rental takers who were concerned they could accidentally damage the Providers' item. Meanwhile, swapping takers also discussed a minor consideration for making the providers feel guilty if they did not appreciate their acquired object. For example, many swapping takers said they would wait awhile before re-swapping an unwanted item because they didn't want to hurt the Providers' feelings.

Responsibilities of Participation—"It's Too Much to Handle"

CC can be characterized as a self-service model of cocreation (e.g., Vargo and Lusch 2004; Zwass 2010) where participants have to actively collaborate in the realization of value in an exchange (Lawson 2011; Young 2011). Consumers need to conduct various activities to fulfill an exchange "such as searching for information, negotiating terms, and monitoring the on-going process to ensure a favourable deal" (Liang and Huang 1998, 31). Although the Internet has lowered "transaction costs of coordinating groups of people with aligned wants and needs" so that P2P exchange can be less tricky, inconvenient, and inefficient, our findings suggest that the online second-hand world may not always be as "practical, convenient, and worthwhile" as Botsman and Rogers (2010, 126–127) anticipated. Indeed, P2P renting and online swapping were both highly involved CC examples, with both providers and takers holding extensive responsibilities for cocreation. These responsibilities create challenges for participants and thus reduce their willingness to participate in the behavior.

For instance, providers described needing to create an inventory of objects to post on the website. Objects needed to be branded and curated as something takers would actually want to swap for or rent. This requirement of object curation is perhaps the highest deterrent for CC providers. Joel as a rental Provider suggested that object curation required too much initial investment: "One of the biggest frustrations I had with [the website] was the difficulty in posting stuff online."

Providers also spoke about wanting to make sure their items were in good condition and therefore more likely to be requested by takers. Indeed, almost all swapping and renting providers shared a social expectation of "quality" and "valuable offerings" when it came to worthwhile disposal. For example, rental Provider Anita complained that she "hate[d] selling things (on sites like eBay)" because it required "having to get them into top condition."

Another effort of object curation had to do with the pricing and valuation of items. To complete an object listing, rental providers needed to decide on multiple rental prices (i.e., hourly, daily, weekly, and/or monthly), a deposit price, and length of time available for rent and their preferred times for contact and rental drop-off/pickup. Such decisions were often described as overwhelming—especially when the Provider had no experience with the website, or renting in general. As rental goods were not as common in online markets, a few rental respondents said they felt challenged with trying to determine what price was fair and what was too high, such that takers would still want to rent from them.

Geographic distance between participants further added to the efforts involved in a rental transaction. Joel found that, due to the long distance between people, there was a loss of efficiency when people had to "drive past a hardware store to borrow an electric drill." Perceived inconvenience diminished with the item's worth as many participants stated they perceived P2P renting as being too much of a hassle only for "smaller ticket items." This finding is similar to the research of Denegri-Knott and Molesworth (2009b), who found that a tremendous amount of work, which may not be invested in lower-value items, was required by sellers to dispose of possessions on eBay.

Inflexibility of Online Systems—"Sometimes the Website Gets in the Way"

The websites had various requirements and restrictions for each stage of use, which had implications for how much *flexibility* users were given to cocreate the experience. This ultimately impacted their ability to create an online community. For example, some websites required users to enter a security code which was sent to their mobile phone on sign-up, while others required users to enter at least a paragraph-long description about themselves before sign-up was complete. These requirements of *self-curation* could have been potential barriers if the user had not owned a mobile phone or had not had his or her phone near at that moment. Although requirements of self-curation can mitigate unwanted behaviors, they "can also deter people from joining and inhibit contributions to the community, particularly if there are too many rules and people feel stifled by them" (Preece and Maloney-Krichmar 2003, 615).

Due to the rental websites having low externalities and critical mass, a common topic of conversation with renting respondents was trying to get more inventory onto the site. One solution offered by respondents was to give providers more flexibility with object curation by lessening the initial commitment to post information about their items. Essentially, this resolution pointed to decentralization, where users could build an exchange community to their preferred specifications and not be constrained by the given system's terms and conditions. We found inflexibility with the initial commitment of object curation (e.g., choosing a price/value, choosing a rental period) to be a pervasive deterrent for getting rental providers involved. Meanwhile swapping providers were generally offered more flexibility and less initial commitment with curating their objects (e.g., many respondents said they could put the option to swap *or* sell and they did not have to choose a price/value until *negotiation* was initiated). Furthermore, some swapping respondents said posting items for swap was generally easier than posting on other second-hand disposition websites (e.g., eBay).

Lack of Product Focus—"Weird Random Things" "Too Broad"

CC websites without a clear product focus were especially lambasted by respondents. Although flexibility was often sought as a CC ideal for being able to access and provide more objects, many also cautioned that the website should show a clear value proposition. For example, many swapping providers thought the items they listed for swap should be, as Corrine put it, "acceptable and desirable things" rather than "weird random things" like "Band-Aids" or "USB drives." This expectation to offer desired objects of the community demonstrated how swapping users normalized what types of objects were acceptable to offer (objects that were being requested and posted by others in the community) and what types of objects were unacceptable (i.e., objects that did not match the swapping website's product focus).

Meanwhile, Joel as a Desired Provider complained the rental websites he used had no guidance on what types of objects were in demand to rent so he had no idea what objects to list. Meanwhile, Desired two-way rental user Tim said the rental website's "marketing was just, 'list anything, rent anything,' and that seems too broad," and suggested the website "should have really done a lot of marketing on very specific categories" so "the critical mass would start to realize, and they could then start to realize they could use other things on that site too."

Discussion and Conclusion

Our research suggests a number of difficulties impeding the success of swapping and renting between peers online. Both these practices are part of the technological phenomenon of CC, and therefore, our findings suggest implications for other P2P websites that disrupt traditional ownership and disposition through CC. We therefore suggest managers of such websites consider five Cs as enabling factors for CC (see Table 8.2).

Perhaps the most crucial inhibitors for swapping and renting involvement were low externalities, stagnating trial, and organically created websites causing leaky user retention. Research indicates that many online communities fail because of an insufficient number of active contributors (Yen, Hsu, and Huang 2011). *Contribution* and user participation is, therefore, of critical importance. CC managers should focus on increasing users' perceived usefulness

Table 8.2 The Five Cs to Enable Collaborative Consumption

Contribution	Marketing activities aimed to increase network externalities (i.e., user participation and involvement)
	o Incentivize object curation and self-curation
	o Increase perceived usefulness
	o Promote compatibility with user's situational needs
Cocreation	Website features allowing flexibility to explore and cocreate the usage experience
	o Less initial commitment to participate
	o Allow market-driven interaction to mitigate leaky user retention
Confidence	Marketing activities and website features that give confidence to users
	o Safety mechanisms to reduce risk of renting (e.g., deposits, insurance, and escrows) and swapping (e.g., website moderators, satisfaction guarantees)
	o Product/user/system branding and curation
	o Open governance features to build and maintain trust
Convenience	Services offered to increase fluidity of use (i.e., reduce transaction costs for providers and takers)
	o Third-party services and storage
	o Less clicks, more automatic interaction, guided involvement
Community	Marketing strategies aimed to bring users together with shared interests
	o Create groups of similar interest to increase commitment to community
	o Focused/shared product category spaces
	o Charity and fundraising options
	o Gamification for reputation seekers

Source: Philip (2016, 305).

(e.g., Schwarz and Chin 2007) and compatibility with the website (e.g., Taylor and Todd 1995) to inspire trial. Users should be incentivized to contribute to the website (e.g., list products to exchange, add content to community forums).

Managers of swapping and renting websites should focus on attracting providers and encouraging involvement with object curation. Websites could offer services or incentives for providers who post pictures. For example, a few points-based swapping websites offered new users a free "point" for posting their first listing, and a clothing rental website offered a service whereby providers could pay a small fee to have a professional photographer conduct a fashion photo shoot with their clothes. These photographs would then be automatically posted to the website as available objects for rent.

Many respondents discussed instances of leaky user retention when discussing the various constraints, including inflexibility, in using some of the websites. Most respondents agreed CC websites needed to be wary of "controlled governance" (e.g., Keymolen 2013). Building a trustworthy community was important, but our findings indicated flexibility of *cocreation* (i.e., to increase user convenience and allow lower involvement efforts when there was a lower level of risk or attachment to the object) as paramount to increasing consumer involvement. Enabling flexibility ensures websites do not attempt to control interactions between peers but rather allow users to develop and contribute to the website, thus fostering feelings of community ownership (e.g., Lin and Lu 2011).

Although the most common strategy for websites has been to build trust between users (e.g., Petri et al. 2010), our findings suggest that the issue of the commons has more to do with risk. Even when trust was given between users, respondents repeatedly held concerns for negative reciprocity, indicating that trust between strangers is unable to reduce uncertainty in the exchange. Instead of focusing only on "trust" between strangers, managers of websites should strive to coproduce *confidence* (e.g., Chantelat and Vignal 2005) in providers and takers. Building confidence by offering solutions and contingencies for instances of failed cooperation reduces the vulnerability in dealing with strangers.

Although most renting sites enable deposits to be taken, this protects only those who rent out. As insurance mitigates risk for *both* parties involved, in that the renter no longer has to worry about paying for accidental damage and the provider no longer has to worry about replacing a broken item, P2P rental sites could provide insurance options. Another way to enable trust is by branding users, products, and the website itself. For instance, users need to brand themselves as trustworthy to others by the use of feedback and comments, their profile, and the effort they put forth in their communication, and online image. Likewise, products need to be branded as items potential takers would actually want; comments and feedback on a specific product, as well as using merchandising techniques like high-quality photos, could increase the desirability of the product. Finally, institutional trust is extremely important. Managers need to brand their site as a trustworthy broker that provides a safe and engaging place for individuals to gather and share items through renting.

Convenience is another important aspect in overcoming the constraints of these behaviors being too much work. Managers should first focus on increasing perceptions of self-efficacy (e.g., Taylor and Todd 1995) and perceived ease of use (e.g., Venkatesh and Davis 2000) by making sure users know what the website is used for and how it works and by enhancing their belief it will be easy to use. This can be done by designing websites with "fluidity of use," where stages of participation are "automagic," easy, and effortless. For example, one swapping website supplied the postage for consumers to send items, taking away the inconvenience of having to go to the post office and figure out shipping costs. In high-density urban areas, it might be possible for a third party to provide storage facilities and facilitate the logistics of rental transactions, thus reducing the high level of effort required of users and providing storage utility for those who rent out (Lamberton and Rose 2012).

Cheung and Lee (2009, 283) define commitment in online communities as "a sense of emotional involvement with the online community, which is characterized by identification with, involvement in, and emotional attachment to the community." Thus, our final enabler has to do with making users more committed to their involvement throughout the exchange, to other users, and to the website *community*.

Based on our qualitative research, most of the websites used by rental respondents offered broad catchall product categories, so there was no common interest around which the community could come together and get involved as like-minded and enthusiastic consumers. The more successful rental websites had a niche product category like clothing, outdoor adventure gear, party equipment, and photography. By having a specific product focus, users could become more involved and get excited about providing and taking rental objects, and engage in conversations about the focal product— perhaps a necessary component for lowering the perception of P2P renting as "hard work." This proposition aligns with our swapping findings, where the majority of respondents perceived the hard work of second-hand exchange worth their efforts because they were heavily involved in the product categories and enjoyed participating in the swapping community. Thus, swapping respondents thought of it more as "fun work" because it was socially engaging and offered a routine of hedonic stimulation. Websites should therefore offer a clear focus to bring the website community closer together.

In conclusion, our research shows that technology, through P2P networks, geolocation apps, and synchronous communication, has certainly *enabled* the growth of consumption in the second-hand world. But are enough consumers ready to actually *transform* their consumption behavior to the point of a collaborative revolution (as Botsman and Rogers envisioned)? Perhaps not. But, as technology continues to weave itself into our everyday lives (i.e., as objects and people become more findable through geolocation tags, search engines, etc.), access to things can become more ubiquitous *and* easy (even within "the long tail"). Thus, the hard work of P2P exchange can lessen and perhaps become more appealing. Our discovery of organically created collaborative transactions suggests that although many websites have failed, there is a hidden world of consumer collaboration still out there that is very much alive and growing.

Note

1. We use the term "taker" to avoid confusion with human–computer interaction (HCI) studies, which define users as peers signed up to and using a website (e.g., Hassenzahl and Tractinsky 2006). Using the HCI lens, the term "user" is too broad because it encompasses both types of CC usage (both provider and taker activities).

References

Albinsson, Pia A., and B. Yasantha Perera. 2012. "Alternative Marketplaces in the 21st Century: Building Community through Sharing Events." *Journal of Consumer Behaviour* 11: 303–315. doi:10.1002/cb.1389.

Anderson, Lauren. 2014. "Mapping Failure: Studying Failure Is a Recipe for Success in the Collaborative Economy." *Featured Content Perspectives.* December 18. https://www.slideshare.net/CollabLab/failure-mapping-the-collaborative-economy.

Appelgren, Staffan, and Anna Bohlin. 2015. "Growing in Motion: The Circulation of Used Things on Second-Hand Markets." *Journal of Current Cultural Research* 7: 143–168.

Banerjee, Abhijit V., and Eric S. Maskin. 1996. "A Walrasian Theory of Money and Barter." *The Quarterly Journal of Economic* 111: 955–1005. doi: 10.2307/2946705.

Bardhi, Fleura, and Giana M. Eckhardt. 2012. "Access Based Consumption: The Case of Car Sharing." *Journal of Consumer Research* 39: 881–898. doi: 10.1086/666376.

Bohnet, Iris, Benedikt Herrmann, and Richard Zeckhauser. 2010. "Trust and the Reference Points of Trustworthiness in Gulf and Western Countries." *Quarterly Journal of Economics* 125: 811–828. doi:10.1162/qjec.2010.125.2.811.

Botsman, Rachel. 2010, May. "The Case for Collaborative Consumption." *TEDxSydney.* May. http://www.ted.com/talks/rachel_botsman_the_case_for_collaborative_consumption?language=en.

Botsman, Rachel, and Roo Rogers. 2010. *What's Mine Is Yours: The Rise of Collaborative Consumption.* New York: HarperCollins.

Braun, Virginia, and Victoria Clarke. 2006. "Using Thematic Analysis in Psychology." *Qualitative Research* 3: 77–101.

Brehm, John, and Wendy Rahn. 1997. "Individual-Level Evidence for the Causes and Consequences of Social Capital." *American Journal of Political Science* 41: 999–1023. doi:10.2307/2111684.

Campbell Mithun. 2012. "National Study Quantifies Reality of the 'Sharing Economy' Movement." *Carbonview Research*. January. http://www.cmit hun.com/national_study_quantifies_reality_of_the_sharing_economy_ movement-2/.

Chantelat, Pascal, and Benedicte Vignal. 2005. "'Intermediation' in Used Goods Markets: Transactions, Confidence, and Social Interaction." *Sociologie du travail* 47: e71–e88. doi:10.1016/j.soctra.2005.09.00.

Cheshire, Lynda, Peter Walters, and Ted Rosenblatt. 2010. "The Politics of Housing Consumption: Renters as Flawed Consumers on a Master Planned Estate." *Urban Studies* 47: 2597–2614. doi:10.1177/0042098009359028.

Cheung, Cristy M. K., and Matthew K. O. Lee. 2009. "Understanding the Sustainability of a Virtual Community: Model Development and Empirical Test." *Journal of Information Science* 35: 279–298.

Dalton, George. 1982. "Barter." *Journal of Economic Issues* 16: 181–190.

Denegri-Knott, Janice, and Mike Molesworth. 2009a. "'I'll Sell This and I'll Buy Them That': eBay and the Management of Possessions as Stock." *Journal of Consumer Behaviour* 8: 305–315. doi:10.1002/cb.295.

Denegri-Knott, Janice, and Mike Molesworth. 2009b. "Love It. Buy It. Sell It." *Journal of Consumer Culture* 10: 56–79. doi:10.1177/1469540509355025.

Durgee, Jeffrey F., and Gina C. O'Connor. 1995. "An Exploration into Renting as Consumption Behaviour." *Psychology and Marketing* 12: 89–104. doi:10.1002/mar.4220120202.

Fehr, Ernst, and Urs Fischbacher. 2003. "The Nature of Human Altruism." *Nature* 425: 785–791. doi:10.1038/nature02043.

Grimshorn, Cornelia, and Marlene Jordan. 2015. "Ownership—A Challenged Consumer Ideal. A Study of Two Collaborative Consumption Practices: Clothes Swapping and Clothing Libraries." Master's thesis, Lund University.

Hamari, Juho, Mimmi Sjökllnt, and Antti Ukkonen. 2015. "The Sharing Economy: Why People Participate in Collaborative Consumption." *Journal of the Association for Information Science and Technology* 67 (9): 1–13. doi:10.1002/asi.23552.

Hassenzahl, Marc, and Noam Tractinsky. 2006. "User Experience: A Research Agenda." *Behaviour & Information Technology* 25 (2): 91–97.

Heinrichs, Harold. 2013. "Sharing Economy: A Potential New Pathway to Sustainability." *GAIA: Ecological Perspectives for Science & Society* 22: 228–231.

Jacoby, Jacob, Carol K. Berning, and Thomas F. Dietvorst. 1977. "What about Disposition?" *Journal of Marketing* 41: 22–28.

Jevons, William Stanley. 1875. *Money and the Mechanism of Exchange*. London: Appleton.

Jowanza, Joseph. 2011. "Community Affair: Social Inclusion and Swapping." All Student Publications Paper 69. http://scholarsarchive.byu.edu/studentpub/69.

Kessler, Sarah. 2015. "The 'Sharing Economy' Is Dead, and We Killed It." *Fast Company*. September 14. http://www.fastcompany.com/3050775/the-sharing-economy-is-dead-and-we-killed-it.

Keymolen, Esther. 2013. "Trust and Technology in Collaborative Consumption. Why It Is Not Just about You and Me." In *Bridging Distances in Technology and Regulation,* edited by Ronald Leenes and Eleni Kosta. 135–150. Oisterwijk: Wolf Legal Publishers.

Keyton, Joann. 2011. *Communication Research: Asking Questions, Finding Answers.* 3rd ed. New York: McGraw Hill.

Kumar, Nirmalya, Louis W. Stern, and James C. Anderson. 1993. "Conducting Interorganizational Research Using Key Informants." *Academy of Management Journal* 36: 1633–1651. doi:10.2307/256824.

Lamberton, Cait Poynor, and Randall L. Rose. 2012. "When Is Ours Better Than Mine? A Framework for Understanding and Altering Participation in Commercial Sharing Systems." *Journal of Marketing* 76: 109–125. doi:10.1509/jm.10.0368.

Lawson, Stephanie J. 2011. "Forsaking Ownership: Three Essays on Non-Ownership Consumption and Alternative Forms of Exchange." PhD dissertation, Florida State University.

Lee, Hsiang-Ming, Tsai Chen, and Min-Li Hung. 2014. "Online Bartering Motivations." *Psychological Reports: Employment Psychology and Marketing* 115: 75–90. doi:10.2466/01.14.PR0.115c15z0.

Leonard, Annie. 2010. *How Our Obsession with Stuff Is Trashing the Planet, Our Communities, and Our Health—And a Vision for Change.* New York: Free Press.

Liang, Ting-Peng, and Jin-Shiang Huang. 1998. "An Empirical Study on Consumer Acceptance of Products in Electronic Markets: A Transaction Cost Model." *Decision Support Systems* 24: 29–43. doi:10.1016/S0167-9236(98)00061-X.

Lin, Kuan-Yu, and Hsi-Peng Lu. 2011. "Why People Use Social Networking Sites: An Empirical Study Integrating Network Externalities and Motivation Theory." *Computers in Human Behavior* 27: 1152–1161. doi:10.1016/j.chb.2010.12.009.

Magenheim, Ellen, and P. Murrell. 1988. "How to Haggle and to Stay Firm: Barter as Hidden Price Discrimination." *Economic Inquiry* 26: 449–459. doi:10.1111/j.1465-7295.1988.tb01507.x.

Makkonen, Juho. 2014. "3 Reasons Why Peer-to-Peer Marketplaces Fail (and How Not to)." *Share Tribe.* May 6. https://www.sharetribe.com/academy/3-reasons-why-peer-to-peer-marketplaces-fail-and-how-not-to/.

Martenson, Chris. 2011. *The Crash Course: The Unsustainable Future of Our Economy, Energy, and Environment.* Hoboken, NJ: John Wiley & Sons.

Marvasti, Akbar, and David J. Smyth. 1998. "Barter in the U.S. Economy: A Macroeconomic Analysis." *Applied Economics* 30: 1077–1088.

Matthews, Delisia R., and Nancy Hodges. 2014. "Swapping Stories: An Exploratory Study of Consumer Exchange Motivations and Behaviour." In *Marketing Dynamism & Sustainability: Things Change, Things Stay the Same,* edited by L. Robinson Jr. 238–241. Ruston, LA: Springer International Publishing.

Moeller, Sabine, and Kristina Wittkowski. 2010. "The Burdens of Ownership: Reasons for Preferring Renting." *Managing Service Quality* 20: 176–191. doi:10.1108/09604521011027598.

Mont, Oksana. 2008. "Innovative Approaches to Optimising Design and Use of Durable Consumer Goods." *International Journal of Product Development* 6: 227–250. doi:10.1504/IJPD.2008.020395.

Murphy, Scott L., and Shuling Liao. 2013. "Consumers as Resellers: Exploring the Entrepreneurial Mind of North American Consumers Reselling Online." *International Journal of Business and Information* 8: 183–228.

Nissanoff, Daniel. 2007. *Futureshop: How to Trade Up to a Luxury Lifestyle Today.* New York: Penguin Group.

Oh, Seongwhan. 1989. "A Theory of a Generally Acceptable Medium of Exchange and Barter." *Journal of Monetary Economics* 23: 101–119.

Owen, William Foster. 1984. "Interpretive Themes in Relational Communication." *Quarterly Journal of Speech* 70: 274–287.

Ozanne, Lucie K., and Paul W. Ballantine. 2010. "Sharing as a Form of Anti-Consumption: An Examination of Toy Library Users." *Journal of Consumer Behaviour* 9: 485–498. doi:10.1002/cb.334.

Ozanne, Lucie K., and Julie L. Ozanne. 2011. "A Child's Right to Play: The Social Construction of Civic Virtues in Toy Libraries." *Journal of Public Policy & Marketing* 30: 263–276. doi:10.1509/jppm.30.2.264.

Parasuraman, A., and Dhruv Grewal. 2000. "The Impact of Technology on the Quality-Value-Loyalty Chain: A Research Agenda." *Journal of the Academy of Marketing Science* 28: 168–174. doi:10.1177/0092070300281015.

Petri, Ioan, Gheorhe Cosmin Silaghi, and Omer Rana. 2010. "Trading Service Level Agreements within a Peer-to-Peer Market." *Proceedings of the 11th IEEE/ACM International Conference on Grid Computing,* Brussels, pp. 242–251.

Philip, Heather E. 2016. *An Examination of Online Swapping and Peer-to-Peer Renting: Exploring the Providers, Takers, and Non-Users of Collaborative Consumption* (Doctoral thesis). https://ir.canterbury.ac.nz/handle/10092/12511.

Philip, Heather E., Lucie K. Ozanne, and Paul W. Ballantine. 2015. "Examining Temporary Disposition and Acquisition in Peer-to-Peer Renting." *Journal of Marketing Management* 31: 1310–1332. doi:10.1080/02672 57X.2015.1013490.

Piscielli, Laura, Tim Cooper, and Tom Fischer. 2015. "The Role of Values in Collaborative Consumption: Insights from a Product-Service System for Lending and Borrowing in the UK." *Journal of Cleaner Production* 97: 21–19. doi:10.1016/j.jclepro.2014.07.032.

Preece, Jenny, and Diane Maloney-Krichmar. 2003. "Online Communities." In *Handbook of Human-Computer Interaction*, edited by J. Jacko and A. Sears. 596–620. Mahwah, NJ: Lawrence Erlbaum.

Rice, Daniel. 2003. "Barter's Back! Internet Barter: The Recent Resurgence of an Ancient Practice." *Proceedings of the Ninth Americas Conference on Information Systems,* Tampa, Florida, pp. 53–58.

Sagar, Reuben. 2012. "50 Shades of Green: The Collaborative Consumption Movement." *The Ecologist.* November 15. http://www.theecologist.org/

green_green_living/1680762/50_shades_of_green_the_collaborative_
consumption_movement.html.

Schwartz, Ariel. 2013. "The Return of Spinlister: How to Revive a Dead Sharing
Economy Startup." *Co-Exist*. August 8. http://www.fastcoexist.com/
1682784/the-return-of-spinlister-how-to-revive-a-dead-sharing-economy-
startup.

Schwarz, Andrew, and Wynn Chin. 2007. "Looking Forward: Toward an Understanding of the Nature and Definition of IT Acceptance." *Journal of the
Association for Information Systems* 8: 230–243.

Sheth, Jagdish N., and Can Uslay. 2007. "Implications of the Revised Definition
of Marketing: From Exchange to Value Creation." *Journal of Public Policy & Marketing* 26: 302–307. doi:10.1509/jppm.26.2.302.

Simmel, George. 1978. *The Philosophy of Money*. London: Routledge.

Song, Jaeki, and Eric Walden. 2007. "How Consumer Perceptions of Network
Size and Social Interactions Influence the Intention to Adopt Peer-to-Peer
Technologies." *International Journal of E-Business Research* 3: 49–66.
doi:10.4018/jebr.2007100103.

Taylor, Shirley, and Peter Todd. 1995. "Understanding Household Garbage
Reduction Behaviour: A Test of an Integrated Model." *Journal of Public
Policy & Marketing* 14: 13–35.

Toivanen, Heini. 2015. "How Does a Facebook Flea Market Create Value? Value
Co-Creation and Value Outcomes in a Digital Platform." Master's thesis,
Aalto University.

Trocchia, Philip J., and Sharon E. Beatty. 2003. "An Empirical Examination of
Automobile Lease vs Finance Motivation Processes." *Journal of Consumer
Marketing* 20: 28–43. doi:10.1108/07363760310456937.

van de Glind, Pieter. 2013. "The Consumer Potential of Collaborative Consumption: Identifying (the) Motives of Dutch Collaborative Consumers and
Measuring the Consumer Potential of Collaborative Consumption within
the Municipality of Amsterdam." Master's thesis, Utrecht University.

Vargo, Stephen L., and Robert F. Lusch. 2004. "Evolving to a New Dominant
Logic for Marketing." *Journal of Marketing* 68: 1–17. doi:10.1509/jmkg.
68.1.1.24036.

Venkatesh, Viswanath, and Fred D. Davis. 2000. "A Theoretical Extension of the
Technology Acceptance Model: Four Longitudinal Field Studies." *Management Science* 46: 186–204. doi:10.1287/mnsc.46.2.186.11926.

Ye, Shun. 2013. "Reciprocity in Online Markets: Empirical Studies of Auction
and Barter Markets." PhD dissertation, University of Maryland.

Ye, Shun, Siva Viswanathan, and Il-Horn Hann. 2016. "The Value of Reciprocity
in Online Barter Markets: An Empirical Investigation." Robert H. Smith
School Research Paper No. RHS 2710505. http://dx.doi.org/10.2139/
ssrn.2710505.

Yen, HsiuJu Rebecca, Sheila Hsuan-Yu Hsu, and Chun-Yao Huang. 2011. "Good
Soldiers on the Web: Understanding the Drivers of Participation in

Online Communities of Consumption." *International Journal of Electronic Commerce* 15: 89–120. doi:10.2753/JEC1086–4415150403.

Young, Grant. 2011. "Platforms for Shared Value Creation." http://sharedvalue .org/sites/default/files/resource-files/Platforms-for-shared-value-creation .pdf.

Zwass, Vladimir. 2010. "Co-Creation: Toward a Taxonomy and an Integrated Research Perspective." *International Journal of Electronic Commerce* 15: 11–48. doi:10.2753/JEC1086-4415150101.

CHAPTER NINE

Access-Based Consumption: From Ownership to Non-Ownership of Clothing

Pia A. Albinsson and B. Yasanthi Perera

Introduction

The act of consumption, the acquisition of possessions, services, and the like, "provides comfort, satisfies physical needs, and ultimately contributes to the construction of one's self and the communication of it to others" (Cherrier 2009, 181). To some extent, "we are what we have and possess" (Tuan 1980, 272, as cited by Belk 1988), and what we possess supports our sense of self. Our possessions are a part of, or an extension of, the self as indicated by taboos in certain traditional societies regarding the living to use the belongings of the dead (Belk 1988). Moreover, consumption assists in social differentiation and attaining status as consumption practices shape both identity and lifestyle (Felski 2000; Giddens 1991). Thus, in helping define who we are, our possessions play a role in identity development (Firat and Venkatesh 1995).

For much of modern history, consumption in the marketplace entailed the acquisition of ownership over the possession in question. Recent developments, however, have moved the consumption practice of sharing, prevalent in the private sphere between family members and friends, in to the modern marketplace with the advent of the collaborative consumption–based sharing economy (also referred to as the circular economy, see Ghisellini, Cialani, and Ulgiati 2016). In 2011, *Time* magazine identified collaborative consumption, later defined as "the set of resource circulation systems which enable consumers to both obtain and provide, temporarily or permanently, valuable resources or services through direct interaction with other consumers or through the mediation of a third-party" (Ertz, Durif, and Arcand 2016, 15), as 1 of 10 ideas that would change the world (Walsh 2011). In fact, the five key sharing economy sectors (i.e., travel, car-sharing, finance, staffing, music and video streaming), currently valued at $15 billion, are projected to increase in value to $335 billion by 2025 (PwC 2015), reflecting the anticipation that consumers will increasingly access goods and services through collaborative consumption opportunities. Much of this collaborative consumption is in the form of access-based consumption (Bardhi and Eckhardt 2012) where an individual accesses a product for temporary use as opposed to purchasing it outright. Such consumption prompts one to contemplate the value of traditional acquisition-based consumption because consumers' relationships with objects change with the utilization of non-ownership models of consumption (Bardhi and Eckhardt 2012).

In this research, we examine the collaborative consumption of clothing. Clothing refers to "enclosures that cover the body and omits body modifications" such as hairdos, tattoos, and other modifications to which the term "dress" alludes (Roach-Higgins and Eicher 1992, 3). Clothes are highly personal in nature. They protect and shield the body, and communicate personal style, status, and values, and "because dress functions as an effective means of communication during social interaction, it influences people's establishing identities of themselves and others" (Roach-Higgins and Eicher 1992, 1). For some, the thought of sharing clothes with those beyond immediate family or friends is unthinkable due to social stigma and attitudinal barriers (Belk 2007). Belk (2007, 136) notes that "materialism, possessive individualism, and the conviction that self-identity must be developed by extension into possessions are all factors that inhibit sharing." In addition, sharing of clothes is further curtailed by contagion, the disgust some consumers feel from the knowledge of others utilizing the same clothes (Gregson and Crewe 2003). Yet the fact that the retail sale of second-hand clothing is projected to increase from US$18 billion in 2017 to US$33 billion in 2021 (ThredUp 2017) contradicts "theories of contamination and disgust" (Roux 2010, 2). In addition, to utilize examples from different yet highly private contexts, the existence of surrogate motherhood and wet nursing indicates that what is intensely personal can be shared, and can be "outsourced" (Belk 2007, 129). Thus, based on these examples, one might argue that it is not inconceivable for consumers to share clothes with relative strangers. Indeed, the existence of businesses that rent tuxedos and wedding dresses as well as the increasingly popularity of organizations like Avelle and Le Tote that provide access to cocktail wear, jewelry, and designer handbags signal growing consumer interest in consumption without the burdens of ownership (Belk 2007; Lawson 2011; Moeller and Wittkowski 2010). Temporary ownership involves a willingness to utilize objects that have been used and will be used by strangers. However, on a practical level, temporarily accessing certain goods through renting is sensible because, unless one is sentimental or attends many formal functions, most would deem it foolish to spend hundreds or even thousands of dollars on formal wear that is unlikely to be worn beyond once or twice. In addition, it is more feasible for a fashionista with an "average income" and an affinity for luxury handbags to rent a Christian Loubatin Sweet Charity bag from a luxury goods rental business like Bag Borrow or Steal for a month or two (US$175 per month) as opposed to purchasing it outright (nearly US$1,500). These are practical decisions. However, our research is unique because it explores consumers sharing ordinary, everyday clothing with strangers facilitated by small-scale Swedish social enterprises.

This practice is unique on multiple fronts—first, as noted, clothing is personal. This category of product is distinct from objects such as cars, vacation homes, and luxury goods based on the required investment of resources. While some consumers' identities are very much connected to their cars, for the large part, we are accustomed to access-based consumption of cars. In addition, when it comes to less-expensive items, for the most part, consumers are also accustomed to access-based consumption of tools and library books. As mentioned in the previous paragraph, consumers engage in access-based consumption of specialty clothing, which are most often used sparingly and are costly. In contrast, the products consumed through access-based consumption in this study consist of everyday clothing that are reasonably priced and that are likely to be accessible to most consumers' budgets. Thus, guided by the broad research question "Why do consumers share mundane clothing with strangers through access-based consumption?" this research examines a particular set of consumers' responses to current marketplace offerings, including fast fashion (i.e., inexpensive trendy clothing offered on a continuous basis by retailers such as H&M, GAP, and Zara). While the extant research on clothing libraries has examined these entities through the lenses of business models (Pedersen and Netter 2013) and social entrepreneurship (Albinsson and Perera, working paper, 2017), to our knowledge, the research presented in this chapter is the first study that examines temporary access-based clothing consumption from a consumer perspective.

We contribute to the literature in three ways. First, in discussing the notion of ownership in relation to personal objects that are intimately connected to one's sense of self, we question whether ownership is becoming passé in a marketplace that is seeing a surge in collaborative consumption and access-based consumption. In doing so, we offer insights into the tension between the desire to own and the desire to be free of possessions. Second, much of what we know about access-based collaborative consumption is gleaned from the study of large-scale ventures, such as Zipcar, in the North American context (Eckhardt and Bardhi 2016). Thus, by examining access-based consumption facilitated by small-scale, grassroots-activist-type organizations in Sweden, we contribute to the literature by extending current knowledge on temporary access. Third, we offer insight into strategies that could assist smaller-scale, access-based organizations working within the social enterprise sphere to garner consumers' attention and participation. In the following section, we provide an overview of the relevant access-based consumption literature.

Access-Based Consumption

Access-based consumption focuses on "transactions that can be market mediated but where no transfer of ownership takes place" (Bardhi and Eckhardt 2012, 881). While consumers are accustomed to the notion of temporarily accessing cars, and perhaps even toys in playgroups, for instance, this chapter examines access-based consumption of clothes and accessories, a more personal type of possession and product category. In terms of the extant literature, two works, in particular, are relevant to our research: the work of Ozanne and Ballantine (2010) on the consumers' use of toy libraries and Bardhi and Eckhardt's (2012) study on access-based consumption of cars.

In their study of toy libraries, Ozanne and Ballantine (2010) posit sharing as a form in which consumers may express anti-consumption values and sentiments. They identify four types of consumers who participate in toy libraries: socialites who participate due to the possibility of socializing and developing community; market avoiders who enjoy socializing but appreciate the opportunity to mediate market influence; quiet anti-consumers who value anti-consumption, frugality, and sharing; and passive members who are socially uninvolved and do not value anti-consumption (Ozanne and Ballantine 2010, 495). Overall, Ozanne and Ballantine (2010) find that consumers are motivated to participate in these facilities due to the desire to save money and build community, among other reasons. However, in a study of access-based consumption in a car-sharing context, Bardhi and Eckhardt (2012) identify consumer motivations based on self-interest and utilitarianism but do not find support for altruism and community-seeking outcomes. These accounts indicate that non-ownership is multifaceted.

Bardhi and Eckhardt (2012) identify the following six dimensions of access-based consumption that are useful in categorizing access-based ventures:

- *Temporality* involves (1) duration of access and (2) usage (Bardhi and Eckhardt 2012). Temporality in terms of *duration* varies between one time/short term (e.g., an Uber ride or a one-night stay at an Airbnb accommodation) and long term (longer-term stay at an Airbnb accommodation or membership-based collaborative consumption services such as Netflix, or toy libraries). *Usage* of physical items can also vary from a few hours to several years (Bardhi and Eckhardt 2012).

- *Anonymity* relates to how access *consumptionscapes* differ in interpersonal anonymity varying from private to public context use (Bardhi and Eckhardt 2012). In private settings, such as Airbnb, there is limited or no interaction with other consumers, whereas in public spaces such as toy libraries (Ozanne and Ozanne 2011) or Really Really Free Markets (Albinsson and Perera 2012) participants are exposed to more people and thus may interact with others to a greater extent.

- *Market mediation* varies from not-for-profit to profit-based access consumptionscapes. While profit-driven collaborative consumption businesses have garnered much attention (Botsman and Rogers 2010; Gansky 2010), not-for-profit, grassroots-level enterprises and nonmonetary practices (Albinsson et al. 2009, 2012, working paper, 2017; Ozanne and Ballantine 2010; Pedersen and Netter 2013) exist within this space.

- *Consumer involvement* varies from self-service to full service. In some platforms/enterprises, the consumer/user becomes the producer of the service, or the boundaries between the producer and user roles are blurred. For example, in a car-sharing context, the user reserves the car, collects it, drives it, perhaps washes and replenishes the fuel, and finally returns it to a pre-specified location. In the context of Airbnb, depending on the host's desired level of involvement, the service can vary from the consumer collecting the key, meeting the house/apartment owner, and being offered snacks and or a meal to the users having to provide meals for themselves.

- *Type of accessed object* pertains to whether the item is a functional or an experiential product (Chen 2009). The nature of access-based consumption will differ (Bardhi and Eckhardt 2012) based on if the good in question is a virtual/digital product in an online environment such as file sharing (Giesler 2006) and software development (Scaraboto 2015) or a physical product such as in car-sharing (Bardhi and Eckhardt 2012) or toy sharing (Ozanne and Ballantine 2010).

- *Political consumerism* is the final dimension characterizing access-based consumption (Bardhi and Eckhardt 2012). Based on the idea that consumers' marketplace actions and choices constitute a "political tool" (Micheletti, Follesdal, and Stolle 2004, vii), this dimension notes that consumers may "use their choice of mode of consumption—ownership versus access—as a strategy to articulate and promote their ideological interests to society, business, and government" (Bardhi and Eckhardt 2012, 885).

Based on these dimensions, we posit that clothing libraries are high in political consumerism, vary in duration and usage, are fairly public and social, are mostly nonprofit in nature, and offer full-service and functional objects. We discuss these characteristics in more depth in our Method section. For the purpose of this study, we find the dimension of political consumerism to be of utmost importance as Cherrier (2009) posits the notion of the political consumption in relation to anti-consumption practices, which, we surmise, might be relevant to our investigation.

Consumer culture has the potential to exploit individuals (Cherrier 2009). In response, consumers engage in political consumption, which entails addressing issues of exploitation, inequality, and oppression through self-education, personal research, and learning (Cherrier 2009). This approach is based on the idea that an individual's actions make a difference; thus, political consumers' primary goals are "to create, diffuse, and teach environmental and social awareness" (Cherrier 2009, 186). Political consumers resist the dominant power of "mass consumerism" through "commitment, consistency, and a sense of duty," which allows them to "reshape and re-structure their everyday life according to a discursive choice against the ideology of unlimited mass production and mass consumption" and to reorient "the meanings of consumption toward justice, equality, and participation" (Cherrier 2009, 186). In returning to the notion of identity, in particular a hero identity, a political consumer "represents a heroic being, who can, consciously and rationally, distinguish between doing the wrong and doing the right in society" (Cherrier 2009, 187). Next, we offer an overview of our research methodology.

Method

Clothing Libraries in Sweden

Clothing or "fashion" libraries and indeed libraries of other goods (e.g., tools and toys) have surfaced in many parts of the world as of late. This study focuses on the Swedish market that, from most accounts, appears to have been the first to offer consumers access to clothing and accessories through a library-based model. Despite mixed reaction to the circular economy (e.g., curtailing of some Airbnb and Uber activities due to legal issues, see Schmidt and Albinsson 2017, and Ranchordás, Chapter 12, this volume) in general, Sweden is regarded highly in terms of social justice and environmental sustainability initiatives. Thus, the development of new collaborative consumption opportunities geared toward sustainable consumption practices might not seem as foreign to Swedish consumers as to those in cultures that emphasize environmental well-being to a lesser extent. Similar to other identity-related research, we situate our study in the consumer culture theory tradition where "the marketplace has become a preeminent source of mythic and symbolic resources, through which people, including those who lack resources to participate in the market as full-fledged consumers, construct narratives and identity" (Arnould and Thompson 2005, 871).

The 10 clothing libraries identified for this study ranged from brick-and-mortar locations (see Figure 9.1) housed in local municipality buildings, public libraries, art galleries, and social enterprises' premises (Figure 9.2) to temporary pop-up events in parks and other public spaces. Clothing library members pay a fee ranging from 20 to 450 SEK/month (at the time of data collection). Depending on the library in question, this allows members to borrow either a specified or an unlimited number of items for a certain length of time (two weeks to several months). The libraries' founders started the enterprises' inventories by donating their own clothes, collaborating with charities and second-hand stores, asking the public for donations, or partnering with designers. While designer clothes constitute a small part of the clothing libraries' inventories, designers lend or donate either part of or an entire collection to the libraries in order to promote their brand while simultaneously supporting a sustainable collaborative business model. Besides the designer options, these ventures carry basic clothing and accessories, fashion items, and a little more elaborate and formal party clothing and accessories. The inventory of each

Figure 9.1 Clothing Library, Stockholm, November 2012

Figure 9.2 Pop-up event at Johanna N. Jewelry Designer, Stockholm, October 2015

library differs based on the ideological focus of the clothing library (Pedersen and Netter 2013) and the founders' preferences (Esculapio 2017). Despite the various differences, the libraries that our consumer informants participated in were all nonprofit social enterprises—they combined an enterprise platform with social value creation in the form of aiding consumers reduce textile consumption, thereby contributing to environmental sustainability efforts.

Data Collection and Analysis

Using open-ended questionnaires, the authors collected 25 consumer narratives from individuals who were members of a clothing library that has been open since 2010. Over the course of its life, this library transitioned from pop-up events to a brick-and-mortar location and back to currently only offering pop-up events with a local retail partner that has a brick-and-mortar operation (January 2015). Twelve additional consumer narratives were collected from members of a second clothing library one week after the organization announced its closing (March 2015). The second library, which opened in 2011, operated a brick-and-mortar location, as well as a second location for returning borrowed clothing. In addition, this library held occasional mobile events using a specially designed bike to attract new members and spread its sustainability message.

The two libraries' founders were instrumental in administering both surveys. In each case, they helped distribute the survey (administered via Qualtrics) through the enterprises' newsletters, Facebook pages, and homepages. Eleven in-depth, follow-up interviews were conducted during October and November 2015 with survey respondents who had indicated an interest in further participating in the project (see Table 9.1 for a summary of select consumer profiles). The in-depth interviews focused on the informants' ideas about non-ownership and their overall consumption ideals and philosophies. In addition, they helped clarify any questions brought up in the narratives. All data was collected in Swedish, and the first author translated the responses to English. Both authors participated in the design of the questionnaire and in the data analysis process. In addition to consumer narratives and interviews, the authors immersed themselves in secondary data, including the websites of 10 clothing libraries, their newsletters, blogs, and social media sites. Furthermore, during a field visit to Sweden, the first author engaged in six in-depth Skype and face-to-face interviews with clothing library founders. These additional data allowed the authors to better understand the clothing library concept and the ideologies behind their emergence in the marketplace and to triangulate the data. During the field visit, the first author engaged in five participant observation sessions, each an hour-long, at various times of the day on five consecutive days at a brick-and-mortar clothing library in order to

Table 9.1 Select Informant Profiles of Clothing Library Members

Informant	Drivers/Motivation/Consumption Ideology	Length of Involvement	Age	Education	Income (SEK/Month)	Gender	Data
Consumer	Likes the idea of not having to consume; uses car pools/sharing and sport equipment pools; buys organic, locally produces and fair trade	Two years	36	Master	25,000–35,000	Female	Narrative
Consumer	Environment/reduce waste as much as possible; recycles and sorts trash; donates to second-hand stores; buys quality and sustainable/organic when possible	Nonuser but love concept	55	Master	>35,000	Female	Narrative
Consumer	Practical, easy, finding solutions to one-time events. Borrow not buy! Market liberal	Two months	26	Master	15,000–25,000	Male	Narrative
Consumer	Great to renew closet without buying	Two years	19	High school	n/a	Female	Narrative
Consumer	Fun to try on new styles, Good NOT to buy. Sharing is cool! I don't buy new stuff in general. Dumpstering, thrifting, reuse. Anti-capitalist, anti-consumption, organic, sustainable, solidarity, vegan; political activist with strong solidarity views. Sharing clothes is great!	Eight months	31	Bachelor	10,000–15,000	Female	Narrative

(continued)

Table 9.1 (continued)

Informant	Drivers/Motivation/Consumption Ideology	Length of Involvement	Age	Education	Income (SEK/Month)	Gender	Data
Consumer	Awesome concept and awesome clothes; great to be able to borrow in addition to traditional consumption; recycles, reduces, and reuses	Three years	37	Bachelor	25,000–35,000	Female	Narrative
Consumer	Great way of adding to regular wardrobe; have to actively work toward an economy where we respect our planet's resources and limits; social justice and equality—these views guide my consumption choices	Four years	29	High school	10,000–15,000	Male	Narrative
Consumer	Good to borrow not buy; recycles, reduces, and reuses when possible; probably could engage in more sharing; use things until they cannot be used anymore, and then repair if possible	Three years	34	Bachelor	10,000–15,000	Male	Narrative
Consumer	I wanted to donate clothing and learned about the cool concept that way; recycles, reduces, and reuses	Nonuser but love concept	30	Bachelor	25,000–35,000	Female	Narrative
Consumer/volunteer	Resents overconsumption; recycles and reuses as much as possible	Four years	34	Bachelor	10,000–15,000	Female	Narrative
Consumer/founder	Variation, fun items, reuse, environment. We should work toward increasing quality of our lives and save our resources	Four years	32	Bachelor	25,000–35,000	Female	Narrative

observe participants' behavior and interactions in the collaborative consumptionscape.

Our unit of analysis is the individual, and the individual's experience with collaborative consumption and sharing in the Swedish clothing library context (Schau, Gilly, and Wolfinbarger 2009). Data analysis consisted of the two authors engaging in individual iterative readings of the consumer narratives and interview transcriptions for coding, and thematic analysis purposes.

Findings

In this section, we first present our findings through discussing the relevant components of Bardhi and Eckhardt's (2012) dimensions of access-based consumption, followed by two emergent themes: *resistance of non-ownership and surviving in the marketplace*.

Type of Accessed Object

Many of the clothing libraries in this study post their inventories online and share the items' travel stories (e.g., "this shirt was in NYC or Reykjavik last week") and size availability. While these narratives add to the sharing experience, the libraries' clothing inventories serve a functional role in the members' lives in that they provide clothing for daily use. Our analysis indicates that, despite the absence of outright ownership, library members extract value from the clothes they borrow. Informants enthusiastically listed items that they enjoyed borrowing from their local clothing library. They expressed their appreciation in terms of "joy for trying new styles, fun and fancy clothes" (female, 36), "having access to quality clothing" (male, 26), and "I borrow what makes me happy, what fits me and what I normally don't buy, a bit more odd items" (female, 37). A member (male, 29) stated: "I borrow mostly long sleeved shirts. I enjoy the possibility of trying on new styles and different items that I normally would not wear. This is the unique thing about the borrowing concept." Most members mirror this consumer in that they often borrowed unique, different, and fun items that they normally would not buy. Thus, echoing Bardhi and Eckhardt (2012), our findings are contrary to Chen's (2009) conclusion that value is derived from functional products only when they are owned.

Lamberton and Rose (2012, 111) identify multiple sources of utility in sharing: (1) "transaction utility," namely, the "deal value perceived in a sharing system," which is apparent from many of the informants' comments listed earlier; (2) "flexibility" that pertains to the "absence of limitations on product use within a sharing system" that is also reflected by the informants' accounts; (3) "storage utility," meaning consumers who partake in sharing typically do not have to store the items on a permanent basis. Though library participants yet needed temporary storage necessary for the borrowed clothing, some comments indicated storage utility. For example, a member (female, 26) noted: "You can use the items for four months but that you can return them and avoid having stuff gather at home for years"; (4) "anti-industry utility" in reference to "psychological gains derived from a decision that denies support of the traditional ownership market"; (5) "social utility," which translates into approval by reference groups; and, finally, (6) those interested in "sustainable or prosocial behaviors" may believe that sharing minimizes negative impact on the environment.

An informant (female, 55) shared:

> I try to consume as little clothes and stuff as possible. I have had a purchasing ban of clothes the last three years (but I have had a few relapses) . . . second hand is okay for me to buy but my closet is over full so to borrow and return the items is good.

This consumer's account illustrates the burden of consumption (e.g., limited storage) and tension between the desire to reduce consumption and wanting to access and wear fashionable clothes on a regular basis. For individuals like this member, clothing libraries provide a feasible solution.

Another (female, 19) expressed her excitement about breaking social norms regarding consumption:

> Being part of something that works towards breaking the exclusivity of ownership is a great feeling. Why is it that we need to buy that next black dress when we already have four hanging in the closet?

Both these accounts, to some extent, comprise elements of anti-industry utility in that they indicate some measure of satisfaction from engaging in a practice that counters typical marketplace exchanges.

Essentially, in this context, users extract their own meaning from the same borrowed item. Per Roach-Higgins and Eicher (1992, 4), "Ultimately, the meanings communicated by the objectively discernible types and properties of dress depend on each person's subjective interpretations of them." Therefore, based on *symbolic interaction theory* (Weigert et al. 1986), a consumer's fashion statement and the reasons for wearing specific items and the source of the items (e.g., buying vs borrowing) can be interpreted differently by the wearer and the observer (Roach-Higgins and Eicher 1992). Thus, consumers extract value from the clothing library offering in different ways. Some find utility in terms of extending the range of available options, while others find that this mode of consumption represents an opportunity for them to exercise their values, thus reflecting utilitarian and symbolic value, respectively (Albinsson and Perera 2012).

Temporality: Exploring Temporary Ownership

Each clothing library (10 libraries identified, 2012–2015) has an individualized set of membership rules, meaning there is variation in requirements regarding the length of membership options, the number of items that may be borrowed at a given time, and the duration of the checkout period. In terms of *duration,* the membership ranged from one month to a year. In cases where the library in question offers only limited pop-up events over the course of a year, membership duration and checkout period ranged from one pop-up event to the next. For membership that lasts a year, the number of items that may be checked out range from five to unlimited, and the borrowing period from four to five weeks. The *usage* of accessed items depends on the member as some items may be worn a lot, while others may not be utilized at all during the time allotted.

Echoing the extant research that consumers interpret value in multiple ways, we find that consumers' reasons for frequenting the clothing libraries differ, ranging from the pragmatic to ideological, and that they essentially derive individual meaning and value from access-based consumption of clothes. For example, some wholeheartedly support environmental conservation efforts and want to reduce their consumption, whereas others are drawn by the possibility of accessing trendy clothing, especially the more exclusive offerings donated by designers (Lamberton and Rose 2012). The main difference between consumers' motivations seems to be whether they are commercially or relationally oriented (Lamberton 2016). Clothing library members appear to hold an expanded idea of ownership as clothing libraries allow for temporary ownership (Bardhi and Eckhardt 2012). This entails a more fluid relationship to the items at hand but the consumer is yet able to obtain the same utility from it as if it were purchased. This mode of ownership (or lack thereof) allows for more freedom with respect to goods: consumers are no longer obligated to care for and store items that do not provide them with value. We posit that this finding aligns with the downshifting and minimalist movements that emphasize value extraction with minimal possessions (Cherrier 2009).

Anonymity and Consumer Involvement

According to Goodwin (1994), consumptionscapes, which in the past were the washhouse, the town square, or the pub, can perform roles of "social support or communality" (as cited in Cova 1997, 313). In this regard, consumptionscapes become "linking spaces" for consumers "for their enactment of rituals of integration and recognition" (Cova 1997, 313). In other words, they function as a way of connecting people. Based on participant observations and data analysis, clothing libraries function as consumptionscapes, and the formation of connection between individuals occurs in multiple ways.

First, there is much interaction between founders and members, as well as among the members in the clothing library context. There is no observable pressure from the founders; they offer honest opinions on how the clothes look on the wearer and provide helpful suggestions on product pairings. The lack of sales pressure and the absence of price tags offer consumers a respite from the mainstream marketplace. This is similar to another collaborative consumption context, toy libraries, which parents regard as a "safe haven" when browsing for toys for their children (Ozanne and Ozanne 2011). Second, most of the clothing libraries in this study have members who volunteer to staff the operations by operating the cash register, washing clothes, merchandising items, sorting donations, or helping with "remake" or social events, thereby further blurring the boundary between users and producers. A member who serves as a volunteer is highly involved in the consumptionscape and can be considered a "prosumer" (Ritzer and Jurgensen 2010). Third, there is intentional effort to foster social connections between library users, as well as between the clothing library community and the public. For example, the clothing library founders organize designer meet and greets, remake events (e.g., where designers or the founders alter the clothing to make them unique based on members' requests), and other occasions where clothing library members gather in support of various local artists. At many of these events, cocktails and other adult beverages and hors d'oeuvres are offered to create an atmosphere that facilitates social interactions. These efforts can be connected to Cova's (1997) assertion that the value in goods stems from their "linking value," the ability to connect individuals with a community.

There is criticism that the sharing economy might not deliver (Ray 2016; Schor 2014) on the promise of developing lasting relationships, being collaborative, and enhancing social capital (e.g., Albinsson and Perera 2012). Bardhi and Eckhardt (2012), for example, found little evidence of relationship building in their study of Zipcar, a collaborative consumption–based business that is owned by Avis. In contrast, in our study, clothing library founders/managers expend effort in developing relationships and a sense of community, but only time will indicate if these relationships are meaningful. At the surface level, Zipcar is akin to a car rental agency with an up-to-date twist. As consumers are accustomed to renting cars, perhaps we do not feel the need to know who else is using the car we borrowed last week and will likely do so next month. Nevertheless, given the personal nature of clothing, given its close association with identity, perhaps we benefit from knowing, from gaining a sense of comfort with others with whom we share clothes? At the heart of it, access-based consumption as a consumptionscape is dependent on the vison of those who facilitate the experience.

Market Mediation

The clothing libraries studied are nonprofit social enterprises. They are market mediated and offer access to any interested party as opposed to providing access to simply family and friends. Market mediation deals with "the motivating factors driving users to provide and rent" items in access-based consumption (Philip, Ozanne, and Ballantine 2015, 1320). The consumers' narratives disclosed issues that limited members' full utilization of the services offered. For example, six informants cited limited opening hours and locations that were often distant from public transportation as challenges to library use. In addition, as most of the founders/volunteers were young, fit females of small to average size (size 10 and below for females) who had donated their own clothing to start the facilities' inventories, the clothing available limits the pool of consumers that could utilize the services. Overall, sizing limitations for most of the assortment but especially designer clothes were a cause for frustration. However, a consumer (female, 31) framed this limitation in a positive manner:

> The sizes can be a limit, but that can be a good thing. It is not supposed to be that everyone should get everything they want in this world. It is healthier to see what the limits are and be happy that others can use the items you can't as it means that different bodies are allowed to wear what your own cannot. Celebrate differences!

In addition, several of the clothing library founders indicated difficulty in obtaining attractive male clothing that appealed to that smaller segment of clothing library users. In the following section, we present consumers' motivations for gaining temporary access to clothing, which include *political consumerism*.

The Clothing Library Member—A Political Consumer

The clothing library participants from whom data was gathered are largely educated, low- to middle-class individuals. Though they are predominantly female, they come from all walks of life, differ in ages, and joined a clothing library for a variety of reasons (see Table 9.1). Their narratives indicate a strong awareness of sustainability issues and the related desire to consume products and services in a conscious manner as a response to what they perceive as both Swedish and global hyper-consumption. In fact, 23 of the narratives indicated environment-related reasons for engaging in access-based consumption, which aligns with the altruistic idea of universalism—"the desire to leave the world a better place" (Schau, Gilly, and Wolfinbarger 2009, 271). Nonetheless, these consumers also find that access-based consumption of clothes allows them to temporarily enlarge their closets by acquiring outfits and accessories for both everyday wear and special occasions (without the need for permanent storage and added expenses) in a sustainable manner as opposed to purchasing.

The following excerpts illustrate a desire to reduce consumption:

I like the principle of not having to consume (buy new). (Female, 36)
    It is great to NOT buy, to have collective/shared clothes are super cool!!!
(Female, 31)
    Good to be able to share clothes in conjunction to regular purchases. It
is good to borrow instead of buying clothes. (Male, 29)

Many members, who are politically motivated on multiple fronts, make conscious decisions with respect to their clothing consumption. These members opt to utilize the local clothing library in lieu of making new purchases. For example, some spoke of their attempts to consume sustainably by not wasting food, eating organic, and using public transportation. A member (female, 26) shared:

I try to keep informed on how we can change our patterns to become a
more sustainable economy—from how we act as citizens and members in
certain events to how we act as consumers. It is important to understand
that the economy is something we shape together, rather than something
that an invisible hand rules or guides.

Another (female, 31) spoke of living simply, and wanting to minimize her ecological footprint, which led her to engage in various measures, including vegetarianism. Yet other members shared:

I work with design and am engaged in the circular economy and sustainability. I am happy to share and am part of sharing services such as car2go
and ride sharing and I try to buy organic foods. (Female, 55)
    My perspective is to reduce consumption as much as possible, reuse, recycle, dumpster dive, borrow, give, and exchange. I think there is actually very
little we need to consume, most things do not lose its utility value with use. It
is about an ideology and a way of thinking about things and resources as old,
new, [or] used without they really lose their utility at all. (Female, 31)
    I try to stay informed on how we can change and work towards a more
sustainable business climate, from how we act as citizens and to how we
can act as consumers. It is important to see that the economy is something
we shape together, rather than an invisible hand running it. (Male 29)

These narratives indicate that these individuals' lifestyles align with conscious consumption. Some communicate the wish for more solidarity in society in terms of the environment. Specifically, they note that as we essentially share nature's resources, it is imperative for us to consume consciously in a manner that is neither wasteful nor detrimental to the environment. Thus, their membership in clothing libraries mirrors their overall consumption beliefs, patterns, and marketplace rituals. For consumers who are actively involved in the clothing libraries, for instance as founders and dedicated volunteers, the findings reflect Cherrier's (2009, 185) hero identity based on some consumers' perception of "living in an uncontrollable world" in terms of environmental degradation and social injustice. Their perceptions of dominant consumption as being exploitative and contributing to environmental degradation lead them to resist the dominant market discourse and participate in the fostering of social change (Cherrier 2009). To a certain extent, if we regard clothing as a type of product, these particularly active individuals reflect the characteristics of market activists (Iyer and Muncy 2008) in that they might avoid the use of a brand or product due to concerns regarding its environmental impact. However, the clothing libraries do not foster the avoidance of clothing; they simply provide a different and more environmentally respectful means of consuming clothes. Therefore, given their active efforts on multiple fronts, including raising awareness, Cherrier's (2009) hero identity is a better reflection of these individuals. The other participants who mention concern for environmental well-being to a lesser extent but yet in varying degrees are akin to the consumers discussed by Iyer and Muncy (2008): global impact consumers who desired to reduce their general level of consumption due to concerns of environmental well-being and simplifiers who desire a lifestyle that is simple with less emphasis on consumption.

Cherrier (2009, 184) also discussed project identity stemming from the theme "emotional solitude" in that consumer culture facilitates an obsession with material goods that fosters emotional solitude indicated by a lack of meaningful relationships and a sense of emptiness; consumers' accounts of participating in clothing libraries do not reflect such concerns. In contrast, some participants mentioned community in relation to the clothing libraries. Therefore, we contend that any emotional solitude that may be experienced in solo participation of the market may be abated by engaging in access-based consumption opportunities that are invested in developing member communities and consumptionscapes, such as clothing libraries. However, we note that for some the clothing library concept pushes up against the boundaries of their comfort zones in that it introduces them to a new context, a different category of goods, with respect to the application of their sustainable consumption practices. However, as indicated in the following section, not all consumers immediately embrace the idea of sharing clothes.

Resistance of Non-Ownership

Clothing library founders note that when first presented with the idea of borrowing clothes, many consumers have to "go home and sleep on it" before making the decision to participate. This is partly because while we, as consumers, are accustomed to borrowing and sharing items from those within our circles, extending beyond a specific circle can be challenging. In addition, the idea of borrowing clothes is novel. We know what to expect when we become a member of a library with books and electronic media. Do the same rules apply to the clothing library? Indeed, many founders report that potential clothing library members, most of whom had not heard of the concept, often raised a variety of worst-case scenario questions such as "What happens if they get stained, or I break something?" or "What if I fall in love with the item?" (Interview, founder) often stemming from their anxiety about the unfamiliar situation. The fear of breaking something mirrors Philip, Ozanne, and Ballantine's (2015) finding in a peer-to-peer renting context. The clothing libraries try to minimize the members' fear by establishing replacement guidelines or making decisions based on a case-by-case basis depending on the specific member's history. As one founder (female, 32) stated:

> Every day wear and tear do happen to one's regular clothes, accidents happen in terms of food spills, fabric catching on something sharp, someone slipping and falling etc. We don't want people to be so scared of wearing our clothes that it becomes a deterrent for becoming a member or using the clothes.

In order to minimize this fear, a typical orientation of a new member entails reviewing membership rules and having a conversation regarding concerns and fears. While some libraries maintain a three-strike rule (to avoid abuse by members), none of the founders interviewed could think of a time when a member had intentionally abused his or her membership privileges.

However, several member narratives referenced some difficulty in accepting that they had the right to use the borrowed items. This discomfort may be construed as stemming from the fact that consumers are accustomed to assuming full ownership of their clothes. With full ownership, consumers are free to do what they wish with the clothes but temporary access means that they must return the clothes for others' use. For example, the following interview excerpt with a female, 37, who has been a member for three years, shows resistance to this resource distribution system:

> When I first heard about the clothing library, I thought it was a great idea, but it took me about a year to go check it out. . . . I was busy but also thought borrowing clothes was a bit weird . . . I am so used to buying my clothes and I never really used to shop second hand.

Thus, for consumers accustomed to ownership of clothes, irrespective of whether they acquire them new or used, the non-ownership model of the clothing libraries is a challenge. However, some of these individuals surmounted this challenge by relating the clothing library concept to their

ideological beliefs, in particular, regarding the environment. This consumer
continued:

> Then I read more about it and also learned more about the detrimental
> environmental effect the production of fast fashion has.

Thus, in this context, consumers are challenged to reflect on their multiple
interests and motivations and clarify what is most important. In this regard,
how the clothing libraries present themselves to the consumer also matters.
The same consumer noted:

> I was amazed by the clothing items offered, it was different from what
> I normally would buy. It made me branch out and try different things and
> it helped me save a lot of money. I have reduced my clothing purchases by
> at least two-thirds.

These accounts reflect a tension between ownership and non-ownership and
some insight into the slowly shifting boundary between the two in terms of
understanding what is appropriate to include in the non-ownership realm.
When integrating this with the previous discussion of why individuals might
choose to forego consumption, we return to Cherrier's (2009) work. In stating that much of consumer research on anti-consumption posits individuals
as being resistant to the dominant cultural practice, Cherrier (2009, 182)
asks: "Is this dualistic model of resistance/dominance adequate to understand the complex set of anti-consumption discourses?" Through integrating
the works of Foucault (1988) and Bourdieu (1984), she (Cherrier 2009) discusses the "paradox of the resistant consumer" and their "necessary dependence on, yet dislike of or desire for independence from the market"
(Featherstone 1995, 23 as cited by Cherrier, 2009, 182). While all of this
culminates in the notions of hero and project identities (Cherrier 2009), it
also adds value to our discussion of ownership.

Consumers are resistant to the notion of sharing clothing due to a variety
of reasons, the most prevalent being the unfamiliarity of such a notion. We
posit that our upbringing teaches us that clothing belongs in the private, personal sphere, not something to be shared with the wider community. This
notion of "I do not share my clothes nor borrow them" becomes a self-descrip-
tor, a part of who we are. Therefore, consumers may be challenged when initially faced with a counter perspective. One of the authors recalls an event
from boarding school where, after observing girls borrowing clothes from one
another over the course of two years, she was finally persuaded by peers to
borrow a black skirt to wear out to town on a Saturday. The lender, who had
to be woken up on a Saturday morning, was not gracious, and the author,
though she used the skirt, felt ashamed because it challenged her view of

herself as someone who did not borrow clothes even though others in this large community did so. Based on messages learned through childhood, at the heart of it, to this individual, having to borrow meant that one did not have something and that one was not self-sufficient; this was shameful. Though our participants did not share details to such an extent, some of them communicated that borrowing of personal items was simply not done. Therefore, in resolving the tension between ownership and non-ownership, to arrive at a space of community or co-ownership, one has to be encouraged to entertain this conundrum within oneself. What does it mean to share? What does it mean to borrow? Are the answers that surface sufficient to prompt participation in ventures such as clothing libraries? At the individual level, we posit that this is how the boundary between ownership and non-ownership can be negotiated, and more product categories included within the realm of non-ownership.

At some point, cars were personal, as were toys and tools, and for many, they yet are. However, external entities, such as rental agencies, toy libraries, and neighborhood sharing groups, influenced this inner discussion of ownership by making sharing opportunities available. Similarly, the clothing libraries, at the very least, by offering access-based options, move the discussion of sharing of clothing into the marketplace. Beyond that, obviously, maintaining an appealing "store" with up-to-date trends makes a difference to consumers, for example, the female consumer (age, 37), whose quotes are mentioned earlier, notes that she initially found the clothing library concept to be unusual. Therefore, had the library not offered attractively displayed fashionable clothes, she might have walked away from the experience with a negative impression that would have likely affected her future interest in such measures. Thus, the clothing libraries must pay attention to how they might best survive in the marketplace and compete with mainstream market offerings.

Surviving in the Marketplace

As we had the opportunity to survey customers of a library that closed, we gained insight from members about measures that would have helped the clothing library attract more members and thereby perhaps remain in operation.

Although most member narratives shared positive feedback on the clothing library concept and their experience with temporary access to clothing, they conveyed some dissatisfaction with the sizes, styles, and the shape of the clothes. For example, one member, female, 34, stated:

Most of the times, the clothes are nicely hung and clean, but due to the amount of clothing they are not always ironed or pressed and one time I got an item and didn't notice a spot until I came home. I immediately called the library so they could put it in the file so I wouldn't be charged for it. I didn't mind it too much as I have made similar calls to car rental companies when I have smelled smoke in the car but still it does create some extra anxiety when you borrow things.

As an earlier quote suggests, informants indicated challenges in finding clothes of their size. Another member (female, 36) indicated that during the busy times of the month, when consumers accessed and returned more clothing, the clothes seemed less well maintained. Other consumers wished for convenience with respect to expanded operating hours and centrally located brick-and-mortar libraries because non-centrally located stores were difficult to access in terms of both time consumption and reach of public transportation. Yet others spoke of the stress of having to remember the due dates and talked about how fast the three or four weeks passed so developing means of online renewals (as some libraries have done) would to help minimize this inconvenience.

As discussed in the consumer involvement section, due to the fact that all clothing libraries depend on members to volunteer in staffing the operations, the accessibility and long-term sustainability of these organizations are limited compared to mainstream retail operations which are "open all hours and days of the week." Thus, we find that many of the participants desire access-based consumption through clothing libraries to be more convenient. To this end, the following might foster further development of clothing libraries:

1. Reliable staffing—Staffing the clothing libraries at a level necessary for effective service and outreach is important. This may be achieved by securing funding through additional revenue streams, grants, donations, and so on to hire employees. Alternatively, these libraries could look globally for ideas and ways to attract dedicated volunteers by collaborating with local nonprofits, universities, and institutions that may require a place for their members to volunteer. For example, secondary school students in Ontario, Canada, cannot graduate without completing a certain number of community service hours.

2. Convenience factors:

   a. Related to adequate staffing is offering consistent operating hours, which are convenient for members and potential borrowers.

   b. Online access—Some libraries offer an online platform with information on their operation. Informants' accounts indicate that they would prefer online presence whereby the libraries offer up-to-date operation information, full or partial list of inventory items, and the ability to extend the checkout period without calling or visiting the library.

   c. Central or accessible locations—The importance of the ease of access was mentioned by many informants. If libraries' resources are limited, partnering with other operations that are easily accessible would benefit consumers.

3. Consumer feedback through consumer advisory board—The participants identified multiple challenges with potential solutions. Thus, soliciting consumer feedback, in general, would be useful. However, more formally, an advisory panel consisting of members could advise the clothing library operators on a variety of issues, including styles and types of clothing to acquire, operating hours, membership drive ideas, and general feedback that could strengthen the operation.

4. Clarity regarding purpose—The clothing library concept is novel, and, as one sees from the findings, majority of the participants relate to the ethos of sustainable consumption. Data indicates that the type of clothing acquired by the libraries is somewhat dependent on the values and social interests of the founders. Thus, thoroughly considering the purpose of the library, what value it aims to create in the world, would be useful in making branding and outreach decisions, including which sorts of consumers to target. For example, in a related study of the social entrepreneur founders, the informants indicated that they were hard pressed for time due to the significant number of speaking and interview requests (Albinsson and Perera, working paper, 2017). A clear understanding of the purpose and market would be helpful in identifying opportunities that truly align with the clothing libraries.

5. Promotion—Related to the earlier point, as clothing libraries are a relatively novel idea, promotion and outreach matters in them gaining marketplace traction. Despite being nonprofit social enterprises, messaging is critical in attracting consumers. A solid understanding of the target market would aid in crafting messages that resonate. In addition, given that this is a novel idea, prompting conversations about access-based consumption, in general, and clothing libraries, in particular (e.g., asking "what does it mean for you to share clothes?"), may be beneficial in helping this idea gain legitimacy and traction.

6. Funding streams—While the clothing libraries assess fees that are used for funding the ventures, in order to develop further or to even provide consistent, reliable service, additional funding must be secured. To this end, the clothing libraries might benefit from securing grants geared toward nonprofits, soliciting monetary donations, or creatively developing the means through which to generate revenue streams within the enterprise.

7. Partnerships—Some informants deemed the inventory as being limited compared to a fully stocked fast-fashion store. To this end, some libraries collaborated with fashion designers to offer unique items that attracted consumers. Thus, this strategy might be adopted by other libraries. In addition, as mentioned earlier, some libraries are not centrally located. Therefore, they could collaborate with organizations that are more centrally located to

offer consumers' convenient access. As we have mentioned the importance of revenue for clothing libraries' sustainability and growth, perhaps partnerships with private-sector organizations would benefit both parties—funding for clothing libraries and opportunity to engage in corporate social responsibility for the businesses.

Discussion

An individual's self incorporates identities based on assigned and achieved positions within social structures, especially those that organize kinship, economic, religious, and political activities. (Roach-Higgins and Eichier 1992, 1)

The notion of positional consumption is based on the idea that "consuming and displaying material objects provides a sense of self that others recognize and accept" (Cherrier 2009, 190). When we started this project, we were hard pressed to understand why consumers would choose to share clothes with strangers through an access-based consumption model. Clothes, especially relatively inexpensive fast-fashion items, are not normally items that consumers consider sharing with strangers. While we understood that strong values pertaining to environmental well-being might influence consumers to engage in sustainable consumption, surely, most consumers would balk at the prospect because clothes are far more intimate than cars, bicycles, or even books.

We are, indeed, more apt to share things with our inner circle (Belk 2007); however, as this research indicates, there are consumers who step beyond their inner circle to engage in formalized sharing opportunities. According to our research, individual consumers interpret the value of clothing libraries in multiple ways. First, access-based consumption of clothes is a practical way in which to better manage personal finances. Sharing/borrowing for a fee in lieu of purchasing makes financial resources available for other projects, including debt repayment, and saving for major purchases. Second, for the majority, access-based consumption of clothing is a means by which they enact their various values, including those regarding environmental sustainability. Consumption based on values pertains to Cherrier's (2009) concept of creative consumption. Creative consumers do not find worth in simply copying what is presented in the media (Cherrier 2009). Through personalization in order to achieve meaning, consumers construct project identities whereby they bypass the meaningless to consume based on their values and beliefs. Such consumption highlights the idea "I know myself therefore I am" (Cherrier 2009, 188). This notion of project identity does not entail resistance to consumer culture but instead focuses on "making a space for oneself and/or detaching oneself from oneself" (Hoy 2005, 90). It entails authenticity, and determining what is excluded and included is determined by values and beliefs and not by cultural impositions. In essence, some of our informants' accounts reflect consuming according to values, and creative consumption to varying degrees, while Hoy's notion of "detaching from oneself" brings identity, and how clothing influences it, to the forefront.

We find the work of Cova (1997) on consumers in postmodern communities relevant to our discussion of collaborative consumption of clothes in the public sphere. In referencing the work of Maffesoli (1993), Cova (1997, 300–301) notes that postmodern communities which are "inherently unstable . . . can be held together through shared emotions, styles of life, new moral beliefs, senses of injustice and consumption practices." Within such contexts, consumers' preferences are unfixed. Individuals "may dress in the morning like the concierge and in the afternoon like a top model," and thus, the postmodern consumer is "a perpetual social movement and unpredictable even in relation to their former behavior" (Cova 1997, 305). This consumer utilizes various marketplace offerings, goods and services, to find meaning and develop an identity (Cova 1997; Elliott 1993). Clothing libraries allow consumers to try out new styles that are quite distinct from their typical look, thereby aiding in identity clarification and development. The ability to borrow one's clothes also lessens "object-person attachment" (Ozanne and Ozanne 2011, 272). Ozanne and Ballantine (2010, 489) report that by engaging in "the toy library experience 'stretched' children in ways parents had not anticipated, with boys trying toys that are typically associated with girls, and less active children becoming more physical in their play." Having access to different styles may allow a consumer to stretch beyond his or her established boundaries, to try different ways of expressing himself or herself, and perhaps to alter his or her self-concept (Albinsson and Perera 2009). Thus, clothing libraries may play a role in shaping and defining consumers' identities and facilitating the expansion of their thinking to position more goods under the umbrella of non-ownership.

We posit that consumers' sense of who they are, and what is appropriate for them, might influence their decision of whether or not to partake in access-based clothing consumption. We find that while those who participated in the clothing libraries appear to hold an expanded idea of ownership, not all informants were initially comfortable with the idea. Culture and socialization teaches us what is appropriate and what is not. For many, this includes learning what is appropriate to share and with whom. These learnings become a part of one's self, so, when faced with various access-based consumption opportunities, one may be challenged if what is being shared is deemed by oneself as being inappropriate to share with others, especially with distant others, or even strangers. Thus, in these situations, while a consumer might reflect on the appropriateness of sharing on a category-by-category basis (tools, clothes, cars, etc.), we contend that those who hold certain overarching ways of defining the self, especially in relation to the environment, for example, "I am an environmentalist" or ". . . conscious consumer," might be more apt to try sharing opportunities. In this regard, we find that consumers' identity projects, in this case facilitated through access-based consumption, are related to Schau, Gilly, and Wolfinbarger's (2009) notion of *self-synchronization,* that is, how consumers inspire to "align oneself with the current state of culture and society" (270) because, for some, the driving motivation relates to the contemporary issue of environmental sustainability.

Finally, the first author's observation and informants' accounts, to some extent, indicate the value found in community. According to Cova (1997), while consumers in postmodern communities value the idea of community over consumption, they do ascribe value to certain goods and services with "linking value," which "permit and support social interaction of the communal type" (Cova 1997, 307). Some consumers involved in the clothing libraries, similar to those in other sharing contexts such as community toy libraries (Ozanne and Ballantine 2010), and clothing exchange events (Albinsson and Perera 2009, 2012), in part, seek out the services of clothing libraries to be connected to others and create community. Thus, Cova's (1997) notion of linking value is relevant because the clothing libraries strive to connect individuals to one another through various communal activities. According to Schau, Gilly, and Wolfinbarger (2009, 272), "Identity is actively broadened to consider one's self in relationship to the community, the nation, or the world." Therefore, we posit that participating in a clothing library opens avenues for social connection. This finding is in contrast to Bardhi and Eckhardt's (2012) finding in the Zipcar context that "consumers are not looking for social value" (Eckhardt and Bardhi 2015) and their assertion that successful access-based business models will not be based on community. Of course, this depends on one's definition of success. If success is being a publicly traded company with millions in profits, Eckhardt and Bardhi (2015) may be correct. However, for founders of grassroots-level collaborative consumption efforts, such as the founders of clothing libraries in this study, success entails creating awareness of the negative effects of clothing production and consumption and starting a dialogue with consumers to change consumption practices. Thus, if one adopts this perspective of success, the clothing library founders indicate that community is an important aspect in the success of access-based organizations.

Conclusion and Future Research

This chapter contributes to the discussion on collaborative consumption in multiple ways. First we discuss how access-based clothing assists consumers in communicating their identity. Specifically, by introducing temporary ownership of intimate objects and how the choice of accessing clothes versus owning them contributes another layer to consumers' identity projects, we add another perspective to the discussion of ownership. In summary, our findings indicate that some consumer segments are open to temporary access of clothing and are working toward limiting their overall need for ownership. Second, we introduce small-scale, social entrepreneurship–based clothing libraries to the larger discussion of access-based consumption literature. Third, based on consumers' experiences as members of clothing libraries, we offer insight into practical strategies that clothing libraries and similar organizations could utilize to succeed in the marketplace.

In terms of limitations, the sample was not representative of the population as the majority of our informants were female, as were the majority of the founders of the clothing libraries. Future research could explore the reasons behind why more women appear to engage in clothing libraries both as social entrepreneurs and as members. In addition, some of the consumers' narratives included the suggestion to integrate more free shop elements, such as free bins, into clothing libraries. As previous research has noted (e.g., Albinsson and Perera 2012), exploring sharing in more permanent sharing structures such as free shops and tool libraries may be in order. Researchers could also explore cultural differences in adopting clothing libraries. While this idea appears to be popular in Sweden and some European countries, we encountered some blog posts from the United States with less positive views. These bloggers oftentimes mentioned clothing libraries as being very helpful for the homeless, or for those with low or no income. However, they did not see the value of clothing libraries for those of middle- and higher-income brackets. This warrants an exploration of cultural differences with respect to the notion of ownership itself. Materialists often believe that gathering stuff, obtaining more things, and owning possessions are key sources to happiness, or unhappiness if one does not obtain the things for which one yearns (Belk 1985). Thus, cultural differences in terms of materialism may also be a fruitful avenue for future research (Habibi, Kim, and Laroche 2016). Many of our informants expressed the burdens of ownership, the toll it takes on their physical and mental well-being, and their desire to declutter their homes. The accumulation of material possessions can be a source of stress in modern societies where there in much overconsumption, and consumers spend significant effort and resources, including time and money, in storing and caring for their goods, most of which sit idle. Thus, for some consumers, sharing may counter the stress of ownership, develop a sense of community, and bring them a measure of well-being in an increasingly complex world.

References

Albinsson, Pia A., and B. Yasanthi Perera. 2009. "From Trash to Treasure and Beyond: The Meaning of Voluntary Disposition." *Journal of Consumer Behaviour* 8 (6): 340–353.

Albinsson, Pia A., and B. Yasanthi Perera. 2012. "Alternative Marketplaces in the 21st Century: Building Community through Sharing Events." *Journal of Consumer Behaviour* 11: 303–315.

Albinsson, Pia A., and B. Yasanthi Perera. 2017. "Social Entrepreneurs and Collaborative Consumption: The Case of Swedish Clothing Libraries." Working Paper, Appalachian State University and Brock University.

Arnould, Eric J., and Craig J. Thompson. 2005, March. "Consumer Culture Theory (CCT): Twenty Years of Research." *Journal of Consumer Research* 31: 868–882.

Bardhi, Fleura, and Giana M. Eckhardt. 2012, December. "Access-Based Consumption: The Case of Car Sharing." *Journal of Consumer Research* 39: 881–898.

Belk, Russell. 1985. "Materialism: Traits Aspects of Living in the Material World." *Journal of Consumer Research* 12 (3): 265–280.

Belk, Russell. 1988. "Possessions and the Extended Self." *Journal of Consumer Research* 15: 139–168.

Belk, Russell. 2007. "Why Not Share Rather Than Own?" *The Annals of the American Academy of Political and Social Science* 611: 126.

Botsman, Rachel, and Roo Rogers. 2010. *What's Mine Is Yours. The Rise of Collaborative Consumption.* New York: HarperCollins.

Bourdieu, P. 1984. *Distinction: A Social Critique of the Judgment of Taste.* London: Routledge and Kegan Paul.

Chen, Yu. 2009. "Possession and Access: Consumer Desires and Value Perceptions Regarding Contemporary Art Collection and Exhibit Visits." *Journal of Consumer Research* 35 (6): 925–940.

Cherrier, Helene. 2009. "Anti-Consumption Discourses and Consumer Resistant Identities." *Journal of Business Research* 62 (2): 181–190.

Cova, Bernard. 1997. "Community and Consumption: Toward a Definition of the 'Linking Value' of a Product or Services." *European Journal of Marketing* 31 (3/4): 297–316.

Eckhardt, Giana M., and Fleura Bardhi. 2015. "The Sharing Economy Isn't about Sharing at All." *Harvard Business Review* 28. https://hbr.org/2015/01/the-sharing-economy-isnt-about-sharing-at-all.

Eckhardt, Giana M., and Fleura Bardhi. 2016. "The Relationship between Access Practices and Economic Systems." *Journal of Association of Consumer Research* 1 (2): 210–225.

Elliott, R. 1993, June. "Marketing and the Meaning of Postmodern Culture." In *Rethinking Marketing: New Perspectives on the Discipline and Profession*, edited by Douglas Brownlie. 134–142. Coventry: Warwick Business School.

Ertz, Myriam, Fabien Durif, and Manon Arcand. 2016. "Collaborative Consumption: Conceptual Snapshot at a Buzzword." *Journal of Entrepreneurship Education* 19 (2): 1–23.

Esculapio, Alessandro. 2017. "Check Out Some Fashion: Clothing Libraries in Sweden." *Journal of Design Strategies* 7. http://sds.parsons.edu/designdialogues/?post_type=article&p=723.

Featherstone, M. 1995. *Undoing Culture: Globalization, Postmodernism and Identity*. London; Thousand Oaks, CA: Sage Publications.

Felski, Rita. 2000. "Nothing to Declare: Identity, Shame and the Lower Middle Class." *PMLA* 115 (1): 33–45.

Firat, A. Fuat, and Alladi Venkatesh. 1995. "Liberatory Postmodernism and the Reenchantment of Consumption." *Journal of Consumer Research* 22 (3): 239–267.

Foucault, M. 1988. *The History of Sexuality*. New York: Vintage Books.

Gansky, Lisa. 2010. *The Mesh: Why the Future of Business Is Sharing*. New York: Penguin.

Ghisellini, Patrizia, Catia Cialani, and Sergio Ulgiati. 2016. "A Review on Circular Economy: The Expected Transition to a Balanced Interplay of Environmental and Economic Systems." *Journal of Cleaner Production* 114: 11–32.

Giddens, Anthony. 1991. *Modernity and Self-Identity: Self and Society in the Late Modern Age*. Stanford, CA: Stanford University Press.

Giesler, Markus. 2006. "Consumer Gift System: Nenographic Insights from Napster." *Journal of Consumer Research* 33 (2): 283–290.

Goodwin, Cathy. 1994. "Private Roles in Public Encounters: Communal Relationships in Service Exchanges." *Proceedings of the 3rd International Research Seminar in Service Management*, May 24–27, La Londe les Maures, 311–333.

Gregson, Nicky, and Louise Crewe. 2003. *Second-Hand Cultures*. Oxford, UK: Berg Publishers.

Habibi, Mohammad Reza, Andrea Kim, and Michel Laroche. 2016. "From Sharing to Exchange: An Extended Framework of Dual Modes of Collaborative Nonownership Consumption." *Journal of the Association for Consumer Research* 1 (2): 277–294.

Hoy, D. C. 2005. *Critical Resistance: From Post-Structuralism to Post-Critique*. Cambridge: MIT Press.

Iyer, Rajesh, and James A. Muncy. 2009. "Purpose and Object of Anti-Consumption." *Journal of Business Research* 62 (2): 160–168.

Lamberton, C. P. 2016. "Collaborative Consumption: A Goal-Based Framework." *Current Opinion in Psychology* 10: 55–59.

Lamberton, C. P., and R. L. Rose. 2012, July. "When Is Ours Better Than Mine? A Framework for Understanding and Altering Participation in Commercial Sharing Systems." *Journal of Marketing* 76: 109–125.

Lawson, Stephanie J. 2011. "Forsaking Ownership: Three Essays on Non-Ownership Consumption and Alternative Forms of Exchange." PhD dissertation, Florida State University.

Maffesoli, M. 1993, January. La contemplation du monde: figures du style communautaire, Grasset, Paris [The Contemplation of the World: Figures of Community Style]. Morph's Outpost (1994).

Micheletti, M., A. Follesdal, and D. Stolle. 2004. *Politics, Products, and Markets*. London: Transaction Publishers.

Moeller, Sabine, and Kristina Wittkowski. 2010. "The Burdens of Ownership: Reasons for Preferring Renting." *Managing Service Quality: An International Journal* 20 (2): 176–191.

Ozanne, Lucie K., and Paul W. Ballantine. 2010. "Sharing as a Form of Anti-Consumption? An Examination of Toy Library Users." *Journal of Consumer Behaviour* 9 (6): 485–498.

Ozanne, Lucie K., and Julie L. Ozanne. 2011. "A Child's Right to Play: The Social Construction of Civic Virtues in Toy Libraries." *Journal of Public Policy and Marketing* 30 (2): 264–278.

Pedersen, Esben Rahbek Gjerdrum, and Sarah Netter. 2013. "Collaborative Consumption: Business Model Opportunities and Barriers for Fashion Libraries." *Journal of Fashion Marketing and Management* 19 (3): 258–273.

Philip, Heather E., Lucie K. Ozanne, and Paul W. Ballantine. 2015. "Examining Temporary Disposition and Acquisition in Peer-to-Peer Renting." *Journal of Marketing Management* 31 (11–12): 1310–1332.

PwC. 2015. "The Sharing Economy." *Consumer Intelligence Series.* https://www.pwc.com/us/en/technology/publications/assets/pwc-consumer-intelligence-series-the-sharing-economy.pdf.

Ray, Augie. 2016. "The Sharing Economy Is Dead. Long Live the Leverage Economy." June 23. http://www.gartner.com/marketing/analysts/augie-ray.html.

Ritzer, George and Nathan Jurgenson. 2010. "Production, Consumption, Prosumption: The Nature of Capitalism in the Age of the Digital 'Prosumer.'" *Journal of Consumer Culture* 10 (1): 13–36.

Roach-Higgins, Marcy Ellen, and Joanne B. Eicher. 1992. "Dress and Identity." *Clothing and Textiles Research Journal* 10 (1): 1–8.

Roux, Dominique. 2010. "Identity and Self-Territory in Second Hand Clothing Transfers." In *NA—Advances in Consumer Research,* volume 37, edited by Margaret C. Campbell, Jeff Inman, and Rik Pieters. 65–68. Duluth, MN: Association for Consumer Research.

Scaraboto, Daiane. 2015. "Selling, Sharing, and Everything in Between: The Hybrid Economies of Collaborative Networks." *Journal of Consumer Research* 42 (1): 152–176.

Schau, Hope Jensen, Mary C. Gilly, and Mary Wofinbarger. 2009. "Consumer Identity Renaissance: The Resurgence of Identity-Inspired Consumption in Retirement." *Journal of Consumer Research* 36 (2): 255–276.

Schmidt, Jessica, and Pia A. Albinsson. 2017. "Navigating the Regulatory Environment in the Swedish Sharing Economy." In *Creating Marketing Magic and Innovative Future Marketing Trends. Developments in Marketing Science: Proceedings of the Academy of Marketing Science,* edited by M. Stieler. 925–929. Cham: Springer.

Schor, Julie. 2014. "Debating the Sharing Economy." http://greattransition.org/publication/debating-the-sharing-economy. Last modified October 2014.

ThredUp. 2017. "ThredUp Annual Resale Report 2017." https://cf-assets-tup.thredup.com/resale_report/2017/thredUP_resaleReport2017.pdf.

Tuan, Y. 1980. "The Significance of the Artifact." *Geographical Review* 70 (4): 462–472.

Walsh, B. 2011 "Today's Smart Choice: Don't Own. Share." http://www.time.com/time/specials/pachages/article/0,2884,2059521_2059717_2059710,00.html. Last modified March 17, 2011.

Weigert, Andrew J., J. Smith Teitge, and Dennis W. Teitge. 1986. *Society and Identity, toward a Sociological Psychology.* Cambridge, UK: Cambridge University.

PART 4

The Sharing Economy in Relation to the Marketplace and the Government

CHAPTER TEN

Commercial Sharing 2.0: Business Opportunities in a Maturing Marketplace

Cait Lamberton

Ten years ago, the "sharing economy," broadly construed, was a "new idea"—proponents like Rachel Botsman, Roo Rogers (Botsman and Rogers 2010), Lisa Gansky (Gansky 2010), and Neal Gorenflo of mashable.com trumpeted its massive potential to change not only the market but society as a whole.

And the types of businesses to which they referred did grow, though estimates of their aggregate value vary widely. Some sources sized the peer-to-peer rental market alone at $26 billion in 2014 (Kapoor 2014), while others noted that in 2015, there were 17 billion-dollar companies in the sharing economy (Newton 2015). In 2016, PricewaterhouseCooper economists (Hawksworth and Vaughan 2016) estimated the size of the five main sharing economy sectors (peer-to-peer finance, online staffing, peer-to-peer accommodation, car-sharing, and media streaming) would be $15 billion globally. Further, PwC predicted that these sectors could offer as much as $335 billion in opportunity by 2025, equaling the revenues offered by the traditional rental sector.

This sharing economy is also referred to as "platform capitalism," "mesh economy," "trust economy," "collaborative consumption," "on-demand economy," "matching economy," "circular economy," "peer-to-peer economy," or "access-based economy." It may involve a variety of transaction types that do not create the costs of sole ownership to a consumer, including renting, lending, swapping, or subscription. In a less-sanguine characterization, it has also been called the "share-the-scraps" economy—a world where humans do only unpredictable, low-pay tasks and software or robots owned by corporations carry out the scalable, profitable work (Reich 2015)—a cautionary indicator for those who would enter the commercial side of these systems, which we will discuss further.

Regardless of the exact numbers involved, terminology by which it is called, or feelings about its overall effect on well-being, substantial growth is predicted for the future. But how can firms identify and respond to opportunities in the sharing economy? Can they do so in ways that are likely to be both economically sustainable and good for participants?

In this chapter, I will argue that we can learn a great deal about the sharing economy opportunities of the future by considering the successes and challenges faced by collaborative consumption firms over the past decade. I focus on *exchange-based* opportunities in the sharing economy—those that are amenable to economic quantification without losing their inherent value. In these systems, efficiency and cost savings are likely to be of paramount concern, resources may be depletable or nondepletable, and participation may be exclusive or inclusive in nature. In prior work, we have referred to these as *commercial sharing systems* (Lamberton and Rose 2012).

Note that in taking this focus, I am *not* addressing opportunities to develop sharing economy organizations that are defined by their lack of anticipated reciprocity, absence of payment, or rejection of quantifiable value (Belk 2010; Hern 2015) or gift systems (e.g., Giesler 2006). Certainly, these relational sharing systems are extremely important and worthy of study, but the decision to monetize such systems may distort their purpose and threaten their well-being. Rather, the opportunities I will discuss here are those whose success or failure is explicitly determined by their economic sustainability. While the focus on financial opportunity makes the use of the word "sharing" a misnomer in some ways (e.g., Hern 2015), I will use this term as shorthand for commercial systems that share three specific elements that make them different from traditional marketplace firms.

1. Transformation of slack resources into a productive outcome.

    One aspect of commercial sharing involves the transformation of excess "slack" resources into a productive outcome, as in the PwC definition:

    Sharing economies allow individuals and groups to make money from underused assets. In this way, physical assets are shared as services. For example, a car owner may allow someone to rent out her vehicle while she is not using it, or a condo owner may rent out his condo while he's on vacation.

In a similar sense, the World Bank argues that, in general, sharing systems "involve the more efficient utilization ('sharing') of physical assets (a house, car, physical space, machinery, tools, appliances, clothes, shoes, bags, accessories) or time (e.g., through tasks such as cooking, cleaning, assembly of furniture, doing DIY jobs, running errands, etc.)" (vanWelsum 2016, 1).

Thus, the first key aspect of a commercial sharing system is its ability to extract value from otherwise-underused personal resources.

2.　Reliance on technology

The second differentiating aspect of commercial sharing is its reliance on technology-facilitated consumer interdependence. As Koopman et al. define the sharing economy, "The sharing economy is defined as any platform that brings together distributed networks of individuals to share or exchange otherwise underutilized assets." Here, technology plays a crucial role as a matchmaker—connecting consumers' needs to nearly instantly accessible resources—in a way for which they are willing to pay.

3.　Access, not ownership

The third important element of commercial sharing, as I will discuss the domain, is that it provides temporary access to a good but not a permanent transfer of ownership. Consumers are willing to pay for this temporary access. In this sense, it is similar to "access-based consumption," as discussed by Bardhi and Eckhardt (2012).

This is a fortuitous time to explore new opportunities in the sharing economy, as we now have the opportunity to assess the survivors and challenges of the past decade. Given this assessment, we can see challenges that the commercial sharing economy itself has generated—and that themselves offer opportunities for new businesses—what I will call the opportunities of "Sharing 2.0." I will begin by considering lessons we can learn from the most successful modern commercial sharing systems. This analysis allows the identification of general principles that can guide sustainable marketplace collaborative systems. However, latent in these principles are the challenges they present—and it is in these challenges that new Sharing 2.0 business opportunities exist. This discussion is captured in Table 10.1.

Table 10.1 Success Criteria, Challenges, and Commercial Opportunities for Sharing 2.0

Success Criteria of Successful Commercial Sharing Systems	Emerging Challenge	Commercial Opportunities for Sharing 2.0
Respond to existing demand and capitalize on ample supply, as relates to optimally shareable products	Lack of supply, demand, and venture capital	1. Finding supply 2. Identifying shareable inventory 3. Finding demand 4. Identifying undepletable resources 5. Supporting the connection of demand and supply 6. Bridging to business to stabilize demand
Offer ways to build trust	Inability to monitor or ensure trust	7. Put behaviorally informed data science to work 8. Help commercial sharing systems build trust
Are seamlessly technology enabled	Technology may facilitate unethical behavior	9. Innovate for reduced psychological distance
Provide cost savings to consumers	Cost savings may be dependent on worker exploitation	10. Proactively support providers/workers 11. Offer platforms with low commissions in semiskilled professions that are currently subject to high rent extraction
Evolve based on their own growth and changes in the market	Traditional market competitors fight back	12. Help commercial sharing systems differentiate from traditional competitors. 13. Communicate broader societal benefits of sharing to public and private sectors

What Can We Learn from the Most Successful Commercial Sharing Businesses?

Virtually any research on collaborative consumption first leads one to the most commercial of the established sharing systems: Airbnb, Uber, and Lyft. Zipcar, long heralded as one of the great successes of the commercial sharing economy, has now been purchased by Avis—whether that makes it a success or a failure remains open to debate. However, any consideration of commercial sharing opportunities should begin by understanding the criterion that made these businesses work and, therefore, the factors by which we might assess opportunities in the commercial sharing space for their economic viability.

So what makes these commercial sharing systems work?

1. They respond to existing demand and capitalize on ample supply. Airbnb grew out of the founders' decision to rent out three air mattresses in their home as a way to pay their rent in the pricey San Francisco real estate market (Vital 2014). Thus, they recognized the demand for affordable lodging, particularly in cities. In the same way, successful sharing systems tap into recognized consumer needs—rather than trying to generate a need that doesn't exist. Because a need already exists, successful companies do not need to persuade consumers or investors of their market relevance. They can scale rapidly on both supply and demand sides, which requires early and often massive financing (Kapoor 2014).

    Supply and demand are, in part, optimal in successful commercial sharing systems because they involve the right types of products and services. Yochai Benkler provides two guidelines for the types of goods that are shareable. First, shareable goods are lumpy, meaning that they are purchased in a given quantity as opposed to in continuous increments. Lumpiness raises the likelihood of excess slack: most homes may simply "come with" three bedrooms, but we only need two. Most vehicles will seat four or five people, but we only sit in the driver's seat. Second, shareable goods are mid-grained, meaning that they are widely available. While not all people have a car, many do. This mid-grained character raises the likelihood that there will be ample supply for those who seek access.

    Shareable goods are also infrequently used, again, raising the likelihood of excess capacity, and often have high costs of sole ownership. The proverbial power tool fits such requirements—it may cost a few hundred dollars but be used only briefly, thus making borrowing a more appealing option than purchase on both counts.

2. They offer ways for consumers to build trust. Because consumers in a commercial sharing system are interdependent, trust is recognized as a crucial factor in overcoming resistance to participation. Uber, Lyft, and Airbnb all have mechanisms by which providers and consumers rate one another. This

data is relied on heavily by sharing system participants, as a means of reducing the likelihood that they'll suffer losses due to their participation.

3. They offer cost savings. Eighty-one percent of respondents to PwC's survey agreed that sharing is less costly than sole ownership, and this appears to need to be the case; environmental or social benefits are unlikely to outweigh a suboptimal price structure. In our work (Lamberton and Rose 2012), we also found that consumers take economic benefit into consideration when deciding whether to own or share. At present, Uber is approximately 20% cheaper than a taxi, explaining why Uber is competing with taxis in many cities—and this is critical to its business model. Further, if a driver travels less than 9,481 miles a year, sole reliance on Uber is also less expensive than sole ownership (Hill 2014).

4. They are seamlessly technology enabled. The role of the firm in commercial sharing systems is often to provide the platform that connects sharing partners to one another. Importantly, that technology has to work perfectly. In fact, failure to develop the right technology at the right time, or overinvestment in the wrong technology, can doom a commercial sharing start-up. Well-designed technology allows the type of matchmaking at the heart of commercial sharing systems.

5. They evolve based on their own growth and changes in the market. Zipcar began with a simple emphasis on the low price of car-sharing. However, the company quickly learned that to build a large following, they would need to evolve—to focus on elements of the experience aside from the car, and to do so at a hyperlocal level, since its target market centered on urban dwellers within a small radius of an existing Zipcar. To grow its market, Zipcar developed creative local campaigns, such as the placement of a couch on a busy Washington, DC, sidewalk, labeled with the message, "You need a Zipcar for this," and developed partnerships with local coffee shops and dry cleaners, where their target market was likely to be a frequent visitor (Patel 2009).

    Other smaller firms have also had to evolve as the dominant players reshape the market. For example, RelayRide began in 2010, intended as a collaborative platform for consumers to borrow cars from one another for short-term use. However, as the concept of ridesharing became popularized by the growth of Uber and Lyft, RelayRide adapted its branding, promoting its cars for longer-term "adventures" and rebranding itself as Turo (www.turo.com)—a more fluent name for international consumers—with a slick logo that turns down the emphasis on a "kumbayaish encounter session" suggested by RelayRide's prior emblem (Tanz 2015). While the platform manages vehicle listing and search, screening of travelers, payment, emergency service and insurance, the direct consumer-to-consumer transfer of underused cars makes this a clear example of a commercial sharing system.

Any commercial sharing opportunity should be evaluated in light of its ability to meet these five criteria. But interestingly, a closer look tells us that substantial challenges are in fact inherent in the ways that commercial sharing firms are attempting to do so. Some of these challenges have undermined the success of now-dissolved commercial sharing firms, and it may be tempting to feel somewhat dispirited by these sharing economy challenges. For the present, I will be more optimistic, considering each challenge in the sharing economy as an opportunity to develop new businesses—and this is what I refer to as Sharing 2.0: the business opportunities for which demand exists *because* of the growth of commercial collaborative consumption. The next part of the chapter considers the challenges that arise from these seven criteria and proposes business opportunities that they offer. I close with a few words of caution and a call to research that can further track successes and failures and, hopefully, help this new business model grow in ways that promote the good of all involved.

Challenge 1: Lack of Supply, Demand, and Venture Capital

Because commercial sharing systems are intended to be profitable, they deal with classic laws of supply and demand. To keep prices low while making money, there must be enough supply and matching demand. Unfortunately, this is tricky in the early days of a commercial sharing system—the system needs to attract enough "providers" to generate ample supply and enough "consumers" to create the kind of demand that attracts providers. Often, creating an appropriate platform and getting the word out about their business, such that supply and demand can be increased, also requires venture capital—but venture capitalists want evidence that supply and demand exist. Are there opportunities for Sharing 2.0 businesses to help address this chicken-and-egg problem and, in doing so, help commercial sharing systems function well?

Opportunity: Finding Supply

Mature commercial sharing systems have presumably solved supply and demand problems. In fact, when Randy Rose and I wrote our commercial sharing paper in 2012, we found that anticipated resource scarcity was a major factor in predicting consumers' propensity to participate in sharing systems. Sharing systems were less familiar at that time, and consumers seemed to intuit the possibility of a commons-sharing problem: if people like them all needed a bike at the same time they did, there might not be bicycles available. In short, the sharing pool could be depleted. Given that, at that time, real inventory management challenges existed for both Zipcar and bike sharing systems, this concern was rational.

However, some work does not find a concern about resource scarcity in either qualitative or survey data. Likely, this is, in part, due to the maturation of firm-directed commercial sharing systems, which have improved their inventory management systems and now have enough funding to raise their overall stock without undermining their ability to provide cost savings. It may also be because many large-scale commercial sharing systems now include contractual agreements that guarantee resource availability. A third factor driving down concerns about resource scarcity may be simply that the most successful consumer-driven commercial sharing systems have reached a scale where consumer-provided supply is very large.

But a lack of supply remains a real challenge for new commercial sharing start-ups, in part because of the growth of the sharing economy. For example, Ridejoy, a carpooling start-up, saw rapid growth in its first year, 2011, with an average 30% increase in its membership per month, and attracted $1.3 million from venture capitalists by 2013. However, as other competitors entered the market and consumers learned to simply pay in cash rather than using Ridejoy's app (thus avoiding the 10% transaction fee that fueled the business), the availability of enrolled cars dropped. When it hit 25,000 users, cofounder Kevin Wang folded the business, stating "You never really have enough inventory," with that number of participants.

Opportunity: Identifying Shareable Inventory

First, an opportunity exists to identify and connect goods that offer ample unused slack for sharing systems. As discussed earlier, Benkler calls these goods "mid-grained" and "lumpy," and they may include items that are expensive but rarely used or that become obsolete as individuals move through their life cycle. This kind of thinking may open surprising untapped markets, for example, seniors who rarely drive likely have gently used vehicles in their garage but primarily use technology for e-mail or to keep in touch with family members. Empty nesters who once needed all the accoutrements for a large family may have many resources that now sit fallow but resist selling them. For such individuals, sharing may be an appealing means of increasing their income without losing pieces of their family history. Businesses that can effectively reach out to owners of such resources and make participation in the sharing economy easy for them may have an important role as brokers. Another opportunity here lies in facilitating overflow demand for new start-ups. "Overflow" provision firms may help new commercial sharing systems to absorb excess demand on systems with high-demand variability, such that bad customer experiences can be avoided.

Opportunity: Finding Demand

Problems can arise on the other side of the demand/supply equation as well, as it can for any business. Tutorspree, advertised as the "Airbnb for tutors," opened in 2011 and closed in 2013. Cofounder Aaron Harris attributed this failure to a lack of consistent demand, saying, "We ended up unable to consistently produce a level of demand on par with what we needed to scale rapidly" (Needleman and Loten 2014).

One opportunity here first lies in a combination of traditional marketing research and creativity. For example, are there other ways to meet recognized consumer needs? Uber has succeeded in part because it meets an established consumer need: transportation. But transportation can take many forms, and new commercial sharing systems offer creative opportunities, such as scooters and boats (Maag 2014). Airbnb satisfies the need for lodging while away from home but primarily in urban areas. What options might work in rural areas? High-end clothing-sharing systems meet consumers' occasional needs, but others have found that kids' fast growth makes clothing sharing appealing for younger consumers (i.e., Kidizen). What about utility or work clothing, to which consumers are unlikely to become deeply attached, or clothing for certain unusual experiences, like spelunking, kayaking, or extreme-weather travel?

A second opportunity on the demand side may have to do with the rapid connection of supplies to areas that experience sudden need. For example, sharing systems poised (and funded) to respond after natural disasters and accept payment from insurance companies may have cyclical but important roles to play in our economy. Further, consumers face micro-upheavals that are far more typical—remodeling projects often make a consumer's kitchen inaccessible for substantial periods, raising their immediate demand either for temporary cooking implements and portable meal-prep equipment or, perhaps, for shared meals. Individuals who are selling homes may need equipment or furnishings to "stage" their property, but have no interest in keeping such items in the long term, and people waiting for their moving truck to arrive are often in need of enough furnishings to keep from eating on their living room floor. Commercial sharing systems that can anticipate and respond to such demands easily may facilitate life transitions while also becoming profitable.

Opportunity: Identify Undepletable Resources: Information, Relationships, Digital Media

Supply and demand become less of a concern if sharing systems, at least in part, focus on nondepletable resources—those that remain even after many users enter the collaborative pool. Information, advice, and electronic media are essentially nondepletable: if a provider offers it to a sharing pool, it can be used repeatedly or even simultaneously by multiple consumers. If consumers would otherwise have paid for this resource, this type of sharing system can be viable.

The opportunity here comes first, in providing research to determine real needs for such resources. Second, there is an opportunity to augment depletable-resource commercial sharing with nondepletable complements. For example, a start-up may offer tool sharing—but until the supply of tools is large, depletion is a possibility. Augmenting the physical tool-sharing offer with the provision of online how-to guides or do-it-yourself stories, also provided by sharing system members, may allow consumers to gain value from participation even if they face slight delay in receiving their tool of choice.

Opportunity: Support the Connection of Demand to Supply

After Rachel Botsman drew attention to the complete waste of power tools in 2010, multiple tool-sharing systems began to spring up. Economodo, CrowdRent, Share Some Sugar, Neighborgoods, Thingloop, OhSo We, and SnapGoods all sought to connect temporary demand for utility products with the apparently ubiquitous underused items already in consumer garages. Media response was rapid and enthusiastic, with these companies garnering rave reviews from *Time* magazine, *the Guardian,* and *Wired,* among others. After all, this was a clear case of strong supply and demand—it should have worked!

Unfortunately, even given apparent supply and demand, the vast majority of these systems failed by 2015. As it turned out, people actually didn't have demand to avoid buying power tools. It was more expensive, but much easier and quicker than sharing, after all. And ease and speed matter. At this point, however, a combination of new economy businesses could be bundled that reduce the pain and time of using a tool-sharing system. For example, courier services can deliver a tool and help you return it with no fuss. Social networking sites have massive penetration, and if a given item is not currently available, a platform owner can decide to simply buy it from Amazon and introduce it into the sharing system.

More opportunities may exist to help commercial sharing systems overcome such real or perceived time and convenience barriers. For example, entrepreneurs may find ways to help consumers fit sharing systems into their daily lives, coordinate exchange of shared goods, or communicate the time savings and ease associated with using new commercial sharing start-ups.

Opportunity: Bridging to Business to Stabilize Demand

Business use often provides a more reliable base of demand than does private consumption. Uber has successfully created a consistent demand level by working with the management services company Concur to develop "Uber for Business," which allows employees to directly expense their Uber trips to their company's accounts rather than having to later seek reimbursement. Not only does using Uber save companies relative to other private car services or taxis, but they can track their costs in real time (Schwartz 2015).

The opportunity here is to help growing commercial sharing systems to build a bridge to business, and to help manage that relationship. If an entrepreneur can effectively connect new commercial sharing businesses with companies that have fairly reliable demand, the commercial sharing start-up may be able to maintain revenue flow while it builds a consumer base—thus being able to show a proof of concept with appeal to both investors and potential individual partners.

Challenge 2: Inability to Monitor or Ensure Trust

Rachel Botsman called for the development of a "trust dashboard" in one of her early TED talks, claiming that reputation would one day be the currency for the sharing economy. In her depiction, such an interface would allow consumers to build their reputation across multiple sharing experiences, giving them a single score analogous to a credit score that would travel with them—from Uber to TaskRabbit to Mealsharing (Botsman 2012).

However, some of the most marked failures have been for firms that have attempted to build trust-rating mechanisms. For example, the firm Rapleaf launched in 2006 with the goal of providing sharing system participants with a "portable rating" that would help them establish their reputation in both the online and offline world. In other words, Rapleaf set off to do precisely what Botsman had suggested. However, Rapleaf suffered from numerous challenges, varying from eBay's rejection of links to Rapleaf's reputation scores (Arrington 2006), later negative responses to limiting users' access to other users' scores (Faulkner 2007), and backlash related to its sale of members' presumably private information to advertisers (Goldman 2010). Within the same year, over 30 other firms, including iKarma and Opinity, offered similar services (Marshall 2006). Only one firm, Trustcloud, has survived in its current form to the present, and boasts only 769 fans on Facebook as of May 2016.

Beyond these obvious business challenges, even established trust systems are suspect by users. Maureen Dowd of the *New York Times* wrote a piece expressing her frustration with Uber's "ratings system," which, she learned, relied on a quid pro quo: if one gave a driver a 5-star rating, the driver would return the favor. Meanwhile, Dowd's lowly 4.2 rating drove drivers away (Dowd 2015).

Psychologically, we can understand why trust and reputation rating is a tricky business:

1. People recognize that collaborative experiences are not completely in their control. Thus, they fear being downgraded in terms of trust due to a collaborator's bad behavior. If consumers feel that their own reputation is not in their control, they may display psychological reactance to others' evaluations of them (Brehm and Brehm 2013; Burger and Cooper 1979).
2. Trust may be context dependent, and many are novices in different aspects of collaborative economy. Novices may fear being "labeled" due to simple

mistakes they make during their learning process. Knowing this, they may avoid participation at all; owning is more familiar and, therefore, an easy default.

3. A unified trust dashboard also requires consumers to give up privacy—and people tend to value their privacy (Acquisti, John, and Lowenstein 2013). Thus, giving up privacy may be acceptable in a close-knit collaborative community but may be aversive in commercial online settings.

Trust is also an issue on the provider side; 69% of respondents felt that they would not trust a sharing economy company until it is recommended by someone they trust (Hawksworth and Vaughn 2016, 9). Business writers cite this reliance on trust as one of the risks that may push investors away from new commercial sharing ventures. As such, commercial sharing systems challenge us to address the importance of trust without ignoring consumers' preferences and concerns.

Opportunity: Put Behaviorally Informed Data Science to Work

The first and most obvious opportunity here is for smart IT firms and data scientists. As described in Ransbotham (2016), violations of trust can be fairly minor: depicting one's house in a better light than it might present in person when posting it on Airbnb, failing to clean the seats in your Lyft vehicle, and smoking in a shared car. Based on economic rationality, if all participants seek their own optimal well-being and this is a "single-stage" game, we can expect this to happen. Historical data, however, makes commercial sharing participation into a multistage game, where behaviors in a prior round may affect the next.

Ransbotham argues that opportunities exist to translate advanced analytics into consumer trust without reliance on a single Big Brother trust metric. First, historical consumer and provider behavior should be displayed rather than treating each interaction as a stand-alone event. Second, using IT capabilities and careful analytics can be used to identify bad actors who transfer from one platform to another with name changes. Third, firms can explore ways of sharing reputation information with other platforms without violating consumer privacy concerns—perhaps via an opt-in system. Data scientists and information technology firms may work well with behavioral scientists to combine superior analytics with messaging and visual formatting that communicates effectively with consumers and providers, while doing more to alleviate than exacerbate concerns.

Opportunity: Help Commercial Sharing Systems Build Trust

Increasingly, commercial sharing systems rely on written contracts to protect both themselves and consumers from risks that may arise in the collaborative context. However, these external means of protecting participants do not necessarily translate into trust. Rather, scholars have argued that "relational governance" mechanisms should augment written contracts (Ndubisi, Ehret, and Wirtz 2016). Such mechanisms include the ability to communicate easily and facilitate conflict resolution, maintenance of a long-term focus, a sense of mutualism, and the promotion of satisfaction. This offers an interesting opportunity: can entrepreneurs facilitate the type of relational governance that supports commercial sharing systems? For example, could a firm offer "nudges" to maintain a long-term focus in a relationship with a commercial sharing system, or broker fast, easy, responsive communication between partners?

Another means of creating trust is by offering a trustworthy technology platform. For example, both www.near-me.com and www.sharetribe.com offer a simple way to create an attractive, relatively seamless means of matchmaking between consumers and firms. The platform www.myturn.com provides a similar service, focused more on industrial or business partners. As technological failures are likely to undermine trust, consulting services that ensure that platforms are usable and seamless may also be increasingly necessary in the commercial sharing economy.

Challenge 3: Technology May Facilitate Unethical Behavior

On one hand, commercial sharing platforms could be expected to generate inclusive, fair transactions. Indeed, online sales appear to be more immune to discrimination than are brick-and-mortar purchases (Morton, Zettelmeyer, and Silva-Risso 2003), presumably because technology occludes the types of personal characteristics that lend themselves to stereotyping and resulting unfair practice.

However, sharing systems can become more exclusive than they are inclusive. In an important recent study, Edelman, Luca, and Svirsky (2016) found that Airbnb guests with "distinctively African-American names are roughly 16% less likely to be accepted than identical guests with distinctively White names," even when rejecting an African American as a guest leads to financial loss for the host.

More generally, critics have argued that massive commercial sharing systems retain none of the "community" feeling that was originally suggested by the emergence of sharing as a mode of exchange (Kessler 2015). Rather, commercial sharing may be as profit motivated and heartless as is any other transaction, making it unlikely to inspire prosocial behavior. What opportunities might arise from commercial sharing systems' proclivity toward noninclusive or unethical behavior?

Opportunity: Innovate in Ways That Reduce the Psychological Distance Created by Technology

This problem raises an opportunity to shape the way that technology platforms are designed. Specifically, firms may seek to develop ways to use technology in ways that do not raise tendencies to discriminate or behave unethically. For example, platforms may be designed in ways that vivid interaction between consumers is made possible and even appealing. Support firms may provide ways for participants to share successful sharing experiences or make sure that prospective participants are exposed to stories that offer authentic understanding of collaborators. By reducing the psychological distance between sharing partners, tendencies toward stereotyping and discrimination may be reduced.

Further, Sharing 2.0 businesses may be able to provide insight, planning, and evaluation services for established commercial sharing systems aiming to reduce the dehumanizing effects of technology—even in very large, geographically dispersed systems. For example, classic cases in early consumer sharing systems like Zipcar called for the creation of normative influencers—the development of consumer interconnections, where a sense of relatedness, ability to see the effects of one's actions on other sharing partners, and affective carrots and sticks could be used to generate good citizenship. But not every commercial sharing system will have the capacity or skills to create such communities, develop meaningful online and offline interactions, or evaluate the effectiveness of such efforts. This presents a substantial opportunity for event planners, communications professionals, behavioral scientists, statisticians, public relations experts, and researchers—partnering with commercial sharing systems to help them rehumanize their tech-based business.

Challenge 4: Cost Savings May Be Dependent on Worker Exploitation

It has been argued that many commercial sharing systems rely on a business model that relies on exploitation to maintain its cost advantages. For example, Uber has faced multiple lawsuits, alleging that its determination that drivers are independent contractors rather than employees is not only false but exploitative, as drivers lack standard employment benefits and protections.

Avi Asher-Schapiro (2015) presents this argument as follows:

> In the long run, however, if the "sharing economy" is disruptive of anything, it is disruptive of hard-fought labor protections. Uber brings on 40,000 new drivers a month. But to avoid minimum wage laws and liability claims, Uber will not admit that it actually employs these drivers—though around 20% work full time.
>
> Uber then extracts millions of dollars from its drivers' labor and invests in ad campaigns and lobbying efforts to spread to other cities. . . . In the short term, Uber is encouraging drivers to take out predatory subprime car loans with the Spanish bank Santander.

Further, the independence associated with participation in the commercial sharing economy is accompanied by high levels of uncertainty and, often, competition among providers. Any objections can lead to providers being "blacklisted," or dropped by platforms, making their earning potential highly precarious.

Opportunity: Proactively Support Providers

While ongoing litigation, union efforts, and some shifts in platform policy are seeking to ameliorate these problems, opportunities remain to support commercial sharing system participants. As the founder of RelayRides stated (Singer 2014),

> "Looking at this as a new paradigm of employment, which I think it is, the question is, What are you giving up?" Mr. Clark says. "At the end of the day, there's a metalayer of support services that is missing."
> He predicts that new businesses will soon arise to cater to the needs of project workers: "There are opportunities to focus on providers, finding ways to make it easier, more stable and less scary to earn in the peer economy."

Such calls offer clear opportunities for support industries to serve participants in the commercial sharing economy—for example, room likely exists for firms that allow providers to better manage their financial resources, provide means of smoothing income flow or align bill payment with their ups and downs in pay, offset risk, or help them identify insurance services that fit their budget. Firms that facilitate connections among commercial sharing providers and offer them negotiation power, such as the Freelancer's Union, also play important roles here; as commercial sharing reaches into new markets, other connective organizations will likely be in high demand.

Opportunity: Offer Platforms with Low Commissions in Semiskilled Professions That Are Currently Subject to High Rent Extraction

At present, the largest and most successful commercial sharing systems are largely "staffed" by nonprofessionals: private individuals who can simply drive a car or provide reasonable residential space. These individuals are those most at risk of exploitation, in part because they are *not* professionals with any particular externally valuable certification or skills, giving them little leverage with the platforms. They cannot simply go to another employer, so there is not upward pressure on wages for retention. In short, commercial sharing systems are profiting by not "sharing the wealth" (Kocieniewski 2016).

However, opportunities exist to extend commercial sharing systems to areas where, in fact, competition for workers does exist and a platform can provide superior rather than inferior compensation. As an example, the market for home health aides is brisk, with high degrees of turnover. Presently, many home health aides are employed by agencies that take more than half of a customer's hourly payment—a process in economics referred to as "rent extraction" (Schor 2014). If a commercial sharing system could take a lower percentage of the payment while offering these workers autonomy over their daily work, it may, in fact, lower existing rent-seeking by agencies. Further, the entry of such commercial sharing platforms into this market would exert pressure on agencies and skilled nursing facilities to compete on wages, ideally creating incentives for the best care workers to remain in their profession.

Challenge 5: Traditional Market Competitors Fight Back

Unsurprisingly, incumbents in industries where commercial sharing systems are growing are responding aggressively to these new offerings. These new means of acquisition threaten their revenue stream in ways unforeseen until about a decade ago, and suboptimal economic conditions drive consumers to solve problems without incurring the cost of ownership.

One way in which traditional market competitors are fighting back is by extending their offerings into access-based models. For example, carmakers are now attempting to develop access-based models, either internally or by acquisition. In 2013, Daimler AG acquired RideScout, a platform that connects taxis, bicycles, car-sharing, buses, and trains to provide customized travel plans for U.S. and Canadian consumers. This purchase fit with its "mobility arm," moovel GmbH, which hopes to offset financial losses resulting from lower rates of car purchase. Audi offers "Audi Unite," a type of "automotive time share" where a lease is shared by three to four consumers, connected by a smartphone app that eases scheduling.

The second way that traditional market competitors are fighting back is through legal means. Hotel chains have pushed for greater regulation of Airbnb (Elliot 2016). Taxi unions have sued Uber, rejecting their immunity from costly inspections, insurance requirements, licensing fees, accessibility, minimum wage, and overtime laws, though with mixed results (Baker 2015). And while Uber recently agreed to pay drivers a $100 million settlement (Mclean 2016), they have not become subject to the same requirements that taxis face and their drivers remain independent contractors. Still, governments are listening: Belgium, France, Germany, Italy, and the Netherlands have made ridesharing services using nonprofessional drivers illegal, and the mayor of Paris set up a 20-agent team to seek out and fine illegal room-sharing hosts.

Opportunity: Help Commercial Sharing Systems Differentiate from Traditional Market Competitors

Part of the reason that traditional marketplace offerings can so effectively push against commercial sharing systems is that they appear to be very similar. However, services that help commercial sharing businesses to clearly differentiate themselves from traditional providers may alleviate some of the pain in this area.

To some extent, this is a job for communications professionals. Zervas, Proserpio, and Byers (2016) found that, in fact, Airbnb both competes with and is differentiated from traditional hotels. Airbnb does not compete for the business traveler but does for budget and nonbusiness travelers. When Airbnb and hotels do compete, we observe the type of price competition that is near and dear to the free market economist: hotels have lowered prices to capture budget travelers, particularly in the high season. Communicating these types of findings, and helping commercial sharing companies to target the segments on which they do *not* compete, may help increase regulators' willingness to protect sharing companies.

There are also opportunities to help commercial sharing businesses differentiate based on enriched experiential and prosocial augmentations for both providers and consumers. Research has suggested that social and prosocial experiences offer unique sources of consumer happiness beyond solo or self-focused spending (Dunn, Aknin, and Norton 2008; Kahneman et al. 2004)—social and prosocial augmentations to a base service may be largely nonreplicable and differentiating from typical marketplace offerings. Thus, an opportunity may exist for arts organizations, educators, historians, nonprofits, or even tour guides to work in the world of commercial Sharing 2.0—coordinating rich creative, cultural, or volunteer experiences for individuals who use sharing systems can help differentiate these businesses further from traditional marketplace offerings.

As commercial sharing systems differentiate themselves in part because they can offer greater variety than does a traditional business, other curation service opportunities may exist. For example, Localeur and Vayable help people to find the "best" properties to meet their needs on Airbnb. What other commercial sharing businesses could benefit from curation or guidance? If a firm existed to help consumers navigate the world of commercial sharing, it might be a valued addition.

Opportunity: Capture and Communicate the Broader Societal Benefits of Commercial Sharing to Both Public and Private Sectors

Given that traditional market competitors will present a largely negative outlook on commercial sharing business, an important opportunity exists for researchers and firms to accurately capture and present community-level and macroeconomic benefits of collaborative consumption. For example, a consulting firm in Australia reported that car share users in Sydney, Australia, reported less car travel, in general, than they had before car-sharing and that congestion and emissions had dropped (Boyle 2016). Uber has pledged to have 1 million female drivers by 202C—facilitating, tracking, and publicizing movement toward this goal may help Uber's large-scale benefit to be appreciated (Marchi and Parekh 2015). Further, it may be important for researchers and community leaders to highlight profits that flow to small supportive businesses of the type I have described as Sharing 2.0 ventures: for example, property sharing companies may sprout rental management, cleaning, or meal-delivery start-ups.

A Caveat

Recent noteworthy efforts have been made both to connect and to distinguish between relational and commercial sharing systems (e.g., Eckhardt and Bardhi 2016; Habibi, Kim, and Laroche 2016). While we are moving closer to a full understanding of these systems' nature, practitioners can take one critical lesson from this literature: *not all collaborative consumption experiences can be monetized without losing the real value they provide in terms of relational richness, emotional engagement, and long-term community building.* In such cases, the addition of extrinsic incentives, rewards, and punishments may well crowd out the intrinsic motivations and rewards that are critical to sharing's survival (e.g., Deci 1971). This may be the case for some of the most fast-growing and inherently appealing collaborative experiences emerging in the marketplace, or those that seem to most acutely meet a need.

Therefore, opportunities for businesses need to be assessed in terms of both consumer and firm goals within the venture—assumptions about either group's motives may lead to problematic design decisions or ill-fated commercial sharing support businesses. Would monetizing an otherwise socially enriching experience undermine its value? Or would extracting profit from a unique collaborative interaction allow the firm to expand and develop its capacity without disrupting consumer experience?

Finally, I would like to close with the mention of a major opportunity: little generalizable academic research on commercial sharing systems exists. Recently, this has begun to change, with major journals devoting special issues to its complexity, mostly in terms of micro-level behaviors or specific contexts (see Price and Belk's introduction to the spring 2016 *Journal of the Association for Consumer Research*'s special issue for an overview). However, an opportunity still exists for researchers to chronicle the way that commercial sharing systems evolve, affect the communities in which they exist, develop reliable paths to success or respond to failure, and adapt to changing macroeconomic and business conditions. Ideally, such work will not only consider isolated commercial sharing companies but be able to take a broader view across such systems. Further, the best research on commercial sharing will recognize that in some ways, it is not at all a new phenomenon but resonates with past patterns explored by anthropologists, sociologists, psychologists, experimental economists, marketing scholars, and strategy scholars—such that our under-standing of these new opportunities and challenges can contribute to those literatures as much as they have contributed to ours.

References

Acquisti, Alessandro, Leslie K. John, and George Loewenstein. 2013. "What Is Privacy Worth?" *Journal of Legal Studies* 42 (2): 249–274.

Arrington, Michael. 2006. "*eBay Bans Rapleaf Links.*" *Techcrunch.* https://techcrunch.com/2006/05/17/ebay-bans-rapleaf-links/

Asher-Schapiro, Avi. 2015. "The Sharing economy Is Propaganda." *Cato Unbound.* February 13. http://www.cato-unbound.org/2015/02/13/avi-asher-schapiro/sharing-economy-propaganda.

Baker, Dean. 2015. "The Sharing Economy Must Share a Level Playing Field." *Cato Unbound.* February 11. http://www.cato-unbound.org/2015/02/11/dean-baker/sharing-economy-must-share-level-playing-field.

Bardhi, Fleura, and Giana M. Eckhardt. 2012. "Access-Based Consumption: The Case of Car Sharing." *Journal of Consumer Research* 39 (December): 881–898.

Belk, Russell. 2010. "Sharing." *Journal of Consumer Research* 36 (February): 715–734.

Botsman, Rachel. 2012. "Rachel Botsman: The Currency of the New Economy Is Trust." *TED Talk.* http://www.ted.com/talks/rachel_botsman_the_currency_of_the_new_economy_is_trust.

Botsman, Rachel, and Roo Rogers. 2010. *What's Mine Is Yours: The Rise of Collaborative Consumption.* New York: HarperCollins.

Boyle, Phillip & Associates. 2016. "The Impact of Car Share Services in Australia." http://carsharing.org/wp-content/uploads/2016/01/The-Impact-of-Car-Share-Services-in-Australia.pdf.

Brehm, S. S., and J. W. Brehm. 2013. *Psychological Reactance: A Theory of Freedom and Control.* Waltham, MA: Academic Press.

Burger, J. M., and H. M. Cooper. 1979. "The Desirability of Control." *Motivation and Emotion* 3 (4): 381–393.

Deci, Edward L. 1971. "Effects of Externally Mediated Rewards on Intrinsic Motivation." *Journal of Personality and Social Psychology* 18: 105–115.

Dowd, Maureen. 2015. "Driving Uber Mad." *New York Times.* May 23. http://www.nytimes.com/2015/05/24/opinion/sunday/maureen-dowd-driving-uber-mad.html?_r=0.

Dunn, Elizabeth W., Lara B. Aknin, and Michael I. Norton. 2008. "Spending Money on Others Promotes Happiness." *Science* 5870: 1687–1688.

Eckhardt, Giana M., and Fleura Bardhi. 2016. "The Relationship between Access Practices and Economic Systems." *Journal of the Association of Consumer Research* 1 (2): 210–225.

Edelman, Benjamin, Michael Luca, and Dan Svirsky. 2016. "Racial Discrimination in the Sharing economy: Evidence from a Field Experiment." http://www.benedelman.org/publications/Airbnb-guest-discrimination-2016-01-06.pdf.

Elliot, Christopher. 2016. "Big Hotels' Plan to Win Customers from Airbnb." *Fortune*. January 27. http://fortune.com/2016/01/27/big-hotels-Airbnb/.

Faulkner, Tim. 2007. "The Rap on Rapleaf, the 'Trust Meter' You Can't Trust." gawker.com. September 6. http://gawker.com/297143/the-rap-on-rapleaf-the-trust-meter-you-cant-trust.

Gansky, Lisa. 2010. *The Mesh: Why the Future of Business Is Sharing*. New York: Penguin.

Giesler, Markus. 2006. "Consumer Gift Systems." *Journal of Consumer Research* 33 (2): 283–290.

Goldman, David. 2010. "Rapleaf Is Selling Your Identity." money.cnn.com. October 21. http://money.cnn.com/2010/10/21/technology/rapleaf/index.htm.

Habibi, Mohammad Reza, Andrea Kim, and Michel Laroche. 2016. "From Sharing to Exchange: An Extended Framework of Dual Modes of Collaborative Nonownership Consumption." *Journal of the Association of Consumer Research* 1 (2): 277–294.

Hawksworth, John, and Robert Vaughan. 2016. "The Sharing Economy—Sizing the Revenue Opportunity." PWC. http://www.pwc.co.uk/issues/mega trends/collisions/sharingeconomy/the-sharing-economy-sizing-the-reve nue-opportunity.html.

Hern, Alex. 2015. "Why the Term 'Sharing Economy' Needs to Die." *Guardian*. https://www.theguardian.com/technology/2015/oct/05/why-the-term-sharing-economy-needs-to-die.

Hill, Kyle. 2014. "A Financial Model Comparing Car Ownership with UberX (Los Angeles)." www.medium.com. https://medium.com/@kaleazy/a-financial-model-comparing-car-ownership-with-uberx-los-angeles-b7becd917095#.z3qrc5f5v.

Kahneman, Daniel, Alan B. Krueger, David A. Schkade, Norbert Schwarz, and Arthur A. Stone. 2004. "A Survey Method for Characterizing Daily Life Experience: The Day Reconstruction Method." *Science* 306 (5702): 1776–1780.

Kapoor, Raj. 2014. "Lessons from the Sharing Economy." *TechCrunch*. August 30. http://techcrunch.com/2014/08/30/critical-lessons-from-the-sharing-economy/.

Kessler, Sarah (2015), "The Sharing Economy Is Dead, And We Killed It." *Fast Company*. September 14 https://www.fastcompany.com/3050775/the-sharing-economy-is-dead-and-we-killed-it.

Kocieniewski, David. 2016. "The Sharing Economy Doesn't Share the Wealth." *Bloomberg Businessweek*. April 6. http://www.bloomberg.com/news/arti cles/2016-04-06/the-sharing-economy-doesn-t-share-the-wealth.

Koopman, Christopher, Matthew Mitchell, and Adam Thierer, "The Sharing Economy and Consumer Protection Regulation: The Case for Policy Change." *Journal of Business Entrepreneurship & the Law* 8 (2): 529–545.

Lamberton, Cait Poynor, and Randy Rose. 2012. "Yours, Mine and Ours: An Investigation of Consumers' Propensity to Participate in Commercial Sharing Systems." *Journal of Marketing* July: 109–125.

Maag, Christopher. 2014. "The Sharing Economy Grows Up: The Emerging Models and Investment Trends." *CleantechIQ.* April 23. http://cleante chiq.com/2014/04/the-sharing-economy-goes-from-gawky-adolescent-to-prom-queen/.

Marchi, Alberto, and Ellora-Julie Parekh. 2015. "How the Sharing Economy Can Make Its Case." *McKinsey Quarterly.* http://www.mckinsey.com/business-functions/strategy-and-corporate-finance/our-insights/how-the-sharing-economy-can-make-its-case.

Marshall, Matt. 2006. "Networker Hoffman Launches Rapleaf—To Track Your Reputation beyond Ebay." www.venturebeat.com. April 24. http://venturebeat.com/2006/04/24/networker-hoffman-launches-rapleaf-o-track-your-reputation-beyond-ebay/.

Mclean, Robert. 2016. "Uber Will Pay up to $100 million to Settle Labor Suits." *CNN Money.* April 22. http://money.cnn.com/2016/04/22/technology/uber-drivers-labor-settlement/.

Morton, Scott F., Florian Zettelmeyer, and J. Silva-Risso. 2003. "Consumer Information and Discrimination: Does the Internet Affect the Pricing of New Cars to Women and Minorities?" *Quantitative Marketing and Economics* 1 (1): 65–92.

Ndubisi, Nelson Oly, Michael Ehret, and Jochen Wirtz. 2016. "Relational Governance Mechanisms and Uncertainties in Nonownership Systems." *Psychology & Marketing* 33 (4): 250–266.

Needleman, Sarah E., and Angus Loten. 2014. "Startups Want to Be the Next Airbnb, Uber—'Sharing Economy' Ideas Are Hot, but Many Lead to Failure; Pet-Sitting Incidents Are Proving Costly for DogVacay.com." *Wall Street Journal,* Eastern edition. May 8. https://www.wsj.com/articles/startups-want-to-be-the-next-Airbnb-uber-1399503252

Newton, Paula. 2015. "The Sharing Economy: Some of Its Successes to Date." www.intelligenthq. June 20. http://www.intelligenthq.com/social-business-2/the-sharing-economy-some-of-its-successes-to-date/.

Patel, Kunar. 2009. "Zipcar: An America's Hottest Brands Case Study." November 16. http://adage.com/article/special-report-americas-hottest-brands-2009/zipcar-america-s-hottest-brands-case-study/140495/.

Price, Linda L., and Russell W. Belk. 2016. "Consumer Ownership and Sharing: Introduction to the Issue." *Journal of the Association for Consumer Research* 1 (2): 193–197.

Ransbotham, Sam (2015), "Data at the Heart of the Sharing economy," *MIT Sloan Management Review.* October 26. http://sloanreview.mit.edu/article/data-at-the-heart-of-the-sharing-economy/.

Reich, Robert. 2015. "The Share-the-Scraps Economy." February 2. http://robertreich.org/post/109894095095.

Schor, Juliet. 2014. "Debating the Sharing Economy." *Great Transition Initiative.* October. http://www.greattransition.org/publication/debating-the-sharing-economy.

Schwartz, Eric Hal. 2015. "A Look at Uber's 9 Biggest Successes and Failures." *DCInno.*June23.http://dcinno.streetwise.co/2015/06/23/sharing-economy-ubers-9-biggest-successes-failures/.

Singer, Natasha. 2014. "In the Sharing Economy, Workers Find Both Freedom and Uncertainty." *New York Times.* August 16. http://www.nytimes.com/2014/08/17/technology/in-the-sharing-economy-workers-find-both-freedom-and-uncertainty.html?_r=0.

Tanz, Jason. 2015. "Once-Radical Relayrides Adapts to a World That Digs Sharing."www.wired.com.http://www.wired.com/2015/11/relayrides-becomes-turo-sharing-economy-here-to-stay/.

vanWelsum, Desiree. 2016. "Sharing Is Caring? Not Quite. Some Observations about 'the Sharing Economy.'" Background Paper: Digital Dividends, World Development Report series.

Vital, Anna. 2014. "How Airbnb Started." http://notes.fundersandfounders.com/post/82297315548/how-Airbnb-started.

Zervas, Georgios, Davide Proserpio, and John W. Byers. 2016. "The Rise of the Sharing Economy: Estimating the Impact of Airbnb on the Hotel Industry." http://people.bu.edu/zg/publications/Airbnb.pdf.

CHAPTER ELEVEN

The Role of Governments in Peer-to-Peer Sharing and Collaborative Consumption

Friedrich Chasin

A Difficult Relationship

Despite the public (Geron 2013) and academic (Heinrichs and Grunenberg 2013) discourse on the potential of the sharing economy to address the social, economic, and environmental challenges of today, there is major skepticism in regard to its future. At the core of this skepticism are governments' concerns regarding the legitimacy of peer-to-peer (P2P) sharing and collaborative consumption (SCC) services.[1] For instance, sharing services often operate in the legal gray area where it is difficult for governments to enforce proper taxation and ensure citizens' protection—a situation that can lead to unfair competition as traditional businesses have to comply with a variety of regulation that do not necessary apply to the sharing businesses (Baker 2014; Wogan 2013). Consequently, governments can go as far as to withdraw their support from sharing businesses and even fine and block them (Tuttle 2013). However, basic motivations behind governmental and sharing practices are arguably aligned. On the one hand, the aim of every government is "to meet the needs of its constituency, to maintain their welfare . . . [and] serving people's basic needs, both physical and economic" (Firestone and Catlett 2009, 296). On the other hand, sharing services are built upon the idea of making use of idle resources and serving economic needs of peers. Peer-providers are given an opportunity to monetize their resources, and peer-consumers are granted access to resources that they are unable or unwilling to get from traditional channels (Hamari, Sjöklint, and Ukkonen 2015). The sharing of idle or underutilized resources has not only economic implications but also affects the ecological and social systems by making the management of resource scarcity a social endeavor (Heinrichs 2013). Therefore, governments should carefully explore opportunities to support citizens' sharing practices that aid in addressing current and future economic, environmental, and social challenges.

In this chapter, I will focus on the challenges and potential resulting from the ambivalent relationship between sharing services and government. On the one hand, legal tensions can arise when governments observe economic activities between peers being executed in legal "gray" areas (Chernova 2013). On the other hand, synergies can emerge when P2P concepts are embedded into governmental policies (Chasin and Scholta 2015). The concept of sharing is not new to the governmental bodies and is exercised across municipalities. For instance, much is written about tackling societal problems through sharing of resources and infrastructures that are possessed by governments, with bike sharing being probably the most prominent example (DeMaio 2009). Other examples are any forms of public infrastructure, including public transportation (Murray et al. 1998), and, for example, an infrastructure of public street-bookshelves (Doctorow 2002). However, the bidirectional relationship of governments and P2P sharing and collaborative consumption platforms is hardly explored with fragmented reports on sharing practices provided by individual municipalities (Botero, Paterson, and Saad-Sulonen 2012; City of Chicago 2014; Johnson 2013; Linders 2012; Stoll 2012). I will shed light on the relationship from both academic and practitioner perspectives by synthesizing my research in this domain. For instance, I will mainly draw upon the results of two completed research projects with the focus on the governments' active role in the provision of sharing services (Chasin and Scholta 2015) and the legal environments of sharing businesses (Chasin et al. 2015). Moreover, I will present findings from ongoing research on the pilot project of the Sharing City Seoul—a governmental initiative that aims at supporting the development of sharing practices in the South Korean capital. Last but not least, I will draw upon my personal experience gained through the active involvement in the development of an IT-enabled P2P collaborative consumption service for the electric vehicles charging infrastructure. The latter serves as a good example of a German sharing service that is heavily challenged by the national legal environment.

The remainder of the chapter is structured as follows. First, different forms of sharing and implications for their relationships with governments are presented in the next section. Subsequent section provides research background and related work in regard to the role of the governments in the sharing practices. Next, the research on the legal aspects of the relationship is presented. This is followed by the exploration of one particular case where governments actively support the development of sharing practices. The last section is devoted to the question of how sharing practices can be integrated into the governmental agenda.

Different Types of Sharing

The terminology around the "sharing economy" is confusing. The phenomenon is interpreted differently with varying scope of practices that are considered part of it (Belk 2014a; Botsman 2013). Consequently, what is true for one type of services that fall under the broader term of the sharing economy is often not true for the others. Therefore, it is imperative to establish a clear understanding of the practices under consideration before moving forward. This is especially important in case of discussing the relationship between governments and sharing economy practices because the relationship varies greatly depending on the economic transaction type that underlies a service at hand.

Five characteristics that help to define the scope of the practices within the sharing economy are presented. I argue for two basic criteria that need to be fulfilled in order to consider an economic transaction as part of the sharing economy: lack of ownership transfer and IT support of the marketplace. Ownership transfer is not aligned with the idea that modern consumers increasingly prefer to distance themselves from ownership as an ultimate expression of personal desire (Chen 2009; Marx 2011), preferring functionality over the product itself, and the experience of using a resource over its acquisition (Firnkorn and Müller 2012; Rifkin 2000). However, even when the two are satisfied, there are still variations of practices that can be distinguished. Figure 11.1 provides an overview of the criteria in the form of a morphological box. The criteria are elaborated in what follows.

Transfer of Ownership

Although some of the research and practice literature might suggest otherwise, there are a number of arguments against considering practices involving transfer of ownership, such as swapping, part of the sharing economy. Arguably, the basic idea behind the sharing economy is the preference for the access to a resource over the ownership, and the preference for the function over the object itself (Bardhi and Eckhardt 2012a). Depending on whether there is a transfer of ownership for the resource at hand, the relationships between involved parties vary. Swapping can be "reduced" to a form of barter, and,

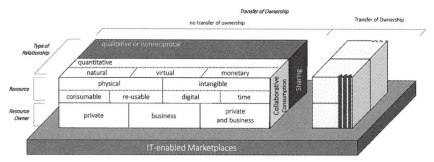

Figure 11.1 Dimensions of economic transactions of the sharing economy

even when the practices might be aligned with the aim of reducing overproduction, the characteristics of the swapping service will be different from renting or true forms of sharing (Belk 2014a).

IT-Enabled Marketplaces

Second criterion that needs to be satisfied for classifying an economic transaction as part of the sharing economy is the presence of an *IT-enabled marketplace* that enables the transactions. What arguably gives the sharing economy the legitimacy to be considered as a new phenomenon is the efficiency and effectiveness of the sharing practices enabled by rapid advances in IT (Botsman and Rogers 2010). Against the backdrop of advanced Internet technologies (most importantly the ability of Web 2.0 to provide user-generated content), "Uber, the world's largest taxi company, owns no vehicles . . . [and] Airbnb, the world's largest accommodation provider, owns no real estate" (Goodwin 2015). Therefore, the scope of the phenomenon's impact is part of its definition, and the use of IT is its inherent characteristic. Without the use of IT, the scope of the sharing practices could not reach the level that we observe today—a level that is changing the consumer behavior and is increasingly challenging the conventional value chains (Chase 2013; De 2013; Owyang 2015; Owyang, Tran, and Silva 2013; Walsh 2011).

Types of Relationship

Belk discusses two different types of relationships formed between parties through a transaction—*qualitative* and *quantitative* (Belk 2014a, 2010). While true sharing is nonreciprocal in nature, self-interest and qualitative relationship formed by it can also be present in some sharing-alike practices (Belk 2014a). A quantitative relationship means that the relationship formed by a transaction is quantifiable by means of a monetary, virtual, or natural equivalent. A payment is, for example, a quantitative assessment of the value provided in the course of the economic transaction from one party to another. A qualitative relationship, on the other hand, cannot be quantified. For example, a qualitative relationship is formed when sharing an accommodation for free creates an expectation that the person on the receiving side will do the same in the future. It is therefore important to distinguish nonreciprocal behaviors or behaviors that form a qualitative relationship (sharing) from behaviors that typically involve some form of quantifiable compensation (collaborative consumption) (Belk 2014a, 1598).

Although both sharing and collaborative consumption practices are different in the aforementioned respect, they manifest a change in consumer behavior towards "non-traditional" forms of consumption. This shift is motivated by environmentally driven resource utilization (Botsman and Rogers 2010), ethical concerns regarding overconsumption (Belk 2014b; Leismann et al. 2013), prospects of and addressing degradation of the natural environment (Anderegg et al. 2010; Oreskes 2004), as well as by expectations of economic benefits (Bardhi and Eckhardt 2012b).

Resource

The resource that is required for the transaction to take place can be *physical* or *intangible*. Sharing and collaborative consumption of intangible resources, for example, *digital* content, is well researched (e.g., Hughes, Lang, and Vragov 2005; Xia et al. 2012). The advent of the sharing economy set focus on the sharing of physical resources—practices that are nowadays represented by highly successful businesses such as Airbnb and Uber. Physical resources can be *consumable* and *re-usable*. For example, sharing a meal is different from lending kitchen equipment. Both behaviors form different types of relationships with the latter creating at least an obligation to return the resource to its owner. Reusable resources hence require responsible handling in a sharing scenario while consumable resources do not.

Resource Owner

The owner of the resource that is shared or collaboratively consumed during the service execution can be owned by either *business* or a *private* individual. Traditional car sharing falls in the category of resources shared by the business. P2P platforms typically offer privately owned resources. However, there are exceptions where intermediary platforms allow both *private and business* resources to be shared.

One subset of economic transactions in the sharing economy is especially interesting for the purpose of this chapter. Those are practices that underlie

P2P sharing and collaborative (P2P SCC) services, in which a *physical* resource is required for the service offering to be performed and *private* people are able to provide the resource. Such services are manifested in the form of P2P digital platforms (Andersson, Hjalmarsson, and Avital 2013) where private peers can share resources either for compensation (collaborative consumption) or as a true form of sharing, therefore forming *quantitative* or *qualitative/nonreciprocal* relationships correspondingly. What makes these services especially interesting from the government point of view is the fact that they address basic societal needs such as transportation, food, housing. P2P car ride (BlaBlaCar)[2], car sharing (Turo)[3] and car taxi services (Lyft)[4] create affordable and flexible mobility solutions for the citizens. Same goes for the apartment sharing service (Airbnb)[5] that, in some regions, presents a preferable alternative to the traditional housing solutions. For instance, from my personal experience, staying several months in Seoul leaves one with few affordable options other than a P2P apartment sharing. Last but not least, dining at private persons' homes (PlateCulture[6]) as well as enjoying home-grown food (RipeNearMe[7]) can be real and often more sustainable alternatives to traditional solutions of the food industry. All these domains touch upon governmental areas of responsibility and are subject to ongoing challenges that municipalities face when establishing infrastructures for their citizens. Second, sharing services challenge governments by demanding new regulations. When private peers share music files, governments have arguably fewer reasons to be concerned. It is rather the music industry that pays closer attention in this case. But when private people start to share vehicles, apartments, parking spaces, store venues, drones, and others, this touches upon a multitude of domains regulated and overseen by municipalities—domains where problems are quickly linked to the government's[8] inability to assure citizens employment, safety, and well-being.

Status Quo in Research

While media regularly cover the topic (Baker 2014; Cannon and Summers 2015; Cellan-Jones 2014; Chokshi 2014), the government's role in P2P sharing and collaborative consumption services is an underresearched topic in academia. This is surprising since, when it comes to the development of the sharing domain, governments can be both a facilitator or a barrier that is impossible to overcome (Chasin et al. 2015). The following introduces results of a literature review aimed at finding articles that address topics where governments and sharing economy come together. Scopus search platform was utilized as a literature database.[9] To assure the quality of the publication, only outlets from the list of peer-reviewed sources according to VHB-JOURQUAL3[10] rating were considered. Table 11.1 summarizes the results in the form of a concept matrix. Three concepts are used for the analysis: influence character,

Table 11.1 Concept Matrix for the Analyzed Articles

Citation	Influence Character			Influence Direction			Influence Impact		
	negative	positive	ambivalent	Gov. -> P2P SCC	P2P SCC -> Gov.	bidirectional	enabling	restricting	demanding
Barnes and Mattsson 2016	x					x		x	x
Buliung et al. 2010			x	x			x	x	x
Cannon and Summers 2015	x				x				x
Chasin et al. 2015			x			x	x	x	x
Chasin and Scholta 2015		x				x	x		
Costantini 2015			x	x				x	
Firnkorn and Shaheen 2014	x				x				x
Gobble 2015	x			x				x	x
Hong and Vicdan 2016	x			x				x	x
Kassan and Orsi 2012			x		x		x	x	x
Kim 2015		x		x			x		
Lindloff et al. 2014			x	x			x	x	
Tal and Cohen-Blankshtain 2011		x		x			x		
Wang and Chen 2012		x		x			x		x

influence direction, and influence impact in regard to the relationship of the governments and sharing services as perceived and presented by the authors of the articles in the sample.

Influence character describes how authors of academic publications perceive the relationship between governments and sharing businesses in their articles. It can be either *positive* or *negative* or *ambivalent*. It is a subject of interpretation and can only serve as a starting point for a more detailed enquiry. The choice of the content and overall connotation of the described relationship between governments and sharing economy services helps to interpret the perceived influence character.

Influence direction indicates if government influences sharing economy businesses (Gov. → SE), the sharing economy businesses influence the governments (SE → Gov.) or if this influence is bidirectional (SE ↔ Gov.). Similarly to the influence character, this dimension describes the perceived influence direction. While the factual direction is bidirectional in nature, the focus in the analyzed research can focus on one of the directions.

Influence impact is the notion of the impact that results from governments and sharing businesses influencing each other. The effect, for example, can be demanding if governments demand sharing economy businesses to fulfill certain characteristics, or if respective services demand financial support or changes in the legal environment from the governments. Analogously, restricting and enabling impacts can occur in both directions.

With the exception of three articles (Barnes and Mattsson 2016; Chasin and Scholta 2015; Chasin et al. 2015), the represented influence is unidirectional. However, since the relationship is bidirectional in nature, ignoring mutual dependencies of governments and sharing economy businesses in research can be problematic. For example, a governmental reaction through introduction of new laws for legal limbos requires a deeper understanding of how the introduced laws will affect the development and proliferation of new sharing services. When analyzing the articles with the unidirectional representation of the influence, it becomes apparent that the choice of the direction can be primarily explained by the authors' expertise. The majority of the analyzed articles come from management, organization, transportation, and information system domains. There, governmental forces, such as the influence of regulations introduced by the New York City on the development of car sharing (Kim 2015), the influence of policy making on innovations in general (Gobble 2015), or impacts of policies aimed at reducing car use (Tal and Cohen-Blankshtain 2011), are external factors. What these studies arguably lack is the reflection on the process of making these policies. The regulations are often represented as given although they are introduced as reactions to the phenomena they regulate. For instance, first regulations that subject private drivers in Colorado, the United States, to background checks and regular vehicle inspections are a direct response to the operations of companies like Uber and

Lyft (Chokshi 2014). By looking at the regulations' origins, implications for the new technological phenomena and their design parameters can be derived.

The ambivalent character of the relationship between governments and sharing economy is not only reflected in the media (Baker 2014; Wogan 2013) but in the research too. On the one hand, there are negative accounts for the influence character, including representations of governments as an evil barrier that needs to be overcome by clever business strategies (Cannon and Summers 2015) as well as criticism of policy makers having a "static view" (Firnkorn and Shaheen 2014), making substantial changes to the law that prevent the natural fostering of the sharing environment (Hong and Vicdan 2016) and crippling innovations that are not yet proven to be harmful for society (Gobble 2015). On the other hand, positive influence character can be observed especially in the context of pro-sharing legislation (Kim 2015; Tal and Cohen-Blankshtain 2011). Depiction of further positive influences in the relationship between governments and sharing economy can be found in the articles that consider the relationship to be ambivalent (Buliung et al. 2010; Costantini 2015; Lindloff et al. 2014), including research on the legal landscape of sharing services (Chasin et al. 2015) and the potential for governments to bring technology-facilitated sharing onto the next level (Chasin and Scholta 2015). The complexity of the bidirectional and ambivalent relationship between governments and the sharing economy is also demonstrated best by the distribution of accounts of influence impacts found in the analyzed literature. Multiplicity of restricting, demanding, and enabling effects in both directions is discussed in the research (compare Table 11.1).

Challenges: Legal Environment as the Backbone of the Sharing Economy

Sharing businesses such as those providing access to private accommodation (Airbnb)[11], cars (Lyft)[12], and clothes (Share Closet)[13] are required to comply with a variety of regulations. However, governments are also required to react when sharing businesses use legislative or regulatory loopholes to enter the market (Kassan and Orsi 2012). Arguably this tense legal environment is demonstrated best by the platform Uber, which enables private individuals to acquire taxi services from drivers of privately owned cars. This business, which amounts nowadays for at least 10% of the taxi market (even according to skeptical estimations)[14], is often perceived by traditional taxi providers as a threat. They demand that the strict regulations that are applied to their businesses should also be applied to Uber drivers (Cellan-Jones 2014). For example, in London, the range of legal requirements for traditional businesses includes the obligation to have a liability insurance, to have a credit card reader installed in the car, to pass English proficiency exam and a test on local geography, to become subject of regular vehicle

inspections and annual criminal background checks, and to pass a manda-
tory physical exam (Wogan 2013). Those regulations do not apply to Uber
drivers because there is no one to be held accountable in case an Uber driver
does not comply with the aforementioned requirements. Furthermore, according to a possible legal argument, an Uber driver is not an employee of
Uber and, therefore, there is no business entity that can become subject of
additional compliance requests. Similar situations can be observed with
sharing platforms that offer resources other than cars, including private accommodations (Vasagar 2014), private cars (Tuttle 2013), and private Wi-Fi
(Silver 2013).

The legal tensions are bidirectional. On the one hand, sharing services
challenge governments with the need for changed or even new legislation.
This becomes increasingly the reality. For instance, the state of Colorado
(USA) signed a legal proposal that subjects sharing service to the state's regulations (Chokshi 2014; Quittner 2014). On the other hand, regulations challenge sharing businesses, which often operate in a legal limbo (*The New York
Times* 2014; Streitfeld 201). Especially regulations in regard to citizen protection (Wogan 2013), fair competition (Cellan-Jones 2014), and taxation (Baker
2014) constrain the emergence and operation of P2P practices. Noncompli-
ance can result in governments issuing fines and ordering platforms to stop
operations (Tuttle 2013). A concrete example is a shutdown of a private taxi
service SideCar in New York (USA) due to its drivers lacking a taxi license
(Chernova 2013). Arguably, the lack of regulations for the new consumption
space is the nexus of the tensions.

A recent study (Chasin et al. 2015) conceptualized the relationship between the law and sharing services. The conceptualization is similar to how
the research on the relationship between governments and the sharing economy was categorized in the research background section. However, this conceptualization aims at providing an instrument to derive specific guidance to
the sharing businesses. The application of the framework can result in better
risk management of potential failures during the development of new sharing
services or even terminations due to incompliance or compliance-driven
changes in the services that can become infeasible. The holistic view on the
relationship also allows governments to identify gaps in the legal environment
of the sharing services. The framework (Figure 11.2) is based on Knackstedt
et al. (2013), who analyzed the representation of a more general relationship
of information systems and law.[15]

The specific case of a P2P sharing and collaborative consumption service
is explicitly reflected in the proposed framework. Any IT-enabled sharing
service comprises two types of service providers. While the intermediary
provides the platform and, in some cases, additional services such as insurance and verification, the peer supplier offers access to his or her private
resources. Correspondingly, the relationship between law and a sharing

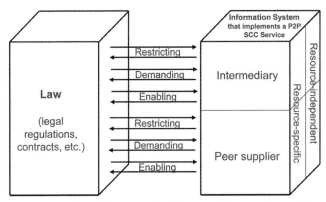

Figure 11.2 Framework of the mutual influence of law and P2P SCC services
Source: Chasin et al. (2015).

service can be separated into the bidirectional relationships between the intermediary platform and the law, and the relationship between the peer supplier and the law. To illustrate this relationship one can recall different bidirectional relationships of the law with the Uber platform itself and its drivers correspondingly. The set of regulations that applies to the platform is different from the one that applies to the owner and driver of the private cab. This is also true for the influence impacts of the platform and peer suppliers on the law.

The second specifics is derived from the fact that one part of the relationship between sharing services and governments is particular in regard to the resource that is being shared or is required for the service and the other part is not. Therefore, we differentiate between "resource-independent" and "resource-specific" parts of the relationship. A specific part of the relationship can be, for example, a requirement for Airbnb to list only those accommodations that comply with hygiene standards set by the local municipality. This requirement is obviously irrelevant in the case of sharing private cars. However, peer suppliers in both cases are subject to become business entities and therefore subject of taxation when their income from a sharing service exceeds a limit set by the local legal body.[16]

To effectively apply the framework, it needs to be instantiated with the local legal environment and specific sharing business or class of businesses. In this case, all facets of the complex bidirectional relationship between peer-suppliers and the law and intermediary platform and the law can be systematically illuminated. The results of such an analysis can help both the developers of a new sharing services and legal experts to understand the requirements for new legislations. An exemplary application of the framework in the domain of sharing private charging stations for electric vehicles can be found in Chasin et al. (2015).

Solutions: Sharing City Seoul—Insights from an Initiative That Brings Government and the Idea of Sharing Together

The Initiative

In 2012, the mayor of Seoul, Park Won-soon, launched the Sharing City Seoul initiative.[17] The initiative aims at supporting the development of sharing practices in the South Korean capital. The birth of the initiative came against the background of challenges faced by a big Asian city with 10 million citizens. These included typical challenges in transportation, housing, and general resource overcapacity (Princen, Maniates, and Conca 2002). However, according to a manager of the current partner of the Sharing City Seoul, one particular problem faced by Seoul is that "people are getting more and more individualized and [form] less connections with neighbours."[18] Similarly, the manager of the Social Innovation Division[19] summarized the problem as "isolated people and broken communities." Seoul's mayor believes in the positive impact of sharing behavior on the society and hopes to improve the situation in the megalopolis through citizens' increased practice of sharing. This is consistent with the research on qualities of sharing, which include social interaction, social proximity, and social bonds (Wittel 2011).

Unlike initiatives of other municipalities to promote sharing (Johnson 2014), the major difference of the Sharing City Seoul is the provision of financial support to sharing start-ups. Several sharing city initiatives were announced with much fanfare but with "little follow through" (Johnson 2014). This does not, however, mean that City Seoul managed to achieve a radical change in the consumer practices of its citizens as for now. Interviews with City Seoul and ShareHub[20] indicate that less than 10% of the population are aware of the initiative let alone make use of it. Nevertheless, during the last years, the list of achievements of the initiative includes support of 57[21] sharing businesses, help in raising total sales of these businesses by 900%, provision of direct financial support, total annual savings for the citizens amounting to 12 billion Korean won (US$4.3 million) and 1.18 trillion Korean won (US$1 billion) for the city itself, creation of over 1,000 new jobs, and reduction of tons of CO_2 emissions (ShareHub 2015). This is impressive considering that other cities' achievements with respect to the sharing economy entailed shutdowns of sharing businesses (Chernova 2013).

The foundation of the initiative are legislations passed by the local government with the "Seoul Metropolitan Government Act for Promoting Sharing" being its core element. The structure of the initiative is depicted in Figure 11.3. On the government side, there is a division called Social Innovation Division (SID), which has its own budget and comprises four permanent members. It advises and works together with other divisions of the municipality such as transportation and housing divisions. As its manager puts it, the members of

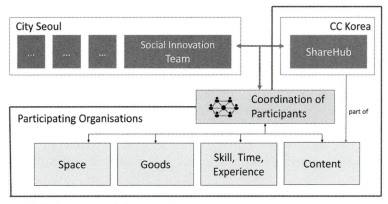

Figure 11.3 Structure of the initiative

the SID are "control towers and think-tankers" and are responsible for finding "new issues" that will be then considered jointly with other divisions. Besides working with other divisions, members of the SID communicate and coordinate their efforts with the ShareHub to optimize the promotion of the initiative and its participating members and to catalyze network activities. The portfolio of ShareHub responsibilities includes hosting a web platform, developing promotion materials, organizing network events and conferences, and evaluating the initiative's progress and providing training for the sharing startups. Furthermore, a committee of 5 permanent members (general directors) from the city government and 10 external experts meet annually to select businesses that will be funded by the government and to define the plan for the next year.

Insights from the Government Perspective

Governments can learn from the initiative's past and present. Interviews with both representatives of the City Seoul and its partner ShareHub were conducted in order to gain a deeper understanding of the challenges that the initiative faces.[22] The insights from the interviews are summarized in what follows. This chapter will primarily focus on the problems that the initiative faces because the experienced challenges and their potential solutions represent the most valuable insights for those governments that plan similar initiatives in the future.

First, it is important to outline that there is a paradox behind the initiative. According to a manager of the SID, the most important component of a successful governmental sharing initiative is to "listen to the citizens" that is to address their needs for sharing resources. However, according to the interview data, citizens in Seoul do not have an inherent desire for sharing and only a small fraction of the population know about the existence of P2P sharing practices. That means, although it is implied that the movement comes from the citizens, this is hardly the case for the city of Seoul. This is why, after four years of work, the major challenge of the initiative remains that people "do not know about the initiative." It means that governments need to be prepared to facilitate demand for sharing and not expect that large portions of the population are ready to start using sharing offerings and just wait for those to appear on the market. In the case of Sharing City Seoul, the words of ShareHub manager describe the situation best: "The government or research teams have a lot of interest in . . . sharing resources, but there is certainly less interest from citizens." This does not, however, diminish the achievements of the initiative. It solely highlights the need to manage expectations of interested governments in regard to the citizens' readiness to participate in sharing.

When governments decide to support sharing businesses, they also face a challenge of positioning themselves in regard to the local and foreign sharing platforms. For example, City Seoul is concerned with the competition on the sharing-based housing market. Local providers such as Kozaza[23] have difficulty competing against international providers such as Airbnb even if the local businesses demonstrate higher compliance with the legislation and have a better impact on the local economy. For the reasons of better control and better connection to the local sharing businesses in the domain of housing, Sharing City Seoul "want[s] to promote more than Airbnb." That means that the City Seoul is searching for ways to promote the local competitors of big players such as Airbnb. They explicitly state that they prefer the market being dominated by the local sharing enterprises as they can better assure that the businesses comply with all the standards necessary. Therefore, the issue of the government's positioning between local and foreign sharing platform providers needs to be clarified upfront and strategies need to be developed in order to provide local businesses with the support they need.

From the organizational point of view, the initiative faces further challenges. The biggest challenge is arguably the need for the SID to coordinate its efforts with the other 144 divisions of the City Seoul. Building sharing houses, for example, falls under the responsibility of the housing division. Even if the representatives of the SID describe this cooperation as "friendly," there is an obvious challenge of combining the sharing agenda with the agendas of the related divisions. Another challenge is connected to the structure of the initiative and the fact that there are two coordinating bodies. After four years of initiative operations, there are still clarity issues regarding the responsibilities of the SID and ShareHub. Their functions, especially in terms of promoting the initiative, overlap. Consequently, every government that plans a sharing initiative requires a concept of how to acquire competency that is needed for the development of the initiative and how to clearly divide responsibilities between parties in case some external partners need to be introduced to the initiative for coordinating purposes.

To summarize, financial support from the governments for the sharing companies might seem to be a panacea yet it is not. Despite financial support that sharing start-ups received from City Seoul, most of those companies still struggle with the market penetration. The ability to develop a market is a crucial component that distinguishes successful sharing businesses from less successful ones. There is a certain level that the governments of today seem to be ready to go in terms of supporting sharing behavior of their citizens. For example, City Seoul plans to aggregate promotion of sharing offerings on a single platform. However, it is skeptical in terms of becoming a platform provider itself. The city also supports businesses but is less enthusiastic about going beyond that and supporting the peer suppliers who participate in sharing businesses. Governments are careful because they do not want to damage the competitiveness on the market.

Insights from the Companies' Perspective

Besides interviews with representatives of City Seoul and ShareHub, in-person interviews were conducted with four sharing businesses that participate in the initiative where the respondents were asked to reflect upon the relationship with the initiative. The remainder of this section presents insights from a P2P parking space sharing (a), P2P clothes sharing (b), P2P apartment sharing (c), and P2P general space sharing (d).[24] The findings go beyond a simple appreciation of the initiative. First and most of all, the need for promoting sharing among citizens is unanimously confirmed and highlighted by the interviewed companies. Sharing businesses are grateful to the government for the advertisement. One successfully operating sharing business stated that it "did not spend a single penny on marketing. It is a big help from City Seoul doing all the advertising work" (b). However, while the government does not differentiate between peer-suppliers and peer-users, companies clearly articulate the greater importance of peer-suppliers in developing the business (see Table 11.2). The clear implication for future governmental initiatives is that there should be a concept regarding how to facilitate participation of potential peer-suppliers in the supported sharing businesses.

The challenge of different responsibilities within the City Seoul division has a further dimension. Apparently, it is often not enough to get support from the city government alone in order to successfully enter the market. City Seoul has 25 district authorities who might have the final say in allowing certain forms of sharing. For example, for the sharing of parking spaces, you have to "set up sensors to let people know where the free spaces are in real time." In order to do so, "you have to get the approval from each district in Seoul"

Table 11.2   Quotations Regarding the Need for Peer-Suppliers for the
              Successful P2P Sharing Service Development

Statement	Source
"It is hard to make people who have the [resource] to participate in this service"	(a)
"It was difficult to get the cooperation from the provider side. As house is a very important capital for individuals in Korea, people did not want to rent houses for experimental purposes"	(c)
"There were many challenges, but the core one was that there were not enough suits provided"	(b)

(space-sharing business). Therefore, any governmental initiative for supporting sharing businesses must analyze its internal structure to make sure all
parties involved into approval process are involved.

The challenges that sharing businesses face can vary depending on the resource being shared. When smart technologies such as sensors are required
for the service to take place, the development of the service is complicated by
the hardware development and additional legal issues in regard to data gathered by the devices. Therefore, support in acquiring peer-suppliers would be
directly followed by the need to resolve potential legal issues. Those companies that have little legal challenges can rather focus on the challenge of pen-
etrating the market. For the latter, the governmental support is utmost
important because "if Seoul City gives a contact on behalf of us, it [works]
smoothly" (clothes-sharing business).

The major achievement of the Sharing City Seoul that needs to be highlighted is the atmosphere that the initiative established in the network. Especially for innovative businesses such as the sharing services, which face many
risks and uncertainties, the atmosphere of support can be a decisive factor in
the business success. The CEO of a parking space sharing business explained:
"For me, they (Government) give us a good atmosphere." The CEO of a general space-sharing business confirms: "If we request something, they always
say yes to us."

The Way Forward

The governments will continue to play a crucial role in the future of the
sharing economy. After the phase of badly needed response to catch up with
the rapid developments on the market, there must be a phase in which governments more actively consider its role in actively shaping the sharing economy and especially its subset of P2P sharing and collaborative consumption
services. In this chapter, I focused on this subset of sharing economy practices

as they are the frontline of practices that can reduce overconsumption and provide a step forward toward a more sustainable consumption in the future. As highlighted in the previous section, first governmental initiatives start to actively participate in the shaping of the sharing economy. It is apparent that some form of sharing and collaborative consumption is not feasible without governmental support. While prominent examples of sharing businesses such as Airbnb, Uber, and Lyft are based on sharing of rather expensive resources, many other resources continue to be underutilized without feasible solutions in the sharing economy domain at the moment. Financial support, adaptation of legal environment to foster the development of sharing businesses, addressing the "dark" side of the sharing economy, and considering the possibility of becoming an intermediary in the provision of sharing services—those are the directions for the governments if they want to utilize the full potential of the sharing economy to contribute to the solution of the societal, economic, and ecological problems of today and tomorrow.

Research has to play its role along the way. Many questions remain unanswered when it comes to the potentials of governments to bring the sharing economy and more specifically the sharing services onto the next level (Chasin and Scholta 2015). One direction for the research is to focus on the hidden potentials of the canonical research on electronic governments[25] to integrate sharing services into the portfolio of e-governments. This means creating sharing platforms that are run directly by the governments and not by for-profit organizations. This would put a government into the role of a trusted intermediary. First, the existence of e-government infrastructures in municipalities can reduce the amount of required investments to provide governmentally run intermediary platforms. Second, issues of trust that are known to be a major barrier in adopting sharing services (Botsman and Rogers 2010; Petri et al. 2011) can be addressed by utilizing higher citizens' trust in governmental platforms. Third, an active participation of governments in establishing sharing service landscapes provides greater control for the governments over the development of the domain, therefore reducing the risk of lagging behind the developments in the practice. Finally, as outlined previously, some forms of P2P sharing and collaborative consumption are unlikely to be adopted by the private sector due to infeasibility. Governments, on the other hand, can use their budgets "to meet the needs of its constituency, to maintain their welfare . . . [and] serving people's basic needs, both physical and economic" (Firestone and Catlett 2009, 296) by means of supporting or even developing sharing services.

Table 11.3 summarize research questions that need to be addressed when considering the path of active support of sharing services by governments (Chasin and Scholta 2015). Questions are divided into three groups. The first group addresses issues related to the existence of different stakeholders in the domain of e-governments. The second group of questions is related to the

Table 11.3 **Research Questions for the Research Agenda on the Role of Governments in Facilitating the Development of P2P SCC Services**

Stakeholder-related	
RQ1:	How can a government participate in establishing a P2P SCC platform as an e-government service for its citizens?
RQ2:	Which form of participation in establishing a P2P SCC platform as an e-government service is suitable for which government?
RQ3:	What are external obstacles and barriers for the introduction of P2P SCC as an e-government service and how can they be addressed?
RQ4:	How does the participation of a government in establishing P2P SCC affect its relationships to other e-government stakeholders?
Acceptance-related	
RQ5:	What is the antecedent structure for the governments' acceptance in regard to establishing P2P SCC as an e-government service?
RQ6:	How can an incentive structure support the governments' attitude toward P2P SCC as an e-government service?
RQ7:	To what extent can citizens' trust in IT-enabled P2P SCC be improved through governments assuming the role of the platform provider?
RQ8:	How do the antecedents of acceptance in regard to providing and using P2P SCC as an e-government service differ from the citizen perspective?
Stage-related	
RQ10:	How can existing e-government infrastructures of services from related stages be adopted to provide IT-enabled P2P SCC?
RQ11:	What are the different resource types that can be best shared and collaboratively consumed over the P2P SCC as an e-government service?
RQ12:	How should a P2P SCC platform be designed to combine low costs of the service with high value and quality for the citizens?

acceptance of sharing services as an e-government service. Finally, the third group of research questions aims at understanding how sharing services can be integrated along the different stages of e-governmental services.

In this chapter, I addressed the role of governments in the P2P sharing and collaborative consumption. Having provided insights into the research on that topic, I presented an instrument to analyze the complex relationship between sharing services and the governmental regulations. The challenge that results from this tense relationship is twofold. For the practice, it arguably represents the biggest barrier for the development of new sharing services. For the governments, it represents a challenge to control the emergence of P2P sharing and collaborative consumption businesses. In the second part of the chapter, I addressed the hidden potentials of the relationship. First I reported on the unique initiative of the Sharing City Seoul to support the sharing economy sector highlighting its experience with supporting sharing businesses and reporting on challenges that such governmental initiative is likely to face. Second, I summarized an existing research agenda for understanding the role of governments in establishing sharing services. It is my hope that the potentials for the governments' role in actively shaping the sharing economy that were outlined in this chapter can be realized and that research can spur this development along the way.

Notes

1. In the following and for the sake of readability, I will refer to peer-to-peer sharing and collaborative consumption (P2P SCC) services as simply sharing services. However, please bear in mind that these services are only a subset of sharing services that require private persons to temporarily share their physical resources.

2. https://www.blablacar.com.

3. https://turo.com.

4. https://www.lyft.com.

5. https://airbnb.com.

6. https://plateculture.com.

7. http://www.ripenear.me.

8. Governments refer in this context to the municipal public bodies.

9. Search string employed on the Scopus platform: TITLE-ABS-KEY(government) or title-abs-key(regulation) or title-abs-key(law) or title-abs-key(legal) or title-abs-key(policy) or title-abs-key(administration)) and title-abs-key("sharing economy") or title-abs-key(shareconomy) or title-abs-key("collaborative consumption").

10. http://vhbonline.org/en/service/jourqual/vhb-jourqual-3/complete-list-of-the-journals/.

11. https://www.airbnb.com.

12. https://www.lyft.com/.

13. http://sharecloset.com/.

14. http://fivethirtyeight.com/features/uber-isnt-worth-17-billion/ accessed on April 30, 2016.

15. For details of the framework's original dimensions see the original publication.

16. It must be noted that there are different ways for how governments can react to the proliferation of sharing businesses. The work by Rauch and Schleicher (2015) is a good starting point for an interested reader.

17. http://english.sharehub.kr/.

18. Interview material. Conducted on March 25, 2016, in the Seoul City Hall, Seoul, Korea.

19. The Social Innovation Division is one of the 145 divisions of the City Seoul and is responsible for the Sharing City Seoul initiative.

20. ShareHub is a partner organization under the flag of the Creative Commons Korea, which is responsible for promoting the Sharing City Seoul initiative. In March 2016, we conducted two interviews with the representatives of the Sharing Hub and one interview with the official of the Sharing City Soul Initiative.

21. According to out interview conducted on March 25, 2016, with the representative of the City Seoul there are already 64 companies that were supported by the initiative.

22. Three 60-minute-long interviews were conducted in the time frame from February 26, 2016, to March 23, 2016: one with the project manager of Social Innovation Division and two with managers of ShareHub.

23. https://www.kozaza.com/

24. Interviews were conducted on March 28, 2016, with (a) and (b) and on the March 29, 2016, with (c) and (d).

25. Electronic government describes the provision of governmental services through Internet platforms.

References

Anderegg, William R. L., James W Prall, Jacob Harold, and Stephen H Schneider. 2010. "Expert Credibility in Climate Change." *Proceedings of the National Academy of Sciences of the United States of America* 107: 12107–12109. doi:10.1073/pnas.1003187107.

Andersson, Magnus, Anders Hjalmarsson, and Michel Avital. 2013. "Peer-to-Peer Service Sharing Platforms: Driving Share and Share Alike on a Mass-Scale." *International Conference on Information Systems* 4: 2964–2978. Milano. http://www.scopus.com/inward/record.url?eid=2-s2.0-84897783206&partnerID=tZOtx3y1.

Baker, Dean. 2014. "Don't Buy the 'Sharing Economy' Hype: Airbnb and Uber Are Facilitating Rip-Offs." *Guardian*. http://www.theguardian.com/commentisfree/2014/may/27/airbnb-uber-taxes-regulation.

Bardhi, Fleura, and Giana M. Eckhardt. 2012a. "Access-Based Consumption: The Case of Car Sharing." *Journal of Consumer Research* 39 (4): 881–898. doi:10.1086/666376.

Bardhi, Fleura, and Giana M. Eckhardt. 2012b. "Access-Based Consumption: The Case of Car Sharing." *Journal of Consumer Research* 39 (December): 881–898. doi:10.1086/666376.

Barnes, Stuart J., and Jan Mattsson. 2016. "Technological Forecasting & Social Change Understanding Current and Future Issues in Collaborative Consumption: A Four-Stage Delphi Study." *Technological Forecasting & Social Change* 104: 200–211. doi:10.1016/j.techfore.2016.01.006.

Belk, Russell. 2010. "Sharing." *Journal of Consumer Research* 36: 715–734. doi:10.1086/612649.

Belk, Russell. 2014a. "Sharing versus Pseudo-Sharing in Web 2.0." *The Anthropologist* 4 (2): 7–23.

Belk, Russell. 2014b. "You Are What You Can Access: Sharing and Collaborative Consumption Online." *Journal of Business Research* 67 (8): 1595–1600.

Botero, A., A. Paterson, and J. Saad-Sulonen. 2012. "Towards Peer-Production in Public Services: Cases from Finland." http://urn.fi/URN:ISBN:978-952-60-4663-1.

Botsman, Rachel. 2013. "The Sharing Economy Lacks a Shared Definition." http://www.fastcoexist.com/3022028/the-sharing-economy-lacks-|a-shared-definition.

Botsman, Rachel, and Roo Rogers. 2010. *What's Mine Is Yours—How Collaborative Consumption Is Changing the Way We Live. Business.* New York: HarperCollins. http://www.wired.co.uk/news/archive/2011-10/13/rachel-botsman-wired-11.

Buliung, Ron N., Kalina Soltys, Randy Bui, Catherine Habel, and Ryan Lanyon. 2010. "Catching a Ride on the Information Super-Highway: Toward an Understanding of Internet-Based Carpool Formation and Use." *Transportation* 37 (6): 849–873. doi:10.1007/s11116-010-9266-0.

Cannon, Sarah, and Lawrence H. Summers. 2015. "How Uber and the Sharing Economy Can Win Over Regulators." *Harvard Business Review* 13: 1–4.

Cellan-Jones, Rory. 2014. "London Braced for Anti-Uber Protests." *BBC News.* http://www.bbc.com/news/technology-27783218.

Chase, Robin. 2013. "The Rise of the Collaborative Economy." *The Market News.* http://pioneers.themarknews.com/articles/the-rise-of-the-collaborative-economy/.

Chasin, Friedrich, Martin Matzner, Matthias Löchte, Verena Wiget, and Jörg Becker. 2015. "The Law: The Boon and Bane of IT-Enabled Peer-to-Peer Sharing and Collaborative Consumption Services Peer-to-Peer Services in a Uncertain Legal Environment." *12th International Conference on Wirtschaftsinformatik*, Osnabrück, Germany.

Chasin, Friedrich, and Hendrik Scholta. 2015. "Taking Peer-to-Peer Sharing and Collaborative Consumption onto the Next Level—New Opportunities and Challenges for E-Government." *Proceedings of the 23rd European*

Conference on Information Systems (ECIS 2015): 1–16. doi:10.18151/7217288.

Chen, Yu. 2009. "Possession and Access: Consumer Desires and Value Perceptions Regarding Contemporary Art Collection and Exhibit Visits." *Journal of Consumer Research* 35 (6): 925–940. http://ideas.repec.org/a/ucp/jconrs/v35y2009i6p925-940.html.

Chernova, Yuliya. 2013. "N.Y. Shutdowns for SideCar, RelayRides Highlight Hurdles for Car- and Ride-Sharing Startups—Venture Capital Dispatch." *Wall Street Journal.* http://blogs.wsj.com/venturecapital/2013/05/15/n-y-shutdowns-for-sidecar-relayrides-highlight-hurdles-for-car-and-ride-sharing-startups/.

Chokshi, Niraj. 2014. "Colorado Passes Nation's First Law Regulating uberX, Lyft." *The Washington Post.* http://www.washingtonpost.com/blogs/govbeat/wp/2014/06/06/colorado-passes-nations-first-law-regulating-uberx-lyft/.

City of Chicago. 2014. "Chicago Shovels." http://www.chicagoshovels.org.

Costantini, Federico. 2015. "The 'Peer-to-Peer' Economy and Social Ontology: Legal Issues and Theoretical Perspectives." *Lecture Notes in Computer Science (Including Subseries Lecture Notes in Artificial Intelligence and Lecture Notes in Bioinformatics)* 9341: 311–322. doi:10.1007/978-3-319-25639-9_45.

De, P. 2013. "The Rise of the Sharing Economy." *The Economist.* May 9. http://www.economist.com/news/leaders/21573104-internet-everything-hire-rise-sharing-economy.

DeMaio, Paul. 2009. "Bike-Sharing: History, Impacts, Models of Provision, and Future." *Journal of Public Transportation* 12 (DeMaio 2004): 41–56. doi:10.1016/0965-8564(93)90040-R.

Doctorow, Cory. 2002. "Public Street-Bookshelves in Berlin Made from Hollow Logs/Boing Boing." *Boingboing.* http://boingboing.net/2012/07/19/public-street-bookshelves-in-b.html.

Firestone, R., and J. Catlett. 2009. *The Ethics of Interpersonal Relationships.* London: Karnac. http://books.google.de/books?id=R1ILxUn8-Z8C.

Firnkorn, Jörg, and Martin Müller. 2012. "Selling Mobility Instead of Cars: New Business Strategies of Automakers and the Impact on Private Vehicle Holding." *Business Strategy and the Environment* 21 (4): 264–280. doi:10.1002/bse.738.

Firnkorn, Jörg, and Susan Shaheen. 2014. "Generic Time- and Method-Interdependencies of Empirical Impact-Measurements: A Generalizable Model of Adaptation-Processes of Carsharing-Users' Mobility-Behavior over Time." *Journal of Cleaner Production* 113: 897–909. doi:10.1016/j.jclepro.2015.09.115.

Geron, Tomio. 2013. "Airbnb and the Unstoppable Rise of the Share Economy." *Forbes.* http://www.forbes.com/sites/tomiogeron/2013/01/23/airbnb-and-the-unstoppable-rise-of-the-share-economy/.

Gobble, MaryAnne M. 2015. "Regulating Innovation in the New Economy." *Research-Technology Management* March–Apri (April): 62–63. doi:10.5437/08956308X5802005.

Goodwin, Tom. 2015. "The Battle Is for the Customer Interface." *Techcrunch*: 1–10. http://techcrunch.com/2015/03/03/in-the-age-of-disintermediation-the-battle-is-all-for-the-customer-interface/.

Hamari, Juho, Mimmi Sjöklint, and Antti Ukkonen. 2015. "The Sharing Economy: Why People Participate in Collaborative Consumption." *Journal of the Association for Information Science and Technology* 14 (4): 1–13. doi:10.1002/asi.23552.

Heinrichs, Harald. 2013. "Sharing Economy: A Potential New Pathway to Sustainability." *GAIA: Ecological Perspectives for Science & Society* 22 (4): 228–231.

Heinrichs, Harald, and Heiko Grunenberg. 2013. "Sharing Economy towards a New Culture of Consumption." *Centre for Sustainability Management Luneburg*.

Hong, Soonkwan, and Handan Vicdan. 2016. "Re-Imagining the Utopian: Transformation of a Sustainable Lifestyle in Ecovillages." *Journal of Business Research* 69 (1): 120–136. doi:10.1016/j.jbusres.2015.07.026.

Hughes, Jerald, K. R. Lang, and R. Vragov. 2005. "Electronic Market Design Principles in the Context of Peer-to-Peer Filesharing Systems." *PACIS*: 852–865. PACIS 2005 Proceedings. 72, Bangkok, Thailand. http://www.pacis-net.org/file/2005/330.pdf.

Johnson, Cat. 2013. "Is Seoul the Next Great Sharing City?" *Shareable*. http://www.shareable.net/blog/is-seoul-the-next-great-sharing-city.

Johnson, Cat. 2014. "Sharing City Seoul: A Model for the World." *Shareable*. http://www.shareable.net/blog/sharing-city-seoul-a-model-for-the-world.

Kassan, Jenny, and Janelle Orsi. 2012. "The Legal Landscape of the Sharing Economy." *Journal of Environmental Law & Litigation* 27 (1): 1–20. http://search.ebscohost.com/login.aspx?direct=true&db=lgs&AN=77049452&lang=de&site=ehost-live.

Kim, Kyeongsu. 2015. "Can Carsharing Meet the Mobility Needs for the Low-Income Neighborhoods? Lessons from Carsharing Usage Patterns in New York City." *Transportation Research Part A: Policy and Practice* 77: 249–260. doi:10.1016/j.tra.2015.04.020.

Knackstedt, Ralf, Mathias Eggert, Marcel Heddier, Friedrich Chasin, and Jörg Becker. 2013. "The Relationship of IS and Law—The Perspective of and Implications for IS Research." *Proceedings of the European Conference on Information Systems (ECIS)*. Utrecht, Netherlands.

Leismann, Kristin, Martina Schmitt, Holger Rohn, and Carolin Baedeker. 2013. "Collaborative Consumption: Towards a Resource-Saving Consumption Culture." *Resources* 2 (3): 184–203. doi:10.3390/resources2030184.

Linders, Dennis. 2012. "From E-Government to We-Government: Defining a Typology for Citizen Coproduction in the Age of Social Media." *Government Information Quarterly* 29 (4): 446–454. doi:10.1016/j.giq.2012.06.003.

Lindloff, Kirstin, N. Pieper, N. C. Bandelow, and D. M. Woisetschläger. 2014. "Drivers of Carsharing Diffusion in Germany: An Actor-Centred

Approach." *International Journal of Automotive Technology and Management* 14 (3–4): 217–245. doi:10.1017/CBO9781107415324.004.

Marx, Patricia. 2011. "The Borrowers (Electronic Version)." *The New Yorker*. http://www.newyorker.com/magazine/2011/01/31/the-borrowers.

Murray, Alan T., Rex Davis, Robert J. Stimson, and Luis Ferreira. 1998. "Public Transportation Access." *Transportation Research Part D: Transport and Environment* 3 (5): 319–328. doi:10.1016/S1361–9209(98)00010–8.

The New York Times. 2014. "The Dark Side of the Sharing Economy—NYTimes. com." *The New York Times*. http://www.nytimes.com/2014/05/01/opin ion/the-dark-side-of-the-sharing-economy.html.

Oreskes, Naomi. 2004. "The Scientific Consensus on Climate Change." *Science* 306 (5706): 1686–1686. http://www.sciencemag.org/content/306/5702/ 1686.short.

Owyang, Jermiah. 2015. "Large Companies Ramp Up Adoption in the Collaborative Economy." *Web Strategist*. http://www.web-strategist.com/blog/ 2015/07/20/large-companies-ramp-up-adoption-in-the-collaborative-economy/.

Owyang, Jermiah, Christine Tran, and Chris Silva. 2013. "The Collaborative Economy." San Maeto, CA: Altimeter Group. http://www.lsed-wealth.org/ media/sal/pages_media/112/f5_collabecon-draft16-130531132802-phpapp02.pdf.

Petri, Ioan, Omer Rana, Yacine Rezgui, and Gheorghe Cosmin Silaghi. 2011. "Evaluating Trust in Peer-to-Peer Service Provider Communities." *Proceedings of the 7th International Conference on Collaborative Computing: Networking, Applications and Worksharing*, 407–414. IEEE. doi:10.4108/icst. collaboratecom.2011.247125.

Princen, T., M. Maniates, and K. Conca. 2002. *Confronting Consumption*. Cambridge, MA: MIT Press. http://books.google.de/books?id=L95ICsAoFIYC.

Quittner, JEREMY. 2014. "Sharing Economy Companies, Get Ready for Regulations." *Inc.* http://www.inc.com/jeremy-quittner/colorado-moves-to-reg ulate-share-economy.html.

Rifkin, Jeremy. 2000. *The Age of Access: The New Culture of Hypercapitalism, Where All of Life Is a Paid-For Experience*. New York: Jermey P. Tarcher/ Putna.

ShareHub. 2015. "Seoul Sharing City Executive Summary." Seoul. http://english. sharehub.kr/wp-content/uploads/reports/executive_summary_report_ 2015.pdf.

Silver, James. 2013. "The Sharing Economy: A Whole New Way of Living." *Guardian*. http://www.theguardian.com/technology/2013/aug/04/internet-technology-fon-taskrabbit-blablacar.

Stoll, Michael. 2012. "San Francisco Pitched as Beacon of 'Collaborative Consumption' | San Francisco Public Press." *San Francisco Public Press*. http:// sfpublicpress.org/news/2012-04/san-francisco-pitched-as-beacon-of-collaborative-consumption.

Streitfeld, DAVID. 2014. "Companies Built on Sharing Balk When It Comes to Regulators—NYTimes.com." *The New York Times.* http://www.nytimes.com/2014/04/22/business/companies-built-on-sharing-balk-when-it-comes-to-regulators.html?ref=davidstreitfeld.

Tal, Gil, and Galit Cohen-Blankshtain. 2011. "Understanding the Role of the Forecast-Maker in Overestimation Forecasts of Policy Impacts: The Case of Travel Demand Management Policies." *Transportation Research Part A: Policy and Practice* 45 (5): 389–400. doi:10.1016/j.tra.2011.01.012.

Tuttle, Brad. 2013. "Sharing Is Hard: Legal Trouble for Airbnb, RelayRides, FlightCar." *Time.* http://business.time.com/2013/06/06/sharing-is-hard-legal-trouble-for-airbnb-relayrides-flightcar/.

Vasagar, Jeevan. 2014. "Berlin Housing Law Threatens Sharing Economy by Restricting Rents." *Financial Times.* http://www.ft.com/cms/s/0/1e8299a0-d065-11e3-af2b-00144feabdc0.html#axzz373wbvD2t.

Walsh, Bryan. 2011. "10 Ideas That Will Change the World." *Time.* http://content.time.com/time/specials/packages/0,28757,2059521,00.html.

Wang, Tingting, and Cynthia Chen. 2012. "Attitudes, Mode Switching Behavior, and the Built Environment: A Longitudinal Study in the Puget Sound Region." *Transportation Research Part A: Policy and Practice* 46 (10): 1594–1607. doi:10.1016/j.tra.2012.08.001.

Wittel, Andreas. 2011. "Qualities of Sharing and Their Transformations in the Digital Age." *International Review of Information Ethics* 15: 3–8. http://www.i-r-i-e.net/inhalt/015/015-Wittel.pdf.

Wogan, J.B. 2013. "How Will the Sharing Economy Change the Way Cities Function?" *Governing.* http://www.governing.com/topics/urban/gov-how-sharing-economy-will-change-cities.html.

Xia, M., Y. Huang, W. Duan, and A. B. Whinston. 2012. "Research Note—To Continue Sharing or Not to Continue Sharing? An Empirical Analysis of User Decision in Peer-to-Peer Sharing Networks." *Information Systems Research* 23 (1): 247–259. doi:10.1287/isre.1100.0344.

CHAPTER TWELVE

On Sharing and Quasi-Sharing: The Tension between Sharing-Economy Practices, Public Policy, and Regulation

Sofia Ranchordás

Introduction

The "sharing economy" is everywhere and nowhere at the same time. In recent years, multiple digital platforms have claimed this "green label" to promote business-to-consumer, community-based, and consumer-to-consumer services (Hartl, Hofman, and Kirchler 2015, 1). Once upon a time, "sharing economy," "collaborative economy," and "collaborative consumption" were terms used to designate sustainable and collaborative practices between friends or individuals based in the same community that shared underutilized goods (e.g., a drilling machine used once a year) (Botsman and Rogers 2010) or exchanged services (e.g., shared babysitting). Nowadays, the sharing economy has converted informal sharing practices into million-dollar businesses, reshaped and questioned the rights and models of labor relationships previous generations had fought for (Prassl 2016; Stefano 2016; Sundararajan 2016), and replaced long-term ownership by short-term access. Law was once again caught by surprise by these innovative practices which forced local, national, and supranational regulators and legislators to rethink existing rules and define new policies and regulations that could embrace the benefits of the sharing economy while at the same time limiting their shortcomings. As this chapter explains, although the benefits and risks of the sharing economy appear to be similar throughout the world, the regulatory and policy approaches adopted have been quite different. Similar to the time when regulators were challenged by the regulation of the Internet and its inherent 'code' (Lessig 1999), now they are asked to balance the interests protected by existing regulations with the intrinsic 'laws of the platform' (Lobel 2015), and the informal rules of an economic system originally based on collaboration rather than on profit.

The rapid changes operated in the informal context of sharing practices have been made possible by technology, in particular by the emergence of digital platforms that allow for a convenient match between the supply of underused goods and their demand. The emergence of user-friendly websites, social media, mobile applications, and the employment of pricing algorithms have transformed collaborative practices into lucrative businesses (Choudary, Van Alstyne, and Marshall 2016; Demailly and Novel 2013, 1). Platforms are "matchmakers" that connect supply and demand (Evans and Schmalensee 2016; Krakovsky 2015, 26–29), and self-regulate these exchanges. The diversity of experiences (e.g., an Airbnb stay in a castle or treehouse rather than a standardized hotel room), lower prices, and the convenience of many of these sharing economy services appear to have come at a cost: unfair competition, higher rents, nuisance to neighbors of home-sharing hosts, regulatory uncertainty in case of accidents, as well as tax evasion, lower wages, and longer working hours (Malhotra and Van Alstyne 2014).

In recent years, local regulators as well as national and state public bodies have tried to respond to the circumvention of existing authorization schemes and regulations. While digital platforms and a part of the literature have argued that they differ from traditional businesses operated by professionals (Hern 2016; Ranchordás 2015), popularizing the Magrittian expression "ceci n'est pas un taxi" (Lobel 2015), few regulators are convinced. This debate reminds us of the historical tendency of regulators to show, at times, excessive skepticism toward novel products and services that break with existing paradigms (Werbach 2016). The initial prohibition of bicycles in some U.S. states more than a century ago illustrates this skepticism (Brenner 2007, 37–38; e.g., *Thompson v. Dodge*, 60 N.W. 545, 546, Minn. 1894).

In 2014, the Brussels Commercial Court prohibited Uber. Soon more European courts in the Netherlands and Germany replicated this opposition to the company (Finck and Ranchordás 2016). This was only the beginning. Since 2014, Uber, in particular the peer-to-peer variant UberX (or UberPOP in Europe), has been the target of multiple lawsuits, and it has been totally or, in most cases, partially "banned" in multiple cities around the world (e.g., Rio de Janeiro, Amsterdam, Brussels, Berlin, Stockholm, Seoul). A few years ago, Uber was one of the first personifications of the sharing economy; however, nowadays this platform appears to almost have been excluded from this concept (Finck and Ranchordás 2016). Uber is not alone in its legal controversies. Airbnb also has encountered legal opposition.

In 2014, New York attorney general Eric T. Schneiderman initiated an investigation to identify illegal Airbnb listings and subpoenaed the platform to provide its New York City records (Schneiderman 2014). As his hypothesis appeared to be correct, this investigation opened the door to more litigation (*Airbnb, Inc. v. Schneiderman*, 44 Misc 3d 351, 358, 360 [NY Sup 2014]). In Berlin, recent legislation driven by the concern that home-sharing was creating a rise in rents prohibits Airbnb as well as other home-sharing platforms such as Wimdu or 9Flats from advertising entire units. Also, Amsterdam, once an "Airbnb-friendly city," has now enacted additional restrictive measures.

This chapter analyzes the tension between existing regulations and policies and the sharing economy. This contribution discusses the regulation of the sharing economy in light of its different variants, existing regulation and public policies enacted to protect the public interest, and the need for a differentiated approach to the challenges of the sharing economy. This chapter invites further reflection on two qualifications which might be essential for the regulation of sharing economy: first, the need to qualify these platforms either as mere digital intermediaries or information society services or strict service providers (e.g., transportation dispatchers); second, the distinction between sharing economy and quasi-sharing economy platforms which capitalize sharing, facilitating at times (but not always) sustainable collaboration (e.g., Uber).

In this chapter, I start by distinguishing between two categories of platforms: those that, regardless of their commercial or noncommercial nature, literally facilitate the sharing of idle capacity (e.g., unused tools, parking space, spare bedroom); and "quasi-sharing economy platforms" that may or may not facilitate the sharing of excess capacity, depending on the user or the different services offered by the platform. The former refers to a traditional community-based and often offline market model that has promoted sustainable production and consumption in the past decades (Cohen and Munoz 2015).

The distinction between sharing economy platforms and quasi-sharing economy platforms, and between these platforms and traditional businesses is relevant for the purposes of this chapter for two reasons. First, regulators have failed to address the challenges of the sharing economy model because, with a few exceptions (e.g., California Public Utilities Commission, Loi Allur in France on Airbnb), most regulators have attempted to understand these platforms through the lenses of traditional professional businesses and their regulations (Dyal-Chand 2015, 247). Second, regulators have been particularly reluctant to accept quasi-sharing economy platforms since they often disguise unlicensed professional practices and may not actively promote the goals underlying the original idea of the sharing economy, that is, efficient use of idle capacity, power parity, trust, sustainability, and peer participation.

The "Sharing Economy"

The idea of sharing goods, space, infrastructures, and exchanging nonprofessional services is not new (Cohen and Zehngebot 2014, 6). Rather, it is intrinsic to humankind: we share to guarantee survival or for altruistic reasons (Belk 2014, 1595). The sharing of goods was nonetheless traditionally stigmatized: ownership granted a better status as citizen, neighbor, or parent (Bardhi and Eckhardt 2012, 883). In 2017, sharing practices have changed: they have become lucrative businesses, which rely upon the idea that peers are indeed able to share and care for shared goods in a sustainable way. In the digital age, the "sharing economy" is no longer a set of practices limited to the exchange of poor-quality goods which no one took care of in the context of poor, working-class, and minority urban communities (Schor 2014, 5). Digital forms of sharing now transcend social classes as affluent college-educated individuals driven by sustainability concerns (O'Rourke and Lollo 2015, 233) who wish to "collect badge experiences, not badge products" (Fromm 2015). Moreover, the global economic crisis required once-prosperous individuals to rethink their consumption values (Bardhi and Eckhardt 2012, 883). Also, in the 21st century, a new generation of users is growing up sharing videos, images, and experiences. With Web 2.0 and social networks, which are defined by underlying sharing practices, the collaborative economy re-emerged under new metaphors (John 2013, 119).

"Sharing economy," "collaborative consumption," and "collaborative economy" are only some of the terms employed to refer to the widespread use of digital platforms to facilitate the access to underutilized goods by consumers other than their owners (Benkler 2006). Such practices take place primarily between peers (consumer-to-consumer) (Ritzer 2015, 413), but businesses can also be involved as it happens in the popular platform Zipcar (business-to-consumer). Belk (2014) defines "collaborative consumption" as a form of citizen coordination to acquire and distribute a resource for a fee or other compensation (Belk 2014, 1597). Belk includes bartering, trading, and swapping, which involve giving and receiving nonmonetary compensation. Although Belk explicitly excludes hospitality networks like Couchsurfing, even these transactions involve a form of direct or indirect consideration (Belk 2014, 1597). In nonmonetary home-exchanges, users might host each other or other individuals within the same network, but there is an expectation of future reciprocity. Therefore, these transactions are not fully altruistic (Bhardi and Eckhardt 2012, 884–886). This distinction may have implications for the regulation of these platforms as, in many civil law countries, the existence of some form of consideration or advantage turns an exchange into an "onerous contract," which determines the application of more stringent rules (Kinsella 1994, 1272).

In this section, I start by analyzing the meaning of the term "sharing," then I discuss the different practices that are encompassed by the broad concept of "sharing economy."

Sharing

In the Web 2.0, "sharing" has acquired two basic meanings: first, it might refer to an act of distribution in the sense of allocating parts of divisible good (e.g., food in the case of private kitchens) or in the sense of having something in common or allowing someone to have access to the same good without affecting its properties (e.g., sharing a room) (John 2012, 4). Second, "sharing" may also refer to an act of communication that allows individuals to share their intellectual resources, opinions, documents with each other. Sharing economy platforms involving transactions typically refer to the distributional character of the idea of "sharing," while collaboration platforms (e.g., citizen participation and crowdsourcing) as well as social networks (Facebook or Twitter) refer to the latter. In addition, in the Web 2.0 the term "sharing" is expected to convey positive social relations. In this sense, "sharing" has been defined as "the concept that incorporates a wide range of distributive and communicative practices, while also carrying a set of positive connotations to do with our relations and a more just allocation of resources" (John 2012, 11).

The Definition of "Sharing Economy"

The concept of "sharing economy" refers to a plurality of possibilities which vary between a strict business mind-set and more social, sustainable, nurturing, and democratic possibilities (Morgan and Kuch 2015, 557) or the popular idea that "sharing is caring" (Ranchordás 2015). In the last years the sharing economy has been framed in contrasting and contradictory ways, ranging from the perception that it is a pathway to a decentralized, equitable, and sustainable economy to the criticism that it creates unregulated marketplaces (Martin 2016, 154–155). In terms of goods and services provided, the sharing economy falls into four broad categories: recirculation of goods, increased utilization of durable assets, exchange of services, and sharing of productive assets (Schor 2014).

In this chapter I distinguish between sharing and quasi-sharing economy platforms: the first category promotes intermediated, sustainable peer-to-peer exchanges that rely upon the communication or distribution of excess capacity (e.g., empty seat in a car offered to someone traveling to the same destination as promoted by BlaBlaCar). In this category, individuals make minimal profits and mainly share costs. The second category, quasi-sharing economy platforms, also refers to peer-to-peer exchanges intermediated by platforms but which might not always imply the literal sharing of an under-utilized good. Uber and Airbnb are the best examples of this second category, which does not exclude the possibility that some individuals might derive significant financial advantages from these practices. Nevertheless, quasi-sharing also means that individuals are not always fully sharing underused goods in a sustainable way: for example, Airbnb, similar to Couchsurfing, started by offering spare bedrooms or couches, but nowadays the platform offers entire apartments, where no one lives on a regular basis, for rent.

Some of the most relevant public policy and regulatory concerns in the context of the sharing economy can be explained by the use of an all-encompassing concept of "sharing economy," which does not fully distinguish between sharing and quasi-sharing platforms. As explained earlier, the concept of "sharing economy" includes not only small-scale, peer-to-peer transactions involving the sharing of excess capacity (the "real" sharing economy, Finck and Ranchordás 2016) but also full-time unlicensed or licensed professional services facilitated by digital platforms. In the first case, technology has allowed peers to be more easily matched with other individuals with similar needs or interests (e.g., two or more people traveling to the same city) and a more efficient distribution of goods with excess capacity (e.g., vehicle parked outside office during the day). In the second, the same technology has allowed the black market and labor exploitation to thrive. The existence of these two categories means that different rules should apply in order to prevent total bans on "sharing" components of the platforms. Not surprisingly, in 2015 and 2016, sharing and "quasi-sharing" platforms like Uber had been featured in the media as the personification of an "extractive mindset" rather than collaborative mentality (Morgan and Kuch 2015, 557).

Both sharing and quasi-sharing economy platforms tend to be characterized by temporary, on-demand, intermediated transactions: access to a good owned by another individual is granted typically for a short period, and supply and demand are matched by a digital platform (Bhardi and Eckhardt 2012, 884). This matching process has been further improved by the use of adjacent networks, namely, Facebook, LinkedIn, and Twitter, that allow users to obtain more information about each other. In the next section, I delve into the additional pillars of the sharing economy.

The Pillars of the Sharing Economy

Nowadays virtually any traditional business uses digital platforms and relies on social media to sell its products, advertise promotions, and provide customer assistance. Nevertheless, not all digital businesses are part of the platform or sharing economy. The literature has attempted to narrow down the principles or pillars of the sharing economy in order to define the boundaries of these practices. Botsman and Rogers (2010) have listed four principles that have determined the success of the sharing economy in the digital age: (i) the existence of a critical mass, (ii) idle capacity, (iii) belief in the commons, and (iv) trust between strangers (Botsman and Rogers 2010, 72–75).

The popularity of peer-to-peer platforms can also be explained by six central elements inherent to the sharing economy: (i) "sharing mentality," (ii) low-threshold participation, (iii) power parity between users, (iv) use of reputational mechanisms, (v) limited transaction costs, and (vi) de-professionalization and increasing automation of labor-intensive services (Haug 1972, 195). In addition, the growing popularity of sharing economy platforms is reflected in the development of the so-called network hospitality where social interaction and trust relationships are mediated by technologies (Molz 2012, 215). This concept is based on the idea of "network sociality" coined by Wittel (2001, 70) which describes the idea of de-localized social interactions or "socialization on the move."

Capacity Maximization

The emergence of sharing economy platforms and the growing popularity of platforms such as Airbnb have revealed that there is an excess capacity in many cities around the world: while New York City and San Francisco might complain about the shortage of housing, there are other residents who have spare bedrooms and are willing to share this excess capacity with strangers (Ellen 2015, 783). Interestingly, the sharing of space with strangers is not limited to the sharing economy. It precedes it. Ownership of the single-family dwellings is a fairly recent phenomenon that came to be a symbol of economic success: affluent individuals did not need to share their spare space (Carp, Hoch, and Hemmens 1996, 2). By contrast, in less prosperous families, different generations would cohabit for many centuries. In the past few decades, the number of single-family dwellings and home-ownership increased with the growing development of the banking sector and differential tax treatment of owner-occupied housing (Chambers, Garriga, and Schlagenhauf 2009, 678). As home-ownership became increasingly important, so did zoning laws, which were designed to safeguard the quality of neighborhoods and real estate prices. Nevertheless, this did not put an end to home-sharing.

More recently but in historical critical contexts, families in Europe have been requested to share idle capacity with strangers. This occurred, for example, in the Netherlands following World War II, giving rise to important litigation on the limits and proportionality of administrative decisions on capacity maximization, and the need to balance the privacy of families with the public interest (Waard 2016, 111–112). With the Syrian refugee crisis in

Europe, several families volunteered in 2015 and 2016 to host asylum seekers. Inspired by the example of Airbnb, mobile applications (e.g., Refugees Welcome) were developed to match hosting families with refugees.

Power Parity and Participation

Sharing economy platforms are forms of citizen participation in the economy. Sharing can be either an act of distribution (i.e. when we share a good with excess capacity, e.g., guest bedroom) or an act of communication (e.g., share pictures on Instagram) (John 2012, 4). Regardless of the digital platform used, sharing in the digital age tends to be an act of direct participation in a community (Dyal-Chand 2015, 243). Although this participation narrative has existed for centuries, particularly in urban centers, the high penetration of Internet and mobile applications and the development of sophisticated digital intermediaries have altered our perceptions of what sharing and collaborative consumption entail.

With the increasing interest of civil society in alternatives to capitalism, some sharing economy practices have materialized the values of participants in grassroots movements who see the potential to contribute to the transition to more sustainable production and consumption (Martin and Upham 2016). Following the Industrial Revolution, technology started facilitating the hegemony of large economic forces that would become the special interests shaping law and policy for the next decades (Cunningham 1983, 259). Since the "participation revolution" in the 1960s, more importance has been attached to the ability of citizens to voice their political and social concerns, particularly in their local communities. Nowadays, technology is promoting power parity between special industries and citizens, assisting skilled and unskilled individuals to participate not only in the political process, by petitioning national and local legislators but also in the economy. Individuals wish to participate in the sharing economy for numerous reasons, including the rejection of established economic forces and monopolies (taxi companies) (Bond 2015, 78) and opting for more affordable and sustainable consumption alternatives (Hamari, Sjöklint, and Ukkonen 2016).

Trust and Reputational Mechanisms

Trust is the core element of many sharing economy platforms, but one of the most salient questions in this context refers to "the lack of trust and how strangers negotiate risk and establish trust with one another on the Internet" (Molz 2012, 218; Bakos and Dellarocas 2011). With the emergence of user-friendly digital platforms and the rising prices of accommodation, trust has been mediated by technology and peer-review instruments and in some cases, it has become a lucrative business (e.g., Yelp for traditional businesses). Before the emergence of hotels and their complex licensing procedures, these sharing practices were provided gratuitously or in exchange for small gifts or amounts of money in most communities around the world (Molz 2012, 217), in particular in urban centers. These practices were often determined by altruism and a cultural perception of hospitality, which relied upon mutual trust in strangers' bona fides.

It does not suffice to have shareable goods with idle capacity. The quality of these goods must also be maintained to guarantee the continuity of sharing practices. In traditional businesses the quality of services and products is regulated by general rules on liability and consumer protection, namely on product liability, misleading advertising, and e-commerce (Benohr 2014, 20; Owen, Montgomery, and Davis 2014). By contrast, in the sharing economy, there is a greater degree of regulatory uncertainty as platforms try to minimize their liability by arguing that they are mere intermediaries that have no control over the listings (Katz 2015, 1072). Instead, these platforms delegate a part of the quality control to users by making available more or less thorough reputational mechanisms.

Reputational mechanisms help the owners of shared goods be reassured that the users will take care of the good and provide incentives to both service providers (Benkler 2006, 59–81). While in the personal sphere, individuals collaborate because they trust each other, in the context of the sharing economy, users rely on online reviews to develop this trust (Resnick and Zeckhauser 2002). Research has shown that Airbnb guests infer the host's trustworthiness from the sellers' personal photos, attaching significant importance to their perception of these elements (Ert, Fleischer, and Mager 2016, 62).

De-professionalization of Services

The increasing popularity of this digital peer-to-peer economy is being driven by the generalized de-professionalization of services and the growing automation of work (Lee et al. 2015, 1603). The polarization of work, that is, the increase in high-wage positions but decrease in middle- and low-wages ones, has resulted in the last decades from the general improvement of technology (Dwyer 2013, 391). This tendency to de-professionalize and outsource labor and employ independent contractors who do not have any specific training or experience is not a new phenomenon, and it is far from being limited to the sharing economy (Barley 2005). Rather, the developments with regards to the Internet and globalization have facilitated the employment of freelancers and other contractors who are not officially employed. In addition, the business model of sharing economy platforms as well as the fact that they are able to maximize the value of networks and match demand and supply more efficiently, and that they often do not comply with numerous regulations has been translated into lower prices. In addition, the automation of labor, the use of complex algorithms, and different types of robots promise an even more de-professionalized economy. Although this has been attractive for consumers, lower prices have also been the result of low wages, the absence of social benefits, limited consumer rights, and regulatory uncertainty regarding the application of liability rules.

The Legal Challenges of the Sharing Economy

Sharing economy platforms such as Airbnb (home-sharing), BlaBlaCar (long-distance transportation) or Eatwith (meal sharing) have disrupted not only existing capitalist and "conspicuous" consumption models (Veblen 1899) but also long-standing national and in particular local regulations and policies (Choudary and Alstyne 2016). Although the "platform revolution" has had an unquestionable impact on national and local regulations, law has remained to a great extent untouched by ongoing business changes while regulators have struggled to apply it to new sharing practices. This struggle results from two factors: first, the innovative and even disruptive character of some sharing economy platforms and the difficulty in applying traditional legal concepts and rules to them (Ranchordás 2015). Second, sharing economy platforms do not fit easily into existing legislative and regulatory regimes designed in the 19th century or the early decades of the 20th century (Freeman and Spence 2014, 2; Light 2016, 3).

In this section, I provide an overview of different legal challenges posed by the sharing economy at the transnational, national, and local levels.

Local Law

From a legal perspective, the rise of sharing economy platforms has raised multiple concerns regarding authorization schemes in terms of the required licenses and permits to drive passengers locally, or to operate a hotel or restaurant. Sharing economy platforms are accused of violating zoning, public safety, hygiene, fire and road safety regulations, which are primarily justified by the protection of the public interest. Regulators and incumbents, that is, taxi drivers, hotels, and restaurants, have been critical of the uncontrolled and unregulated development of sharing economy platforms. In most cases, the public bodies competent to regulate and enforce regulations and policies in this context are situated at the local level.

Not only do municipal public bodies have more information regarding local problems and the expertise to regulate them, but they also have a legitimate interest in regulating subjects which benefit primarily locals (Macey 1990, 284). Zoning law is an example of this reasoning. From a public-interest perspective, zoning rules which aim to govern allowable construction and land use by dividing cities into separate geographic zones for residential, commercial, and industrial uses (Steele 1986, 714) serve mainly the interest of local citizens (Macey 1990, 284). They aim to make the city more livable and orderly, and allegedly safeguard the fluctuation of housing prices, even though empirical research has delivered mixed results on this aspect (Quigley and Rosenthal 2005, 69). However, it is worth noting that sharing economy platforms might also produce externalities that cross the borders of a municipality. This is the case of the environmental impact of platforms like Uber and Lyft, which, from a precautionary perspective, might call for a federal rather than state or local intervention (Light 2016).

The study of the legal challenges of the sharing economy is nevertheless largely a discussion of the impact of technology on local law (Moss 1998; Shkabatur 2011). Sharing economy platforms such as Uber and Lyft might be global players, but they also have an impact on local traffic, congestion, and public transportation (Davidson and Infranca 2016, 2; Light 2016, 7). Sharing economy platforms challenge the core of local administrative law by disregarding authorization schemes, zoning regulations, required fire and hygiene inspections performed by local authorities.

At first blush, local regulators who are generally responsible for the regulation of the most common sharing economy sectors, notably local transportation, hotel and restaurants licensing, and accommodation, appear to have a paradoxical relationship with more commercial variants of the sharing economy. On the one hand, multiple cities have affirmed their interest in cultivating a "sharing mentality" and incentivizing the participation of citizens in local affairs, namely, in the management of infrastructures and idle capacity of public goods (e.g., playgrounds, public transportation) (McLaren and Agyeman 2015). On the other, as the next sections show, cities still enforce 19th- and early 20th-century regulations, which might no longer be effective to safeguard the local public interest.

Local Private Transportation

Local transportation has been among the most regulated economic sectors for decades (Schaller 2007, 490). Price regulation is necessary since consumer demand is typically immediate, for example, because passengers taking a cab are not flexible regarding the waiting time or they do not have other public transportation options. This results in the consumer's limited ability to negotiate the price or seek alternative service providers (Gallick and Sisk 1987, 118).

Taxi regulation in the United States emerged in the 19th century and in particular in the 20th century during the Great Depression, when an excessive number of illegal taxis started colonizing the streets of New York city causing numerous accidents (Bond 2015, 78). Although taxi regulations were enacted to serve the public interest, the extensive regulation of this sector has been criticized for a number of years due to its ineffectiveness (Cairns and Liston-Heyes 1996,1), excessive burdens, and outdated character in light of the emergence of technology that reduces the informational asymmetries that were at the outset of taxi regulation (Cohen and Sundararajan 2015). Despite its potential outdated character, taxi regulations continue to serve the public interest. For example, by collecting the fingerprints of drivers, the identity and criminal background of drivers are verified in an attempt to protect the safety of drivers. Uber and Lyft have opposed the collection of fingerprints and refused to comply with the new safety regulations imposed by Austin, Texas. In addition, taxis must use taximeters and practice regulated fees in order to guarantee reasonable fares, despite the weather or demand. Uber has challenged this regulation, for example, in London, arguing that its pricing application should not be compared to a taximeter. Indeed, the algorithms used to determine pricing do not operate on the grounds of flat rates but rather take into account the hard rules of supply and demand. More importantly, taxi regulations also guarantee that conventional taxis cover all the segments of a city, providing universal access to private transportation to citizens, regardless of their disabilities or remote residence (Leiren and Aarhaug 2016). Regulatory authorities are therefore concerned that if several taxi drivers are driven out of the market by ride-sharing platforms, there will be a deficit of private transportation services in the less lucrative areas as it usually is the case of the countryside (Leiren and Aarhaug 2016).

Local regulators have responded in divergent ways to the emergence of ride-sharing platforms. While New York City requires Uber and Lyft drivers to register and obtain a license, in many cities where the platform is allowed to operate, drivers have no contact with local government and operate regardless of traditional taxi regulations. Uber drivers only need to register online, send a number of personal and vehicle identification documents, have a driving license, and a vehicle to drive. A large number of cities have nonetheless been critical of this business approach. In Berlin, for example, local regulators prohibited quasi-sharing platform Uber to offer unlicensed peer-to-peer services (UberPOP) in 2014. This decision, justified on the grounds of public safety, was later upheld by the court in 2015. At the time of writing, the mentioned platform has reduced its presence to a mere taxi-hailing platform in the German capital. Uber remains undeterred by judicial challenges and continues its battle to convince other local cities to change their regulations. Lobbying and "regulatory entrepreneurship" have become an important part of Uber and other innovative digital platforms that feel that current legislation and regulations are impeding their disruptive operations. As the literature correctly points out, some of these companies "are in the business of trying to change the law" (Barry and Pollman 2017).

Zoning

Zoning law is a fairly recent part of local law designed to protect the value of an existing area, by excluding or limiting prejudicial uses (e.g., factories next to residential areas), and promote the consistent development of cities. Among the first examples of local planning and zoning regulations in the United States is the 1880 San Francisco ordinance limiting the operation of public laundries, which was later invalidated by the U.S. Supreme Court in *Yick Wo v. Hopkins* due to the violation of the equal protection clause. At that time, laundries were mostly operated by Chinese immigrants. San Francisco continued, nonetheless, to expand its zoning restrictions to slaughterhouses, saloons, and dance halls. By 1913 multiple U.S. cities, including Boston and New York City, had instituted local land use provisions, namely, on the height of buildings. The original goal of zoning was, however, to protect homeowners in residential areas from devaluation by the construction of industrial facilities or apartment complexes in the surrounding areas (Weiss 1986, 7).

In order to minimize urban negative externalities such as high living costs, pollution and high rates of criminality, modern land use law and zoning regulations emerged in order to maintain the quality and character of neighborhoods and protect homeowners from devaluation by industrial and commercial uses of property (Fischel 2004, 317).

More recently, the constitutionality of municipal restrictions on home-sharing through digital platforms in the United States was challenged by Jefferson-Jones who, relying on the historical value of zoning regulations (e.g., improvement of public safety, character of neighborhoods, and property value), argues that sharing economy practices can promote these historical regulatory goals (Jefferson-Jones 2015). By limiting these transactions—often to protect the vested interests of the hospitality sector—cities are adopting regulatory takings without providing compensation to users and in violation of the Fifth and Fourteenth Amendments (Jefferson-Jones 2015, 560). While this argument is controversial, it reminds us of the need to rethink the underlying public interest goals of local regulations, the question of whether they are still necessary in the digital age and the existence of alternatives, and the question whether existing local law is well suited to regulate the digital services provided by home-sharing platforms (Gottlieb 2013, 4).

Landlord-Tenant Law

The sharing economy is currently challenging existing landlord-tenant law relationships and housing association regulations on the limits of sublease. As an increasing number of tenants are being evicted both in the United States and in Europe due to the illegal sublease of units on home-sharing platforms, the literature has also underlined the need to rethink the impact of the sharing economy on existing landlord-tenant law, social housing regulations, and housing association agreements.

To illustrate, in 2015 a Swedish tenant who was in the process of moving to a new residence decided to sublet her apartment on Airbnb to avoid double costs. Since Swedish law requires the housing association authorization to consent to every sublease, the host applied to seven short-term rentals. The Stockholm Rental Tribunal ("Hyresnämnden") considered that the host was engaging in an illegal commercial activity and decided in favor of the housing association (*Hyresnämnden i Stockholm*, No. 8741–15, August 17, 2015). In the Netherlands, housing associations and municipalities are also dealing with similar problems as social housing tenants have tried to illegally earn additional income by renting a spare bedroom to tourists on a regular basis.

The existence of illegal home-sharing practices is not new: tax circumvention has been of common concern in most jurisdictions, even before the emergence of sharing economy practices. To illustrate, in Hungary, the provision of illegal hospitality services to tourists in Budapest and in the touristic area surrounding Lake Balaton has existed for decades. Considering the deep roots of the "Zimmer Frei" culture in the country and the thriving black economy in the real estate and hospitality sectors (Arvay and Vertes 1995, 27; Belyó 1995, 125), the Hungarian legislature regulated home-sharing in 2009, before the worldwide success of Airbnb and similar platforms (Section 2, point h of the Decree Government Decree 239/2009).

Labor Protection of Service Providers

At the time of writing, one of most controversial legal aspects of the quasi-sharing economy concerns the qualification of service providers using the platform to be connected with consumers. If these platforms are not operating within the nonprofessional, sporadic, and sustainable collaborative economy that originally characterized the sharing economy, but are mere businesses with an "app," then they should internalize the costs of employing these individuals (Dyal-Chand 2015, 294). This question has been at the center of the litigation against Uber. The thin line between an employee and an independent contractor is often defined in many jurisdictions in light of the extent of control by the digital platform: Do Uber, TaskRabbit, or other platforms determine the prices? What should the contractors wear, when should they start and stop working, or how should they address customers? Uber determines and controls the terms and form of payment, and it can easily deactivate a driver when his or her ranking is lower.

Level-Playing Field and Competition Concerns

Sharing economy platforms are currently disrupting existing regulatory models and changing the way in which businesses compete. To illustrate, the circumvention of existing regulations regarding professional regulations (operational licenses and permits) means not only that sharing economy service providers are operating illegally but also that they are benefiting from a more favorable competitive position. They can charge lower prices than registered service providers that need to comply with a long list of requirements. Sharing economy platforms are hence challenged for disrespecting the existing level-playing field and promoting unfair competition. While hotels and restaurants are required to register and obtain municipal business permits, comply with strict fire, hygiene, and safety standards, pay taxes, apply for expensive licenses and undergo labor inspections, home-sharing hosts (e.g., Airbnb or VRBO) and private kitchens (e.g., Eatwith) often only need to upload a description of their services and include their social media profiles. Competition concerns go further than the level-playing field argument. First, multisided markets pose greater challenges and turn the operation of defining the relevant market into a complex task. Second, the algorithms used by digital platforms to fix prices as well as the information shared by the different service providers within the platform might raise the risk of collusion between competitors.

First, contrary to many traditional businesses disrupted by sharing economy platforms, these new businesses do not operate on one-sided markets. Instead, actors operate in two or multisided markets as they interact via intermediaries or platform (Evans 2003; Evans and Schmalensee 2016). The customers of these businesses have different preferences, there are externalities associated with being connected through a network, and an intermediary is necessary to internalize the externalities created by one group for the other (Evans 2003). In other words, the fact that more Uber drivers join the network creates membership externalities for the riders, generating a positive feedback loop. This produces an impact on how the relevant market and market power of these businesses are defined (Russo and Stasi 2016). However, knowing what market we are referring to is a first, but challenging, task since often customers on one side do not pay directly for the product (e.g., Spotify) so a small-but-significant-non-transitory increase in price (SSNIP test) might not always help us to define the borders of the relevant market (Russo and Stasi 2016). This challenging task is listed here as a competition concern, but further elaboration is left for future research due to its rather technical nature.

Second, Uber's model might also be opening the door to other and greater competition concerns: if it is true that Uber drivers are independent contractors who benefit from the same pricing algorithm, then it would be fair to argue that pricing agreements, more specifically, price fixing, are taking place since competitors have agreed on a pricing structure, instead of competing against each other (Gata 2015, 4). Without further research into the need to use this algorithm to guarantee the well functioning of the platform, it is not possible yet to argue that Uber is facilitating anticompetitive price fixing between its drivers (Gata 2015, 4). In the United States, Uber is currently facing a class action lawsuit in New York instituted by Spencer Meyer, a customer from Connecticut, for allegedly conspiring with drivers to guarantee they charge the same prices. This is guaranteed by the price algorithm integrated in the Uber application which includes the ability to "surge price" during periods of higher demand (*Meyer v. Kalanick*, U.S. District Court, Southern District of New York, No. 15–09796). In this lawsuit, it is alleged that drivers cannot compete on price because both the standard fare and the surge pricing fare have already been fixed by Uber. Kalanick is involved in this lawsuit not only as the cofounder of Uber but also, and primarily, as an occasional driver who allegedly conspires with other drivers and provides them with the software to set prices. Kalanick's defense is that the pricing agreement is not horizontal, as suggested by Meyer in the lawsuit, but rather vertical (between Uber Technologies and the different drivers). In March 2016, Judge Rakoff (U.S. District Court), in refusing Kalanick's attempt to dismiss the lawsuit, compared this case to the traditional "hub and spoke conspiracies" where all the individuals were aware of the conditions negotiated in each vertical agreement. In August 2016, the lawsuit was halted while Uber appealed the denial to compel arbitration.

Platforms as Information Society Services

At the time of writing, the Court of Justice of the European Union (CJEU) is expected to shed light on the qualification of Uber. In 2015, a Spanish court raised a relevant question in a preliminary ruling to the CJEU (Asociación Profesional Elite Taxi, Case C-434/15): is Uber a mere digital intermediary ("information society service") that does not provide any local transportation services, or is it a transportation service (e.g., a transportation dispatcher)? If the CJEU decides that Uber is a mere information society service, then EU Member States must comply with the E-commerce Directive (2000/31/EC) and the Services Directive (2006/123/EC). This implies, for example, the exclusion of liability for the listings posted by individuals and the inability of Member States to ban the operation of Uber.

As an information society service, the platform would benefit from the freedom to provide services guaranteed by Article 56 of the Treaty on the Functioning of the European Union (TFEU), the Services Directive, and the E-Commerce Directive. However, if Uber is qualified as a local transportation operator, then national and, more specifically, local authorities remain competent to regulate the platform. The Services Directive removes administrative barriers to trade in the EU and limits national restrictions to proportionate public interest restrictions. According to Article 9 of the Services Directive "authorization schemes," that is, authorization, licensing or permits regimes must be justified by the public interest and should not be disproportionate so as not to unreasonably hinder the principle of freedom of establishment. This directive is, nonetheless, not applicable to local private transportation.

In the European context, the possibility to hold information society services liable for third-party behavior under certain circumstances, notably for comments and listings posted on the platform, is not totally excluded. In 2013, the European Court of Human Rights (ECtHR) upheld a ruling by the Estonian Supreme Court imposing broad liability and a monitoring obligation on a news website (*Delfi AS v Estonia*, ECtHR, Application No. 64569/09, October 10, 2013). While the website had removed all offensive comments and threats that targeted a director of a ferry services company, it refused to compensate for damages. The ECtHR considered that the platform's filtering and notice-and-take-down instruments were also insufficient because they failed to prevent a number of insults or threats. In the case of sharing economy platforms, content in this sense is limited in many cases to peer-review mechanisms and the description of listings.

In the United States, information society providers (ISP) also benefit from similar immunity for the host's listings. Existing dispositions on the liability of ISP aim to safeguard not only innovation and the development of the Internet but also free speech. Section 230 of the Communications Decency Act encourages responsible practices regarding online content and limits the liability of ISPs. Not surprisingly, the application of these rules to Airbnb and other sharing economy platforms has also been discussed in the literature, as the statutory definition of ISP appears to encompass the services provided by these intermediaries: "any person or entity that is responsible, in whole or in part, for the creation or development of information provided through the Internet or any other interactive computer service" (Interian 2016, 138).

Nonlegal Challenges of the Sharing Economy

The expansion of these digital platforms that rely on the sharing of idle capacity has also been challenged on nonlegal grounds thus raising public policy concerns. While the sharing economy generates multiple benefits, it also creates social costs, including nuisance for neighbors, potential rising rents, and reduced perception of safety in buildings where Airbnb hosts have access to shared premises. In addition, a common public concern is the taxation of the sharing economy, in particular the collection of hotel taxes, income tax, and, in some countries, VAT (Kaplan and Nadler 2016, 103). Airbnb, for example, already collects local taxes in many cities, including San Francisco, Portland, and Amsterdam. Barter transactions have, however, been taxed for many years, but the taxing of the sharing economy remains partially contested (Ring and Oei 2016). However, as platforms have access to the users' data, these agents could potentially be converted into tax withholders, providing an effective remedy of the black market.

In the home-sharing sector, the media have publicized the complaints of long-term residents about the rising prices of rents and shortage of housing

(Malhotra and Alstyne 2014, 24; Lee 2016, 230), the de-characterization of neighborhoods, and the need to separate commercial from residential areas not only for the sake of real estate prices but also to guarantee the quality of living of long-term residents. City officials in the United States, notably in New York City, have also voiced their concerns regarding fire safety, the need to maintain an available rental inventory for people living in NYC, and increased levels of noise, traffic, alleged parking problems, complaints from neighbors (McNamara 2015, 158). Moreover, several home-sharing platforms offer not only spare bedrooms and entire units but also shared rooms, including couches in studios or in a living room. Shared living also raises the question of offline privacy for both hosts and tourists (Ellen 2015, 784). Although both parties have willingly consented to share their space, there is great potential for conflicts.

Public policy concerns also arise from "too much sharing," particularly when shareable goods are not built to be used by different people on a regular basis. When goods are shared and not owned by different individuals, they might make individual and selfish decisions regardless of the overall social welfare, namely, by consuming too much of it. While an Airbnb host can be compensated for some damages, his or her neighbors might not be compensated for such selfish decisions. Not surprisingly, as Elinor Ostrom's work demonstrated, shared commons often (but not always) have a "tragic ending" (Ostrom 1990). While most shared goods are not "commons" in a traditional sense (Hardin 1968, 1243), the argument that these goods might not be well taken care of, that users might disregard overall community, and that products might not be repaired or replaced as they approach the end of their life is a relevant one. According to recent research, the replacement of shared goods might indeed be avoided as they approach the end of their lives, which might have an impact on the long-run future of the sharing economy (European Parliament 2016).

The Future of the Sharing Economy

The capitalization of sharing practices has challenged long-standing assumptions underlying public law and in particular local law: licenses and permits attest someone's ability to drive safely, cook a meal in hygienic conditions, and host a guest in a safe environment. These regulations were and are enacted to address the power imbalance between hosts and guests who might be in a more vulnerable position, as some scandals at Airbnb accommodations have already revealed, as well as to address a number of market failures such as information asymmetries between parties, variable prices, and potential for discrimination (Edelman, Luca and Svirsky 2015). The sharing economy supposedly relies upon a different idea: power parity between users. The answer to the regulation of the sharing economy may thus lie in looking back at the specific regulation of these practices in order to draw the line between the sharing exchanges which are closer to a collaborative rationale and those that are purely commercial businesses enabled by technology, unskilled labor, and good old shadow economy.

Regulatory Approaches

From a traditional perspective, regulation has been regarded as a governmental mechanism to achieve the "appropriate balance between competitiveness and consumer protection, misuse of regulatory protection by self-interested incumbents" (Morgan and Kuch 2015, 563), address regulatory capture, and solve market failures, such as information asymmetries (Cohen and Sundararajan 2015). In the digital age, some of these market failures have changed and new insights are needed. To illustrate, while information is now widely available thanks to the peer-review mechanisms, consumers still know little about why they see some reviews and not others, how algorithms work to determine prices, and how much platforms like Amazon know about their preferences and how they will use them. In this complex context, law is expected to play a more important role in the regulation of the sharing economy. As Morgan and Kuch (2015, 564) underline, "[Law] is much more than an infrastructure of repression and denial, risk, and mitigation."

With a broad interpretation of existing law, sharing economy platforms would be easily qualified as illegal businesses, resulting in a total or partial ban of peer-to-peer activities. Therefore, in the last five years the literature and regulators have tried to find answers for the current regulatory uncertainty in the sharing economy. While in the early years of the sharing economy revolution these platforms benefited from few regulations, regulators and law enforcers soon decided to take action on both sides of the ocean. The literature responded by suggesting new approaches including differentiated regulatory response as long as platforms do not conduct business like professionals (Miller 2016, 151); self-regulation (Cohen and Sundararajan 2015, 116–117; Koopman, Mitchell, and Thierer 2014, 542); and temporary or experimental regulation (Ranchordás 2015; Finck and Ranchordás 2016).

The growing use of platforms with an "extractive" rather than a collaborative mind-set (Morgan and Kuch 2015) and the recent scandals involving the safety and privacy of sharing economy users indicate that self-regulation might be insufficient to address the challenges of the sharing economy (Dyal-Chand 2015, 304). Therefore, other scholars suggested that since the sharing economy is "a nascent version of a mature system of capitalism," or "coordinated capitalism," it should be addressed from a new perspective that considers the specific institutions of this new economic model and its power relations and imbalance (platforms vs. peers) (Dyal-Chand 2015, 288–292).

In this section, I advance some regulatory suggestions that address some of the problems described in the previous sections.

Sharing Economy vs. Quasi-Sharing

A first option for the regulation of the broader concept of the "sharing economy" would be to distinguish between pure sharing economy practices that fit within certain limits (sharing limited to 30 days a year, one listing per person, low mediation fee, community-based exchanges, and gratuitous transactions) and quasi-sharing platforms that are mainly digital mediation businesses using unskilled labor. The first category refers to small-scale sharing where little to no profit is made from the capitalization of sharing idle capacity. Examples are home-exchanges where hosts can swap houses without paying for their stays. In the second, platforms adopt a professional approach toward mediation, charge, for example, a 10–20% fee, for the matching, process the payment, provide guidance to the users, and monitor the individuals not only by doing adequate background checks but also by controlling the quality of the services. If we place the emphasis on the intermediation aspect of these platforms, national and, in the case of EU member states, EU law would also be applicable, and as mentioned earlier, exempting the platforms from a number of obligations and liability. For the sake of simplicity and while awaiting the decision of the CJEU in a case involving Uber, I will not explore this position and will focus on the local regulation of sharing economy platforms.

In recent years, several cities have imposed limits on the number of days hosts can share their houses but the enforcement of these regulations has proven to be difficult. Some of the first sharing economy specific regulations emerged in California with the California Public Utilities Commission requiring the registration of Uber and Lyft as common carriers (Ranchordás 2015a). In the hospitality sector, San Francisco started regulating home-sharing in 2014, legalizing this practice under certain conditions ("San Francisco Ordinance No. 218–14). As of February 1, 2015, home-sharing platforms are permitted but strictly regulated to avoid the establishment of illegal hotels and the deterioration of the housing market. Ordinance 218–14 amends the Administrative and Planning Codes to allow platform hosts to rent their properties without violating the City's Residential Unit Conversion and Demolition Ordinance (Administrative Code Chapter 41A) or the Planning Code. Hosts must, however, register in order to rent their primary residential units for periods of fewer than 30 nights. Hosts must also be permanent residents in San Francisco and have liability insurance. These elements sound familiar to most of us but as mentioned earlier in this chapter, not all quasi-sharing economy platforms embrace a monitoring obligation.

Not surprisingly, cities like Paris and Amsterdam have started to conduct investigations to identify infractions and have threatened platforms to sanction them. The tension between platforms and regulators is growing by the day, and the winners in the "sharing wars" are unpredictable (Rauch and Schleicher 2015). Cities that were initially depicted as "Airbnb-friendly" or "a role model for sharing cities" (Bergren Miller 2015) like Amsterdam are now adopting more restrictive policies as research shows that many individuals are using platforms to pursue unlicensed businesses, renting multiple units, or leasing houses year-round while benefiting from more favorable conditions designed to facilitate occasional sharing.

The good and bad aspects of these platforms are that all the data public authorities need to guarantee that hosts are abiding by the rules is in the hands of platforms. In addition, the imposition of a stronger monitoring obligation on platforms (e.g., prohibition of hosts to have multiple listings or visits to the units) would actually be a preferable option to the raids conducted by public authorities, possibly resulting in fines and evictions. Amsterdam has recently required Airbnb to take action against illegal listings, namely, individuals with multiple listings who were not the subjects that the city wished to benefit with its "light regulation" of home-sharing. A report on home-sharing in Amsterdam published in March 2016 revealed that while users were very optimistic regarding Airbnb, residents were very critical and many hosts were not complying with the city's already-favorable regulations. Amsterdam allows local residents to lease their houses for a maximum period of 60 days a year, with the maximum occupancy limit of four persons. The Dutch city is now adopting a more stringent policy, requiring Airbnb to enforce local regulations.

Distinguishing between platforms and expecting platforms to monitor their users can be a challenging task from a practical perspective. Nevertheless, the application of existing regulations designed for traditional offline businesses would result in the prohibition of many of their services. It remains important to inquire whether sharing economy participants would be willing to accept top-down or self-imposed regulatory and governance monitoring and sanctioning mechanisms and whether their existence would improve collaboration. While, in principle, the original idea of the sharing economy suggested trust in strangers and the desire to manage all transactions in an informal way, the truth is that humans do not trust each other and peers are not equal. This is particularly true in the context of quasi-sharing transactions, where the participants are often not driven by collaborative incentives but by the maximization of economic gain or efficiency concerns.

Conclusion

Sharing economy platforms have disrupted the ownership-based consumption model as well as our perception of property (Kreiczer-Levy 2015, 63), traveling, and hosting (Guttentag 2015, 1192). The hoarding of goods, resulting from the development of a bourgeoisie eager to display wealth

(Botsman and Rogers 2010), was replaced for some of us by a more sustainable perception of the need to share idle capacity. The sharing of infrastructure and goods with excess capacity (e.g., vehicle parked outside office during the day) enables a more efficient use of resources (Cohen and Zehngebot 2014, 6). However, when we read in the media that some individuals are buying apartments in Las Vegas without the intention of living there but just for the sake of renting them on a regular basis on Airbnb, we can conclude that the sharing economy narrative might have failed in some cases.

This contribution explained this original narrative, distinguished it from the category of quasi-sharing, and discussed the regulatory and public policy restrictions to the different concerns raised by this new form of platform economy. The solution to the ongoing legal controversies involving sharing economy platform might imply refining our understanding of these platforms and imposing stricter monitoring obligations on these intermediaries. However, it is also important to underline that many of the same ongoing controversies result from the maintenance of outdated local law authorization schemes. While traditionally justified by the public interest, these outdated regimes might no longer reflect reality. The sharing economy is only exposing some of the vices of an outdated regulatory system that needs to be rethought in light of innovations such as mobile applications and smart algorithms. The complex relationship between traditional regulatory systems and instruments and the new challenges posed by the sharing economy require further research on, for example, how reputational mechanisms protect the public interest and consumers, solve the underlying information asymmetry that justified originally the need for regulation, and make permits and authorization schemes redundant.

References

Arvay, J., and A. Vertes. 1995. "Impact of the Hidden Economy or Growth Rates in Hungary." *Statistical Journal of the United Nations Economic Commission for Europe* 12 (1): 27–35.

Bakos, Yannis, and Chris Dellarocas. 2011. "Cooperation without Enforcement? A Comparative Analysis of Litigation and Online Reputation as Quality Assurance Mechanisms" *Management Science* 57: 1944.

Bardhi, Fleura, and Giana M. Eckhardt. 2012. "Access-Based Consumption: The Case of Car Sharing." *Journal of Consumer Research* 39: 881–899.

Barley, Stephen R. 2005. "What We Know (And Mostly Don't Know about Technical Work)." In *The Oxford Handbook of Work and Organization*, edited by Stephen Ackroyd et al., 376. New York: Oxford University Press.

Barry, Jordan M., and Elizabeth Pollman. Forthcoming. "Regulatory Entrepreneurship". *S. California Law Review* 90. www.ssrn.com.

Belk, Russell. 2014. "You Are What You Can Access: Sharing and Collaborative Consumption Online." *Journal of Business Research* 67: 1595.

Belyó, Pál. 1995. "The Hidden Economy in Hungary." http://www.ksh.hu/statszemle_archive/1998/1998_K2/1998_K2_125.pdf.

Benkler, Yochai. 2006. *The Wealth of Networks: How Social Production Transforms Markets and Freedom*. New Haven, CT: Yale University Press.

Benohr, Iris. 2014. *EU Consumer Law and Human Rights*. Oxford: Oxford University Press.

Bergren Miller, Anna. 2015. "Amsterdam Is Europe's First Named 'Sharing City.'" *Shareable*. February 24. http://www.shareable.net/blog/amsterdam-is-now-europes-first-named-sharing-city.

Bond, Andrew T. 2015. "An App for That: Local Government and the Rise of the Sharing Economy." *Notre Dame Law Review Online* 90: 77.

Botsman, Rachel, and Roo Rogers. 2010. *What's Mine Is Yours. The Rise of Collaborative Consumption*. New York: HarperCollins.

Brenner, Susan. 2007. *Law in an Era of "Smart" Technology*. New York: Oxford University Press.

Cairns, Robert D., and Catherine Liston-Heyes. 1996. "Competition and Regulation in the Taxi Industry." *Journal of Public Economics* 59: 1.

Carp, Jana, Charles Hoch, and George Hemmens, eds. 1996. *Issues and Innovators in Shared Housing*. Albany: SUNY Press.

Chambers, Matthew, Carlos Garriga, and Don E. Schlagenhauf. 2009. "Accounting for Changes in the Homeownership Rate." *International Economic Review* 50 (3): 677–726.

Choudary, Sangeet Paul, and Marshall W. Van Alstyne. 2016. *Platform Revolution: How Networked Markets Are Transforming the Economy—And How to Make Them Work for You*. New York: Norton Press.

Cohen, Boyd, and Pablo Munoz. 2016. "Sharing Cities and Sustainable Consumption and Production: Towards an Integrated Framework." *Journal of Cleaner Production* 134 (Part A): 87–97.

Cohen, Molly, and Arun Sundararajan. 2015. "Self-Regulation and Innovation in the Peer-to-Peer Sharing Economy." *The University of Chicago Law Review Dialogue* 82: 116–133.

Cohen, Molly, and Corey Zehngebot. 2014. "What's Old Becomes New: Regulating the Sharing Economy." *Boston Bar Journal* 58: 6.

Cunningham, James V. 1983. "Power Participation, and Local Government: The Communal Struggle for Parity." *Journal of Urban Affairs* 5(3): 257–266.

Davidson, Nestor and John J. Infranca. 2016. "The Sharing Economy as an Urban Phenomenon." *Yale Law & Policy Review* 34: 217–279.

Demailly, Damien, and Anne-Sophie Novel. 2013. "Économie du partage: enjeux et opportunités pour la transition écologique." Studies N°03/14, IDDRI, Paris, France, 32 p.

Dyal-Chand, Rashmi. 2015. "Regulating Sharing: The Sharing Economy as an Alternative Capitalist System." *Tulane Law Review* 90 (2): 241–309.

Edelman, Benjamin G., Michael Luca, and Dan Svirsky. 2015. "Racial Discrimination in the Sharing Economy: Evidence from a Field Experiment." Harvard Business School NOM Unit, Working Paper No. 16-069, http://papers.ssrn.com/sol3/papers.cfm?abstract_id=2701902.

Ellen, Ingrid Gould. 2015. "Housing Low-Income Households: Lessons from the Sharing Economy." *Housing Policy Debate* 25: 783–784.

Ert, Eyal, Aliza Fleischer, and Nathan Mager. 2016. "Trust and Reputation in the Sharing Economy: The Role of Personal Photos in Airbnb." *Tourism Management* 55: 62–73.

European Parliament. 2016. *The Cost of Non-Europe in the Sharing Economy: Economic, Social and Legal Challenges and Opportunities, European Parliament Research Advice*, available at http://www.europarl.europa.eu/thinktank/en/document.html?reference=EPRS_STU(2016)55877.

Evans, David S. 2003. "The Antitrust Economics of Two-Sided Markets." *Yale Journal on Regulation* 20 (2): 327.

Evans, David S., and Richard Schmalensee. 2016. *Matchmakers: The New Economics of Multisided Platforms*. Boston: Harvard Business Review Press.

Finck, Michele and Sofia Ranchordás. 2016. "Sharing and the City." *Vanderbilt Journal of Transnational Law* 49: 1299–1369.

Fischel, William A. 2004. "An Economic History of Zoning and a Cure for its Exclusionary Effects." *Urban Studies* 41: 1–47.

Freeman, Jody, and David E. Spence. 2014. "Old Statutes New Problems." *University of Pennsylvania Law Review* 163: 1.

Fromm, Jeff. 2015. "Affluent Millenial Travelers Embrace the Sharing Economy." *Forbes.* December 16. http://www.forbes.com/sites/jefffromm/2015/12/17/affluent-millennial-travelers-embrace-the-sharing-economy/#d3a97f77a240.

Gallick, Edward C., and David E. Sisk. 1987. "A Reconsideration of Taxi Regulation. *Journal of Law, Economics & Organization* 3: 117.

Gata, João E. 2015. "Sharing Economy, Competition, and Regulation." *Competition Policy International*, November. https://www.competitionpolicyinternational.com/assets/Europe-Column-November-Full.pdf.

Gottlieb, Charles. 2013. "Residential Short-Term Rentals: Should Local Governments Regulate the 'Industry'?" *Planning & Environmental Law* 65 (2): 4.

Guttentag, Daniel. 2015. "Airbnb: Disruptive Innovation and the Rise of an Informal Tourism Accommodation Sector." *Current Issues in Tourism* 18: 1192.

Hamari, Juho, Mimmi Sjöklint, and Antti Ukkonen. 2016. "The Sharing Economy: Why People Participate in Collaborative Consumption." *Journal of the Association for Information Science and Technology.* doi: 10.1002/asi.23552 (Forthcoming).

Hardin, Garrett. 1968. "The Tragedy of the Commons." *Science* 162: 1243.

Hartl, Barbara, Eva Hofmann, and Erich Kirchler. 2015. "Do We Need Rules for 'What's Mine Is Yours'? Governance in Collaborative Consumption Communities." *Journal of Business Research* (Forthcoming).

Haug, Marie R. 1972. "Deprofessionalization: An Alternate Hypothesis for the Future." *The Sociological Review* 20: 195.

Hern, Alex. 2016. "Uber and Airbnb Call on EU to Support 'Collaborative Economy.'" *Guardian*. February 11. http://www.theguardian.com/technol ogy/2016/feb/11/uber-airbnb-eu-support-collaborative-economy.

Interian, Johanna. 2016. "Up in the Air: Harmonizing the Sharing Economy through Airbnb Regulations." *Boston College International & Comparative Law Review* 39: 129–161.

Jefferson-Jones, Jamilla. 2015. "Airbnb and the Housing Segment of the Modern 'Sharing Economy': Are Short-Term Rental Restrictions an Unconstitutional Taking?" *Hastings Constitutional Law Quarterly* 42: 557.

John, Nicholas A. 2012. "Sharing and Web 2.0: The Emergence of a Key Word." *New Media & Society* 15: 1–16.

John, Nicholas A. 2013. "The Social Logics of Sharing." *The Communication Review* 16: 113–131.

Kaplan, Roberta A., and Michael L. Nadler. 2015. "Airbnb: A Case Study in Occupancy Regulation and Taxation." *University of Chicago Law Review Dialogue* 82: 103.

Katz, Vanessa. 2015. "Regulating the Sharing Economy." *Berkeley Technology Law Journal* 30: 1067–1126.

Kinsella, N. Stephen. 1994. "A Civil Law to Common Law Dictionary." *Louisiana Law Review* 54 (5): 1265–1305.

Koopman, Christopher, Matthew Mitchell, and Adam Thierer. 2014. "The Sharing Economy and Consumer Protection Regulation: The Case for Policy Change." *Journal of Business, Entrepreneurship & Law* 8: 529.

Krakovsky, Marina. 2015. *The Middleman Economy: How Brokers, Agents, Dealers, and Everyday Matchmakers Create Value and Profit.* New York: Palgrave MacMillan.

Kreiczer-Levy, Shelly. 2015. "Consumption Property in the Sharing Economy." *Pepperdine Law Review* 43: 61.

Lee, Dayne. 2016. "How Airbnb Short-Term Rentals Exacerbate Los Angeles's Affordable Housing Crisis: Analysis and Policy Recommendations." *Harvard Law & Policy Review* 10: 229.

Lee, Min Kyung, Daniel Kusbit, Evan Metsky, and Laura Dabbish. 2015. "Working with Machines: The Impact of Algorithmic and Data-Driven Management on Human Workers." *CHI'15 Proceedings of the 33rd Annual ACM Conference on Human Factors in Computing Technology*, doi: 10.1145/2702123.2702548.

Leiren, Merethe Dotterud, and Jørg Aarhaug. 2016. "Taxis and Crowd-Taxis: Sharing as a Private Activity and Public Concern." *Internet Policy Review* 5(2): 1–17.

Lessig, Lawrence. 1999. *Code 2.0 and Other Laws of Cyberspace, Version 2.0.* New York: Basic Books.

Light, Sarah. 2016. "Precautionary Federalism and the Sharing Economy." *Emory Law Journal* 66 (Forthcoming).

Lobel, Orly. 2015. "The Law of the Platform." *Minnesota Law Review* 101: 87–166.

Macey, Jonathan. 1990. "Federal Deference to Local Regulators and the Economic Theory of Regulation: Toward a Public-Choice Explanation of Federalism." *Virginia Law Review* 76(2): 265.

Malhotra, Arvind, and Marshall Van Alstyne. 2014. "The Dark Side of the Sharing Economy." *Communications of the ACM* 57 (11): 24.

Martin, Chris J. 2016. "The Sharing Economy: A Pathway to Sustainability or a Nightmare Form of Neoliberal Capitalism." *Ecological Economy* 121: 149–159.

Martin, Chris J., and Paul Upham. 2016. "Grassroots Social Innovation and Mobilization of Values in Collaborative Consumption: A Conceptual Model." *Journal of Cleaner Production* 134 (Part A): 204–213.

McLaren, Duncan, and Julian Agyeman. 2015. *Sharing Cities: A Case for Truly Smart and Sustainable Cities.* Cambridge: MIT Press.

McNamara, Brittany. 2015. "Airbnb: A Not-So-Safe Resting Place." *Journal on Telecommunications & High Technology Law* 13: 149–170.

Miller, Stephen. 2016. "First Principles for Regulating the Sharing Economy." *Harvard Journal on Legislation* 53: 149–200.

Molz, Jeannie G. 2012. "CouchSurfing and Network Hospitality. It's Not Just about the Furniture." *Hospitality & Society* 1: 215–225.

Morgan, Bronwen, and Declan Kuch. 2015. "Radical Transactionalism: Legal Consciousness, Diverse Economies, and the Sharing Economy." *Journal of Law & Society* 42 (4): 556.

Moss, Mitchell. 1998. "Technology and Cities." *Cityscape* 107.

O'Rourke, Dara, and Niklas Lollo. 2015. "Transforming Consumption: From Decoupling, to Behavior Change, to System Changes for Sustainable Consumption." *Annual Review of Environment and Resources* 40: 233–259.

Ostrom, Elinor. 1990. *Governing the Commons. The Evolution of Institutions for Collective Action.* New York: Cambridge University Press.

Owen, David, John Montgomery, and Mary Davis. 2014. *Product Liability and Safety: Cases and Materials.* New York: Foundation Press.

Prassl, Jeremias. 2016. *The Concept of Employer.* Oxford: Oxford University Press.

Quigley, John, and Larry A. Rosenthal. 2005. "The Effects of Land Use Regulation on the Price of Housing: What Do We Know? What Can We Learn?" *Cityscape* 28 (1): 69–137.

Ranchordás, Sofia. 2015. "Does Sharing Mean Caring? Regulating Innovation in the Sharing Economy." *Minnesota Journal of Law, Science & Technology* 16 (1): 413–475.

Rauch, Daniel E. and David Schleicher. 2015. "Like Uber, but for Local Government Law: The Future of Local Regulation of the Sharing Economy." *Ohio State Law Journal* 76: 903–963.

Resnick, P., and R. Zeckhauser. 2002. "Trust among Strangers in Internet Transactions: Empirical Analysis of eBay's Reputation System." *Advances in Applied Microeconomics* 11: 127–157.

Ring, Diane M., and Shu-Yi Oei. 2016. "Can Sharing Be Taxed?" *Washington University Law Review* 93 (4) (Forthcoming).

Ritzer, George. 2015. "Prosumer Capitalism." *The Sociological Quarterly* 56: 413–445.

Schaller, Bruce. 2007. "Entry Controls in Taxi Regulation: Implications of US and Canadian Experience for Taxi Regulation and Deregulation." *Transportation Policy* 14: 490.

Schneider, Nathan. 2014. "Owning the New Sharing." *Shareable*. December 21. http://www.shareable.net/blog/owning-is-the-new-sharing.

Schneiderman, Eric. 2014. Report of the Office of New York State Attorney General Eric T. Schneiderman, Airbnb in the City. http://www.ag.ny.gov/pdfs/Airbnb%20report.pdf.

Schor, Juliet. 2014. "Debating the Sharing Economy." Great Transition Initiatives. http://www.greattransition.org/images/GTI_publications/Schor_Debating_the_Sharing_Economy.pdf.

Shkabatur, J. 2011. "Cities@Crossroads: Digital Technology and Local Democracy in America." *Brooklyn Law Review* 76: 1413–1485.

Steele, Eric H. 1986. "Participation and Rules—The Functions of Zoning." *American Bar Foundation Research Journal* 11(4): 709–755.

Stefano, Valerio. 2016. "Introduction: Crowdsourcing, The Gig-Economy and the Law." *Comparative Labor Law & Policy* 37(3): 1.

Veblen, Thorstein. 1953 (1899). *The Theory of the Leisure Class: An Economic Study of Institutions*. New York: The Macmillan Company.

Waard, Boudewijn de. 2016. "Proportinality in Dutch Administrative Law." In *The Judge and the Proportionate Use of Discretion*, edited by Sofia Ranchordás and Boudewijn de Waard, 109–139. London: Routledge.

Weiss, Marc A. 1986. "Urban Land Developers and the Origins of Zoning Law: The Case of Berkeley." *Berkeley Urban Planning Journal* III: 7–24.

Werbach, Kevin. 2016. "The Song Remains the Same: What Cyberlaw Might Teach the Next Internet Economy." *Florida Law Review* (Forthcoming). www.ssrn.com.

Wittel, Andreas. 2001. "Towards a Network Sociality." *Theory, Culture & Society* 18: 51–70.

Case Laws

Rechtbank Rotterdam, November 6, 2015, ECLI:NL:RBROT:2015:7899, available at http://uitspraken.rechtspraak.nl/inziendocument?id=ECLI:NL:RBROT:2015:7899&keyword=%22Airbnb%22.

Stockholm Rental Tribunal, *Hyresnämnden i Stockholm*, No. 8741–15, August 17, 2015.

Thompson v. Dodge, 60 N.W. 545, 546 (Minn. 1894).

About the Editors and Contributors

Editors

Pia A. Albinsson (PhD, New Mexico State University) is associate professor of marketing and currently holds the John W. Guffey Jr. Professorship in the Walker College of Business at Appalachian State University where she has been teaching since 2009. Her research interests include consumer activism, sustainability, collaborative consumption, and advertising effectiveness. Her research has been published in numerous journals such as *Consumption, Markets, and Culture, Psychology and Marketing, European Journal of Marketing, Journal of Macromarketing, Journal of Public Policy and Marketing, Journal of Consumer Behaviour, Journal of Marketing Theory and Practice, Journal of Hospitality Marketing and Management, International Journal of Wine Business Research,* and *International Journal of Retailing and Distribution.*

B. Yasanthi Perera (PhD, New Mexico State University) is assistant professor of business ethics at Brock University. Her research focuses on social responsibility. In particular, she examines individuals' consumption and disposition patterns, and their participation in social media-driven activist efforts that are directed toward businesses. At the organizational level, she examines businesses' sustainability efforts and various facets of for-profit social enterprises such as blended value creation and their management of social and financial aims. Her work has been published in numerous outlets, including the *Journal of Consumer Behaviour* and *Journal of Marketing Theory and Practice.* Yasanthi has teaching experiences in multiple areas of management, including business ethics, organizational behavior, team dynamics, and entrepreneurship.

Contributors

Paul W. Ballantine is professor of marketing and head of School (Business and Economics) at the University of Canterbury in Christchurch, New Zealand. His research interests include retailing, consumption behavior (particularly the negative aspects of consumption), and social and ethical issues in marketing. His recent publications have appeared in outlets, including the *Journal of Retailing and Consumer Services, Journal of Marketing Management, International Review of Retail, Distribution and Consumer Research, Journal of Brand Management,* and *Journal of Consumer Behaviour.*

Russell Belk is York University distinguished research professor and Kraft Foods Canada chair in marketing, Schulich School of Business, York University. He is past president of the International Association of Marketing and Development and is a fellow, past president, and film festival cofounder in the Association for Consumer Research. He also co-initiated the Consumer Behavior Odyssey and the Consumer Culture Theory Conference. He has received the Paul D. Converse Award, two Fulbright fellowships, and the Sheth Foundation/*Journal of Consumer Research* Award for Long Term Contribution to Consumer Research and has approximately 600 publications. His research tends to be qualitative, visual, and cultural. It involves the extended self, meanings of possessions, collecting, gift giving, sharing, digital consumption, and materialism.

Friedrich Chasin (MSc, University of Muenster/University of Sydney) is research assistant at the University of Muenster and private lecturer at the South Westphalia University and the Osnabrück University of Applied Sciences. His research interests include green information systems, sustainability, and peer-to-peer sharing. For the past two years, he has been studying the phenomenon of peer-to-peer sharing by studying corresponding businesses in Brazil, Germany, and South Korea. His special focus is on the design-oriented research where he has been developing peer-to-peer sharing services for the electric vehicle domain since 2013.

Isobel M. Findlay (PhD, McGill University) is professor emerita, management and marketing, Edwards School of Business; fellow in co-operatives, diversity, and sustainable development, Centre for the Study of Co-operatives; and university codirector, Community-University Institute for Social Research, University of Saskatchewan. Coauthor of *Aboriginal Tenure in the Constitution of Canada* and *Business Communication NOW* and coeditor of *Journeys in Community-Based Research* as well as journal special issues on cooperatives and on engaged scholarship and quality of life, she is lead author of articles and chapters on Indigenous cooperatives and community economic development; Indigenous education, humanities, justice, and quality of life; communications, culture, and communities; and diversity and equity in the workplace. Isobel works closely with communities, cooperatives, nonprofits, and the public and private sectors designing and conducting research to promote and support economic development, community entrepreneurship, quality of life, and environmental sustainability.

David Golightly (PhD) is senior research fellow in the Human Factors Research Group, University of Nottingham. His background is in the study of learning, problem solving, and expertise, particularly involving the use of technology. He also investigates methods for capturing and integrating user requirements in user-centered design and implementation processes. David completed his PhD in psychology, studying display-based problem solving. Following on from leading commercial user-centered design and user experience IT delivery projects, David has been working in research since 2007. In this work David has explored and published on a number of themes related to innovative forms of interaction, design, and socio-technical systems, particularly with relevance to transport and mobility. His current projects involve the modeling of demand in complex work situations and design principles for adopting new technology.

John Harvey (PhD) is senior lecturer at Nottingham Business School (Nottingham Trent University). His research interests include altruism, gift giving, and interdisciplinary issues in economic anthropology.

Florian Hawlitschek is research fellow at the Institute of Information Systems and Marketing, Karlsruhe Institute of Technology. His research interests include trust, the sharing economy, live biofeedback, and Internet user behavior and psychology. His research has been published in journals such as the *Swiss Journal of Business Research and Practice* as well as on international conferences such as the International Conference on Information Systems, the European Conference on Information Systems, the Hawaii International Conference on System Sciences, and the Australasian Conference on Information Systems.

Katharina Hellwig (PhD, University of Lausanne) is postdoctoral researcher and lecturer at the Marketing Institute of the University of Lausanne. She studies collaborative consumption communities, alternative modes of consumption, and branding in the context of the "sharing economy." Her work has been published in renowned academic outlets such as *Psychology & Marketing,* the *Journal of the Association for Consumer Research,* and the *Advances of*

Consumer Research; she has obtained funding from the Swiss National Science Foundation and the Swiss Academy of Humanities and Social Sciences.

Andreas Kamilaris (PhD, University of Cyprus). He has worked as postdoc researcher at the Department of Building, School of Design and Environment of the National University of Singapore, as project manager of the Social Electricity Online Platform European project at the University of Cyprus, and as senior researcher at the Insight Centre for Data Analytics of the National University of Ireland (NUIG Galway). From September 2016 till now, he has been working at the Institute for Food and Agricultural Research and Technology (IRTA, Torre Marimon) in Barcelona, through the European P-SPHERE project, collaborating with the Autonomous University of Barcelona (UAB), performing research on big data analysis and applications in the agri-food sector. His work is funded by a Marie Skłodowska-Curie fellowship. His research interests include Internet and web of things, web technologies, smart cities and agriculture, big data analysis, and wireless sensor networking.

Cait Lamberton (PhD, University of South Carolina) is associate professor and Fryrear Chair in the Katz Graduate School of Business at the University of Pittsburgh, where she teaches consumer behavior at the undergraduate, MBA, and PhD levels. Her research has focused on decision making both from an individual perspective, for example, among items in differently organized assortments, and from a societally embedded angle, as related to dyadic decision making, sharing systems, public goods, and tax payments. This work has been published in the *Journal of Consumer Research, Journal of Marketing Research, Journal of Marketing, Management Science,* and *Journal of Public Policy and Marketing,* among other outlets. Dr. Lamberton was named Marketing Science Institute Young Scholar, received the Association for Consumer Research's Early Career Award for Distinguished Scholarly Contributions, and received the American Marketing Association's Erin Anderson Award, given to one female academic researcher annually in recognition of outstanding scholarship and mentorship.

Felicitas Morhart is professor of marketing at the University of Lausanne (Switzerland). She graduated in communication science at the University of Munich and earned her PhD in business administration (2008) from the University of St. Gallen (Switzerland). Her work lies at the intersection of marketing, positive leadership, and business ethics, such as her work on brand-specific transformational leadership, brand authenticity, and collaborative consumption. Her work has been published in the *Journal of Marketing, Journal of Consumer Psychology, Journal of Management Inquiry, Journal of Advertising Research,* among others.

Lucie K. Ozanne (PhD, Penn State University) is associate professor of marketing in the College of Business and Law at the University of Canterbury in Christchurch, New Zealand. Her research interests include sustainability, collaborative consumption, transformative consumer research, and corporate social responsibility. Her research has been published in numerous journals such as the *European Journal of Marketing, Journal of Macromarketing, Journal of Public Policy and Marketing, Journal of Consumer Behaviour, Journal of Marketing Management, Journal of Business Ethics,* and *Journal of Business Research.*

Heather E. Philip recently graduated with her PhD in marketing from the University of Canterbury in Christchurch, New Zealand. Her thesis examined aspects of collaborative consumption in peer-to-peer exchange networks, and she has been published in outlets such as the *Journal of Marketing Management.*

Francesc X. Prenafeta-Boldú (PhD, Wageningen University, the Netherlands) is the director of the Program on Integral Management of Organic Waste (GIRO), at the Institute of Agrifood Research and Technology (IRTA, Catalonia, Spain). He has been visiting scholar at the subdepartments of Industrial Microbiology and of Environmental Technology (Wageningen University), as well as at the Dutch research institutes of Agrotechnology & Food Innovations (ATO-DLO), TNO Environment, Energy and Process Innovation (TNO-MEP), and Fungal Biodiversity Center—the Royal Netherlands Academy of Arts and Sciences (CBS-KNAW). His scientific career has focused on environmental biotechnology and engineering, microbial ecology, and agricultural sciences, with the objective of finding sustainable solutions to biologically related environmental challenges. Some of this research has been published in *Applied and Environmental Microbiology, Applied Microbiology and Biotechnology, Biodegradation, Bioresource Technology, Chemosphere, FEMS Microbiology Ecology, FEMS Microbiology Reviews, Fungal Biology, Journal of Chemical Technology & Biotechnology*, and *Science of the Total Environment.*

Sofia Ranchordás (PhD, Tilburg University/Antwerp University) is associate professor with a chair in European and comparative public law at Groningen Law School in the Netherlands and affiliated fellow of the Information Society Project at Yale Law School. She was previously assistant professor of administrative law at Leiden Law School and Tilburg Law School and a resident fellow of the Information Society Project. Her research interests include the regulation of digital platforms, rating and reputational mechanisms, the sharing economy, temporary and experimental legislation, and comparative administrative law. Her books and book chapters have been published by Edward Elgar, Routledge, and Hart Publishing. Her research has also been published in a number of international law journals, including the *European Journal of Legal Reform, Statute Law Review, Theory and Practice of Legislation, Vanderbilt Journal of Transnational Law, Lewis and Clark Law Review,* and the *Minnesota Journal of Law, Innovation, and Technology.* Her scholarship has been featured in numerous media outlets, including the *Wall Street Journal, Boston Review,* and the *Frankfurter Allgemeine Zeitung.*

Wendy Ritz (Doctor of Business Administration, Kennesaw State University) is assistant professor of marketing at Florida State University Panama City. Prior to obtaining her terminal degree, Wendy had more than 20 years as an international sales and marketing manager with Fortune 500 B2B companies. Her research interests include sales, international marketing, marketing strategy, digital marketing, and ethics. Her research has been published in *Harvard Business Review.*

Marlyne Sahakian (PhD, Graduate Institute of International and Development Studies, Geneva) is assistant professor in the Department of Sociology at the University of Geneva. Her research interest is in understanding resource consumption patterns and practices, in relation to environmental promotion and social equity. She is currently coordinating research projects on household energy and food consumption. She writes regularly for journals in the field of sustainability, with a recent edited volume titled *Food Consumption in the City: Practices and Patterns in Urban Asia and the Pacific* (Routledge 2016). She is also a founding member of SCORAI Europe, a network in the field of sustainable consumption research and action.

Andrew Smith (BSc, MSc, PhD) is the professor of consumer behavior at Nottingham University Business School and the director of the newly established Neo-demographic Laboratory for Analytics in Business (N/LAB). He is also an associate of the Horizon Institute (Digital Economy Research). To date he has published book chapters and numerous papers in many leading academic journals on various aspects of consumer psychology and behavior. He has led and contributed to a number of publicly funded and commercially sponsored research projects.

Timm Teubner (PhD) is assistant professor at the Institute of Information Systems and Marketing, Karlsruhe Institute of Technology. His research interests include electronic markets, auctions, Internet user behavior and psychology, and crowd sourcing, as well as peer-to-peer sharing schemes and platforms. His research has been published in numerous journals such as the *Journal of the Association for Information Systems, Electronic Markets, International Journal of Electronic Commerce, Business & Information Systems Engineering,* and *Economics Letters.*

Marco Wolf (PhD, New Mexico State University) is associate professor of marketing in the College of Business at the University of Southern Mississippi, where he has been teaching since 2008. His research includes do-it-yourself consumption/retailing, coproduction, and prosumption. His research has been published in the *Academy of Marketing Science Review, Psychology & Marketing, Journal of Marketing Theory and Practice, Journal of Consumer Behaviour, Journal of Research in Interactive Marketing, Journal of African Business, Global Journal of Business Research, International Journal of Marketing Studies,* and *Educational Leadership Journal.*

Index

between ownership and non-
ownership, 201
Third-party certification, 143
Time banks, 106, 120
Togetherness, 34
Toy library, 60, 167, 186
Trabant, 42–44; conserving and
individually modifying the car,
43–44; information sharing
amongst owners, 42–44; symbolism
(economic stagnancy), 42
Transaction costs, 135–38
Transformation of slack resources, 216
Trust, 116, 139–40, 219–20; build, 116,
226–27; as currency, 139; ensure,
225–26; online, 116, 132, 169
Trust dashboard, 225

Uber, 46
Uberisation of work, 10
Upcycling, 47
Usage, 187, 195
Usage risks, 170–71; individual risk,
170; object curation, 170; social
guilt risk, 170
User representation, 144–45
Users, 6; nonusers, 163; one-way
users, 163; two-way users, 163
Utilities (consumer), 31
Utility, 193–94; anti-industry, 194;
flexibility, 193; social, 194; storage,
193; sustainable and prosocial
behaviors, 194; transaction, 193

Values, 35; benevolence, 62;
frugality, 35; ingenuity, 35;
universalism, 62
Verification and signaling, 140–41
Vicarious sharing, 83, 86–87;
commons-based peer production,
86; open-source software, 86
Voluntary simplicity, 47
Voluntary simplifiers, 32

Waste, 160; definition of, 160
Web 2.0, 82, 99, 114–15, 119, 123,
240, 267; definition of, 267
Web design, 143–44
Web of Things (WOT), 120
Well-being, 51; economic, 51;
psychological, 51
West Germany (post WWII), 32–33;
differing economic development
between East and West Germany,
32–33
Wikipedia, 86
Wirtschafts-Ring System (WIR), 52
Worker exploitation, 228
World Commission on Environment
and Development (WCED), 54
World Social Forum, 55

Zero Marginal Cost Society, 130
Zimrider, 104
Zipcar, 5, 53, 64, 186, 196, 220, 221,
228
Zoning, 275; law, 275